W9-APA-972

The Library

COLBY JUNIOR COLLEGE

COLBY JUNIOR COLLEGE FOR WOMEN
PARATI · SERVIRE
MENS · ANIMUS
CORPUS
1837

Foreword

No OTHER COUNTRY in Latin America is more important to the United States today than Argentina.

Of all the republics of the Americas, none has been more of a constant source of difficulty—and at the same time, held more of our hopes for the future.

Yet the fact is that we probably know less of the Argentine people, the things that make them what they are, and why they think, act, and behave as they do, than we know of the peoples of most of the countries of Europe. Or, if it need be said, of many other parts of the world.

Because Argentina is the key to much of what lies ahead in our Western Hemisphere, this book has been written. Over a period of some years I have observed the people and events of Argentina on many levels. This has extended from close relationship with many government leaders and officials as well as with men and women of every social, political, and economic background, from the owners of the great cattle-raising *estancias* to the dirt farmers on whose land I have hunted.

My friends, associates, and I have all disagreed from time to time about political activities in this perplexing country. But we have all shared the same feelings and deep affection for its people. I have flown tens of thousands of miles over all parts of the Argentine republic: the tropical jungles bordering Brazil; the Andes and its foothills, the broad expanse of the pampa; twice to lower Patagonia, the Straits of Magellan and Tierra del Fuego; never over Cape Horn but within sight of it, and to the great cities as well as the interior of the rich and beautiful land to which I had been accredited.

The aim of this book is not, however, to serve as a memoir or a survey of the ever-changing political situation. That field has been covered from every viewpoint. Rather, it is to present a picture of the Argentine people, their collective personality, as it were. There has been no desire to point a finger at faults or foibles, though these naturally emerge, or to say that our way is better and their way worse. No programs of action are urged, no indictments issued. Rather, this is an attempt to help explain what the Argentines are like, the kind of growing pains they have gone through and how and why they are what they are today. By the same token, it may also indicate what they may be expected to do tomorrow—the *mañana* of which all Latin Americans speak.

It is essential that these things be understood, for few Latin American republics affect us so strongly politically, economically, and militarily. Argentina's riches, possessions, political and economic power, her leaders and development, have all given her a unique position. She has been a source of food for Britain and much of western Europe, as well as the key supplier of many of the free world's raw materials.

And even though our dependence on Latin American markets and sources can be generally said to decrease as we move southward from the United States—and Europe's dependence and importance to Latin America to increase proportionately—Argentina today has never been more vital to us. Her constantly changing role vis-á-vis the Soviet Union affects our whole defense picture, both because of Argentina's own geographic and political position and because of her influence on her Latin American neighbors. Argentina's role with the Latin bloc in

the United Nations has also become more and more decisive as we have come to realize that Latin America's
votes can—and have—often meant a difference between
passage and disapproval of many of the measures that
concern us so deeply.

No other Latin republic has been so reluctant to ratify
conventions or to adopt measures that we in the United
States have been anxious to see approved. It is the Argentines who have spoken up most often and most loudly at
Inter-American sessions. And generally the impression
has been created that each time an Argentine succeeds
in opposing us, somehow he has scored a victory for himself and for Latin America.

But the fact that the Argentine government and its
leaders are distinct from the Argentine people and frequently in disagreement is becoming increasingly clear
to many in the United States. Events in recent years have
emphasized this even more.

Yet it is hard for most North Americans to understand
the difference between the two—and to determine where
government and people agree and where they do not.

This book will attempt to answer some of these questions frankly, realistically, honestly, in terms of people
rather than of products, and in terms of the personality
of a nation fully as much as in political events. In a situation as fluid as that which has existed in Argentina since
the military took over exactly ten years ago today, it is
inevitable that some of the points made in these pages
will have changed and others become more sharply emphasized. Argentina's growing economic crisis—with
black markets, meatless days, spiraling inflation, and rising unemployment, plus a growth of communist activity

—erupted in a violent series of events, including the destruction of the famed Jockey Club in April, 1953. Other events are sure to take place, for no one can accurately forecast just what will happen on the Rio de la Plata.

Some of these points have been covered in this work, but this book, it must be emphasized, is not intended as a critical study in this field. Rather, its aim is to help explain, fully, completely, and with candor, those factors that make the Argentine people tick. This includes many things usually left unspoken or concealed because of a refusal to look squarely at the facts, as well as because of lack of knowledge. And often this has meant simply an avoidance of the kind of honesty Good Neighbors must have with one another.

Those of us who have known many Argentines for long periods of time—lived with them, worked with them, and enjoyed their sports and amusements, their books and fiestas—have not let this affection blind them from looking closely. Not everyone will agree with everything said here. That is expected. And, of necessity, much of what follows must be purely interpretive, based not on documents or statistical studies, but on less scientific research, analysis, and interpretation.

Perhaps the greatest hope one can express is that as an Argentine who read the manuscript put it: "A really honest look at one another may enable us to understand each other's viewpoints more than all the pious statements we have heard for so many years."

New York City   JAMES BRUCE
June 4, 1953

Acknowledgment

ONE DAY in 1947, not long after I arrived in Buenos Aires as United States Ambassador to Argentina, I had a call from a traveling correspondent bearing a letter of introduction. The note was highly commendatory in its description—but what its writer told me in his own incisive way, I had, in the interim, discovered in the pages of my caller's book, *Argentine Diary*, for in Ray Josephs' volume and in his dispatches to leading United States newspapers and magazines, he had established a mark as a correspondent with a remarkable grasp of Latin America.

In our discussions about Argentina and Latin America in the years since, complementary experiences have been exchanged and the vantage points of an ambassador and a roving correspondent produced a mutual admiration for the people of the Argentine and a conviction that the North Americans need to know the South Americans better. From these discussions came the impetus for this work.

And for it, Ray Josephs has made available his seasoned research in the field—a fund of published and unpublished source material—and has given of his unsparing professional aid in every phase of its writing and editing.

The "without whose help" phrase in book acknowledgments has become so much a cliché that today only the first words need to be mentioned to produce a chuckle. Nevertheless, no preface to *Those Perplexing Argentines* would be complete without my publicly expressing my deepest appreciation for Ray Josephs' generous and unstinting assistance.

JAMES BRUCE

Contents

Those Perplexing Argentines

Chapter I

Those Perplexing Argentines

THE AVERAGE North American, trying to conjure up some sort of realistic picture of the average Argentine, is more often than not likely to think of a romantic gaucho in a black sombrero, galloping over the *pampa* by day and serenading a lovely dark-haired *señorita* by night.

Or he may visualize a dashing polo player who travels around with a string of fleet ponies, frequenting the better after-dark gathering places of Paris and Manhattan, and dancing the tango.

To a somewhat lesser extent, the average Argentine, visualizing his North American brother, has a similarly distorted viewpoint.

The fact is that although many books, articles, and editorials about Argentina's politics, meat and wheat, and international relations have appeared in our press in

1

recent years—so that the once-prevalent charge that we are little interested in what happens there can no longer be made—rarely have we in North America sought to understand the people behind the headlines from Buenos Aires.

Unfortunately, the differences between *Argentino* and *Yanqui* have long been more emphasized than the similarities.

What are these differences? How did they come about? Why is it that though we both come from similar backgrounds, fought not-too-dissimilar wars for independence, and have so many similar characteristics, we don't get along better than we do?

Ask an average Argentine about our differences and he'll probably tell you: "We'll never really get along for our basic conflict is economic."

Yet the fact is that actually we are not economic competitors, though most Argentines *think* we are. And international legends die just as hard as generalizations made on the basis of superficial impressions.

Talk to an Argentine and he will tell you that the United States has always refused to admit the product of which they are proudest, their incomparable meat, because we fear it is both better and lower-priced than ours. In part, as shall be pointed out presently, we did bar their meat and still do, primarily because of the prevalence of foot-and-mouth disease on their vast flat grazing lands. But Argentines in general feel that we have banned all of their products because we feared competition; and to some small extent this has been true.

It makes no difference when you explain that we have always been important purchasers of Argentina's cereals, wool, hides, and quebracho extract for tanning. You may also explain that though we produce wool we are a big wool importer, that though we produce hides we import them from the Argentine. You can also make clear that the meat question is today academic since Argentina cannot keep her commitments, let alone provide an exportable surplus for the States. Even when you show that our principal exports—cars, refrigerators, machine tools and the like—are, for the most part, not produced in Argentina, the average Argentine is not convinced. It is a significant clue to Argentine character that most Argentines like to believe this competition between us is strong because it automatically ranks them with the United States even if only for argument's sake. It also represents a kind of Argentine national defense mechanism often impossible for North Americans to understand.

Many Argentines see our economic strength as a constant menace to their own vaunted sovereignty and desire for Latin-American leadership. They will insist to you that most *Yanquis* are hard-boiled businessmen, dollar-chasing representatives of soulless corporations. Though they have never personally encountered anyone even remotely resembling this caricature, many believe the picture nevertheless. Some see us as unscrupulous financial promoters or as Hollywood characters who constantly change wives. All too often, they will say, we are good enough at mechanical and technical things. "But," they add, "you lack the culture so vital to full living. We work to enjoy life. You work because you do not know what else to do."

Some North Americans and Argentines enjoy warm personal relationships. They may regard us as *simpático* individuals. *Simpático* is a word that does not translate exactly, and defining it as warm, likable, and agreeable hardly gives the Argentine flavor. Yet relatively few Argentines really like us, for, despite all the endless series of official speeches, proclamations, and exchanges, it must be conceded that a real warmth between our countries does not exist. Misunderstanding has often occurred over little things, for, though we are fundamentally alike in many ways, our psychological approaches are often different.

Growing up as a nation, we in the United States have begun to get over some of our sensitivity to criticism. The Argentines, being less mature, are still far more likely to resent any real or fancied slight.

We both have the same excessive interest in ourselves —a fact which peoples of other countries are likely to see more sharply than either one of us. We like to discuss ourselves and never tire of being admired.

Most of our ancestors came from Europe. We fought similar wars for our independence and established governments which, regardless of the directions in which they have since moved, were based on the same kind of constitutions. We both enjoy similar temperate zone climates and geography; we both produce many of the same crops.

We both tend to be in a hurry. The Argentines tell us: "You aren't willing to take time out for courtesies or the little gestures we consider so important." Other Latins, however, make almost exactly the same accusation against the Argentines.

We both think we are generally right even if we are not certain exactly where we are going. We are both likely to be realistic and mercenary despite bursts of generosity.

Most Argentines want the same things most North Americans want—a comfortable home, a car, good clothes for ourselves and families, a chance for our children to get an education and succeed, and a secure future.

If these things are admittedly so, why then do the Argentines puzzle us and we puzzle them?

Distance is one major factor. It has always been easier for Argentines to visit Europe than the United States. Buenos Aires is the Latin American capital farthest from us, a thousand miles more distant from New York than Moscow. Establishing the personal contact which brings understanding is difficult when it takes so long and costs so much to travel between two countries. We get along better with Mexicans than we used to, partly because so many of us have visited their country and because so many Mexicans have come to the States to study, work, and play. Our easy contact with Canadians is certainly one of the reasons for our friendship.

Unfortunately, our relations with the Argentines have frequently been thoughtless. Hasty and ill-prepared goodwill wooing missions often did more harm than good. Our sudden and repeated past "discoveries" of Argentina sometimes were announced with the astonished surprise of an explorer first locating a strange, long-lost civilization. Some of this carelessness in our Argentine relations was the result of our indifference to their national sensitivity. If, for example, Argentines made ludicrous movies about us we would probably laugh them off and pay little attention. When Hollywood made a horror called "Argentine Nights" featuring a group of

brotherly comics as inter-American advocates, it caused
a national scandal down there.

Too few Argentines, especially officials, have studied
or traveled widely in the United States. Consequently,
while many know our history from books, they do not
always appreciate our enthusiasm, our impetuousness
and our way of doing things. Little attempt was made in
the past to close the physical or mental gap between us.
Our wooing efforts were often based on the ostentatious
approach of showing how good, powerful, and mighty
we were, rather than on establishing a mutuality of interest.

Our wartime Office of the Coordinator of Inter-American Affairs quickly discovered how this produced anything but the desired results. In order to tell the Argentines something about the States, the Coordinator's Office,
early in the war, placed a series of full-page advertisements in many Argentine newspapers inviting Argentines
to visit us. They were full of the glories of the United
States—the invitation being designed as an indirect way
of telling our story.

The Argentines, however, merely regarded this as
boasting and decided to boast back. Many turned away
from the advertisements convinced that Manhattan was
not superior to Buenos Aires, whether in night clubs,
opera, or modern buildings. Even though they had never
visited America, they were sure their Iguazú Falls were
more spectacular than our Niagara, their Nahuel Huapí
National Park grander than our Yellowstone, their subways more like art museums than the crowded underground of New York. The campaign brought us no closer.
As those who directed it soon learned, the look-what-

sibly half are completely or partially primitive Indians or Negroes. "Our population," say most Argentines, "is Latin America's largest in the only terms that matter."

Taught the theory of the superiority of the white race, Argentines have long emphasized the lack of any other blood in their veins. As far back as 1920, census statistics were twisted to show this. *Mestizos* with mixed white and Indian blood were often listed as white. Immigration from Negro countries was never permitted, despite the long-time absence of most other immigration bars. Argentines tell you that not only is their country Latin America's whitest, but the hemisphere's. On more than one occasion, Argentines have remarked: "We are the *only* white nation south of Canada."

Argentines tell you there are few Negroes in Argentina; they are almost a rarity. There was a highly popular Cuban night-club pianist, known as *Bola de Nieve*—Snowball—and an American Negro who was a singing waiter-bartender in another well-known Buenos Aires after-dark spot appropriately called "The American Bar." Argentines adored the singing Mills Brothers in much the same way Frenchmen have lionized Negro entertainers. But you see no Negro servants, elevator men, dockhands or taxi drivers. For this reason, the color line is not a conscious point. No hotel, restaurant or night club has any signs or unwritten rules to bar Negroes. There simply are none around the capital.

Argentines have great pride not only in their country but in themselves. Compliment an Argentine and he will not try to convince you that you are flattering him unduly. Instead, he will probably accept it as his natural right—without that depreciating modesty we sometimes try to convey. Argentines also like to hand out compliments, possibly because they want others in return. More likely, however, the reason lies in their temperament: they enjoy doing things a bit more dramatically than we.

If an Argentine wins a promotion or achieves almost any other triumph, major or minor, he is likely to get more vocal bouquets than a newly-elected governor in the States. His friends usually give him a *homenaje,* a testimonial banquet featuring verbose and flowery speeches. At the end the guest of honor invariably receives an elaborate illuminated parchment scroll duly immortalizing the achievement and destined for his office wall.

Because his country's richness has supported him with such little effort, many an Argentine often expects all, or almost all, from the weather and the land. "*Dios* (God) *es Argentino,*" say the Argentines. His benefactions, they are convinced, prove it—more *pesos* to spend than their Latin neighbors, handsomer homes to live in, better cars to drive, finer schools for their children.

One Argentine physician expressed it this way: "Since so much of our wealth has come from nature, and incidentally come with comparatively little help, we have been willing to accept that which falls our way unthinkingly, regarding it as our natural right. We ride the waves and drift, letting the self-seeking *caudillo,* boss, map the course. Our only reservation is that he not interfere overly much with our pocketbooks, personal dignity, and pleasures. The very abundance of material things—food, drink, the soil of the *pampa*—has made us careless of our liberties."

Many an Argentine admits he and his countrymen

have slipped into the yoke of dictatorial control because
President Juan D. Perón is attempting to readjust Argentina's historic maldistribution of wealth. To these Argentines it is of secondary importance that this has meant
the strangulation of many of the democratic essentials.
Such Argentines see in democracy only the rights it
offers, forgetting the duties it imposes.

Early settlers wanted material things rather than freedom. Unlike the French, Argentines have not had to gain
their sense of social consciousness in fighting feudalism
or foreign powers. Nor have they, like ourselves, fought
for democracy and national unity from a need and desire
for freedom.

"Our masses," a university professor once said, "have
never been forced really to battle for their rights. And
the upper economic stratum has wrestled primarily only
to keep the status quo of its privilege. This may change—
there are signs. But no one can be certain."

Argentines have never had much chance to see democracy in action in their own country. Currently, while
Argentines have a form of democracy, they do not enjoy
much of its substance. This does not mean democracy is
a lost cause. "But," most Argentines admit, "Argentines
are not yet ready to fight and die for it."

Just as Argentines have never developed any strong
convictions about democracy, so, often for the same reasons, they have not produced a strong national culture.
"Our culture," one cynical Argentine once explained,
"has been superficial and borrowed, lacking depth: an
offshoot of continental Europe."

Argentines are great imitators. But they do not like
to feel they are copying anybody. They borrowed their

art from France, their music from Italy, their movies from Hollywood, their gadgets from New York. And the militarists, who currently run the country, did much of their studying in prewar Berlin, Rome, and Madrid.

Just before World War II, José Maria Cantilo, Foreign Minister of Argentina, said:

"We feel ourselves closely associated with Europe by the immigration we have received from her, which has contributed so much to our greatness, our European capital which has developed our agricultural and livestock industries, our railroads and other industries. But even more than that there still lives in our spirit the memory of the men who discovered and populated our land, as well as the cultural tradition they bequeathed us.

"From Spain we received our blood and our religion. From France and Great Britain as well as the United States we received the doctrinal direction of our democratic institutions. If to the Mother country we owe the basis of our literature, French culture has contributed largely in the formation of our intellectual life while Italy and Germany have contributed to important aspects of our evolution. European influence predominates in the higher education of our universities just as European methods are used in our schools."

Most Argentines have always considered France, not Spain, their spiritual home. They used to go to Paris for their ideas, their education, their clothes, and their fun. Some rich Argentines, in fact, even learned French before Spanish. It was regarded as the true mark of one's education. Slavish acceptance of all that came from abroad, in preference to anything produced at home, is no longer the rule. World War II, cutting off both products and

ideas, helped cause the change. Still, while protesting
their independence, most Argentines would probably prefer a pair of English shoes or a radio made in the States
to a domestic product. Somehow, he would figure, anything made at home is not *quite* as good.

The patriot plays up the nationalistic pride in local
production. But many an Argentine confesses: "It is
primarily for the working people—Perón's followers." In
the best men's shops in Buenos Aires British fabrics will
always be preferred to the national. The most expensive
ties will be Italian; the best shirts Swiss. Even though
they do not carry any imported items, shops often have
names like Larry, Jenny, Daisy, Kent. Popular brands of
cigarettes include Clifton, Sportsmen, American Club.
The foreign name and spelling gives that little extra
touch of swank, even though the item is made at home.

But the visiting North American will stock up on locally produced *Industria Argentina* products, for when
the Argentine puts his mind to it, he can produce goods
as fine as those found anywhere. One reason is that the
Argentines undoubtedly have the highest educational
level of all Latin Americans. More has been done there to
make education available to everyone who wants it than
in any other Latin American Republic. Although private
schools rated highest, the state's standard education was
always, in the past, free for all. This helped produce a
keen, alert, literate populace, especially among the
porteños (dwellers in the port city of Buenos Aires)
where education, at all levels and in all forms, was most
abundant.

Buenos Aires has always had the most avid and assid-
uous readers. It is said Argentines buy more books and

support more publishers per capita than almost any other country. Their great publishing industry is currently, with Mexico City, the center for all books published in Spanish—an honor possibly taken from Spain after Franco made ideas dangerous.

Often, it is true, Argentines read superficially, yet they know the literature of all Europe and, increasingly, of the States. Books in French and English are popular. The latter can be traced to the influence of our films and to the number of popular new writers first published in English.

Despite Argentine interest in books, however, few native writers have gained international fame, though it is hard to tell why the most widely translated was the notoriously anti-Semitic Gustavo Martínez Zuviría, who wrote under the pen name of Hugo Wast, and who in 1943 served as Minister of Education under the military government which seized power that year.

Here again, the reason may lie in the lack of motivating struggle and the absence of deep feeling and knowledge essential for truly good writing. Even Argentina's experts on many subjects are not full-time professionals in their field. Rather, they are doctors, lawyers, dentists, businessmen, who, as a hobby, have taken an interest in art, literature, or one of the social sciences. They learn enough to move into the local expert category. Many can write with facility and technical terminology on almost any subject so long as there is not too great a demand for facts. Too often, however, this has not been accompanied by the kind of solid, long-term study which marks the real authority. In many cases, for example, in analyzing books written by Argentines dealing with their own country, one finds philosophical ramblings and generalized dissertations, rather than hard, well-organized data.

In many instances, the most extensive studies on certain aspects of Argentine life have not been done by Argentines at all. The Argentine—and in general the Latin American—approach to intellectual achievement has the flavor of the romantic countries. It is characterized by the glitter and drama of language itself, by an intoxication with words. Much of this writing is impressive, on first reading. But penetrating studies of Argentina's rural life for instance, such as those made by Dr. Carl Taylor of the United States Department of Agriculture, or economic studies such as those made under the sponsorship of Columbia, the University of California, North Carolina, and of other top United States schools, cannot be found.

Like many another Latin American, the Argentine likes the intellectual fun of knowing, but not the hard digging and spadework. Many Argentines say their population is not large enough to support men of top ability in most full-time research and writing fields. Exceptions are economics, law, and medicine where institutions are able to afford their services and abilities.

When Argentines read their own writers—and others—they are generally on the lookout for what they are certain will be a "catch." Listening to a speech, overhearing a conversation, or being told about some new development, they do not take the words at face value. Instead they try to find a hidden meaning. This applies in both everyday things and international affairs.

"We constantly suspect an ulterior motive because others have used us unfairly in the past," one Argentine explained. During the most extensive United States goodwill wooing period, for instance, most Argentines were certain we would want something in return for our favors, therefore they ought to be automatically opposed.

Argentines love to be in the know—and they don't have to be shown twice. There is hardly anything which does not interest them—at least for a while. This interest extends to both themselves and the world. Argentines have always been preoccupied with history, especially their own. Practically all leading Argentine writers, politicians, and statesmen have been sometimes historians. Most streets in Argentine cities and towns bear the names of historic personalities or eventful dates—Calle Bernardino Rivadavia, 9 de Julio, 25 de Mayo and scores of others. Practically every Argentine schoolboy can tell you how President Rivadavia established the first National Bank, negotiated the first foreign loan, and founded the national charitable organization known as the Sociedad de Beneficencia. He will tell you how the first *junta* or governing board was established on May 25, after the Revolution of 1810, and exactly why July 9 became Argentina's second Independence Day.

Argentines have also been keenly interested spectators of what goes on in the world. Until recently even their provincial dailies made many of ours look like crossroads bulletins, so extensive was the space devoted to international affairs. The Perón regime, with its concentration on domestic events, has brought local news to page one. Yet despite the attempted shift of focus, Argentines today, as in the past, know more about us than we about them—which has not made them like us any more. Their interest in international affairs has, however, all too often left them simply spectators. They are concerned with how events may affect prices of their meat and wheat. But otherwise even in contrast with our rank and file citizen, they have generally seen little practical, personal bearing in the world's critical developments. An Argentine ex-minister offered this explanation: "You in the States have been interested because you or your sons and daughters faced the possibility of being involved in war. We never felt we would ever actually have to fight—so it was all, in a sense, academic."

An Argentine Congressional Committee tried to expose Nazi plotting within the Army back in the early days of World War II. Argentines seethed with sudden indignation when they learned what had been done to mold the thinking of their military officers into totalitarian patterns. But they soon lost interest and allowed it to pass with the headlines. After all, they would tell you, the races and the *futbol* (soccer) games were more exciting and the steaks were as good as ever. In a way they felt it stimulating to watch the propagandists of both sides working in Buenos Aires. They enjoyed a spectator's sideline role.

Even when, on June 4, 1943, the Army officers pushed out the civilian government and took over, reaction was far different from what an unknowing outsider might have supposed. For one thing, most Argentines did not consider it a revolution at all. A majority regarded the step only as a *coup d'état*, an overthrow by the palace guard, an officers' movement of "outs" wanting "in." Most Argentines thought that small handful of top Army brass was acting in what it considered its traditional role as the country's protector. The Army, it was believed, was appalled by the increasing flagrant graft and corruption, a new, threatened political steal, and the fear that relations with the Axis might be broken at a time when Berlin had a good chance of ultimate victory.

The fact is that, after the military seizure of power, some of those within the Army turned it to their own ends. They added democratic trappings and constitutional methods to what they did, even though they had little sympathy with such concepts. In a sense this was in keeping with the Argentine tradition of legalizing every illegal step via the proper formula. Yet the mass of population seemed little shocked. From colonial days they had known authoritarian governments.

Often, opposition groups have forced such regimes from power with cries of "reform" and "an end to tyranny." But the facts show that the new government, whether dubbed Liberal or Conservative, often ended up applying even more restrictions on individual freedom of action than before. Perón, for example, enlisted labor's support. He took steps to give those at the bottom of Argentina's economic ladder some of the advantages denied them for generations. This shored up his own position and helped ensure his continued power. But the Argentine people and Perón both knew that the 1943 "revolution" was hardly an authentic one, either in the traditional French or American sense.

This kind of self-deception applies fully as much to the Argentines' sense of honesty. Argentines *are* honest. Their idea of what this means is, however, far different from ours. Argentines have a good record in the payment of international debts and their reputable firms have always been most trustworthy. Cattle have always been sold by verbal bids. Yet shops, particularly those away from the well-lighted centers of the big cities, consider it imperative to install heavy, iron gates and shutter their windows. There is not much pilfering of tires, radiator caps, windshield wipers, and other automotive equipment frequently stolen in some poorer Latin countries. Yet it is not unknown, particularly in times of scarcities. "Anyone foolish enough to leave something where it can easily be stolen deserves to have it taken away," is the Argentine reaction. "It is one's duty to protect one's own property. The citizen and the law have no obligation to insure."

In every downtown city street, for example, an attendant watches parked cars for a small tip. Even the smallest buildings have custodians; private watchman's agencies are found everywhere.

The small *picardia*, or what might be called native trickery, is part of the basic pattern. Many an Argentine personally adds his restaurant bill to be sure a few extra *pesos* weren't quietly slipped in when he wasn't watching. Constant vigilance in dealing with one's fellow man is considered the mark of the Argentine city dweller. Ruth and Leonard Greenup, who have looked into the matter, say the *picardia* originated when Spain imposed a heavy tax on everything moving through Buenos Aires in order to maintain Lima and Panama as political and commercial centers. Early *porteños* surreptitiously loaded thousands of tons of tallow and hides onto English and Dutch ships riding at anchor in the Rio de la Plata. Circumventing the Spanish throne was as popular as our Boston Tea Party. Smuggling and bribing became the rule. Succeeding immigrants, especially those from southern European countries where such customs were generations old, continued these habits.

Many Argentines, in fact, regard rules and regulations as an attempt at intimidation and a reflection on their own personal *dignidad,* or dignity. For decades Argentines refused to stand in line to buy tickets at their theaters and movie houses or to board buses and trolleys. "It's submission against one's personal dignity," they explained. In the last few years they have reluctantly begun lining up. In part the government has forced them into a *fila,* line. In greater measure, it is because they have apparently come to realize that with the country's public transport becoming more chaotic and equipment not being replaced, the long accepted pushing and shoving might eventually break down the whole system at one time. More recently Argentines—to their surprise—have had to line up to buy scarce foods. But the government soon discovered the queues became centers for anti-government talk, and broke them up.

The every-man-for-himself idea still persists at post-offices and sports events. An Argentine considers it his right to shove ahead to the front of the line no matter who may be there first. He feels he would not be showing his proper status as a man if he meekly waited his turn in the back.

This desire to assert one's self, to achieve self-respect, to keep one's face and not be made ridiculous, extends from the poorest Argentine news vendor to the highest official in the land. And it affects every phase of Argentine life.

Argentines definitely believe familiarity can destroy self-respect. They watch for any possible infraction. They maintain a sharp difference between the formal address of *usted* (you) in contrast with the more intimate *tu* (thou). No matter how old the acquaintance, they are unlikely to unbend, even conversationally, except to true intimates. Our habit of immediately calling many newly-introduced persons by their first names strikes the more formal Argentines as presumptuous. Yet the fact is that they do it in a different way. A distinguished acquaintance might be addressed as *Don* Rafael, or *Don* Jaime, the *Don* being used before the given name as an honorary mark of respect. Employing *Don* before the family name, however, would be an insult.

An Argentine who knows a person extremely well often adds the diminutive *ito* for masculine and *ita* feminine. Thus Juan becomes Juancito. Best-known example was that of President Perón's wife, Evita, literally "Little Eva." At first she insisted upon being known as Dona (the equivalent of Don as a mark of honor for a woman) Maria Eva Duarte de Perón, the full family name an Argentine lady of society might use. Then she apparently began to realize that being known by the diminutive of her given name was a rare thing. So the full name was dropped for Evita. In mid-1951, when plans were afoot to have her run for the Vice Presidency, slogans were posted throughout the country: "Perón—Evita" and *"Perón Cumple"* (in other words Perón does it, keeps his word, fulfills his promises), *"Evita Dignifica"* (Evita dignifies or makes it meaningful).

The Argentine concept of *dignidad* takes many forms. All Latin Americans share this concept, but the Argentine form is most acute. To an Argentine, *dignidad* means no man can be criticized in front of his friend. Employees have been known to resign for lesser cause. Even office boys and porters, streetcar conductors and the sanitation men are treated with the same sort of *dignidad*, lest they become enemies. Argentine students must be strictly obedient to teachers, just as the private obeys his officer. Anything less would be *contra la dignidad*. Much of this applies chiefly to one's personal affairs. Friendship and intimacy are generally regarded as different—a distinction which, if misunderstood, is likely to confuse and perhaps get visiting North Americans into difficulties.

Under the Perón government's recent act of *desacato*, disrespect, anyone, Argentine or foreigner, who publicly criticizes the President, a Cabinet member, a Congressman, or even his family, faces severe penalties. A political opponent or a news correspondent who sends out a dispatch needs only to be accused of disrespect—and have this fact sustained by the offended party or the prosecutor—and he is guilty.

If, for example, an opponent charges a certain Ministry has exceeded its budget, and the Minister regards this as disrespectful, nothing else is needed to secure a conviction. While many an Argentine has found this hard to believe, the fact is that the law could be, and has been, sustained.

Real or fancied charges considered disrespectful still bring challenges to duels. Although they are officially illegal, it is rare that one has been stopped. In fact, when, as in most cases, political figures are involved, details are often reported in the press. If the papers do not carry stories, café gossip speculates on who is participating and what is allegedly involved.

How great the Argentine regard for *dignidad* can become is graphically illustrated by an incident witnessed in December, 1947. In its widely distributed airmail edition, *Time* magazine carried a story describing the tremendous, super-patriotic, flag-waving show the government built round the ceremonial return to Argentina of the remains of the parents of General San Martín, currently Argentina's greatest national hero. It ended by quoting an alleged remark by a youthful onlooker: "Next year they are going to bring back the bones of his *horse.*"

Though the reference had been laughed at by anti-Perónists, its appearance in a United States publication was taken even by them as a national insult rather than simply an amusing instance of journalistic color. The Argentine Ambassador in Washington protested. One Argentine paper demanded the *Time* correspondent's expulsion. Another said the Argentine press "would never have been so irreverent as to publish such items as the fact that George Washington drank eighteen glasses of wine with each meal, or that he married a rich widow because he had been told she was a good administrator."

To help placate many aggrieved feelings I flew up to Mendoza. Accompanied by the Governor of the Province and a military Guard, I proceeded up the approaches of the Andes to the monument erected in commemoration of the famous Army of the Andes. There I placed a wreath in honor of the heroes of the Army of the Andes and made a speech in Spanish about the achievements of General San Martín.

This was not hard for me to do, because I had read much about him, and considered him one of the great men of world history. His crossing of the Andes is comparable to the crossing of the Alps by Hannibal and Caesar.

The next day my speech was carried by all the daily press of the cities of the Andes plus very favorable editorial comment, as well as by the papers of Buenos Aires. Good feeling was restored, and the incident was closed.

Finally, by way of *desagravio*, compensation, the National San Martín Institute publicly laid a wreath on Washington's monument in Buenos Aires. This didn't quite add up in North American eyes, but to many Argentines it was a sober, fitting way of closing the incident in a manner befitting the *dignidad* of those affected.

The Argentine sense of humor, incidentally, is a much-debated subject. It is like much of our humor because it is based on exaggeration. However, many North Americans, French and others find that Argentines almost completely lack a spirit of real fun. One formerly sensed something of the national brand of wit in the political revues at the old Maipo Theater in Buenos Aires, where political take-offs were a part of the *porteño* scene. Argentine humor also appears in the routines of such famed Argentine comedians as Pepe Arias and Luis Sandrini whose style, in their heyday, was low key and apt to dwell on the complexities of life. One can also see the national sense of humor in some of Argentina's most popular cartoonists. Tristan's political drawings, however, make much of butchered legs and arms, while Luis Medrano simply caricatures *porteño*, city-dweller types. Nini Marshall, an Argentine comedienne who recreated an immigrant servant girl character à la Gracie Fields, developed a style of comedy that proved Argentines certainly could enjoy some kinds of jokes. One who did not enjoy Nini's style, however, was Evita Perón. It is said that after a row, Nini left the stage and that unofficially her films were banned. This, in effect, placed her in professional exile in her own country.

There is something essentially sad about the Argentine character that is quickly apparent, especially to the newcomer. It shows in Argentine music, dress, and conversation, and, despite his optimism, in the average Argentine's outlook. Many of the stories popular in Buenos Aires are not locally created, but imports dressed up in local verbiage. Many of the comic strips are translations from abroad. Most locally produced humorous films are with few exceptions not really funny. Rather, they are drawing-room farces filled with talk.

Argentines love conversation. It goes on endlessly and everywhere. In the universities students enjoy nothing better than securing permission to debate with their professors. Such debate is also carried on in city cafés and out on the *estancias* during the frequent pauses for sipping the national beverage, *maté*, the bitter herb tea. Like ourselves, the Argentines often get carried away when they speak, oblivious to the noise they make. The bang of their cups in playing *bidou* (the favorite café dice game) and the din of music in the background seems only to spur them on.

Young Argentines soon learn how to reason on their feet or across the table. What one says and how one says it are fully as important as the facts. The speed of the response and the way the answer is phrased are considered telling. Often a conversation is really a game of matching wits. As one Argentine explained: "When you grow up in a big Argentine family, a good resounding voice and an ability to keep talking is essential if you want to get your viewpoint and will across."

Argentines love the sport and drama of argument. They like to punctuate what they say with verbal thrusts and stinging barbs. Points are often made to win the approval of listeners rather than overwhelm opponents with logic. A stranger, first seeing a pair of Argentines in conversation, often feels that an explosion is imminent. To Argentines, a good rousing argument is a vital part of living. They like talk for talk's sake. Contradicting one's friends or enemies is routine.

Many an Argentine will take almost any other side of an argument, either out of pure contrariness or simply for the sport of it. At other times he will do it for the impression, the attention, and the spotlight it brings.

The Fascists won Argentine support with talk of their economic theories. Russian ideas have caught on in some quarters. The Frenchman's ability to converse has always delighted Argentines who are likely to say: "If we want to talk with North Americans we must talk about their business. Otherwise there is nothing to say."

In their talk, Argentines frequently balk stubbornly and are not overly sure of what they want, but are prepared to shout until they get it. This extends to international questions. One diplomat of long experience in Argentina phrased it this way: "If, somehow, Argentina had taken the lead in continental solidarity, she would probably have exceeded our fondest hopes for real inter-Americanism. When, for various reasons, she got on the other side of the fence, the more we and the rest of the Americas pushed one way, the more Argentina shoved the other."

In their international debating, Argentines have always been strong on principles and ideals. Often there is more talk than action. Our very unwillingness to give sufficient lip service to these things—despite the fact that we often wear our hearts on our sleeves—makes Argentines regard us as people lacking in soul and without their "broader basic concepts."

The habit of contradiction, and the refusal of the average Argentine to take orders may, however, someday be their country's salvation, for, no matter who is in control, the Argentines, although moving slowly, have always somehow managed to contradict.

In their constant conversation and debating, Argentines are able to make the proper gesture and the right compliment. They do this naturally. When you visit them, for example, they will say, "You are in your own house" (*esta en su casa*). This implies an invitation to drop in at any time. The fact is, however, that a foreigner will rarely, even now, be invited to a true Argentine home unless he is extremely friendly with its owners. You are not expected to pay a visit without a formal invitation. "We are like you Yankees," one Argentine said. "Our invitations mean about the same thing as your 'Let's have lunch some time.'"

The North American who is invited to an Argentine home finds Argentines gracious hosts. Their friendly gestures have incomparable charm. Praise anything your Argentine host has and he will say: "*Es suyo,*" it's yours. Again, taking it would be unthinkable. Yet at the moment he says it, the Argentine undoubtedly is as sincere as we with our luncheon gesture.

For those he knows, the Argentine can be the world's

most courteous and charming individual. Unknowns get short shrift. Relatively few Argentines have any sense of public politeness. They frequently bump into people while scurrying round town, refusing all written or unwritten rules about keeping to the right or left, or giving the right of way to man, beast, or vehicle.

Yet, a friend, even a casual one, receives a warm *abrazo*—the bear hug, back-slapping greeting—when two Argentines meet, even after a short interval of not seeing one another. The *abrazo*, incidentally, is more than a greeting of friendship; it is used just as much in times of sadness or distress, serving in a sense as a symbol of friendly intimacy, the public limit to which Argentines will go. Occasionally even men who privately detest one another will extend the *abrazo* at an important public function as a sign that despite present circumstances they have known one another over a long period and can still be gracious. Though the *abrazo* appears highly demonstrative, it is a formality; it is an extension of the inevitable handshake, or the round of handshakes, of any Argentine introduction.

Carlton Beals, describing the rigidity of well-to-do Argentine manners, says: "At a strictly formal function, the slightest deviation from etiquette means social ruin. The fixed greeting, the precise repetitions of your own name, are typical. Even sex, though more open and coquettish, more sly and daring, always is more protected by fixed rules."

Yet outside his immediate circle the Argentine man seldom hesitates to ignore formality and offer the most extravagant remarks, or *piropos*, to the passing *señoritas* on the streets. Such *piropos* come from Argentines of all ages, *porteños* or provincials. They will stand idly on the sidewalk or sit in a café, one eye ever alert for a *chica* whose looks or features may be worth a second glance and a *piropo*. Most *señoritas* don't seem to object, at least not too vocally. An attractive girl will hear such expressions as "What a potato," which is equivalent to "What a peach," or the more elegant, "What lovely eyes you have, little angel."

The *piropo* may be picturesque or provocative. The Argentine male has become so expert at the art that he seems to know exactly the right thing to say, poetic, clever or bright. He also senses to whom to say it. Some *señorita* or *señora* may feel above such things. Yet attractive U. S. women who know Spanish and have spent some time in Argentina often miss the *piropos* when they return to the States. One woman confessed when she returned to the States: "Somehow, I get a feeling I'm slipping. *Nobody* notices me any more."

In days past—and it was not so long ago at that—the *piropos* of Argentina's *caballeros* on the streets would be accompanied by a slight pinch on the *señorita's* posterior. In theory, at least, Argentines tell you, this practice enabled a belle to poll her popularity by counting the black marks when she returned from a stroll. The custom—especially when it was publicized by visitors—gave Buenos Aires a reputation the city fathers were not especially anxious to enjoy. First the municipality ordered the arrest of any man against whom a pinching complaint was made. Subsequently, this became a bit of a racket. So the girls were held until the police could determine the background of the complainant, and action was taken accordingly. Currently, the experts insist the pinch, if experienced at all, is little more than a gentle pat. And old-time *porteños* sadly insist life in Buenos Aires lacks yesterday's zest.

Despite all the colorful Latin implications and the romantic aura of tradition found in so many aspects of Argentine life, the average Argentine's thought is extremely practical. Many Argentines consider themselves idealists, yet they are perhaps the most materialistic of all Latins. A majority of city-dwelling Argentines are very money-conscious. Their talk deals with purchases and profits. Like most practical New Englanders, they are likely to want to know: "What's in it for me?"

Often the complaint about our being materialistic comes from upper-class Argentines who inherited their wealth, or at least did not have to work hard for it. They look down on the first-generation *nouveau riche* still aggressively gathering their fortunes.

Argentina's materialism extends to a desire to get something for nothing. Thus, again like Americans, Argentines are strong on bargains. Shops often feature sales and mark-downs, real or contrived. To limit such *saldos*, the government now requires retailers to obtain special official permits before advertising sell-outs. Nonetheless, since Argentines insist almost anything can be accomplished for a little under-the-table *coima*, palm-greasing, no one can be sure the official permit makes the sale any more authentic or legitimate. This unfortunate practice, of course, is not limited to Argentina.

Most Argentines are bargain-seekers because underneath their frequently sad faces they are optimists, certain everything will eventually turn out all right. Their love of gambling and of taking a chance to get something for nothing is traditional. Should his cattle and crops go without water for any appreciable time, an Argentine may face ruin. Contrariwise, if weather is favorable, he may be in the money. But he feels he cannot do much about rain, anyway. And, as with roulette at the great Atlantic seashore resort of Mar del Plata, win or lose, the Argentine feels it is something beyond his control.

If things go well, he is pleased. But if they go badly, he is not likely to be too concerned. Impassivity in moments of danger or reverses is a characteristic much admired.

As can be expected of a nation which has produced some of the world's finest horses and horsemen, and where these things are revered almost above womankind, physical courage is a national trait, and individual hero-ism not unusual. The Argentine's courage, however, is not the reckless, foolhardy variety or the sort that makes him eager to fight and die for ideals, frequently cited history to the contrary.

Thus, Argentines are law-abiding, yet unresponsive to discipline. They are freedom-loving, but unwilling to take a stand and die for it.

Someone once said, in fact, that Argentina's great trouble is chronic indecision—leaving a way out without becoming involved. "*No te metas*" is a favorite expression meaning: "Don't get yourself mixed up in anything which can only cause you trouble." It is much like our World War II Army expression: "Never volunteer for anything —you'll only have headaches." Most Argentines share this feeling. They want to keep out of anything which might cause them any personal disturbance.

The Spanish philosopher José Ortega y Gasset, after

34381

living in Argentina, said that the national motto seemed to be "Mind your own business." Ernesto Sabato gives this example:

"Suppose, let us say, there is an argument or an altercation of some sort between a bus driver and a passenger. The average Argentine looks on with ironic detachment and remains aloof. And if the police take a hand in the matter and seek a witness, nobody has seen anything, nobody was there, nobody heard a word. There is more than a grain of truth in Ortega's characterization. The average Argentine employs a kind of philosophy that always sees the pro and con of every fact, which makes it hard for him to find motives strong enough to justify a positive attitude."

Argentines want most to live peacefully. They seek a tranquil existence, hence are willing to talk but go along rather than fight back. Some feel this characteristic has stemmed from the vast flat *pampa* where the temperature is mild all year round and the cattle are placid, bland, and phlegmatic. True, the trait of tranquility is more notable in the interior than in Buenos Aires. Yet even among those Argentines who are excitable and passionate in other ways, the desire to keep out of trouble, to remain uninvolved, to refuse to upset oneself unduly, is traditional.

This is not to imply that Argentines do not admire those who make up their minds about what they want and go after it. The Nazis set their goals in Argentina and proceeded to pursue them without deviating. The Argentine military, following their example, did the same in 1943 when it marched to the Casa Rosada—Buenos Aires' rose-colored government house—and took over. But Argentines have often noted that the United States while protesting Argentina's strangulation of democracy, has rarely been able to decide what to do about it.

"You have switched from one side to another," they say. "You have talked and been blamed for economic sanctions, yet you have not followed through. You have threatened to isolate us; then you have sought our friendship. Thus, one day you have encouraged democratic resistance—and the next pulled back. What, in view of this, can you expect from us?"

The Argentines' habit of indecision stems in part from the Latin habit of *mañana* or putting off anything important until tomorrow. Argentines are not as much given to the custom as, say, Mexicans or Central Americans. Yet *mañana* is still part of the national tradition, particularly when it involves doing something distasteful. Argentines, particularly those in official activities, are apt to procrastinate further, promising to resolve the matter *pasado* (the day after) *mañana*. But should this draw demands for action they say: "You North Americans dash around to fill and keep the schedule, regardless of accomplishment. We get the same results when it is all over, for we find things frequently take care of themselves."

The *mañana* habit is on its way out in Buenos Aires. In September, 1951, for instance, one of my friends ordered a number of custom-made articles—shoes, hats, suits, etc.—a brief time before his departure. Every store delivered the things on time, exactly when promised.

Such speed is not so common when one has a house to build, painting to be done, a car to be fixed. On the other hand, as Argentines are quick to point out: "In the United

States, few builders or craftsmen any longer keep promises, so what is the great difference?"

Mañana to the average Argentine also means taking
time out to savor things, to enjoy life. Though the *porteños* of Buenos Aires are far more businesslike than
other Latins, they still believe a certain number of pleas-
antries must come first. One first inquires about a colleague's wife, his children, and perhaps uncles, aunts
and other relatives, then business. Such preliminaries are
considered an essential in being *simpático*. The man who
is all bustle and accomplishment might be considered full
of effervescent agitation but hardly *simpático*.

Simpático gestures vary widely. Franklin D. Roosevelt, for example, was considered highly *simpático*. His
graciousness, his personality, the way he phrased things,
the interest he expressed in them, were all noted. Argentines do not generally love a person who is *simpático*.
But the feeling does establish a relationship that can
help solve many problems. An Argentine politician who
lacks this quality is rarely accepted. He may achieve
power in other ways, but he will never receive the intense
loyalty from his followers which permits him to hold on
and on, despite things which would force a *Norteamericano* from office.

The fact that many of Perón's followers regard him as
simpático is one reason for his success not often appreciated outside the country, for Argentines believe more
in loyalty to persons than to ideas or principles. With
innate knowledge of this point, Perón and the militarists
seek constantly to create the feeling that Argentina is
under fire from the United States and Britain. Their aim
is to arouse an allegiance which can help keep them in

power. They also seek to make Argentines feel a sense of fealty and pride in the fame, if not the notoriety, which Perón has brought their country.

Argentines of top families have, to put it mildly, frequently been critical of the Peróns. Many spoke openly against them in their homes. They felt Evita's radio-actress-girl-about-town background was detrimental to their country. They said she conducted herself poorly, particularly on her famed European trip when she saw the Pope, was decorated by Franco in Madrid, and spent a good deal of her time buying expensive gowns in Paris.

Both peronistas and their opponents express a certain pride in what Perón has done to make Argentina better known and give her a more important role in hemispheric and world affairs. "You must hand it to him," they say in effect. "He has made the others sit up and take notice."

Since Argentines of every group have always been determined to articulate their strong faith in their own destiny, this phase of Perón's activities has been astutely exploited. During inter-American conferences when the question of Argentina's possible break with the Axis was in world headlines, many Argentines were delighted at the banner type and the long dispatches reporting what London, Washington and Paris were saying about them. Such newspaper stories not only further the national feeling of importance, but are somehow regarded as an indication of outside approval.

Fearful of their own sovereignty, even pro-democratic Argentines still nurse the idea that the United States has designs on them and that the British would seek to exploit them. Most tell you so openly. They do not believe it in quite the way the Nazi propagandists wanted, nor do they all accept the government's version of foreign designs. But they believe it nonetheless. And it helps explain why Argentine officials often put up a tremendous display of resistance to United States proposals at hemispheric conferences even if they later back down.

"You have to remember we never overlook what the home reaction will be," one delegate confessed.

In international relations, Argentina used to view Europe as a somewhat arbitrary but well-loved parent, and the United States as an obstreperous and greedy older brother. To carry the analogy still further, Argentines have always been jealous of the rich, powerful brother, in the same way children are jealous, realizing they could never be the first nation in this hemisphere. When Argentines talk of holding the Number One position in the world south of the Rio Grande, they concede that the States holds first place north of it. This, to most, is eminently right and proper. "But," they ask, "if you *Norteamericanos* run things up north, why are you unwilling to admit Argentina should run things down south?"

Argentina's Army officers, deep in their hearts, feel this with special conviction. Those who know the military mind say that the egotism of the General Staff is quite equal to that of the military leaders of Germany or pre-war Japan. Even pro-democratic Argentines may still feel it.

Even though they finally entered the war on our side, Argentines feel their basic position is neutral. "Such countries as Switzerland, Portugal, Turkey, Sweden, Ireland, all had a definite role during World War II," they say. "Our role, even today, is not unlike theirs."

Since the beginning of their independent life, Argentines have always tried to avoid entangling alliances. "We want to keep out of other people's wars. We want to run our affairs, to sell our goods to all, to extend special friendships with those countries which buy from us. Why should we be forced to take sides?"

In part this stems from the Argentines' realistic idea that they must take care of themselves first. Because they did not want to be swept away, Argentines waited to see how both opponents were really doing before making up their minds in World War II. Pearl Harbor was, we insisted, a direct attack obligating Argentina to keep her pledges to join us. Most Latin Republics quickly agreed. Argentines, feeling neither threatened nor attacked, wanted to remain neutral. To us this may seem purely opportunistic. Yet, as one Argentine reasoned: "When one is a small country, this makes a kind of sense which you, in a big country, really do not quite understand."

For years Argentina has been in the convulsions of a social revolution far deeper than her military coup. Regular processes of what might have been an ordinarily democratic change have been thrown aside. The disturbed atmosphere has been stirred up by those who wish to play up their own interest—the Communists, the Fascists, the nationalists, and other groups we shall presently examine.

And so Argentina moves ahead. She is puzzling to us; more often, puzzling to herself.

Chapter II

Meet Some Argentines

THE PORTEÑOS OF THE CAPITAL

YOU WILL probably encounter him first on the Calle Florida, a narrow, brightly-lit street that runs for a mile through the heart of Argentina's Capital of Buenos Aires.

His suit is somber, his shoes brightly polished, his tie, probably black and worn with a tiny pearl stickpin. He carries his gloves correctly. There's a white kerchief in the breast pocket. On his head is a carefully brushed hat. At first glance you won't know if he is a banker or a clerk. His mustache won't provide a clue—most male Argentines wear them, as one put it, "to demonstrate our virility." Neither will you get a revealing hint from his air of affluence or his heavily slang-flavored Spanish, with its references to the newest show, the latest deal, and the high-scoring *futbol* star.

His pace seems brisk yet unhurried—whether it's eleven in the morning or seventeen in the afternoon (5 P.M.) on the twenty-four-hour Continental clock system used in Argentina. He considers the promenade an essential of his day. Automobiles are banned from Florida until late in the evening so he will not have to dodge the fast-moving man behind the wheel who is likely to consider his car as much a weapon as a vehicle. On Florida, there is always time to keep an eye on the passing *señoritas*, to whisper the newest *piropo*, or to stop in at his favorite café for a coal black *café espresso* or a *vermouth con soda*.

Banker or clerk, shopkeeper or waiter, the *porteño* probably carries a calling card listing his profession, titles, and often his honorary connections. Doctors of philosophy generally use the term "Doctor" throughout their lives. Engineers retain their title of *Ingeniero*, architects that of *Arquitecto*. The *porteño* has a pride in himself, what he does, and where he lives—and rarely fails to express it, for there is something about Buenos Aires that gives most of its people a sense of being in what to them is the greatest city in the New World. Smaller than New York? Or, if you insist, even Chicago? "Yes, in numbers," he will say. But that is obviously not important to the three-million-odd city-dwellers and the additional million or more inhabitants of the suburbs of Buenos Aires.

Buenos Aires to them is not only big. Its metropolitan area has more than one-fourth of Argentina's eighteen million population, and because of the desire for higher wages, bright lights, and other attractions of the big town, Buenos Aires is growing faster than the rest of the country. Apply the same percentage to New York, they say, and it would have approximately forty millions. For a proper comparison you would have to throw in Washington too, for Buenos Aires is a federal district, the center both of national government and business, art and intellect, sports and fashion, transport and communications—and the hub point of a continent now in crisis.

To the resident of Buenos Aires the thing that makes his town and his role in it so stimulating is that Buenos Aires is obviously the *center* of everything. It is a town, he will tell you, of which a man must be proud. A town where you can hear the best tangos and perhaps, someday, write one yourself. A metropolis where you need your best clothes all the time, and where the men—who dress up more than the women—first introduced the ultimate in urban formality—a summer straw hat done in the shape of a Homburg.

It is a city whose people like to take two hours for lunch and three for dinner—even though, to their dismay, they now have to finish their meal in half the time. *Porteños* love crowds, excitement, bright lights, and the glass-fronted, modern movie palaces that line Calle Lavalle. In Buenos Aires, even the Recoleta Cemetery looks as though it had been dressed up. That is the effect given by its highly ornate family vaults built above ground like miniature houses of the dead. The Argentines love their metropolis, take an interest in all its activities, and proudly feel that no other world capital has half as many attractions. They are self-conscious about their town. They closed down their public houses of ill repute in the late thirties because foreigners wrote books like "The Road to Buenos Aires." Though the exposé named no names and offered more allure than alarm, the incident provoked national indignation. Films offending *por-teño* sensitivity are so vehemently booed that theater owners withdraw them rather than risk violence.

Many observers feel the city dweller lacks a sense of proportion and the ability to think objectively, particularly when he hears himself discussed. Yet he enjoys his own particular brand of witticism, especially the *cachada*. This is the fine art of poking sly, often caustic fun at an individual in a group without letting him know what is happening. The victim's shoes, or his favorite sports club, or his taste in *señoritas* are praised. Compliment is piled on compliment, until, as the *porteño* puts it, "praise runs from the ears." Everybody is in the know save the butt of the jest. The *porteño* relishes every compliment—yet aware of the *cachada*, and being like many an Argentine unsure of himself, he is likely before too long to break down. The skillful *porteño cachadisto* can keep up a running *cachada* for as long as an hour without the victim's being quite sure of just what is going on.

With all the activity of *porteño* life, the capital produces in most citizens a concentration on one's own affairs, a kind of coldness and indifference that possibly marks big-city people everywhere. The farther you get into the interior, the friendlier the people.

Buenos Aires is, first and foremost, a man's town. This is evident in the numerous clubs and in the café life of the city. The Richmond is one of the favorite cafés. The Odeon Bar—not to be confused with the elegant restaurant—is favored by Argentina's jazz fans. The financial crowd frequents the Boston Bar, shippers go to the Fragata, and *políticos*, real and would-be, favor Del Molino, on the plaza near Congress.

Visitors just down from the United States sometimes feel that since Argentines spend so much time in their cafés they can't get much business done. *Porteños* disagree. They that feel the café is an essential part of their normal routine. As one man put it: "We accomplish as much over a café table as you do in your office. And it's far more convenient. A telephone call costs only twenty *centavos*, though it used to be free. Besides, there is no eavesdropping secretary to listen in. One's friends are here with the inside story of the Finance Ministry's latest move—or the newest scandal. Besides, *señor*, in what office can one get all of this service, plus food, and those lovely *señoritas* passing just outside the window all at the same time?"

Whatever happens in Buenos Aires—and to a relative degree in the interior—is pretty thoroughly worked out in the cafés beforehand. The Argentine café has a social and political significance hard for an outsider to visualize. It may be a smart place in town, a neighborhood café which spreads out to the sidewalk, or a remote provincial *boliche*. All have a collection of tiny, marble-topped tables, back-breaking chairs, and a long service bar presided over by a portly, chit-dispensing proprietor at the elaborate, imported National Cash Register. Many have an adjoining *salón para familias*, a family gathering place often marked only by the fact that its tables boast a few stained cloths, a couple of artificial flowers in a stiff little vase, and a *señora's* room.

Step into any Buenos Aires café, summon the waiter with the *porteño's* penetrating hiss, order what you want, and you can sit as long as you please. The café is part political club, part gambling casino. All day long, and even far into the night, the smack of the *bidou* cup, rolling out the three dice in the absorbing Argentine game, makes the place noisier than a bowling alley. The higher the decibel count the better regular patrons seem to like it. Stakes are rarely high however. Usually men play only for the round of coffees or drinks—a point which they insist encourages moderate drinking.

Supplementing the cafés are the *confiterías*. They have some features of a tearoom, an old-fashioned ice cream parlor and a New York Schrafft's restaurant. They provide a place to drop in for tea, a snack, a morning pause and a sandwich. *Confiterías* are for ladies and youngsters as well as for men. *Bidou* is banned. They offer the fanciest pastry to be found anywhere this side of the Riviera. You may choose the pastry you like best from the large trays brought to your table. You get a check for the total and a return for those you do not touch. Many *confiterías* in Buenos Aires and in the larger provincial cities are more elaborate than our most stylish pink satin Park Avenue bonbon shops. Others look like relics of gaslight Paris with lavish use of marble, great glittering crystal chandeliers, red velvet and lace, and an air of having rejected all attempts at modernization since opening day.

Both the cafés and the *confiterías* fit in with the *porteños'* habit of staying up late. *Porteños* never seem to get tired enough to want to go home early. After the *ciné,* theater or concert, they jam the downtown *confiterías* and cafés. Neighborhood places are likely to be just as crowded. Time and place are, however, highly important. With his determined sophistication, the *porteño* is well aware that the *noche de moda* at the Embassy night club on the Plaza San Martín is Thursday—and that no one who is anyone would go on a Monday. On Saturday at midday one has a *copetin*—generally a sweet cocktail—at Harrod's big, walnut-paneled tearoom, patterned after its London store. Only *señoras* and *señoritas* drop in during the week.

The *porteño's* skills at producing goods, buildings, and money, and his faults and foibles often resemble those of our own city-dwellers. He has the same insincerity, overbearing manner, and materialistic viewpoint so often charged against our big town residents. Yet, the Parisians, the Madrileños, and the Milanese possibly understand the residents of Buenos Aires better than we. The reason lies both in the things the *porteño* likes to do, and in the way his mind works.

Save where their dominant characteristic is Northern Italian, Slavic, or Teutonic, they are likely to appear somewhat more delicately formed than we. This, and his interest in gossip and fashionable chit-chat, sometimes causes unknowing visitors to regard him as effete. Such impressions are highly deceiving.

Actually it is money which dominates a good deal of *porteño* thinking. You hear more talk of prospects and deals than you probably would in New York or any other large American city with, say, the exception of Houston, Texas, during its boom-town period.

All over Buenos Aires you see *casas de cambio*—money exchanges—where dealings go on day after day in pesos, dollars, pounds, and francs. Figures of the day's buy and sell offers are posted in their windows like stocks. And they are as familiar to the average *porteño* as our Coca-Cola signs. Buenos Aires has Latin America's busiest stock exchange, and the most commodious and active banks handling the largest number of business transactions.

The *porteños* are strong individualists. They are self-satisfied, imperturbable, uncooperative. Not only do they dislike lining up for tickets, they have never accepted traffic lights. They are convinced it would be beneath their dignity to be governed by anything "so mechanical and without soul."

The *porteño* seeks many of the same things the North American seeks. He doesn't care for any old car; he wants a new Detroit model, with freshly-scrubbed white wall tires—of which Buenos Aires seems to have more per capita than almost any other world capital. It does not bother him that his car costs two to three times what it does in the United States and represents a far greater percentage of his income, for what he cannot buy directly, he often gets on the installment plan. *Créditos*—so much down and so much a month—are available for every kind of product and service, even funerals. "Without them," many a *porteño* insists, "I could not keep going." The Buenos Aires Banco Municipal de Prestamos, municipal pawn shop, is as big as a major United States department store and serves hundreds of thousands of customers.

Both the *porteño* and his wife are usually socially ambitious. Appearance, which is regarded as a basic sign of one's social status, is a first consideration in Buenos Aires. The male *porteño* keeps his hair so slick that other Latins say Argentines are born with a bottle of *gomina*—the favorite hair tonic—in one hand. Buenos Aires has more *peluquerias*, or barber shops, than almost any other capital. These glittering palaces of gleaming glass and polished brass have white-smocked barbers, manicurists, sports magazines, and, in all likelihood, even a tattered copy of *Esquire* imported from the United States. With all their interest in *señoritas,* the Argentines have no such publication of their own. There are barber shops in scores of cafés, clubs, subway and rail stations and rare is the *porteño* who doesn't look—and smell—as if he has just come from one.

The *porteño* probably spends a far greater percentage of his income on clothes than most American males. Even the poorest manage to keep their suits neat and well pressed. In front of the Naval Club in the center of Buenos Aires, there's a blind pencil seller who wears a black Homburg—and no one thinks it odd.

In part this tradition of dress stems from the Spanish and British influence. The smartest men's shops all have English names: Warrington, Rhoder's, The Brighton— though they are no longer, and perhaps never were, empire outposts. The *porteño* would not be seen dead in one of the garish neckties sold in the United States.

If he is above the lowest economic rank, he will somehow contrive to have his clothes made to order, usually by a special little tailor he has discovered. His suits will be cut a bit more tightly than ours, the shoulders a bit broader. Essentially, however, they will be highly conservative. Few white collar workers would think of appearing in town with sports jackets or loud shirts. In the last decade more informal, made-to-order clothes have been noticeable. The Casa Braudo has grown prosperous by offering one pair of trousers gratis. But most *porteños* still regard such establishments contemptuously as manifestations of "Made-in-U.S.A." civilization.

The *porteño's* wife will, in nine cases out of ten, also

cling to her own little dressmaker rather than buy ready-made clothes. The dressmaker may have only a sewing machine in a tiny flat, or maintain a chic establishment in the smart northern district. Several of the big Paris *couturiers* have their only foreign branches in Buenos Aires.

The women of Buenos Aires have a knack of wearing their clothes smartly. They dress with more formality than their sisters in the United States, preferring darker colors. Black is considered stylish as well as utilitarian since most Argentines observe old-fashioned mourning customs.

Not having an opportunity to engage in as many activities as American women, the *señora* and *señorita* of Buenos Aires spend much more time on dress. Local fashion magazines are plentiful. Copies of *Vogue* and *Harper's Bazaar*—both American and French editions—are also widely followed. Many a dressmaker can copy a model simply from studying the illustration. Scores of shops sell fabrics of all kinds, both domestic and imported. Time spent shopping for just the right handbag, the correct shoes, the exact scarf and gloves to go with an ensemble is considered well invested.

The *porteña* frequents her beauty parlor even more than does her North American sister. For her, as for her father, brother, or husband, keeping up appearances and the impression of well-being is all important.

This concept has spread even to the remote areas of Argentina. Even small towns have numerous *salons de bellezas*. One little-publicized yet vital factor in Perón's "emancipation of Argentina's working class," was the fact that for the first time many women could afford a weekly

trip to the beauty shop. One housemaid told us: "Before
Perón, we servants never enjoyed such luxuries. Now we
do. Other things may be costlier. But to us life has always
been expensive and we have had nothing to show for it.
Now at last we can feel like ladies."

Every Argentine woman and most Argentine males use
scent. The number of perfume shops in Buenos Aires
runs into the thousands. Their windows are filled with
bottles, lipsticks, brushes, all carefully arranged in multicolored geometric patterns. There are innumerable vari-
eties of colognes and toilet waters.

As we have noted, while in the past such Buenos Aires
shops as Harrod's featured imported goods, and many
porteños were reluctant to buy things made in their own
country, today most consumer items are labeled *Industria
Argentina,* the stamp required for all locally manufactured items. These run a wide range. Most fabrics used in
men's and women's suits are now national, although
British woolens are imported and sold at higher prices.
Nationally made shoes dominate. So do domestically-pro-
duced women's gloves, alligator and other leather bags.

In the past, Argentine hides were usually shipped to
Britain for treatment, made into finished goods, and sent
back for sale in the smart shops. Today it would be hard
to find British-made shoes in Buenos Aires. Argentina has,
in fact, become a shoe exporter to neighboring countries.
Some unusual designs are even sold on Manhattan's
fashionable Fifth Avenue.

Shop window displays are more symmetrical than im-
aginative. Exclusive men's shops show racks of shirts
folded back so their collars are hidden. Ties are knotted
and ends spread with the greatest precision. The smaller

shops follow the lead, neatly displaying their wares on little metal stands against highly polished woodwork. Most shops give carefully written receipts for each purchase. Packages are tied with a little wooden handle fitted into the string so that they may be carried delicately. The rude, disinterested sales clerks so frequently found in the United States are rare in Buenos Aires.

Face and show are all important for the *porteño*. Even the lowliest clerk who will not be paid for another week is likely to spend his last *peso* treating a friend to a vermouth or tram fare, rather than give any indication he lacks money. As his income rises, the *porteño* thinks first of buying things to wear for himself and his family, then of improving his home. He wants an apartment in an attractive building. The exterior is more important than the quarters themselves, for few but intimate friends are likely to come up for a visit. The *porteño* wants to display what he has, not guard it in the bank. Savings accounts per capita are far lower than here.

When he dies, the *porteño* wants a funeral with matched black horses, possibly from Casa Miras, a funeral establishment so aggressive in its merchandising that it has an advertisement on every page of the 356-page Buenos Aires telephone directory. *Porteño* families faced with the problem of burying old Uncle Maximiliano in the style befitting the family name have been known to rent a vault for a night in swank Recoleta Cemetery and next morning move the remains to a less expensive resting place.

Argentina benefited economically from both World Wars, and nowhere in the world wealth and prosperity were more ostentatiously displayed than in Buenos Aires.

Even today the *porteño* often feels that his city is the world's lushest, the last sanctuary of well-being in a globe torn by what he regards as "purposeless conflict."

He cannot understand why prices of food and clothing are skyrocketing. Still he knows he is far better off than most other people in the world. "Our government may be bad," he will say, "but what the rest of the world is going through is barbarous!"

The most important *porteños* in the public eye—and those who show off to the greatest degree—are the new, top-notch industrialists. Some have progressive labor and public relations ideas, but most have the same characteristics our industrial leaders had a generation or two back. There is little public ownership of shares or accounting of profits. *Porteño* industrialists don't feel the public has a right to know much about their enterprises. Their social behavior and their economic and political creeds are inferior to those of similar groups in the United States, England, or prewar Germany. They make deals where they may, forget scruples when these interfere, and pile up what they can—making certain that as much as possible is invested outside Argentina, just in case they lose their influence in government circles or there is a serious political crisis. Though he may work energetically to succeed, once the self-made industrialist has completed what he has set out to do, he will give himself the leisure to get the fullest enjoyment out of life.

The *porteño* wants to set his own pace, and he hates to lose any of his personal rights and privileges. One unusual demonstration of this occurred shortly after the military coup, when Vice-President Admiral Saba H. Sueyro died. Even though he was virtually unknown, two days of national mourning were decreed, one a Sunday. For the first time in as long as anybody could remember, Buenos Aires racetracks, movies, cafés and *confiterías* were all shuttered tight. *Porteños*, who in many cases had not even begun to think about the government's interventions, were more upset by the period of enforced mourning for Sueyro than by almost anything else the militarists had done. "Imagine," one man commented, "we couldn't even go for a walk on the Florida. It was intolerable. It was uncivilized."

The *porteño* most of all fancies himself a cosmopolitan living in the heart of civilization. He knows that when he sits down at a dinner party in Buenos Aires at twenty-two in the evening (10 P.M.), the first question may well be: "What language shall we speak tonight?" In the course of a day he may converse in Italian, English, and French, as well as in his own Spanish. He will probably transact business in a foreign bank, get his clothes French dry-cleaned at a Japanese *tintoreria*, and buy his coffee from *Los Dos Chinos* (The Two Chinamen). The radio that wakes him comes from Belgium. His bathroom fixtures were probably made in Holland, and he may ride to work in a German car, or on a subway built by the Spanish. He has only to go down to the docks—as many a *porteño* loves to do on any pleasant holiday afternoon—and see there the ships of every nation in the world tied up to take their fill of what Argentina produces.

True, this could, to a certain extent, be said about New York City. Yet New York's polyglot cosmopolitanism is likely to be found at one of two extremes: the very bottom in the poorer districts—Italian, Armenian, Greek, Puerto Rican—or in a smattering among the very top society. In Buenos Aires the international flavor goes all the way through. Yet while the *porteño* feels this affinity with those across the Atlantic, he has not, at least up until now, had much desire to share their difficulties or tighten his own belt in order to aid them more.

In part it is because he loves his own rich food too well. He knows Buenos Aires' restaurants are among the world's finest, rarely serving him a poor meal. Many have been in business for a half century. Their menus are extensive. Naturally, they concentrate on beef, but it is hard to name any French or Italian dish they do not serve. There are none of the spicy dishes which North Americans, who know Mexico, are apt to expect everywhere South of the Border.

For instance, look at the menu at a typical first-class restaurant like La Cabaña or La Estancia, both of which are extremely popular with Argentines as well as with tourists. Prices are not nearly as high as at the top luxury hotels, the Alvear Palace or Plaza. The Cabaña's menu shows on its lists nineteen kinds of cold meats including suckling pig, small tongues, antipasto, mushrooms in oil; five soups of the regular kind, plus three soups of the day; thirteen different kinds of so-called pastas, including ravioli, cannellóne, taglierini; and five different kinds of rice in many different styles. There are seven regular salads and fifteen different kinds of fish including the Argentine specialty, *pejerrey* from the Rio de la Plata. The regular grill lists lamb, calf, sweetbreads, intestine, udder, lamb kidneys, veal kidneys, black pudding, special sausages, criollo and Italian sausages, rib roast, veal chops, grilled lamb, lamb chops, tenderloin steaks, entrecots, and a mixed grill.

These, it might be emphasized, are simply the regular listing. Under cold meats of the day there are an additional twelve items, fifteen different specialties, or what we might term entrees, and by actual count thirty-nine different desserts.

This is by no means the biggest menu to be found in Buenos Aires. A restaurant such as the Grill of the Hotel Plaza is far more expensive and has a longer menu. Even small second and third class places offer a far greater variety of food than most of our restaurants.

The *porteño* not only eats his heavy lunch and dinner, but pauses for food at least once—and perhaps twice—between each meal. He will probably stop for coffee late in the morning, or a sandwich and a *café con leche* (coffee with milk) before lunch. Most people have tea in the afternoon, crowding into one of the scores of Paulista coffee shops if they don't have a favorite *confitería* near by.

There are no drugstores with soda fountains. But a group of quick lunch places, known as Vascongadas and run by a Basque, are patterned roughly on some of our milk bars. They have become popular, and they feature such specialties as *"waf-lees americanos con Crema Chantilly,"* and *"Ays Krim Sodas,"* in almost as many flavors as Howard Johnson himself serves.

Since even a *porteño* snack is tremendous, the chief complaint is liver trouble caused by overeating. Those who don't die with liver ailments are generally living with them. Yet on the other hand, they do not seem to have the number of strokes, cardiac conditions, ulcers and other afflictions that trouble us so much. They have, incidentally, made their town a fairly healthy place.

Buenos Aires's vital statistics compare favorably with New York, Chicago and other large North American cities. Few deaths from malaria are recorded and, in recent years, none from yellow fever.

Because perhaps he is essentially sad and wants constant diversion to spice his passion for tranquility, the *porteño* supports more film houses than almost any other world capital. Buenos Aires also has as many as twenty-eight legitimate playhouses running during the season. Its racetracks and stadiums are the hemisphere's finest. Taking their sports seriously, Argentines build gigantic coliseums in which to view them.

The *porteño* likes to think his Spanish is perfect, but he drops his d's, slurs his s's and mispronounces his double l's and his y's by strict Castillian standards. His Spanish lacks the softness of Mexican and the poetry of Colombian Spanish. It has plenty of flavorsome Italian phrases.

In the course of a ten-minute conversation, his frequent gestures remind North Americans of the once-popular "handies." The open hand swept from under the chin means *"no se,"* I don't know. His finger holding down his eyelid means *"ojo,"* watch out. Twirling an imaginary mustache indicates something is *"macanudo,"* very O. K., a term that's completely *porteño*; its use by a North American stamps him as one of the *cognoscenti.* Palm out, tilting from side to side, means *"mas o menos,"* more or less.

The inhabitant of Buenos Aires is likely to look down on an Argentine from the interior. And while many of the secondary cities have their own individual personalities which we shall examine later, they ape the customs of Buenos Aires. The street with the smartest shops resembles Calle Florida. Fashions are advertised as "directly from the capital." If you leave for the capital on a train in remote Bariloche you find your destination listed as "Plaza Constitution," not Buenos Aires. Trains from the north head for the Presidente Perón, formerly the Retiro Station.

No matter what his position in life, the *porteño* feels the big town gives him something special. He is likely to think of the interior as a remote and uninteresting region or as a place he has come from but wants to forget.

As Argentine nationalism rises, the number of *porteños* who seek to give the impression that their Buenos Aires is an adjunct of Paris rather than the great port of the *pampa* constantly decreases. More and more Argentines show convincing pride in their country. The inferiority complex is still strong, but the emphasis on *Argentinidad*, the rise of nationalism, and the increased domestic travel (due to unfavorable foreign exchange rates) are all having their effect.

Chapter III

The Middle Class Is Argentina

SOMEONE ONCE defined the middle class as that group which sets up a budget and tries to live within it. While the definition may apply in some countries, it certainly does not to the Argentine. Most of Argentina's middle class would have difficulty in living within a budget, and as a rule they do not even try.

The *estancia* owners—those proprietors of the great landed cattle-raising estates whom we shall examine presently—were the group on whom Argentina's wealth was built. For years it was they who controlled both its economic and its political destiny.

On the other hand, it was the working class at the other extreme of the economic ladder on whom Perón depended for the popular force which enabled him first to obtain personal power after the Army officers had seized control of the civilian government.

Today, however, many believe the middle class is the group on which the Government as well as the country must depend for its future.

Why is this so?

The reason lies first in the fact that Argentina is (with the exception of her close neighbor Uruguay) the one Latin American republic which has a sizable middle class. Again like Uruguay, Argentina is the only country without a large Indian, Negro, or *mestizo* population.

Most Argentina observers define the middle class as that vast group which lies between the *estancia*-owning families at the top of the economic ladder and the agricultural and city laborers at the bottom. The city laborer and factory hand, the *obrero*, regards himself as being in the working class. The white-collar employee, the *empleado*, is legally and by his own concept, someone in the middle class. Some artisans or skilled workers, particularly if they have their own little businesses, also consider themselves middle-class Argentines. So do the teacher and the professional, even though they might actually earn less than laborers or artisans.

Many middle-class Argentines are second or third generation sons and daughters of European immigrants. They received more education than their parents. Many became merchants, or intermediate or even top government officials. Others work in the shops and the offices of the big packing plants and the utilities. Many have gone into small businesses of their own.

Because until comparatively recent times Argentina had no sizable industry, she developed no early industrial middle class. The middle class began with Argentina's period of stepped-up immigration, primarily in the cities. The most sizable recent increase in the middle class is the result of the arrival of Europeans who fled from Europe because of Hitler. Many brought special skills and merchandising initiative to the country, opened small businesses which have produced excellent returns to their owners and have given employment to many Argentines.

In Argentina's middle class are the descendants of the Italians, Spaniards, French, British, German, Swiss, Turks, and Syrio-Lebanese who were attracted to the Argentine in its period of greatest immigration. They now form the basic component of the mixture that has made Argentina different from most other Latin countries.

In the middle class are Argentina's intellectuals. Though exact numbers cannot be determined they have an importance far beyond their numbers. Among the intellectuals are the top newspapermen, whose prestige is often higher than that of journalists in the United States; many of the professors and teachers who write the erudite articles in the magazines and the papers; the painters, sculptors, and top musicians. They correspond more to the intellectuals of France than to any such group in our country. There is hardly one who does not have the title of Doctor, the term being used by almost every Argentine who gains a university degree. Practically every Argentine intellectual will have a book or two to his credit, even though it may have been published privately.

This group of Argentina's middle class might be said to be essentially pro-democratic and liberal in ideas on politics as well as on books, music, art. They are the most receptive to new ideas, to new approaches and concepts even though more conservative than might be supposed.

The non-intellectual Argentine middle class, as we have noted, is generally far more concerned with itself than with political progress and the democratic freedom. They may in a sense ape the possessions, customs, and the manners of the *estancia*-owning families from the very form of writing its family names down to copying the style of the gowns so elegantly displayed in the pages of the magazines *Atlantida* and *El Hogar.* But most members of the upper middle class realize that it is impossible for them to reach a position comparable to that of the great landowners or of those fashionable families that have inherited generations of wealth.

The upper middle-class Argentine may buy acreage out in the provinces, but rarely will he feel able to build a large *estancia* house or maintain the style of even the lesser *estancia* owner, no matter what he manages to accumulate. The age when new families can be added to the upper stratum has ended. New membership in the Jockey Club, for example, is confined to members' families and to the diplomatic group.

Argentina's middle class sets its own basis of morality and ambition as well as the daily conduct of life. It includes the most strongly nationalistic—hence anti-U.S.—Argentines, as well as many who admire the things we make if not the things we do. Thus many of the appeals for the made-in-U.S.A. devices that provide comforts and better living have a strong appeal to Argentine middle class men and women—as witness the successful adver-

tisements for refrigerators and cars which fill the pages of
the Argentine magazines.

While many American publications stress self-help,
publish do-it-yourself articles, and advocate household
budgets and the apportionment of income to this and that
purpose, most Argentines simply do not believe in such
things. They may have their own concept of what they
will spend for certain items, but their ideas are not based
on the methodical apportionment of many of our families.

The reason the middle class is now considered the key
to so much that is happening in Argentina lies in these
factors:

1. Perón's first appeal for support was established on
opposition to the wealthy *estancieros*. They were a national target, and they have not fought back or struggled
with effective results. Instead, they have been content
to return to their mansions and their clubs and sit things
out.

2. More recently Perón has attacked the industrialists
who may be middle class or of the top wealthy group.
Often it is hard to distinguish. In Buenos Aires the concentration of wealth is not generally as apparent as it is
on the *estancias*. The great mansions in which so many of
the landed aristocracy lived are gradually disappearing,
and they were conspicuous and pretentious symbols of
wealth.

3. The working class, both in the city and on the
estancias, has received almost all the benefits that Perón
can provide without putting the country into bankruptcy.
Yet while mass appeals have been to the *descamisados*, a
good proportion of his followers came from white-collar,
government employees.

4. Therefore the only group with undoubted resources and economic power plus the ability to change things is the middle class. In the United States the middle class has been the basis of our growth and development.

Hitler made Germany's frustrated middle class the basis for his rise to power. Some Argentine observers feel that the revolution of 1943 was a middle-class seizure of power from the landed oligarchy.

Ysabel Rennie, for example, explains: "Denied entrance by the front door, the middle class entered by the rear. Thirteen years of fraud and systematic frustration had left the democratic majority among Argentina's middle class millions disorganized and without real hope of power. The 30's had also convinced a majority of the middle class that democracy was a cheat. In the Army hierarchy, which was a stronghold of the Argentine bourgeoisie, middle class resentment, nationalism, and a belief in direct action fused. The Army dictatorship was middle class because its dictators were middle class; their outlook bourgeois: they did not love the landed oligarchy or the economic regime this group stood for. They feared the working class and were determined to make only such concessions as were necessary in order to keep it satisfied without altering in any way its fundamental position of subservience.

"They feared leftist revolutionary ideologies which could in any way rob them—the middle class—of their comfort and prerogatives. They feared the post-war for what it could bring of social unrest and alien doctrines. . . . There was nothing they feared more than a working-class revolution."

Whether this explanation holds or not, the fact is that

today it is the middle class to which Perón and the militarists are turning in order to achieve the vitally-needed balance of power in the event that labor, the Army, and the Church become more restive.

Many middle-class Argentines have, in recent years, become cynical and disillusioned with the military government which dominates them. They have not had the comparative increases in earning power, housing, and social benefits which the poorer classes have gained.

Many members of the middle class have become resigned. Others are beginning to realize in some degree their own latent power. A good deal of the opposition, particularly that which stems from the opposition political parties, could be said to be middle-class opposition. So today it is the middle class to whom the propaganda is now beginning to appeal, the middle class which many Argentine observers today feel may hold the true balance of power.

Chapter IV

How the Argentines Live

PICK UP a copy of the Argentine magazine *El Hogar*—The Hearth. Leaf through its multicolored pictures of homes and apartments. Read the elaborate, detailed descriptions of these new places.

"With the maximum comfort," numerous advertisements say, describing apartments with "elegant atmosphere, ample and numerous closets, air-conditioning, hot water, electric refrigeration, kitchen and pantry, laundry and centralized drying room, built-in incinerators."

With the kind of glowing prose which marks copywriters the hemisphere over, these advertisements describe the "living-room" (there is no equivalent word in Spanish so Argentines use the English which they pronounce "lee-ving"), the *comedor* or dining room, the *dormitorios* or bedrooms, the large "poetic garden" with

65

its "play space and toys for the entertainment of your children." There is a modern solarium on the terrace for your sunbath, a master antenna for your radio. And all of this in Buenos Aires' smartest location.

Such an apartment is, of course, not the apartment of the typical Argentine city dweller. No more would the model in *House Beautiful* or *Better Homes and Gardens* be the typical North American's apartment. But this description does pretty well represent the ideal of what a good many Argentines would like to have—and what an increasing number of wealthy urban Argentines do have, or are actively in the market for.

How the Argentines live, and how they would *like* to live, provide an important clue to their character, what they are, and what they want.

In examining how they live we must once again make clear distinctions among the *porteños* of Buenos Aires, the residents of the secondary cities, and those who live on the land, as well as among the Argentines of wealth, the middle class, and the worker group.

The description of the luxury apartment in *El Hogar* is extremely significant because it stresses what almost every Argentine, whatever his means or whatever his location, seeks most: "Maximum comfort." This idea remains constant, though the standards of what constitutes comfort vary. In the past, even lower-middle income Argentines—i.e., minor officials, small shopkeepers, etc.— had servants. Often they hired immigrants recently arrived from Spain or Italy, who would work for board, room, and wages lower than even the lowest minimums. Since Argentine families generally included several children, help was essential. In the lower middle-class families, the maid was often a slave of all work. She had an ugly little room, generally furnished with only an iron bed and a dresser. She waited on the family day and night and rarely expected more than a day off every two weeks. Often, despite her tiny stipend, she managed to save enough to buy a ticket so that a relative from the old country could come over to begin the same upward climb.

Servants are more expensive today. But percentage-wise, far more Argentines have them than North Americans.

The trend toward apartment-living became evident as Buenos Aires' population began swelling. More and more Argentines wanted to live in the city, for work or pleasure. The influx of city-dwelling Europeans, particularly the French, whose standards were always considered chic, hastened the trend.

As a result, Argentines in Buenos Aires, and many of the secondary cities—Córdoba, Rosario, Bahía Blanca, Mendoza, Mar del Plata—have erected more modern apartments than almost any other kind of structure. Hundreds of thousands of Argentines who do not want to live within the city limits have been building small modern houses in the suburbs. Near the capital they extend for miles to the north, west, and south. In the secondary cities they have moved right out into pasture land. The actual need for living quarters is not the only reason for the rush of apartment building. Many Argentines feel that if it is not possible to invest in land, an apartment house is the next best thing.

The apartments and homes Argentines build are likely to be larger than ours, for average families are bigger. Rooms are more spacious, ceilings higher. Heavy doors, tile walls and floors, solid knobs and plates have been dressed up in a modern motif though retaining their Spanish heritage. Even the courtyard patio has a new twist: it is now an indoor garden.

The modern houses have wide windows and balconies. They are built back from the street instead of flush with the sidewalk as of old, and many of them have swimming pools on their roofs. Homes are now being built to give the *señora* of the house more of an opportunity to do some of her own work with the labor-saving devices that Argentines eagerly seek.

In an Argentine apartment, the size of the kitchen is often regarded as a key to a *señora's* respectability. All over Buenos Aires tiny *garçonnières*, where Argentine males carry on their extra-curricular dalliances, have kitchens not much bigger than telephone booths. The elevators of these buildings are only large enough for two so as to avoid embarrassing encounters. But the average better Argentine apartment or house has a kitchen far larger than most of ours. The modern kitchen is also likely to have far more storage space, marble topped tables and counters, built-in incinerator and often an electric instead of a gas stove.

North Americans, however, are likely to feel that many Argentine homes are cold both in style and actual temperature. Argentines prefer formal draperies, large, heavy, overstuffed furniture, lamps with many frills and flounces, and less use of color and art on the walls. As in the United States, home decorating and styling tastes have been strongly influenced by the films. Argentine movies often follow styles they have adopted from American pictures, so much so that often film interiors do not resemble actual Argentine rooms at all. But since life often imitates the movies, some of the ideas introduced on the screen are beginning to appear in the new homes and apartments.

Every *porteño* who can afford it wants to live in the Barrio Norte, the smartest residential district. Many of its newest, most expensive buildings have replaced wealthy town houses which can no longer be adequately staffed and maintained and on which taxes are becoming prohibitive. Thousands of older homes have been converted to schools, government institutions, or embassies—our own United States Embassy residence is the former Alvear-Bosch family's mansion.

Many of these fabulous places were originally done in French style and resembled Parisian mansions. Furniture was generally imported. Dining rooms might easily seat up to fifty. Formal ballrooms were not uncommon, for entertaining away from home was rare.

One reason Argentines have been able to move ahead so fast with their building is that throughout most of the country temperatures do not get as cold as in the United States. Buildings are lighter, central heating less complex, cellars smaller. As a result, reinforced concrete is widely used. With it the Argentines and Europeans working in the country have done startling things.

The French- and Italian-influenced modern school was already firmly entrenched when the big Argentine urban building program got under way. As a result, the work of architects and planners is comparatively free of incongruous relics of the past. Ultra-modern buildings, even now, are unusual in many United States cities. In Buenos Aires, as in Rio, São Paulo, Mexico City, and elsewhere in Latin America, almost nothing else has gone up in recent years.

The red-roofed, stucco-walled style we call Spanish is generally missing. They call it *Californiano* and avoid it.

Emphasis in new Argentine homes, office buildings, and public structures is on the crisp, the functional, and the contemporary. With concrete are combined glass brick, broad fenestration, sharp lines, and flat roofs. Even in the tallest structures steel beams are practically unknown. Argentines proudly boast that Buenos Aires' thirty-two-story Kavanagh Building was among the first to prove that skscrapers could be built of reinforced concrete. With few open-hearth furnaces and no blast furnaces in Argentina, builders had to find materials other than steel. Concrete proved ideal, and Argentina has an abundance of cement, gravel, and stone. Today in erecting most Argentine buildings concrete is usually mixed on the spot.

Use of hollow tile, masonry, and other materials in original ways was also dictated by necessity. True, there were no permit restrictions on new construction during World War II, but inability to get essentials from the States or Europe did tax resources. In many cases, fugitives from Hitler turned their talents to producing things Argentina formerly imported. Argentines, many of whom were trained in the United States, also took advantage of the situation to try their new theories. United States firms with branch plants in Argentina found they could locally create tubs, hardware, and other fixtures considered impossible to make only a few months before Pearl Harbor. Today, practically every construction item except elevators is produced in Argentina.

Argentines have had a stronger sense of drama than we in setting off their buildings. Property is generally selected with an eye toward achieving an effect on the passerby, fully as much as on the occupant. Hollywood bathrooms, streamlined kitchens, and rumpus-room gadgetry which run our costs upward are not used. Elbowroom, however, is far more generous than in comparable units in the United States. Many Argentines get claustrophobia when they first see our hotels and apartments. Two laps around your room in the Plaza or the Alvear Palace Hotels in Buenos Aires seem nearly a quarter mile.

Labor to do the building job has also proven surprisingly ingenious, especially considering the limited number of technical schools. Complex craft restrictions and strikes which affected much of our building were infrequent in Argentina. Construction trades, as with us, are well organized. But there are fewer rules and less observance to those that exist.

The Argentine artisan refuses to be regimented either by boss or union. It is difficult to make him stick to a specified number of bricks per load, or to blueprints, either. But if he is enthusiastic and proud of the work, he achieves speed and perfection without overtime, bonuses, or bribes.

Workmanship can be excellent—and it can be very bad. Rarely is it impersonal: it shows the fierce individuality of the builders. Many masons are Italians and Poles; other laborers come from Galicia in Spain. They work hard with noisy cheerfulness. They cook their steaks at midday, bringing the famous Argentine rolls, their own salads, fruits, and a bottle of red wine. They may take two hours for lunch and finish with a siesta—stretched out on the sidewalk if no other place is handy. But they do a good job, topping off the construction with a palm branch to show they have finished. The end of a job calls for an *asado*, or barbecue celebration.

Generally the person in charge of building is the architect who works with a construction firm. Architects often arrange the financing and then put up big signboards in front of the building explaining their role. Every subcontractor also displays his name, for Argentines take great pride in their building achievement. The architect also signs his name on the front of the structure, a permanent record of his genius (or lack of it) that many feel encourages public interest in better architectural design.

In much of the smaller home construction around Buenos Aires, the owner often pitches in. Sometimes he hires himself a foreman and a few assistants, sketches a plan on the back of an old envelope, and gets things done over a long series of week-ends.

When visitors from the United States express surprise at the modernity of Buenos Aires building, Argentines will say they are an expression of cultural maturity, "not the technological wealth you admittedly possess."

"Our emergence seems sudden," they add, "but much spadework is due to our *avant-garde* writers, artists, and intellectuals. Usually, they were willing to accept theories which, often as not, were developed, but not always carried out, in Europe or in North America—Frank Lloyd Wright's ideas, for example."

When the discussion continues Argentines are willing to concede that they still have a long way to go before they solve their housing problem. Despite the vast amount of building, apartments and homes are extremely difficult to find, both in Buenos Aires and secondary cities. This is particularly true of apartments, where rents have been officially set at a low figure. One of the first steps taken by the military government after it gained power was to order an automatic 20 per cent reduction for all tenants—and at the same time to require that certain minimum standards of heat, light, and maintenance be supplied. Tenants gleefully pointed out that this, at least, was one worth-while act of the militarists. Property-owners, however, were angry, particularly when they found there were no exceptions for those who are incapable of meeting the costs.

Frequently the Argentine who needs a place to live has to pay "key money," thus giving owners their profits despite the squeeze imposed as rising costs and low-rent ceilings get closer.

Yet despite difficulties, Argentines continue to buy and build apartments. Besides the fact that they consider them good investments, they are the easiest item in which to invest. Investors can find page after page of land and building advertisements. Auctions are held daily. Realty deals are constantly reported. Most Argentines feel that the ownership of property serves as a hedge against inflation. They are convinced that the more prices go up, the more the value of land and buildings will rise, in even greater proportion.

Some feel the great national mortgage banks have helped keep Argentina's inflation spiraling by their liberality in granting mortgages. Yet, many an Argentine is certain that good property will more than repay its complete investment in ten years. Some, in fact, have done it in less. The important trend now is toward what is known as *"propiedad horizontal"*—in other words, co-operative ownership.

The Argentine's love of chance is shown by one little-known fact about property purchase. Many of the mortgage institutions hold lotteries semi-annually. If your mortgage number is one of the scores drawn, your mortgage is publicly burned and the property you are purchasing is yours. The institution takes full-page ads to advertise winners.

The tremendous growth of suburban living around Buenos Aires and other big Argentine cities has many a similarity to and many a difference from such life in the United States. Once Buenos Aires' suburbs were considered distant. Now they are part of the metropolitan area with every square meter of land daily becoming more valuable.

The after-office commuter rush at Presidente Perón Station is almost as busy as Grand Central or the Long Island Railroad. You ride for twenty to twenty-five minutes—and you are in Olivos, one of the typical Buenos Aires suburbs. It is not unlike Great Neck or New Rochelle around New York, Winnetka near Chicago, and Grosse Pointe near Detroit.

Not so many years ago most Argentine suburbanites were fairly well-to-do foreigners. Today, more and more *porteños* have found living away from the center of town desirable. And the commuter pattern gets more like that in the United States. Not so long ago, many an Argentine went home for lunch, but few do any more, for transportation is increasingly difficult. And like many of our suburbanites, the suburban resident generally sees little of his community other than its shopping district, its central plaza filled with school children in white smocks, his own street, and his route to town. Occasionally, he passes the time of day with his neighbors or goes to his local club for relaxation.

But his major interest is his home. Suburban houses around Argentine cities are generally two stories high— the ranch style hasn't yet become popular. Argentine homes are built to the owner's personal tastes rather than to any mass-scale plan. Frequently they do not even conform to any elementary conception of zoning. There are no Levittowns, or any great uniformity of building or styling, even in the new Perón-planned villages. Two identical Argentine houses next to one another would be considered a concession to Detroit belt-line production methods.

Argentines love parquet or tiled floors, terrazzo or marble stairways and house fronts, and shiny surfaces. Like as not, the Argentine suburban home has no central furnace, although they are coming in. Probably it will not even have a cellar, but the garage will be ample to store practically all the impedimenta an Argentine family accumulates, plus the bottled gas that is used in many suburbs where there are no central mains.

Most Argentine suburban homes also have balconies, either to the front or back, adorned with flowering vines. This is also standard in town apartments, for the owner's sun bathing, and for washing and drying clothes. Having laundry done at home or having a laundress come in once or twice a week is customary.

Rare is the Argentine home without a garden, tiny as

it may be. The owner generally has a gardener to cut the front lawn and neatly prune the trees to their last inch to encourage faster growth.

When the *señora* of the house wants to go shopping in Olivos she has her choice of thirty-three groceries and thirty-four butcher shops, but there's not a single supermarket anywhere. The idea has never been tried, although it is successful in Mexico, Cuba, Venezuela, and other Latin countries. There are several *farmacias*, or drugstores—but none with soda fountains. Beauty parlors are prevalent, but most suburbanites prefer those in town.

The real change, however, is that in contrast to bygone days, the *señora* herself frequently goes to the grocer rather than simply trusting her maid. "*Pero,* with prices what they are," she will tell you, "even we Argentines have to worry about getting the best possible value."

The suburban resident may contribute to some of the local charity drives, although far less than in a typical United States community. He will also be far less likely to participate in community organizations, parent-teacher associations, or similar civic affairs. Not many such groups exist. During the war the British had a Community Council in Olivos to raise funds and knit socks for their soldiers, but today the town has no sizeable woman's club.

The Peronista Party has, however, seen to it that every community in Argentina has its branch. The Peronista Women's Party is well-organized.

Many an Argentine buys or rents a place in the country for a "*casa del week-end.*" (Since *fin de semana* does not have the same connotation, the Argentines have adopted "week-end" directly from English.) He plants trees, fences off his area, and builds accommodations for guests, who will probably be his children, grandchildren, and other members of the family.

His retreat is hardly likely to be any quieter than that in town. "But," he will tell you, "this noise is my own noise and that of my family. And, after all, that is something no man regrets having."

Improved worker housing is a prime government objective. While there are fewer outright slum areas in the center of Buenos Aires than in many of our own cities, there are districts where housing conditions are deplorable. Moreover, housing costs in Argentina have always been far greater in proportion to income than those in the United States. This is one reason why many Argentines, including white-collar workers and often young middle-class couples, live with their parents.

Before the Perón Government came into power, the Argentine economist and statistician, Alejandro H. Bunge, reported that from 140,000 to 150,000 Buenos Aires laboring families lived in overcrowded, monotonous tenements. Often these are set around a big patio. A family may have only a single room or two for which they pay a fifth to a third of the husband's salary. Some tenements in the older waterfront area of the Boca have, in the past, crowded as many as 120 lodgers into ten rooms—something that would be hard to beat in Moscow or in Manhattan's Puerto Rican districts. Three or four persons to a room is still not infrequent in some tenements. Occupants share with other tenants the use of kitchens, the water closet and the primitive trickling cold shower.

There is little wonder why many an Argentine worker buys his weekly lottery ticket in the hope that "someday, somehow, he will win and be able to buy his own house."

Many workers hungry for their own places have started to build with the most haphazard material. Often they buy a lot far from their place of employment or band together to buy land and supplies. When one room or two are finished they move in, then they save to add another and another. Meanwhile, they seek what relaxation they can at the movies, the café, the *confitería* or the club— all of which offer an escape, even though temporary.

Workers' housing conditions in Buenos Aires have been so bad, in fact, that one of the first steps taken by the military government was to make some rather dramatic moves to show that it was at least proceeding in the right direction. In December, 1943, half a billion *pesos* were appropriated for low-cost housing. Reduced taxes and interest rates, plus preferential allocations of materials and small-house plans were offered those who would immediately proceed with building. As of the beginning of 1952, no one was sure how much of this housing was ever actually completed, or to how many families Perón helped give new quarters. Several attractive-looking worker villages were constructed near the new broad Avenida General Paz, which circles Buenos Aires. Additionally, a large number of workers' apartment houses similar to those found around Rome and other Italian cities were erected. Others are still rising. Not unnaturally, favored party followers have had first choice of quarters to show what all faithful peronistas may some day expect.

In recent years, an attempt has been made to get as many workers as possible away from the capital's center. As one official explained: "Providing housing in suburban areas where factories have also been built may also help our urban transport problem. It is your Greenbelt idea in actual practice."

Workers' houses being built on the outskirts of the capital are being reproduced in many of the smaller communities. While there are no large cooperative housing developments like those found around New York, neither are there row houses as in Philadelphia and Baltimore. The first public housing project built in the Western Hemisphere by a municipal government was constructed in Buenos Aires in 1910. But housing never has been able to keep up with the community's growth. In 1945 the military government set up a new federal housing agency under the Administración Nacional de La Vivienda (National Housing Administration) designed to build twenty thousand new homes yearly for both urban and rural workers. But these have hardly met the demand. New workers' apartment houses are usually eight to ten stories, simply and sturdily built. The grounds, fresh with the newness of landscaping, include an inevitable playground and the sign: "In the new Argentina Perón is creating, only the children are privileged."

Chapter V

The Capital of the Argentine

IF THE *porteños* and the growing middle class are the new, vital force in Argentina, then the city of Buenos Aires can be said to be their center, for they have made their capital into a unique metropolis—and Buenos Aires, in turn has helped mold succeeding generations of its residents.

Physically, they realize, Buenos Aires lacks the breath-taking bays, and the sheer, precipitate beauty of Sugar Loaf mountain which stands guard at the entrance to the harbor of Rio de Janeiro, capital of Brazil. They know it hasn't the towering mountain backdrop of Chile's capital of Santiago across the Andes from Argentina. But, they insist, neither has Buenos Aires the lazy, indolent air of many another Latin American metropolis.

If you want to flatter a *porteño*, particularly if he co

from the middle class, then you will tell him at once that Buenos Aires looks much like Paris. You will point out how even its tall, light-clustered lampposts, its street signs and sidewalk cafés resemble the "City of Light." You will admire its older buildings and shops, its *confiterías*, the vast Mercado del Plata, the central produce market where cabbages and tomatoes, meat and roasting chickens are displayed the way Cartier shows diamonds.

Driving in from the airport over the cobbled streets of the suburbs, which also have the look of Paris, you will marvel over the fact that the Argentine capital covers more land than any other city in the southern Americas—even more, it is said, than sprawling Los Angeles.

Buenos Aires gives an impression of space in its broad new *avenidas*, its far-flung residential neighborhoods, the sweep of its tree-filled squares and plazas. The resemblance shows in its two great Diagonals, broad avenues laid out like the spokes of a wheel from the central Plaza de Mayo, cutting across the regular squares. And the *porteño* likes to think that outlying areas near Palermo Park look like Paris' Bois de Boulogne. Here are some of the town's more imposing mansions, and many ultra-modern apartment dwellings which rival our most spectacular new architectural designs.

If you want to upset a *porteño*, tell him Buenos Aires is like Chicago in its vast stockyards and meat-packing plants, in its flatness, in the brashness of its politicians, and, of course, in its hustle and bustle, pride in accomplishment, and constant desire for the newest and best.

Like Chicago, Buenos Aires was constructed on a waterfront so wide that you cannot see the other side. The

Rio de la Plata, the Silver River, is neither silver nor a river. Rather, it is an arm of the Atlantic Ocean, an estuary into which the Paraná and Uruguay rivers pour their waters heavy with top soil. Churned with sea water, this mixture produces an ugly brownish color. Optimistic Spaniards, who believed the river would lead them to rich silver mines, gave it its name.

Though Buenos Aires' early development was not favored by natural beauty, it was aided by a natural central location. *Porteños* recall Buenos Aires actually had two beginnings. In 1536, Pedro de Mendoza arrived from Spain with an imposing expedition of some two thousand colonists to settle in the region. Plagued by famine, pestilence, and Indians, Mendoza abandoned the land and sailed for home with most of the surviving expediton members. In 1580, Juan de Garay began anew. Gradually the town began growing.

Early in the eighteenth century Buenos Aires was a sprawling village of mud and straw huts, incomparably poorer in material goods and cultural development than such renowned centers of wealth, religion, and art as Mexico City and Lima. As a dependency of the Viceroyalty of Peru it was restricted and discriminated against in favor of Lima. But in 1776 the Viceroyalty of Rio de la Plata was created, with Buenos Aires as its capital. With this political, economic, and social impetus the town developed swiftly, and came into its own as a port.

In the nineteenth century, railroads pushed out from Buenos Aires to provincial capitals, connecting them with the port city but not with each other. Rail lines and highways were centered in Buenos Aires, and cross traffic was difficult. To get from one part of the country to another one had to go first to Buenos Aires and proceed from there. Now air travel is developing in the interior, bringing provincial cities closer together. And this has reduced the immediate need for many cross-country highways.

The military government seeks to foster this trend. It has lavished some of its most elaborate construction on a brand new General Pistarini Airport at Ezeiza, some forty minutes from the center of Buenos Aires over the broad highway that rings the city. This airport's size equals any in the States, including New York's vast Idlewild, and is regarded as a Perón showcase. Some 6,500 acres of the development's total 17,300 are devoted to the airport itself. The rest of the area features four huge swimming pools, a large children's vacation camp and a model village for airport employees outfitted in every detail. Although traffic is nowhere as great as at big United States fields, Pistarini Airport has a vast array of buildings designed to prove the boast that it is the finest and most completely equipped in the Americas. An eight-story aviation-office building is set at one end of the field. Nearby is a large new hotel. Shops of all kinds supply travelers and the constant stream of visitors, who number thousands on holidays.

They stroll the promenade watching the planes of Panagra, Scandinavian Airlines, Air France, British South American, Braniff, and their own Aerolineas Argentinas take off.

If the airport is the center of Buenos Aires' new air age, in town everything revolves around the Plaza de Mayo, for this is not only the center of the capital, but the hub of the Argentine republic.

The Casa Rosada, office of the President and traditional seat of government, stands at the eastern end of the Plaza. Tall, splendidly uniformed San Martín grenadiers guard its entrances. All Argentines know that the man who sits in the Casa Rosada and controls the Plaza de Mayo and the forces headquartered in the buildings around it, commands the power to rule them with a force possessed by few American heads of state.

On the President's right, as he surveys the Plaza, is the Banco de la Nación, the country's financial heart. Beyond it is the neo-classical Cathedral, seat of the power of the church and last resting place of Argentina's liberator, General San Martín. Directly across the Plaza is the Intendencia Municipal (municipal building), headquarters of the capital's government, its huge police force and its vast array of services. Next is the historic Cabildo, where revolutionists met on May 25, 1810, to set up Argentina's first government.

Round the streets of the Plaza scurry many of the *colectivos*, little jitney buses which drive in from their far-flung routes to the suburbs. Like Chicago's Loop, the Plaza is also a center for the giant busses which are patterned after those of Paris. Everyone calls them "man butchers," because they proceed with the recklessness of juggernauts.

It is in Plaza de Mayo that Perón makes his speeches. There victories are announced and solidified. There the nation's sorrow and triumphs are publicly exhibited. There the newest, biggest signboards proclaim the Argentines' loyalty to Perón or announce a new government drive. Strings of lights go up on national holidays; symbols of mourning are displayed when a top official dies.

Manifestations and demonstrations are an important part of Argentina's political life. During the June 4 movement in 1943, the militarists marched into Buenos Aires and seized control with only a comparatively few shots fired. But *porteño* students had to do something more dramatic to demonstrate their feelings. So they overturned a number of busses and trolleys owned by a British company and set them afire. This was apparently intended to demonstrate that somehow they had been relieved of a foreign yoke. During an important state funeral at the Cathedral on the Plaza, students are likely to break the police line to draw the hearse themselves as a further expression of their feelings. None of these incidents compare to the paroxysm of peronista grief upon the death of Evita Perón on July 25, 1952. The whole country was plunged into mourning, paralyzing all normal activity. Outside the Ministry of Labor building hundreds of thousands waited for hours in rain and chill to file past her bier. Three thousand or more were injured and four died in the crush before the Army came to help the police maintain order.

Out from the Plaza stem the broad Diagonales Norte and Sud. A block away is the big ten-story headquarters of the First National Bank of Boston, which houses the United States Embassy offices.

A few blocks west runs the Avenida 9 de Julio, whose breadth of four hundred feet makes it one of the world's widest boulevards. Under the avenue are extensive underground parking areas—the inspiration, Argentines will tell you, for the huge garage under Union Square in San Francisco. The center of the *avenida* is the Plaza de la Republica, marked by an immense obelisk commemorating the city's four-hundredth anniversary.

Porteños never seem to stop rebuilding their town. Pavements are always torn up for some new project and construction proceeds endlessly. But to insure cleanliness little metal boxes are used to keep even the dirt from street excavations from littering the thoroughfares. During World War II when we halted building, "hot money" seeking unrestricted refuge kept Buenos Aires' boom going. For a time the biggest structures were erected by German, Spanish, Italian, and British firms, each contributing its national taste to the design. Public buildings were usually designed in the French style with heavy statues, tremendous chandeliers, and wide sweeping stairways. Massive Spanish doorways and fittings were still popular. Banks and offices appeared to come straight from Victorian London. Elaborate hotels and offices along tree-lined Avenida de Mayo looked like reproductions of Madrid buildings.

In the newer parts of the city, however, Argentines have built ultra-modern buildings in so-called Mediterranean Modern. Structures are lighter in color, and balconies are used not only as places where the resident can relax and as a device for achieving sharp, clean architectural lines. There are only a few skyscrapers. The tallest is a thirty-two-story apartment house on Plaza San Martín downtown. Such heights are not encouraged, however. Official regulations limit all buildings on the Diagonal Norte and the Avenida 9 de Julio to fifteen floors. Interestingly enough, many *porteños* say they do

not like skyscrapers so they avoid them, but in the next
breath they explain that the soil of Buenos Aires is not
reinforced by rock like Manhattan and could not support such structures.

The town has spread out—not up. To help solve the
increasing traffic problem on its original narrow downtown streets Buenos Aires long ago began a unique city
planning program. Every fourth street was cut back by
an ingenious process that began as long as forty years
ago. Markers were put down and owners informed that
by a certain day fifteen to twenty years thereafter, all
property extending beyond the line must be removed at
the owner's expense. Thus as older structures were replaced, new buildings were built only up to the line.

Streets like Corrientes, now a theatrical center, Córdoba and Belgrano were widened in this way. It cost the
city practically nothing but foresight. The Avenida 9 de
Julio has been broadened in much the same fashion so
that it will eventually run south from near Retiro Park,
behind the port, as far as the great railroad station of
Plaza Constitution. Argentines still chuckle over the fact
that although private buildings had to move back out of
the way the Ministry of Public Works put up its own
skyscraper right in the path of the approaching avenue.
The avenue now carefully detours the federal structure.

Since the income level of Buenos Aires is far above
that of the interior, all of the largest shops are concentrated there. Most manufacturers have set up their plants
around the city's outskirts, with the result that about 75
per cent of the nation's industrial establishments are
located in the metropolitan area. Since the country's most
enterprising citizens have concentrated in Buenos Aires,

they have often paid too little attention to secondary markets. Today, however, many Argentine businessmen are extending their operations to the interior, and with them have gone products and methods bearing the imprint of the metropolis.

Buenos Aires' modern look, its dynamic bustle, its air of progress, often make visitors forget that real growth and development are comparatively new. Away from the main avenues, the signs of the sleepy river town that was the old Argentine capital are still apparent. A visitor need only go to the southern, less stylish suburbs of Avellaneda and Lomas de Zamora to see the mud roads, and the high-ceilinged, windowless shops, and stuccoed houses with patios to note how Argentines have kept old and new side by side.

Although quick to adopt new things, and self-consciously desirous of being up to date, Argentina's *porteños* and provincials are also extremely traditional in some of their building tastes. The first floor of Harrod's great department store, for example, has hardly been changed since it was opened. It keeps its old-fashioned showcases, furniture, mirrors, and carved glass, for they have become symbols of distinction. The modern changes have been limited to the upper floors, lest anybody think that Harrod's could possibly resemble any of the vulgar new establishments. In this it has caught the spirit of the Argentine *porteño*—wanting change yet somehow fearing it, anxious for the new yet not willing to relinquish the old.

Chapter VI

The Cities beyond the Capital

MOST TRAVELERS who come to Argentina for the first time make the mistake of arriving in Buenos Aires. A more interesting approach is to fly one of Panagra's big planes down the west coast of South America to Santiago, Chile. There the traveler can change to a local plane or train to cross the Andes and see the country. If you stop off in some of the provincial cities and get the feel of the broad *pampa,* you will have a better idea of what has supplied the riches that have made the capital, and Argentina, for Buenos Aires, dominant as it is, is not Argentina. The country's essential wealth has always come from the area outside its leading city. Yet we examine Buenos Aires and the other cities before we discuss the land because less than 26 per cent of the Argentine people live on the soil.

Rosario, second to the capital in industry and population, is Argentina's Chicago. Some 203 miles up the Rio Paraná from Buenos Aires, it is a great port and grain center. Ocean liners can reach its three-mile waterfront, and river boats bring Bolivian and Paraguayan products to its docks. Eight railroads enter the city, most of them from the grain districts.

Its tall grain elevators handle millions of tons a year, and its packing houses are enormous. There is hardly a *rosarino* who does not have something to do with grain or cattle products—the tanning of leather, canning, sausage-making, and preparation of meat for shipping abroad directly from Rosario.

The busy city looks like a copy of the capital: streets have the same names, cafés boast similar fittings, shops are branches of those in Buenos Aires. Its inhabitants, however, are not as smart or gay as the people in Buenos Aires. Rosarinos roll down their shop shutters not long after dark, and dine earlier than in Buenos Aires.

Rosario once aspired to national leadership and was considered as a possible federal capital. But its inhabitants do not feel the intense rivalry with Buenos Aires that, for example, the citizens of the port of Guayaquil, in Ecuador, feel about Quito. In some ways the *rosarino* considers himself superior to the *porteño* because, he says, "We have everything they have without the hustle and bustle."

They have built the country's best national modern art gallery, and one of the most original schools, the Escuela Experimental Carrasco in the workers' district of Alberdi. The marks of a good businesslike, comfort-loving, middle-class population are everywhere—in the wide streets, the clean hotels, the expensive cars.

Some Argentines feel Rosario lacks the personality it should have, considering its economic importance.

Rosario, like Chicago, is a freshwater port, a great wheat and packing center. It is not the capital of its state but a town that has made its way by sheer commercial and industrial power, often against both local and federal politicians. Waldo Frank feels a telling analogy is in its architecture: "You can pick it out in the commercial and residential streets, among the still prevailing, hideous late nineteenth and early twentieth-century houses. It is flamboyant; it is not always good, it is probably never as good as the best new architecture in Mexico. But it is vitally poetic and full of promise. Surging dramatic towers, exterior spiral stairs, summing to impressiveness. The functional perpendicular of office buildings is somehow counter-balanced by the use of horizontal subsidiary forms that give the measure of the *pampa*."

Some visitors to Córdoba, who have heard native sons describe it as the Argentine Rome, the American Seville, and the City of Professors, are shocked to find it is no longer a sleepy colonial town. Crowded, rushing, and dynamic, Argentina's third city is located almost exactly in the center of the country in the broad valley of the Rio Primo. Around it are miles of rich wine and ranch country, within are booming industries. Yet its chief attractions consist in its colonial character and its proximity to the famous Córdoba hills, a popular and highly lucrative all-year-round vacationland. The *córdobes* have made *tourismo* one of their big industries.

Unlike most Argentine cities, which have a broad, flat
appearance of regularity, Córdoba occupies a confined
position as at the bottom of a well, among red clay hills
that bury it under dark dust with every wind and mud
with every rain. Most of its upper and lower classes are
descendants of colonial Spaniards, who have preserved
more of the good and the bad from those days than have
any other Argentines. The middle class come from Italy,
France, modern Spain, Poland, England, and Arabia.
Assimilation is more complete than in any American city:
the idea of separate neighborhoods for different nationalities is almost inconceivable to Córdobans—as it is to
most Argentines.

Luis Guillermo Piazza, a *córdobes* who wrote about
his city in the magazine *Americas*, admits that it is not
nearly as cosmopolitan as the port cities. But for this
reason, he says, *córdobes* always consider themselves
more authentic Argentines, and speak mockingly of "the
others," "the ones from the port." Their rivalry with the
porteños is mutual and starts afresh every day. It dates
from the Independence, when there were civil wars between the provinces and the port, and might be compared
with the enmity between the North and South in the
United States. Today the *córdobes'* attitude is more like
the attitude of Bostonians toward New Yorkers, one of
irony and scorn rather than real dislike.

Despite the town's progress and growth (to some 350,-
000 inhabitants) its people know each other better than
in most cities. This is obvious to the visitor on the streets,
in the parks, at the movies, and in the churches.

Few *córdobes* lunch out; the custom of going home to
eat persists despite its inconvenience. As night falls the

people stroll along the Calle San Martín to see and be seen. The Spanish-American custom survives intact; the streets are closed to traffic in favor of wandering crowds.

Once the spiritual center of the country, Córdoba is conservative and staunchly Catholic. On Sunday, *córdobes* all go to Mass according to a timetable that varies inversely with age. The old go very early, the young as late as possible after the festivities of Saturday night. The sweet shops fill up at noon, and then everyone has a chance to look, talk, and even dance. At the siesta hour the young people drive or stroll in Sarmiento Park near the lake and wood. Great crowds pack into the *futbol* stadia. Later the movies draw their biggest crowds of the week, as thousands of families wind up their Sunday holiday.

Culturally the city's institutions are older than those anywhere in southern South America. Córdoba's famed university, part of the life of every *córdobes*, was founded in 1613. It typifies the complexity of the city and its people, which cannot be reduced to statistics or generalizations. From this new-old university have come all the doctors who have brought fame to Córdoba. In colonial days these "doctors" were theologians, who brought new life to church doctrines. Later they were lawyers, innumerable and renowned. Today they include engineers, architects, philosophers, physicians, accountants, and lawyers—everyone with a university degree is grouped under this respectful title. The Córdoban sense of humor has not overlooked this superabundance of graduates: all Argentines know the saying, "Once there was a Córdoban who was not a doctor."

Although realistic about their shortcomings, Guillermo

Piazza says: "*Córdobes* are imbued with localism and firmly believe the world ends at their boundary. Go to Buenos Aires? Just for a few days, long enough to have a good time. See Europe? A magnificent idea, but it is far, so expensive, and after all, one can find out all about it from books. Visit other Latin countries? Too typical, too native, too poor. Go to the United States? Why? What could one learn there? And besides, it is too rich."

If you approach Argentina from Santiago de Chile, your first stop on the eastern slopes of the Andes will be Mendoza. Patriotic Argentines consider it the cradle of the continent's liberty, for it was here, in 1817, that General José de San Martín trained his famous army of the Andes, which was to cross the mountains and liberate Chile and Peru.

Mendocinos appropriately call their town the "Garden of the Andes." The products of their gardens—wine, grapes, and fruits—are the thriving industry of the Mendoza region. Over three hundred years ago the Spaniards brought grapevines from Europe and planted them on terraces watered by the Inca Indian irrigation systems. *Mendocinos* channeled the mountain snows into canals to develop hundreds of orchards. They claim their famous wines and grapes can hardly be bettered by France, and brag that their grapes are sent as far afield as the smart Madison Avenue grocery shops in New York.

The town of Mendoza (population 109,879) is so thickly planted with trees it looks like a park—clean, green, and full of life. Small irrigation ditches along many of its streets water the sturdy trees and countless gardens. After the disastrous earthquake of 1861 the town had to be almost completely rebuilt. Buildings are low, and houses outside the central part of the city are made of unbaked tiles for greater earthquake resistance.

Chiefly of Italian and Spanish descent, the inhabitants are the most progressive and friendly of all provincial Argentines. They seem happier, less worried and prejudiced than the Córdobans. They love to entertain, and their town has become quite a tourist center. Besides its wine and grapes, it features mild, dry days, vivid sun and skies, and thermal springs.

The port of Bahía Blanca, on the southern edge of the *pampas*, is the most important Argentine city below Buenos Aires. Five hundred and sixty miles south of the capital, it has become the nerve center for the whole of Patagonia, which stretches west to Chile and south to Cape Horn.

To guard against a Brazilian invasion, General Rivadavia built a fort at Bahía Blanca in 1828. It became a center of local campaigns against the Indians. In 1838 a great Italian immigration began, largely from Genoa, which contributed to the agricultural development of the area.

Now its 106,258 inhabitants like to call their port the Liverpool of Argentina. From its grain elevators and docks are shipped great bales of Patagonian wool, oil, hides, wheat. The town, with its port and its hinterland, has an authority of its own, a lesser but definite power behind it.

The capital of the wealthy province of Buenos Aires is La Plata, just thirty-five miles southeast of Buenos Aires. When the latter was named national capital in 1880, citizens decided to build a new town for their provincial capital. They planned a model municipality, built on a perfect three-mile square transversed by broad diagonals.

Buenos Aires is too close for La Plata to escape its shadow. But its 217,738 people are proud of its fine buildings, large plazas and parks, excellent observatory, unique Museum of Natural History, its famous university, and its technical schools for women.

Its port, one of the best in the republic, ships meat, gasoline, and hides. Many industries, including Swift and Armour, have built plants in La Plata to avoid crowded Buenos Aires. La Plata refines the oil and processes the meat it ships.

The seaside resort of Mar del Plata might have been mentioned in the chapter on Buenos Aires. But when half a million people arrive every summer to swell its normal population of one hundred thousand, it becomes one of the larger cities of the republic. Eighty years ago it was a fort where neighboring *estancieros* found refuge from the Indians; today it is the largest, richest, most ostentatious resort in South America. Two-hundred fifty miles south of the capital, Mar del Plata has become an Argentine tradition.

After the enterprising landowner Patricio Peralta Ramos opened its first bathing beach in 1887, the well-planned town became the summer abode of the first families of Argentina. They, and the *nouveaux riches* who followed, built luxurious homes more like suburban mansions than beach houses. Now the city clerks, salesgirls, and businessmen with large families also flock to Mar del Plata beaches. There are hundreds of pensions and inexpensive hotels as well as the fashionable and expensive hotels. Trains, busses, cars, and planes run day and night between the capital and its resort during December to March, the mid-summer season.

Many Argentines prefer to live in the provincial cities rather than in Buenos Aires. Older people especially are content to accept what they have, refusing to be disturbed by the speed and bustle, the superiority and overriding manner of the *porteño*. "We feel peace, quiet, and tranquillity are our greatest assets," they say. "If Perón lets us live without molestation, we are willing to go along."

Yet when the provincial city-dweller moves to the metropolis his ambition is aroused. He probably becomes one of the most active members of a political group or labor union. He starts reading the newspapers more carefully. When he hears of plans for new factories he is sure Argentina is on the march toward industrial greatness, for what he sees, in contrast to his home town, convinces him that Buenos Aires is the world's greatest city. And so more and more provincials join the move to the capital.

Chapter VII

Where the Argentines Come From

A FAVORITE characterization of Argentina heard in other Latin American countries is that it is an American nation financed with British capital and peopled with Italians who speak bad Spanish. This evaluation is somewhat exaggerated, but it contains much truth. Argentina is not only a great crucible which has fused her people into a new group; it is a melting pot, still bubbling furiously, in which the citizen's country of origin is frequently a more decisive influence in determining his daily pattern of thought and activity than his country of adoption.

Not until this century did a new Argentine type emerge —a combination of recent European immigrants and the *criollos*, Argentines of Spanish decent, and *mestizos*, of mixed Spanish-Indian blood. As a people, Argentines are much younger than we. Some immigrants to Argentina

98

came just to do a job, intending to go home sooner or later, and retained their native customs and language through second and third generations. Many a third-generation Anglo-Argentine, for instance, still talks of "being out here," or "going back home," even though, in many cases, he has never been "home" in all his life.

Cut off from Europe during the war, sparked by nationalism, and affected by many other causes, the Argentine of today is still in the process of fusion. To understand him and perhaps know where he is going, we must find out where he came from.

The Europeans who first came to North America and those who went to Argentina were motivated by different reasons. The first Spaniards wanted gold and silver, not farmland and homes. They were soldiers, would-be gentlemen, and later merchants, notaries, and lawyers. Some of the earlier arrivals married Indians, and the *mestizos* resulted.

Argentina's greatest period of immigration—the nineteenth century—was also ours. But whereas our Homestead Act gave new arrivals land to develop, in Argentina the best land was already spoken for. Some immigrants of the late 1890's and early 1900's did get acreage in distant Mendoza and Santa Fé, but some of it was so poor it had to be abandoned.

Since most of the land was in the hands of the *estancieros*, immigrants became farm or city laborers, small tradesmen, or artisans. The *criollo* is traditionally a landlord or a *peon*: the immigrant and his sons became Argentina's middle class. It emerged as the country's most stable element. This group began producing a striking change in Argentina's social, cultural, political, and economic life—and it was this change that pushed Argentina to first place in the southern half of the Western Hemisphere. The real significance of the middle class is only now becoming apparent.

Yet nowadays many Argentines frequently attribute all virtues to their country's ancient stock and all evils to recent immigrants. Perón, although of recent French-Italian stock, is guilty of this error. Other second- and third-generation Argentines follow the same line. You often hear the expression: *verdadero criollo* (truly creole) to indicate something that, by its very nature, is strong, brave, hearty, honest, and patriotic. Yet it is the recent immigrants who in the relatively short period of sixty years have changed Argentina from a mixed population like those in other Latin countries to an almost pure white group—alert, progressive, energetic.

Between 1857, when the first attempt was made to compile some immigration statistics, and 1930, when immigration was restricted, at least six million new people came into the country. Forty-two per cent were Italian, 33 per cent Spanish, 8 per cent Russian and Polish, 4 per cent German and Austro-Hungarian. The remaining 13 per cent included British, French, Portuguese, Uruguayans, Brazilians, Armenians, Lebanese, **and Turks.**

Numerically, the Italians have been most important, and their influence is everywhere. You notice it in the expressions, gestures, and accent of Argentine speech, in the names of the people, their food, their appearance. Italian habits and thinking have affected the Argentines. Yet Argentines have never been especially interested in learning Italian. They feel it is too close to their own

Spanish and that all important Italian literary and technical works are translated into Spanish.

Many of the Italians who came to Argentina in the last century crossed the Atlantic just to help harvest the wheat crop. Since seasons in Europe and South America are reversed, laborers sometimes spent one harvest season in the Old World, the next in the New. Those who came and went with the seasons were called *golondrinas*, swallows. Probably half of them stayed because they liked the country or just did not want to bother to return to Italy. Competition was keen, and opportunities few, but hundreds of thousands continued to come, legally or illegally.

The Italians blended readily with the Argentines, who shared their religion and temperament. They presented few problems of assimilation. Although they helped make Buenos Aires one of the world's largest cities, they did not live in "little Italys"—there is no Italian district in Buenos Aires and never has been. Even first-generation Italians often boast of having become hundred per cent Argentines. Second-generation Italians are definitely not Italian-Argentines—they are Argentine.

The early Italian immigrants—Lombards, Piedmontese, and Venetians—were chiefly peasants, laborers, and farmers. Many of them worked their way up from farm hands to tenant farmers, who treated the new lands with almost the same respect they might give their own. They became wheat, corn, and flax producers, or raised sugar and tobacco in San Luis, grapes in Mendoza. They got along well with British, Irish, and Scotch managers who had emigrated earlier. Some stayed near the cities to raise truck gardens, or process the food for export.

Southern Italians flocked to the cities, contributing in part to Argentina's urbanization problems of recent years. These were the artisans, skilled mechanics, bricklayers, masons, and factory workers. Many set up their own bakeries, tailor shops, small businesses. Frequently the Italians had the drive and ambition native *criollos* lacked. Starting humbly, some built fortunes in industrial construction work and in trade.

During World War II, Argentines of Italian stock showed much less sympathy for Mussolini than those of German background did for Hitler. There was no strongly Fascist newspaper in Argentina—the few Italian dailies were mostly anti-totalitarian. Many Argentines of Italian descent took a lead in Acción Argentina, a popular wartime democratic group which at one period included thousands of members. Some of them were arrested or ran into trouble with the government for their anti-totalitarian activities. Again in contrast to the Germans, Italian immigrants rarely retained their native citizenship and did not finance organizations in their homeland.

The Spaniards who came to Argentina in the last fifty years were different from the Andalusian adventurers of the sixteenth century and from merchants and professionals who came from Castile and Aragon in colonial days. Many of the new arrivals were Basques from the western Pyrenees region of Spain, or *gallegos* from the far northwestern province and former kingdom of Galicia. Both groups were sober, hard-headed, hard-working people, who favored city life. Many are still humorously called *gallegos*—a term sometimes indiscriminately applied to all Spaniards. To an Argentine, a *gallego* is his servant, his apartment house porter, or his corner grocer.

He uses the term affectionately and perhaps a little contemptuously.

Since the advent of dictator Francisco Franco in Madrid, official Argentine relations with Spain have grown increasingly warm, though the cordiality freezes when one side or the other feels it is losing a commercial advantage. Even those Argentines who do not come from Spain have nurtured the idea of *hispanidad* and the cultural ties with the "Mother Country." It gives them a feeling of superiority useful in their own dealings with Chile, Peru, and Uruguay.

Spain has played up this feeling for all that it is worth. More and more Spanish theatrical companies have arrived in Buenos Aires in recent years to make extensive and expensive tours. Madrid stock companies have always been popular in Buenos Aires playhouses, but during the civil war the poverty and distress on the Iberian peninsula halted the flow. At the outset the traveling Spanish theatrical companies seemed innocent enough, but it was soon discovered that they served as propaganda agents for Franco. Their methods were not open or direct but a great many of the new jokes were directed against the United States. Radio programs put on by the Spanish companies sang of the glories of the old country and its happy life and introduced more criticism of Uncle Sam. Spanish films and newsreels, often given theater owners at reduced rates, aimed at cementing the ties between "Mother Spain and her children in the New World."

Under a special cultural accord, a flow of books, teachers, films, and periodicals moved across the South Atlantic. It worked well for Spain, but Argentina did not benefit proportionally. *La Prensa*, seeking to point this

out in its independent days, cited cases of incoming shipments of hundreds of thousands of Spanish books carefully selected to sell Franco's ideas. "The only Argentine
publishers who can get anything going the other way,"
Prensa added, "are those who appear on United States
and British blacklists for publishing Axis literature."

The influence of Spanish cultural institutions has also
been strengthened. Spain fostered the idea that she was
among the first to fight Communism, and that liberal
winds from the United States in the North "might easily
mean the breaking up of the old *estancias*."

While not as spectacular or as crude as the Nazis,
Franco realized that even the slightly-faded grandees
moved more freely in high places in Argentina than any
other Spaniards. Under a cloak of culture they were welcomed in wealthy Argentine families, schools and
churches. At first Perón approved of this, but he shifted
his position as his program moved toward winning greater
support of the masses. As a result, Franco's representatives no longer emphasize their nobility.

Far different from the Spanish is the British influence,
which was long all out of proportion to the number of
English who lived there. Bartolomé Mitre, President of
Argentina from 1862–68, once said that Britain was the
"principal factor in the country's political, social, and economic progress." The British did more than anyone else—
including the "natives" as the English called them—to
develop "the Argentine"—another British phrase. They
built the railroads, the water works, the power plants, the
trolley systems. They taught the *estancieros* how to breed
their cattle and sheep, started cotton-raising, and carried
Argentine goods to the rest of the world.

Britain's prestige began rising from the time the Spanish Armada suffered its famous defeat. In the past century, Argentina was Britain's principal source of meat and wheat. Men and money were needed to protect this vital life and trade line. The City of London, not Wall Street, became the key source of Argentine financing. We were too busy expanding and developing our own country to take any notice.

With every pound invested, more and more Britons crossed the South Atlantic. Some were contract men sent to do specific jobs. Others went to Argentina for lifetime careers, managing utilities, railroads, or retailing establishments. A United States businessman, amazed at seeing a London department store in Buenos Aires, was even more surprised to find the imposing Banco de Londres, Bank of London; *The Standard,* an English daily newspaper, now the accepted dean of the Argentine press; not to mention the British stenographers, clerks, and general managers in the railroad offices, the English shopgirls and English bosses in the department stores, and English superintendents in the packing plants.

Many English settled down permanently, buying land in the province of Buenos Aires and elsewhere on the *pampa.* But they often kept their ties with home and, like the Germans, maintained dual citizenship and traveled with both British and Argentine passports. Many Scottish and Welsh immigrants settled in the sheep-raising country of Southern Patagonia.

The Britons in Argentina introduced their ways and words. The Saturday noon closing hour custom became the *sábado inglés,* English Saturday. An Argentine's word of honor is the *palabra inglés.* When an Argentine wants to tell you that he will be exactly on time instead of half an hour or an hour late as usual, he may pledge: *"hora inglés,"* British time. The British introduced their sports and sports terms. They brought in *futbol* (soccer), golf, and tennis and helped develop Argentina's polo.

The English in Argentina considered themselves a race apart. They set up their own homes, clubs, and churches on the exact pattern of "home." Round Buenos Aires are suburbs with names like Hurlingham and Temperley.

Early in 1948, Sir Clive Baillieu, an old friend, came to the Argentine accompanied by Lady Baillieu as chief negotiator in the sale of the British railroads and the purchase of Argentine meat and grains.

The world grain market traditionally had been established by the Liverpool Stock Exchange, but so many economic dislocations had happened that quotations in Liverpool were no longer the criteria for the world grain markets. The Argentines had sold various grains to European countries at prices which were considerably higher than had been established internally in many countries of the world, including the United States.

It came to a question of arriving at a formula and we were instrumental in establishing one constituted by prices ruling at Chicago, plus cost to Gulf ports. This formula was agreed to by President Perón and resulted in the expedition of the trade agreement with Great Britain.

There was some criticism in England itself of the barter of capital assets for food commodities which would be in current consumption, but owing to the economic situation that was existent at the time it seemed a very sensible arrangement all the way around. The formula thus established was also used afterward in several sales that Argentina made to the United States Armed Forces.

The practical English businessmen learned from experience what the Argentines wanted and would buy. Any British concern which packed its goods so carelessly that the product arrived smashed found that the British Consul General in Buenos Aires made certain the Board of Trade back in London heard about it. The Board—Britain's Ministry of Commerce—saw to it that the exporter reimbursed the injured importer and packed his product more carefully next time. The British Foreign Office negotiated treaties favorable to British manufacturers, provided them with essential information, and sent such star Empire salesmen as the Prince of Wales to learn to tango with the debutantes in Buenos Aires while persuading their fathers to buy British.

Since World War II Britain has lost much ground in Argentina. At one time a Briton discussing foreign affairs with an American could say: "You may take Canada from us, but you will never get the Argentine." Today Britain is no longer either the largest customer or the strongest influence on the Rio de la Plata.

The Perón government purchased practically all the British railroads from their private owners. Many of the public utilities have also been taken over, often at the government's own price. The great British-Argentine newspaper and magazine empire, Editorial Haynes, which published the daily El Mundo, the magazines El Hogar and Mundo Argentina, and operated Radio El Mundo and its network, is now owned by prominent peronistas.

Many Britons who live in Argentina have watched

their superior position decline and doubt they will ever
regain it. But the British influence will continue to be a
strong factor in Argentine thinking and daily habits for
a long time to come.

While the Irish who came to Argentina were never as
powerful or numerous as the English, they were among
the country's earliest agricultural settlers and their influence is felt in many ways. Early in the nineteenth century, when cattle were considered valuable only for their
hides and tallow, most Argentine *peons* would brand,
lasso, or skin the beasts, but they refused to dig or do any
other work they thought beneath them. Irish immigrants,
who were not bothered by the *criollo* scorn of manual
labor, earned fantastic wages for digging ditches and
building fences.

The Irish who worked hard did well. Many of them
came earlier than the British and Italians, they were able
to acquire land and marry Argentine girls with whom
they had Catholicism in common. At home they might
have been small farmers, clerks, or tradesmen, but in
Argentina the Irish proudly represented the Empire.
They forgot the traditional animosity toward Britain, and
they and their descendants often took a lead in British
community affairs.

You do not have to travel far on the *pampa* to encounter an Irish *estancia*, and the Irish brogue can be
heard at many a country livestock show. The Buenos
Aires telephone directory contains Irish names in nearly
all professional and trade categories. Many of the
Maloneys and O'Connors can only speak Spanish, but
the Irish-*porteño* somehow seems to introduce a hint of
the old country into the vernacular.

Numerically, the Germans have never been important in Argentina, but they have exercised a strong influence. They are chiefly concentrated in the northern territory of Missiones, where they mingle with the German colonists across the river in Brazil, and in the southern lake district, where their Chilean neighbors are also of German extraction. The Nazi Party announced in 1938 that there were 236,000 German residents in Argentina, and it tried to make each one an active propagandist.

Nazi influence rose as official representatives made German commercial, shipping, and banking houses an instrument of Hitler's policy. The two-hundred-odd German schools, which for years had taught their charges the glories of Germanic literature and arms, stressed the grandeur of Hitler and National Socialism. The German Embassy flooded the country with pro-Nazi material by subsidizing newspapers, movies, and publishing houses.

But many German-Argentines fought Hitler's propaganda. Among these were the refugees from Nazi Germany and Central Europe who came to Argentina in the thirties—probably around 65,000 altogether. Many of them remained in Buenos Aires or settled in provincial cities to start some of the new, smaller industries, the handicraft arts, and many smart continental style shops.

After Argentina finally declared war on Germany in March, 1945, the government seized the most valuable German properties, worth some $40,000,000. But in many cases Nazi sympathizers were put back in charge. Senator Harley Kilgore's Military Affairs Committee reported that the Germans had more than $250,000,000 in Argentina at the end of the war. The State Department's Blue Book on the Argentine situation in 1946 warned that the

Germans "possess today in Argentina the economic organization—industrial, commercial, and agricultural—which they need to provide a base for the reconstitution of German aggressive power."

Now the Nazi threat has been replaced by the Russian. Our officials encourage trade between Western Germany and Argentina. During 1951, it rose from the previous year's $25,000,000 to $82,800,000. Most of this trade skirted currency shortages and exchange regulations.

Despite Nazi influence in Argentina, there has never been a strong anti-Semitic feeling. There are estimated to be about four hundred thousand Jewish residents in the nation, about two-thirds of them in Buenos Aires. Some of them are of German descent, others Russian and Eastern European.

The stream of Jewish immigrants began coming to the Americas in 1889, as a result of the Russian pogroms of Alexander III. The first group to come to Argentina were city merchants, not farmers, but they were eager to work the land sold them by the Argentine consul in Paris. When they arrived they discovered that the properties they had bought were gone. After getting their money back, they made a colonization contract with an *estanciero* of Santa Fé and traveled north. There they found neither food nor shelter was available. They ate wormy flour and slept in wagons. They could not see their land nor get implements to work it. Many of their children died in an epidemic and were buried outside the railroad station. Some of the colonists returned to Buenos Aires; others stayed on, living on the charity of railroad workers and passengers.

Luckily a visitor came through the town and saw

their plight. He became concerned and hurried back to Europe to tell Baron Maurice de Hirsch, a multimillionaire financier and philanthropist, about it. Hirsch became interested, and founded the Jewish Colonization Association to help his persecuted fellow-Jews.

Their colonies were among the first to introduce cooperative dairy processing, a cheese industry, and related activities. Even today thousands of Jewish agricultural colonists remain on the land. In recent years more and more have left it for greater opportunities in the cities. Buenos Aires has many doctors, lawyers, and other middle-class Argentines of the Jewish faith whose parents or grandparents were among the agricultural settlers.

Those who have worked hard have found many opportunities. Some feel they have had more of a chance to get ahead than they would have had in the United States, where competition is keener. On the other hand many still live in poverty not unlike that of New York's lower East Side.

After the military officers assumed power in 1943, rabid nationalists in their camp let loose a wave of anti-Semitic activities. Nationalist newspapers ranted against the Jews, and extremists tar-bombed synagogues, Jewish newspapers, and shops. Unruly mobs broke up Jewish meetings and attacked the homes and offices of "Jews, Communists, and bankers," whom they linked as one. There was even talk of seizing Jewish farmlands, of expelling Jews from public offices, schools, and the professions. Gradually, however, those who led the anti-Semitic attacks lost ground as the government made it clear it did not favor the persecution of any racial group.

Now Perón has organized the Jewish community like

every other. So long as they do not oppose the regime, Argentine Jews feel they are "reasonably safe." This to a certain extent is a situation that applies to nearly everyone else. Argentines are not naturally anti-Semitic, nor do they have any strong religious or racial prejudices.

Another little-known, but important group in Argentina, are the Syrians, Arabs, Lebanese and others from the Middle East. Most Argentines call them all *turcos*. Argentina is said to have more than a million of them, never clearly classified or identified. They have learned Spanish easily—better, many say, than most foreigners who come to Argentina. A large number have married into lower middle-class Argentine families. Many are keen businessmen and have gone into textiles, retailing, and smaller types of manufacturing. They have not been active politically, and for a long time have kept strictly to their own organizations. But they are a vital group in Argentina.

In 1775, about one-third of the population was reportedly black. In 1825, a fourth of the province of Buenos Aires was colored. What happened to the Negroes has never been quite clear. Many people suspect the government quietly put as many as possible into dangerous military service where they got killed in fighting the Indians. In contrast to the States, the remaining blacks increased more slowly than the whites and were swallowed up by the growing population and waves of immigrants. As we have noted previously, there are hardly any full-blooded Negroes in Argentina today.

What are the possibilities of mass immigration in the future? "We would welcome one or two millions of Europe's starving men," Perón declared in 1946. His five-year-plan of that year set the goal at 5,000,000 immigrants—later reduced, on second thought, to 250,000. Technicians and skilled workers were preferred, and Spanish and Italians would be most easily absorbed, but there was to be no discrimination. "All we want are immigrants who are healthy and willing to work," said Miguel Miranda, Perón's economic adviser. At that time other government spokesmen spoke of opening Argentina's doors wide, of increasing its population to 40,000,-000 in not too many years. A special immigration commission went to Europe to help sign up people.

The grand plans were mostly talk. Between 1945 and 1951, 2,500,000 people came to Argentina, but 1,500,000 left it. Most of those remaining were immigrants, though the number includes executives who came to work in foreign firms and embassies.

In February, 1952, Perón revised his immigration program. Henceforth Argentina would admit only agricultural workers and a few skilled technicians. The postwar flow of immigrants was attracted to Argentina's factories rather than farms, thereby creating a drain on food supplies and congested urban areas—especially around the capital. Foreigners arriving in Argentina from now on cannot take up residence within a radius of sixty miles of Buenos Aires and will have their passports endorsed so that they cannot obtain urban work.

It is one of Perón's greatest ambitions to have Argentina reach the twenty-million mark before his second term ends in 1958. He has, in various ways, sought to encourage larger families. However, the Argentine birth rate cannot be forced.

A survey by the United Nations Educational, Scientific and Cultural Organization, released late in 1951, showed that during the first half of the century, Argentina led all the world's countries in population increases. Her figure was 251 per cent, followed by Cuba with 231 per cent, Colombia with 217 per cent, and Brazil with 191 per cent. Yet Argentina could, it is admitted, support millions more. Many still believe colonization the solution.

It is interesting to note that while Argentina has derived so much from Europe, her contributions have been small. Government gifts of wheat and other foods have gone to Italy, Spain, and France. There was even a contribution of forty thousand tons of wheat to Norway, although that country fought Argentina's admission to the United Nations at the San Francisco Conference.

One other foreign influence is worth noting—that of France. Argentina's attachment for France has been based more on sentiment than on immigration. France has never been one of Argentina's leading customers, and there have never been many French in the country. Though they have never launched a systematic drive to spread their culture, the French astutely and assiduously cultivated Argentine leaders of thought. For years the French-Argentine Institute has taught French and entertained visiting French lecturers. French dramatic companies headed by distinguished stars frequently come to the Argentine for a repertory season. When Maurice Chevalier arrived in 1951 he was treated like a hero. Stories and pictures in all Argentine papers recorded every move he made, dwelling especially on his visits to places he had not seen in twenty-five years.

The French tradition of freedom which aided us in our own revolution is, in no small measure, responsible for the high regard in which France has always been held in Argentina. When Paris was liberated in 1944, the joy of Buenos Aires knew no bounds. As far as the *porteños* were concerned, it was the highlight of the war. Thousands of men and women streamed into the downtown streets, cafés, and theaters weeping with joy and happiness and singing the "Marseillaise." The military was determined to suppress any such demonstration, lest cheers for French democracy be transformed into a protest against the lack of it at home. Police drove their horses into the crowds, knocking many down indiscriminately as they sought to enforce decrees against unauthorized processions. The Argentines were undaunted, and kept on singing. A Mexico City newspaper cartoon of the event was captioned: "Paris has fallen, but fighting continues in the streets—of Buenos Aires."

In the latter part of the last century Argentines began adopting French manners and modes. Then Argentina was anxious to get rid of a feeling of inferiority as a rough, tough, pioneer country. As merchant steamers began making regular calls and more hotels, banks, and newspapers were established, Buenos Aires turned to Paris as guide in culture and civilization. Wealthy Argentine families made trips to France, bought French furniture, pictures and draperies, and carried them back to set up new homes in imitation of what they had seen abroad.

France's influence is still important in Argentina. But gradually Argentines are turning northward to the United States. Until politics and the dollar shortage barred most of our magazines, the number of French fashion magazines found in the Argentine capital was small compared

to the number of North American publications. Today
the Hollywood films which display our manners and
morals, our homes and sports are making our influence
stronger than that of the French. The Argentine youths
of university age are no longer longing only for France—
they are going to the United States. The older generation
does not like it and sighs for the good old days. But the
good old days are obviously at an end.

Chapter VIII

This Is the Land

ARGENTINA'S SOIL, as every citizen will tell you, is startlingly rich and miraculously fertile. He quotes experts who say its black, alluvial deposit, "the cream of soils," varies in depth from seven to eleven feet—a seemingly almost inexhaustible agricultural treasure. Nature here, the Argentine adds, is heavy, lazy, and prolific, providing —with rare exceptions like the 1951 drought—an almost ideal combination of warm sunshine and abundant rainfall.

All this, you quickly realize, is Argentina's *pampa*, the plain which is the country's heartland. It is so vast and so productive of grain and beef that, as its output has varied, so has risen and fallen the price of bread and meat in many of the world's markets. Though the number of Argentines who actually live on the *pampa* is relatively small, a drought, a frost, a plague of locusts, or a cattle disease will affect millions of others.

Argentina's *pampa* actually covers only a fifth of the country's total area, but its wide grazing lands and cultivated fields produce 90 per cent of Argentina's grain and 60 per cent of its livestock, not including sheep. The *pampa* is really a huge agricultural factory, turning out countless tons of meat and cereal for an insatiably hungry world.

Land and climate have a great effect on the people of every country. In few places, however, have they helped mold the national character more than in Argentina, where they have contributed to its agricultural riches, its cities, and the temperament of its people.

Most North Americans do not realize that Argentina is essentially a temperate-zone country, as are only two other Latin republics, Chile and Uruguay. The rest are wholly or largely within the tropics. Much of Brazil, for example, has a climate that saps the energy of its people, takes away their desire for work, and stands as a barrier to European immigration.

In Argentina you can find almost every type of land and climate, from tropic jungle to frozen waste. Within its four major physical divisions are many areas similar to our own.

The *pampas*, for instance, might be compared to our Middle West and Great Plains. They produce wheat, corn, oats, flax, hogs, and beef cattle. Around the cities of Buenos Aires, Rosario, and La Plata are thriving truck and dairy farms.

Northwestern Argentina is similar to our states of Arizona, New Mexico, and western Texas. Here are most of Argentina's mineral resources: gold, silver, copper, tin. The irrigated areas produce wheat, corn, sugar cane and, as has already been mentioned, grapes and wine. After a drought, this is Argentina's dustbowl: if you ride the train to Mendoza or Zapala you don't need to be told—dust gets in your eyes, on your clothes, in your mouth. Outside the window you can see the wind blow it. The cloud raised by a passing car over an unpaved road is dense and black.

In the northeast is the Argentine Mesopotamia, the gently rolling grassland between the Paraná and Uruguay rivers, where cattle and sheep graze. The Paraná basin is potentially great cotton country, similar to our South. Bordering Paraguay is the subtropical Chaco, where the quebracho tree grows. It is valuable for its wood and for its bark, which contains a high percentage of tannin, used in the tanning of leather.

The third division of Argentina is Patagonia, which roughly covers everything south of Bahía Blanca. It extends to the beautiful lake country, but is best known as the arid, windswept plateau land which reaches to the Straits of Magellan. Most of it is devoted to sheep-raising —the only cropland (chiefly alfalfa) is found along the rivers. The boisterous, roaring wind of Patagonia is legendary. Against it a man—or a plane—makes headway only by strenuous exertion.

The final division is the Andes, which reach from the dry north to heavily glaciated, ice-covered southern Patagonia. In the north they are higher than our Rockies, more austere, more barren. In the lake country they are lower, greener, and more friendly.

Her land and climate have meant that Argentina has,

and always has had, a predominantly agricultural society which revolves around the output of the *pampa*. The other areas complement the *pampa's* production.

Argentina rose to its important position among the world's nations by exporting its agricultural products. Most Argentines, as Carl Taylor explains, know that Mendoza means wine; Tucumán, sugar; Misiones, *yerba*; the Chaco, quebracho; Rio Negro, fruit; Patagonia, sheep; and the *pampa*, Argentina's famed cattle.

They also know that their country's raw agricultural products have, in the past, constituted more than a third of Argentina's annual wealth. And they know that farm products furnished almost four-fifths of the raw products for Argentina's industry.

These ideas, as Mr. Taylor explains, are not merely learned in school. They are part of the country's proud tradition.

"It is highly doubtful," he adds, "that the whole population, old and young, foreign born and native born, know as much in a broad way about anything else that concerns the whole of Argentine society as they do about its agricultural products. And it is also a safe wager to say that if a stranger were to ask the first hundred Argentines he met in any part of the nation or the world to justify their universal pride in their country, a marked majority would recite the facts just cited. They would not demonstrate their membership in Argentine society by telling you what they think of *Yanquis* or Englishmen, or by discussing Parisian styles. They would recite the chief prides of Argentina, her agriculture and agricultural products."

What is the *pampa* on which Argentina has built her

wealth and position? And what is this land where wealthy
estancieros and their employees live?

It is the grassy, treeless area, virtually without stone
or gravel, which extends in a semicircle with an average
radius of 350 miles around the city of Buenos Aires. The
pampa includes the rich provinces of Buenos Aires and
Santa Fé, the southern part of Córdoba and San Luis, and
part of the new province of Eva Perón, formerly La
Pampa territory.

Nowhere else in Latin America do naturally fertile
soils cover such large areas. Away from the *pampa*, in
Santiago del Estero, are poor soils and scrub lands. In
Mendoza's foothills, as we have noted, irrigation has
been necessary to produce rich areas of specialized fruits
and vegetables.

But the *pampa* needs little help. Sweeping almost without variation from the west bank of the Plata and the
mild Atlantic on out to the Andean foothills in the west,
it is the area which has produced the greatest wealth with
the least effort.

Looking at the *pampa* from a plane, it seems endless,
stretching on and on like a huge patchwork rug. There
are no hills or wooded slopes, but flat, absolutely flat, land
like a tabletop. From a train—the most important transport of the *pampa*—the horizon appears a half-circle. The
rails behind you are parallel straight lines stretching out
endlessly. Everything is close at hand or on the horizon.
There is no middle ground. Only the tops of distant
windmills are visible, and the *pampa* seems to curve only
as the earth curves.

The rich prairie grass seems to go on forever—green
clover or succulent lucerne, monster sunflowers grown

for oil, and lazy, gentle cattle bred, as Christopher Isher-
wood says, "into walking packets of meat."

Pasture goes beyond the eye's visioning. In some ways
it is like our own prairie land, but the *pampa's* grass crops
are more lush and lighter. Rainfall is greater; temperature
extremes less.

Although there are few geographic barriers to transportation and few topographic contours to condition
patterns of settlement, the *pampa* is not a well-traversed
land. It has comparatively few of the concrete or asphalt
highways we know. Most public roads are unmacadam-
ized, and often barely passable in certain seasons. In the
last ten years road-building has moved ahead rapidly.
Today concrete roads join the capital and the provinces
of Santa Fé, Córdoba, and many key points in the province of Buenos Aires.

Many thousands of miles of dirt road have been improved. The general absence of stone over the *pampa* has
made hard-road construction expensive but, on the other
hand road-builders do not have to worry about expensive
bridges or tunnels. Hundreds of miles of private byways
follow the wire fences and divide the land into innumerable rectangles, orderly pastures, and farmlands. All roads
lead eventually to the railroad stations—the points from
which cattle are shipped to market.

Every Argentine knows the fascination of the *pampa*,
whether he has seen it or not. He has read about it from
childhood, heard its music, probably hummed the nostalgic popular song, *"Adios, Pampa Mia."* He knows the
thick *ombu* tree of the *pampas*—it is the theme of countless poems and songs. Even in the capital, he knows the
impressive *ombu* in the parks and plazas. No one knows

the origin of the tree, which botanists consider a gigantic shrub or bush, but it has become Argentina's national tree. Its gnarled roots reach out over the ground and give it a sturdy appearance. At night the *ombu's* leaves are noxious. One rarely sees a nest in its branches, but its generous spread of branch and almost evergreen foliage afford magnificent shade to men and animals on the *pampa*.

Around his residence the *estancia*-owner has planted great squares of huge, shaggy eucalyptus trees and tall, stately Lombardy poplars. If he is a man of wealth, his park also contains his polo fields, tennis courts, and swimming pools.

In his description of the *pampa*, Archibald MacLeish, former Librarian of Congress, explains how the railway stations "come every twenty minutes as though laid out, not by geography, but by clocks." "Argentina of the *pampas*," he writes, "Argentina of the enormous plains, Argentina flowing out into the morning beyond the hills like a sea beyond capes. . . Argentina without towns, with few roads, with fences straight and wide apart as meridians on a map. . . It is a country in which the distances from house to house are too great for the barking of dogs even on the stillest night, a country in which the cocks crow only twice because there is no answer. It is a country so level that even time has no hold upon it and one century is like another; a country so empty that the watchers at night put their eyes along the ground to see the circle of the horizon; a country in which the sky is so huge that men plant islands of eucalyptus over their houses to be covered from the blue; a country in which space is so great that all the visions end in eternity. It is a country of grass, a country without stone. . . A country in which green goes on and on like water and the gulls follow the plows as seagulls follow ships, a country in which the women are always together under the dark trees in the evening, their faces fading into loneliness with the night."

Waldo Frank, describing the *pampa*, says: "It is a land so vast in its monotony, so undifferentiated in its forms, that it ceases to be, like other land, material you can work with; it becomes a mood, at last a spirit, which invades you."

Two centuries after Buenos Aires' founding, the *pampa* still belonged to bands of savages. Early Argentine settlers held only a thin strip of land close to the sea and the river, where they pastured their cattle at great peril. The Indians were exterminated only after long and relentless campaigns in which no quarter was asked and none given.

Before Argentina's railroads were built, the *pampa* was a disorderly, barbarous region, in some ways like our own wild West. Its gauchos were the equivalent of our cowboys. The *pampa* did not approach true economic status until its lands were finally fenced with wire. After that the owner of the land was on his way to becoming the personage around whom everything in Argentina was to revolve.

Chapter IX

The Owners of the Land

APPROXIMATELY TWO HUNDRED families have long owned the great bulk of Argentina's richest land. They have developed the strains of the world's finest cattle and grown the wheat, corn, and linseed which has brought them fabulous financial rewards. For years they dominated the nation's economy, society, and politics.

Some of the first *estancieros* were scarcely more than cattle rustlers. Others were poor Irish immigrants, or small-time *políticos*. Acres and acres of land were parcelled out as rewards to soldiers. A *caudillo* paid his supporters by the acre as he might write a check; the dictator Rosas gave away animals as liberally as he did land.

Whoever they were, the *estancieros* knew that land meant wealth and increased their holdings as much as possible. The early sheep- and cattle-breeders took little

interest in improving their stock or in running their
estancias as businesses. They let their herds run at will
on the vast, unfenced range, and slaughtered them for
hides, tallow, and salt beef.

The fence, the railroad and, in 1877, the first refrigera-
tor ship, changed all that. The British would not eat lean,
tough Argentine beef, so the *estancieros* began breeding
imported beef cattle on fenced-in pastures. To feed them
properly they had to plow some of their land and grow
alfalfa. This required farm hands, so the *estancieros* called
for more immigrants.

The great *estancias* developed according to a feudal
pattern. Those workers born on the land lived and died
on it. Whatever schooling they received was given them
by the *estanciero*. Their food, save for a few items, came
from the land. Their only contact with the outside world
was an occasional visit to the nearest town.

In the early nineteenth century the large landowners
became the aristocracy of Argentina, the traditional ruling class. The top landowning families intermarried to an
astonishing degree, as can be seen in the names of the
leading *señoras* of today who retain their family names.
They form a closely knit caste. Rarely does an outsider
break into their social set.

The story of the Menendez family illustrates how some
landowning families have become millionaires. José
Menendez, a Spanish immigrant, migrated from Havana
in 1875. In Buenos Aires he married a pretty, black-
haired girl of the middle class, borrowed a few thousand
pesos from an uncle, bought several hundred sheep, and
began traveling south. It took four years to walk to the
Straits of Magellan, and on the way three children were

born and the small flock of sheep increased to a few thousand. Don José and Doña Maria had six children, two of whom died. The net income of each child—and of the estates of each of the two deceased children—is said to average about a million dollars a year, after taxes.

This fortune was built up in one of the most sparsely settled portions of the world, where a constant wind rarely blows less than forty miles an hour and where virtually the only inhabitants are Ona Indians and shepherds. The herds of sheep now run up into the millions, and the barns are equipped with all the latest electrical devices for shearing. Five thousand sheep is the average number sheared each day.

Originally an *estancia* meant only livestock: a grain farm is a *chacra*. The owners of the large sugar plantations in Tucumán and the vast vineyards in Mendoza and San Juan consider themselves *estancieros*, though they are not of the cattle aristocracy.

Properties of less than 25,000 acres are still the exception in Argentina. One count not so many years ago showed 259 individual Argentines holding land and properties averaging 47,000 acres each. Fifty families in Buenos Aires Province—where land is most expensive— held more than 75,000 acres each. The largest holdings, of up to more than half a million acres, are chiefly in the territories.

The Perón government has tried to break up these enormous holdings, but has not had much success. The big landowners do not want to sell, and most of them have held on to their property. When it is sold, the buyers in many cases are men who have made their fortunes in industrial or import-export activities and want a place to invest their money, since it is so difficult to transfer profits abroad. Thus the land has not been divided among the actual farmers; it has simply been transferred from one absentee owner to another.

Estancieros seldom want to sell less than five hundred acres. Occasionally a group of tenants join together to purchase a tract and subdivide it, but for the most part the farmer has little opportunity to buy his own place. Even if he does, he cannot afford the expensive machinery, the price of which is increased by import taxes. He cannot sell his produce cooperatively because the big *estancieros* who surround him force him to accept their price. Yet the promise of dividing the land produces hope in Argentine hearts and helps to win elections.

On the statute books are homestead acts designed to break up the huge estates which date back to Spanish land grants. But most of the laws are ineffective. On various occasions the government has promised to cancel the taxes of any *estanciero* who sets up his own colonization project, but few have done it, for, as one authority expresses it, there is probably no society in the world whose members prize the ownership of pasture and farm land as do the Argentines. But the idea that a wider distribution of land ownership would help develop a better and more democratic social order is held by many Argentines, including the city dwellers who do not know much about agricultural economics.

The crippling inflation which has spiraled since 1950 demonstrates this most clearly. Formerly, when funds could be freely remitted, many *estancia* owners and their large families lived abroad, mostly in Paris, for at least part of the year. It was their lavish spending that first made the Argentines known throughout Europe. Today many live with one foot on the soil and the other in Buenos Aires—unhappy at home yet afraid to leave. With interests in Argentina's cattle and crops, as well as in the nation's culture, they have long dominated both Argentina's rural and urban life.

Those who dislike them call them the oligarchy, and the impressive Jockey Club on Calle Florida in Buenos Aires was their citadel. The less vehement admit that the *estancia* system, with all its faults, did build up Argentina's great cattle industry.

You will get many varying stories about how much and how great is the *estanciero* control of Argentina's economy. Under today's highly partisan conditions, it would be hard to justify most of the statistics from either side. For one thing, the *estanciero* is generally a bitter enemy of the Perón regime. He hears talk about breaking up his estates, an idea which he considers Communist no matter what Perón calls it. He knows his taxes are rising, although they are not nearly as high as in the United States. He is also aware that taxes plus the increased cost of working his land may eventually force him to sell some of his property in order to continue to live at his accustomed standard.

The *estanciero* insists Perón will someday destroy Argentina's cattle industry which, he points out, depends on large land areas where cattle can be moved from place to place, fed on grass, fattened on alfalfa in summer and on cereal grains in winter. "The small farmers," he tells you, "often raise just enough for themselves, and little for domestic sale or export. And without exports, Argentina dies."

He sounds just like an American businessman when he explains how the cost of everything he needs to run his *estancia* has gone up. Wire, windmills, pipes, wood for posts—all have risen ten, fifteen, twenty times in the last few years. "We now have to waste half our time simply arguing with officials to settle endless disputes," he continues. "We suspect that lots of our workers deliberately try to get fired in the hope of getting severance pay so that they can go to the city and get factory jobs. Nobody in the government understands—or wants to understand —our problems. On the other hand, we are constantly singled out as the group that is ruining Argentina."

It is especially noteworthy, however, that more and more of the *estancia* owners were saying, as early as 1950: "We, ourselves, are partly to blame. We are responsible for not having taken the lead ourselves and for letting Perón with his demagogue promises win over many who would have been on our side."

With all this, it is surprising to find that the Sociedad Rural Argentina, the *estancia* owners' major organization which pioneered in improving the breed of Argentine herds and which runs the famous cattle shows, has done comparatively little about current conditions, except to have some of its leaders make a few mild speeches. Some Argentines think this policy has been weak-kneed. Others feel it is in the Argentine tradition—that the *estancieros* have been cautious because they felt they could not accomplish anything.

Many an *estanciero* sees himself as a generous, benevolent father to his workers, one who shares their joys and sorrows and is interested only in their welfare. He cannot understand why his more intelligent workers are leaving the *estancia* for jobs in city factories. And he does not much care for the minimum wage rate the government has set for rural workers.

Because of increased costs and labor shortages, many *estancieros* are turning to operations which require less labor. Instead of running *criadeganados*, breeding and rearing ranches, they become *invernadas*, fattening and feeding specially purchased young cattle.

Others are renting more of their land to tenants, or raising cereal crops themselves. But breaking the rich sod of their grazing lands seems almost sinful to many a proud *estancia* owner.

The reorganization of *estancias* as family-owned business corporations is becoming increasingly common. Children of an *estanciero* often form a stock company, dividing the shares among themselves to avoid both inheritance and income taxes. An elder son may assume the responsibility for running the place as a business, rather than leaving it to a *mayordomo* and his foremen.

One illustration of this tendency is the *Estancia X*, four hours outside of Buenos Aires and one of the largest land holdings near the capital. Once rated as one of the world's largest sheep farms, its owners were host and hostess to world-famed personalities. He calls his *estancia* a small place—only 25,000 acres. For many years he played polo, and both he and his lovely wife had as many friends in London and New York as in Buenos Aires.

Today, because he is older and busier, the owner spends fewer hours on his polo ponies and more and more on managing the *estancia*. He can, and frequently has, shod his own horses. He operates on his animals with the skill of a veterinary. A practical carpenter, he can also fix his electric light plant. He keeps increasing his herds of Romney Marsh and Hampshire Down sheep, cattle, and hogs. He imports bulls from Scotland and England to vary the blood strain and produce better cattle.

"I want to keep this business a paying one," he explains. He obviously believes that he and those like him are being discriminated against and that a combination of taxes and price restrictions are making things increasingly difficult. However, selling his land to be broken up into small portions is the last thing he would want to do.

Whether he and his friends will be able to maintain their position no one knows. Their days may be numbered. Whether or not this is best for Argentina is hardly the question—the country, and the world, have changed. But with the changes in Argentina have come a decrease in beef production and the rationing of meat into virtually none for export. Maybe before too long the government will realize that it is not practical to ruin the lowest cost agricultural production in the world in an effort to create an industrial economy which at best could only be third rate.

Chapter X

The Workers of the Land

JUST BEFORE President Perón's first election, groups of campaign workers wearing large peronista badges visited scores of *estancias* in the Province of Buenos Aires. They showed their area maps and big black record books to the tenant farmers and *peons*. "What acreage do you want after the election?" they asked.

The requests were carefully noted. No specific promises were given. Yet the inference was clear: once Perón was in the Casa Rosada, the land they had indicated would be theirs.

Perón knew the *peons* and tenant farmers hungered for land. So his promise "Give the land to the one who cultivates it" won him many a vote. No politician had ever before favored agrarian reform.

Argentina's tenant farmers, or *colonos*, rate far below

133

the *estancia* owners on the economic and social scale. Yet they produce from two-thirds to three-fourths of the wheat, corn, and flax which are the country's most important crops. These farmers and their families are the real middle class of Argentine agriculture. Unlike the *estancieros*, there are hundreds of thousands of them, and their number is increasing. They are seldom mentioned by anyone writing about life and conditions in the Argentine, partly because they are not a homogeneous group.

You will see the *colono* in the vineyard, sugar, cotton, and fruit districts as well as the cereal belt. Sun-tanned, leather-skinned, quiet in manner, the average tenant farmer is ignorant but shrewd. He works hard all week and spends his Sunday afternoon in a nearby *boliche* (the bar adjacent to a country store), talking, bowling, and drinking his highproof *cana*—a sweet, fiery rum.

Many *colonos* in the livestock-producing districts possess more capital and produce far more than the very small landowners who raise cattle. If, in addition, they have managed to acquire even a little bit more than the average three hundred acres, their neighbors recognize their superiority. For the most part, however, they tend toward the lower levels of the middle class. The range runs all the way from the *colono* who is just a little better than a *peon*, or common worker, to one who is just a little lower than an owner-operator. Their per capita income is about a quarter to a third that of a United States farmer. Still, this amount is greater than most Latin-American agricultural producers.

The average Argentine tenant farmer used to be so deeply concerned with his day-to-day tasks and family affairs and so unconscious of his importance in the national economy that he was unconcerned about politics.

"Now that the government in Buenos Aires is involved in almost every phase of our lives," he tells you, "that is no longer true." Once he did not care to vote, or obediently follow the political dictates of his landlord, but now he is aware of his citizenship and his ballot. In the past he rarely joined groups to make his opinion felt, but now he has been practically forced to do something. Perón's party representatives are everywhere. The prices of products are set by the government. Whether the tenant farmer can get implements and housing may depend more on what the government does than what he himself is able to do.

Hence the keen interest in what is happening in Buenos Aires. News from the capital is followed with tremendous interest since the doings of the government have become a part of everyday life.

The *chacerero* is in almost the same position as the *colono*. He is a tenant farmer who uses his land for diversified crops. At present few *chacereros* make enough money cropping to buy much land. Some, however, are beginning to emerge to ownership status.

Though his housing is likely to be as comfortless as the *colono's*—dirt floors, side walls of hardened mud or adobe brick, and roofs with few supports—the *chacerero's* slight independence comes from the fact that he uses his land for some subsistence farming. When prices are good and farming is done on a real share basis, he can actually get a few thousand *pesos* ahead. On the other hand, if he rents for cash, his landlord often raises rents with price increases. Thus often he does not make any money when prices rise—and when prices drop he is penniless.

Most authorities agree there is no segment of Argentina's population more important to the nation's life and yet less conscious of his importance than the Argentine farmer. The explanation lies chiefly in the history of the country's economic and social development, and the institutionalization of the class structure.

The fathers and grandfathers of most *colonos* came to Argentina as poor immigrants after most of the land was distributed. They never have owned land. Most of them started farming as hired men, and rose to the status of tenants. The *colonos* of today are occupying the highest tenure status their group has ever enjoyed. Nevertheless, most of them feel they never will be farm owners unless they are assisted in Buenos Aires. Naturally they are interested in Perón's plans. As many put it: "Only if he or somebody there helps us will we ever achieve independence."

This faith in Perón is, however, beginning to disappear, for many have found that instead of having the local *acopiador* as middleman, the government has taken the middle man's role for itself—and frequently left them with even less than they had before.

In the past, the Argentine landowner collected from a fourth to half of what his *colonos* produced. Sometimes a roving sharecropper would contract to till a piece of land for a period of two to five years. Since the *colono* was not paid for any improvements he made for his landlord, he generally was not interested in improving the property. Often he plowed in April, let the land lie untouched until June, then put in his wheat and waited for it to ripen.

Since he saw and handled money only when his annual crop was sold, he usually had to go to the *acopiador* for funds to carry him over. The *acopiador* usually owned a general store where the *colono* purchased his potatoes and supplies at any price the *acopiador* set. He also sold the jute bags in which the crop had to be delivered. And the *acopiador* owned the threshing machine, which he rented at so much a bushel. Only the *acopiador* would extend credit.

Thus the *colono* was often heavily in debt by the time his grain was threshed. The *acopiador* could corner the crops in his districts before they were sold to the big exporting firms, knowing that most *colonos* had to sell at the time prices were at their lowest.

Many *colonos* considered themselves lucky if they were able to pay off their debts and begin the new year in the clear. Naturally, therefore, they were easy prey to Perón's promises of a better life in return for votes.

The *peon* working on the Argentine *estancia* had even fewer opportunities, but since he expected little he was not disappointed. If you saw him on an *estancia* at the time of a celebration, dressed in the costume of a bygone day, you would have found it hard to identify the *peon* as Argentina's truly forgotten man.

But the fact is that he was for a long time the man to whom few, if any, Argentines paid much attention. City workers were organized and began getting improvements long before the militarists came into power. But the Argentine *peon*, the man of all work on the *estancia* or the tenant farm, in the vineyards of Mendoza, the sugar fields of Tucumán, the quebracho forests or cotton plantations in the Chaco and the *maté* fields in Misiones was taken for granted. He, in turn, often took his own position for granted.

Perón, however, has improved the position of the rural worker. His Statute of the Peon and other acts provide minimum wages, a day off each week, medical and pharmaceutical assistance, etc. The government has set up many rural workers' organizations, especially for agricultural rather than pastoral laborers.

Frequently the *peons* have been hired hands so long they seemingly do not care to get ahead. But sometimes, with the help of a sympathetic employer or a colonization project, a *peon* will become a tenant farmer or even a small landowner.

More and more farm laborers are shifting to city jobs. Their ranks are more than filled, especially in the north and west, by waves of men of even lower status who flow in from Paraguay, Bolivia, and Chile. They go into the sugar, cotton, *yerba maté*, and lumber industries in the north. Other migrants, as in our own country, take unskilled, low-paying jobs as cotton, sugar beet, or fruit pickers. They face the same abuses our migrants encounter—inadequate housing, company stores which charge exorbitant prices, and relatively little food to eat despite the richness of the land on which they work.

Yet whether he works as a hired man all year round or on an itinerant basis, the Argentine worker is not and never was a serf, nor is he quite as badly off as some Indians and *mestizos* in many other Latin American countries.

Chapter XI

The Gaucho Tradition

LOOK CAREFULLY in almost any Argentine home, and
somewhere you will find a calendar painting of a full-
faced, deeply tanned man in a pair of big, baggy trousers.
He will have spurs at his heels, a massive silver coin-
decked belt round his waist, and a guitar slung over his
saddle.

He is riding the endless, flat expanse of the *pampa*,
under a blue, starlit sky. He is so ugly that his ugliness
produces affection. His horse looks like the father of all
horses.

The painting will be by Florencio Molina Campos.
With eleven others in similar vein, it illustrates the calendar long issued annually by Alpargatas, a Scotch-Argen-
tine firm which makes the famous rope-soled sandals

worn by laboring men and women throughout the country.

In poorer Argentine homes, the Molina Campos calendar occupies a place of honor. In others, it hangs in the kitchen, the pantry, or the den. Molina Campos has romanticized and glorified the gaucho. His work expresses the spirit and tradition which Argentines like to remember.

The heroic legend of the gauchos who lived a nomadic and adventurous life on the *pampa* before it was fenced in and fought with the liberating armies in the wars against Spain remains one of the strongest influences on Argentine character today.

The gaucho lives not only in the Molina Campos paintings and in the reproduction of his work. He appears in movies, songs, and stories. You will see him in the costumes children like to wear, just as our children wear the Hopalong Cassidy costume. You even see the gaucho on candy bar wrappers. He signifies a nostalgic yearning for the past—a romanticized past which realistic historians say never existed.

Nothing quite upsets an Argentine as much as having an enthusiastic young woman from North America ask him to show her a gaucho. "They have disappeared," he will explain. "As dead as the dodo."

Yet many an Argentine rural worker keeps the idea alive by wearing the traditional gaucho spurs and belts. The cossack-type of trousers tucked into knee-high, leather boots have changed very little since gaucho days. The gaucho's short bolero jacket, the kerchief knotted round the throat, and the poncho of sheep or vicuna wool are in everyday use. Even *estancieros* like to borrow the gaucho's dashing costume, especially at fiesta time. In the smaller cities you find many an Argentine wearing the long scarf outside rather than inside his topcoat, and the narrow-brimmed, high-crowned hat that resembles those seen in the drawings and pictures of bygone days.

The gaucho emerges in the Argentine's mind's eye as a lean, brown-bodied figure, constantly riding the *pampa* as free and easy as the wind. The muscular and vigorous gaucho's only serious aims in life, so the Argentine is convinced, were to ride superbly, to mount and dismount a galloping horse, to throw and tame a wild colt single-handed. The Argentines' delight in mastering animals doubtless stems from this. The gaucho tradition of horsemanship is still vigorous; and horses are still very much a part of even the city man's life. Most Argentines ride well, and they love doing it in a dashing, whirling, daring style to show off their skill at its best.

The gaucho combined the Spaniard's dignity with the Indian's savage skill. He lived not as a herdsman or breeder, but by taming the wild horses and then riding them in pursuit of wilder cattle. Two things sealed his fate: the invention of barbed wire to fence in the *estancias* and prevent animals from roaming away, and the British preference for tasty beef from well-bred cattle.

The gaucho's sense of personal liberty still marks many an Argentine. In his day laws were unwritten and often crude. Dictator Rosas and the lesser *caudillos* established their rule in their own territories as they saw fit. None of them were more effective than their strength to enforce their will. The man who could hold the respect of the gauchos in his locality and command them in war was the chieftain. For over two hundred years such men ruled most of Argentina's interior. Often they inspired both devotion and terror.

When Argentina achieved independence from Spanish rule, the city of Buenos Aires assumed the right to represent all those living in the former viceroyalty. The gauchos and *caudillos* unanimously opposed this threat to their power. To this day, the conflict between the capital and the interior remains.

The gaucho, says Argentine legend, was a poker-faced, seemingly emotionless individual, something of a mystic and fatalistic brooder. Argentines still show little outward emotion. Yet it took only a word or a signal to change the soft-spoken rider into a hard-fighting warrior. He had courage, but no moral or intellectual qualities. From the gaucho model, Argentines have developed the nonconformist individualism which can be detected in the modern Argentine. It manifests itself, for example, in his refusal to obey traffic lights. The municipality of Buenos Aires was forced to discontinue the use of the few it had installed some years ago and has never attempted to try any since. The gaucho's suspiciousness and wild independence may be responsible for the Argentine's failure to establish many truly cooperative ventures in the nation. Internationally, these characteristics show up at hemisphere and world conferences and in Argentina's procrastination in ratifying treaties.

Work was beneath the gaucho's dignity as a man. He left it to his woman whom he called a *china* (pronounced chee-na), a Quechua Indian word which simply means *hembra*, or female, in the sense in which the word is applied to animals. *China* has since acquired a somewhat more affectionate connotation, and is still applied to girls of the lower classes in the provinces. Because the gaucho refused to tie himself to one woman, many an Argentine man—perhaps even more than most Latins—still feels all women outside his family circle are his potential prerogative.

The Argentine's mustache also comes partly from the gauchos. Most gauchos had large, flowing mustaches, and sometimes beards. Per capita, more Argentine men are said to wear such adornment than perhaps those of any other country in the world.

John White calls the gauchos a completely new and original race, which developed during the colonial period. "The gaucho was the most picturesque and romantic type of man produced on earth in modern times. Unfortunately, he was destined to pass into oblivion. But before he disappeared, he played a tremendously important part in Argentine history. It is no exaggeration, in fact, to say that it was the gaucho who made Argentina. First he helped the Spaniards win the country from the Indians by providing an effective barrier between the civilized towns and the raiding savages. Later, he formed the mounted militias which won freedom from Spain, not only for Argentina but for Uruguay, Chile, Bolivia and Peru. Then after many years of civil war, he finally forced the city and the Province of Buenos Aires to join the federation. It was then, and not until then, that Argentina became a nation."

Domingo Sarmiento, who is known as Argentina's schoolmaster President, felt the gauchos must be exterminated. In his remarkable study of the gaucho mentality, *Facundo*, or *Civilization and Barbarism* (published in 1845), Sarmiento denounced the gaucho tradition as

dangerous, uncivilized and primitive. To him it represented the worst and most savage elements in Argentine
character. Sarmiento distrusted the gauchos' illiteracy,
rough sports, *cana*, and gambling.

Now that Perón is reviving the gaucho idea once more,
Sarmiento's name rarely appears as one of the national
heroes of whom Argentines hear day after day. Perón,
seeking to develop his own *caudillo* status against a modern setting, has not only followed the dictator Rosas'
"bloody precedent," as Fleur Cowles points out in her
comparison of the two regimes, but has also adopted
many traditions stemming directly from gaucho days and
has glorified Rosas.

Argentines of all classes drink *maté*, the herb tea which
has come down from gaucho days. *Maté*, incidentally,
can be described as Argentina's national drink although
it is also popular in Uruguay and in Southern Brazil. It
is made from *yerba maté* leaves placed in a gourd, atop
which boiling water is poured. One drinks it by sipping
through a metal straw. Argentines claim *maté* has all the
vitamins supplied by a full vegetable diet, particularly
Vitamin C. It contains less caffeine than coffee or tea, and
in contrast to the other beverages which are acid, is alka-
line in reaction. This is important in view of the heavy
meat consumption of Argentines. Some authorities even
claim *yerba maté* is responsible for the low incidence of
cancer of the alimentary tract.

Argentina's epic poem, *Martin Fierro*, tells how the
gauchos used the *maté* gourd in much the same way as
our Indians smoked their peace pipes, passing it from
one member of the group to another around a fire at midday or sundown. Every Argentine can quote at least a

few passages from *Martin Fierro*. The ballad is still so popular that country merchants often stock copies of it along with their staples of salt, flour, and sugar.

The author, José Hernandez, was born in Buenos Aires Province in 1834. He followed Rosas to the bitter end, and fought the civilizing influences of Sarmiento. When the last gaucho *caudillo* in Entre Rios was beaten, Hernandez wrote his long poem on the life and sufferings of the gaucho. It was published in 1872. Like *Gone with the Wind*, it glorified an epoch which had ended.

Martin Fierro tells the story of his own life with the wit and vaunt that characterizes his people. Taken prisoner by the army one night when he was drunk in a *pulperia* where a murder had been committed, Martin is pressed into frontier service against the Indians. He escapes, turns bad, and is persecuted by the police, who do not understand his love for freedom, his desire to live "as free as a bird in the sky." He does not consider himself bad: he never fights or kills until he has to. Finally, he takes refuge among the Indians.

In *The Return of Martin Fierro*, he leaves the Indians and comes back to the society he fled. Some Argentines feel Hernandez had a change of heart, that he realized Argentina was coming of age and brought his gaucho back to an orderly world.

Whatever its poetic merits, the book was, and is, a tremendous success, and it is considered a true picture of the life and language, the thought and rather simple wisdom of the nineteenth-century Argentine gaucho. Thousands read it today, appreciating its proud, lonely philosophy, its roughness, its countless allusions to the old ways of the land. "The breath of the *pampas* runs through its disheveled, untamed, vigorous verses," one critic said of it.

In 1926 Ricardo Guiraldes wrote the classic novel of the *pampas, Don Segundo Sombra.* Many other Argentines have written of the gaucho, and are writing of him today. The interpretations change constantly, much as our own history changes as we re-evaluate our heroes and traditions. But the gaucho spirit and inheritance continue to affect Argentina.

Chapter XII

The Argentine Worker

A VISITING United States industrial engineer, anxious to see a new, widely-publicized Argentine industry in operation, journeyed out to its plant one day not long ago only to find the place closed because of a fiesta. Next day he was busy with other matters, but the morning after he made the journey once more. Again the plant was closed—another holiday.

The following week he telephoned the manager and inquired: "How do you get any work done? Every other day seems to be a holiday."

A moment later he regretted putting the question—but not because it was embarrassing. For the next ten minutes, in a torrent of words, the manager described the difficulties with which he had to deal and bewailed the fact that another two-day holiday was just beginning.

The number of paid holidays, all sanctioned by the Perón government as one way of winning the favor and support of the growing number of workers, is beyond the comprehension of most North Americans, and, it must be admitted, of many Argentines as well.

The official holidays became so numerous, in fact, that in 1951 the Argentine Chamber of Commerce reported that for every two days an Argentine worked, he was officially entitled to one day of rest. Some holidays were subsequently cancelled. But the vacation schedule is still more liberal than that of the greatest of the "feather-bedded" industries in the United States.

The law formerly declared eighteen legal holidays compared with eight in the United States. Then the General Confederation of Labor (C. G. T.), the over-all labor organization which is to all intents and purposes a government agency, added nine more in 1951 by decree or by work stoppages. These were all observed by the Federation's claimed six million members and by most other workers as well.

Big rallies bring everything to a dead halt and virtually paralyze industry for the work-week. Celebrants journey to and from Buenos Aires at government expense in order to participate. It is customary after a big peronista day such as October 17 to declare the next day a holiday also. And in addition to all these, each branch of Argentine industry also has special days on which none of its craftsmen will work. There is a day for the barbers, another one for the waiters, a third for the metal workers.

The net effect of these holidays is a tremendous loss of manpower which businessmen say might better be used turning out production needed if the industrial drive is to succeed. Besides official holidays, there has been a sharp increase in absenteeism in the last few years, sharply affecting production. Most workers have taken the not unnatural attitude that if others do not work, why should they.

To meet this difficulty a new system of attendance bonus clauses was put into contracts between the unions and various industries. Pay raises of as high as 30 per cent were awarded those who worked every day. Absence of as few as three days for any cause except a death in the immediate family during a payroll period of two weeks to a month cost the worker his entire increase. An absence of just one day reduced his increase as much as 50 per cent. Lateness was also reflected in the pay envelope. The clause had an effect immediately. In many industries where absenteeism was formerly as high as 12 to 15 per cent, the percentage dropped to almost zero. In 1951 it was 8.4 per cent.

The question of the productivity of Argentine workers is one of the major factors industrial observers use in measuring how far they believe the country can grow industrially. On several occasions Perón himself has stated that one great fault of the Argentine is that he is lazy. The New York *Times* reported he told that to a visiting United States Congressional delegation not long after his second election in November, 1951. And while Perón didn't mention them, statistics based on the United Nations Bulletin of Statistics for August, 1951, showed just what this meant. Based on 1937 as 100, the 1939 productivity of Argentine workers was listed as 99, that of Canadians at 101, and that of the United States the same.

Sweden was higher with 105. But by 1949 the Argentine figure was down to 88, Canada was up to 103, the United States at 121, Sweden at 124. In 1951 the Argentine worker had gone up a bit to 91, Canada was 110, Chile 116, Sweden 128, and the United States 130.

Four factors contribute to an Argentine worker's productivity: his actual skill, his willingness and ability to cooperate, his labor unions (which in the past were a part of his job but now dominate and control its every aspect), and finally how well the worker is prospering under today's conditions.

Engineers say that, although some Argentine plants are highly efficient and use all the devices of modern industry, in general their over-all efficiency rates lower than ours. Argentine industry uses more manpower per job because manpower used to cost less. Production requiring hand operations could sometimes be turned out at lower rates than in the United States. But Argentines have not created the mass hand production methods of either the Germans or the Japanese. While well-adapted to modern factory methods, Argentines have not been large-scale producers for international markets, and they will probably not be in the foreseeable future.

During the early stages of most new manufacturing industries, managers and chief technicians are usually brought in from abroad. If their announced purpose is to train local personnel and then step out, they have generally been welcome. But if they have intended to stay, especially in recent years, there has often been strong resentment. Some concerns, especially United States firms, have successfully overcome this by sending their most promising Argentines to plants in North America for observation and experience. Most of them come back enthusiastic.

Argentine workers have few, if any, of the native handicraft traditions which many North Americans associate with many Latin countries. There is little native pottery, weaving, or carving, although some is produced in remote parts of Córdoba and in the Andean regions. Paraguayan lace, a highly fragile, delicate product, comes from Argentina's far north as well as from Paraguay. Such items are so rare that they are sold only locally or in a few city curio shops.

The Argentine white-collar and industrial worker is in many ways like our own, with some notable exceptions. Argentines themselves will tell you that the lack of team spirit and cooperation which the Argentine considers a sign of his individualism makes it almost impossible for Argentine industry to achieve our type of group planning, assignment of authority, and minimum minute supervision.

Most Argentines do not believe that individual ability assures success in industrial enterprise. In business as well, many young men feel it is possible to get ahead only with the right family background or influence. They are convinced that those who are in power seek to hold them back.

Few Argentine business leaders train successors other than a son, a son-in-law, or an especially close relative. In most cases, an Argentine who moves up to a more important job is suspicious of the aims and desires of those below him and feels that they might be trying to force him out. This idea is seen in the political field: few of those who shared power with Perón in the first days of the military regime are still active. Men who showed signs of strength or popularity have been forced out, lest they consider themselves partners in the regime's success rather than subsidiary figures.

Most Argentines prefer to plan a project and let somebody else worry about seeing it through. It has often been said that on paper they are wonderful administrators and production schedulers but getting the task accomplished is something else. This stems in part from the Spanish disgust for manual labor.

Argentines are neat, orderly, and systematic in operating their own personal business affairs. Most shops and their clerks like to write out bills and receipts for every order, change of routine, or stock notation. They are strong on filing systems, indexes, and reminders. Peuser, the big commercial stationer, has a Buenos Aires shop that is a marvel to behold. The National Cash Register Company has found that many an Argentine storekeeper buys an elaborate machine even before he buys his stock.

This does not necessarily mean that all financial accounts are perfect. Argentines freely admit that everybody who runs a business has to keep several sets of books. The favorite café story is that three is the minimum: "One for myself, another for my wife, and the third for the governmental inspectors who, naturally, expect to get the least."

Often Argentine white-collar or industrial workers start better than they finish. Workers on all levels are likely to begin with much more brilliance, enthusiasm, and interest than they can sustain after the project on which they are working becomes routine. When the novelty wears off, and the thing that makes the job interesting disappears there is a sharp drop in output.

Most Argentine workers want fame and glory for themselves. They are not likely to give credit to equals or subordinates or to laud their achievements. Usually they consider themselves superior to the next fellow and take an inordinate pride in the clothes they wear to work, the food they bring to eat, and in their taste and opinions.

Betty de Sherbinin says the typical Argentine worker is competent and amenable. He has a "realistic frame of mind and is firmly convinced that everyone from the priest to his employer is working him for something. . . . He is a European transplanted to South America. He has a sense of decorum and dignity. . . . He is not stupid and has brought with him from Europe a broad hearty sense of life, and an ability to enjoy sun, red wine, good food, a joke, and the opposite sex. Despite the difficulties that have faced him in Argentina through the poor years in the 30's, despite the fact that he feels he's not getting his share of the prosperity of the present, he has in the past availed himself of what opportunities existed."

Many Argentine white-collar and industrial workers, especially those in Buenos Aires, are highly ambitious. They want to get ahead, the easy way if possible, with more effort if necessary. Many lower-paid civil service employees must get an extra job or two to make ends meet. They may not put in too many hours working, but they do aspire to rise and constantly look for new openings.

Adult night schools offering "improve yourself" techniques and correspondence courses are popular. Dale Carnegie courses have been given in Spanish for many years. At the higher level, technological education has surged forward. Many a worker's son goes to the University of La Plata or Córdoba for specialized courses in electrical and mechanical engineering. The University of Buenos Aires offers other courses in civil and industrial engineering. Announcements of new developments are seen not only in the trade publications but in the daily papers as well.

The average Argentine city worker will tell you that he wants a house in the suburbs or a place in town with a garden, more money to raise his family more comfortably, and security that someone else, his employer or the government, will provide for the future.

He does not much care that his union is officially controlled or that his newspapers do not carry the truth he would like to be able to read. He is inclined to feel that while these things are regrettable, they are beyond his control. Of much more immediate interest is a raise which might allow him to move away from his crowded residence, a shorter work day and more holidays with pay. Because many factories are far from where their workers live, an Argentine generally leaves home earlier and gets home later than our worker does. He sees nothing wrong with taking advantage of every convenient fiesta.

Before 1943, no government had ever really taken an interest in the Argentine worker or his union—and the workers knew it. The dominant Confederation of Labor and other central trades unions had, with the help of the Socialists, won some labor laws: an eight-hour day, a forty-hour week, seven-hour shifts for night workers and six for those in dangerous occupations, pregnancy benefits, child labor rules, and the beginnings of a social security fund. But one of Ramirez' first acts was to put all unions under control and confiscate their funds. Argentine workers had never been strongly militant, but they struck in protest—and were forced back to work at gunpoint. Perón was not so shortsighted: "I am a trade unionist," he declared—and went to work to take over the unions. Argentine workers had heard much about freedom, justice, and class struggle from their leaders, but had received little in the way of bread. Perón gave them bread.

As head of the new Department of Labor in the military government, Perón worked round the clock studying labor conditions. He decided that if the regime were to survive it had to have a popular base, and that base would be labor. Perón set up a National Institute of Social Security, began a low-cost housing project, decreed ten- to fifteen-day annual vacations for all workers, increased wages, lowered rents, etc. He participated in collective bargaining negotiations and helped organize new unions.

With his assistance the packing-house workers signed the first collective bargaining agreement in the industry. This new Federation de la Industria de la Carne became one of Perón's chief sources of support, and helped put him back in power after his return from the prison island of Martin Garcia in the Rio de la Plata on October 17, 1945. The rough, tough packing house workers from the southern Buenos Aires district of Avellaneda had rarely appeared in the elegant streets of the capital, but on that day they came in by the hundreds, coatless and well-armed to demonstrate for Perón. They were termed the *descamisados*, shirtless ones, and the word became a symbol of peronista social justice.

When American Federation of Labor investigators visited Argentina a few years ago, they were invited to take off their coats since it was a warm day. The next day peronista papers pictured the United States visitors in shirtsleeves, saying this demonstrated their support of peronista principles. The American Federation of Labor wrote a strongly anti-Perón report.

Despite the handouts and fine promises, some unions held out from the start. But by fair means and foul, the Perón government gradually took them all over. Labor leaders who resisted were imprisoned, exiled, persecuted, and replaced by Perón's followers. If a whole union held out against him, as some did, he built a new one in the same field and made it the recipient of wage boosts and workers' benefits. The old one, unable to do anything for its members, withered away. Even the dissident railroad engineers and firemen of La Fraternidad, one of the oldest and most independent unions in Argentina—and one of the last to be taken over by peronistas—went on strike, lost, and were drafted into the "civilian service of national defense." They were forced to return to their jobs or face court martial.

Today the government works overtime to make sure the workers are told it is thinking only of their welfare. The official press and propaganda bureau overlooks no opportunity to make it clear that all advantages came as gifts from Perón and Evita, the "defenders of Argentina's workers." In the controlled press, in speeches, in interviews, the worker is told that everything is done for his benefit.

The average man, dazzled by gifts, is shown models of dream housing projects like Ciudad Evita which will be erected for all workers when Perón's plans are carried out. Workers are promised profit-sharing plans and more benefits, and they will usually cheer at the right time and vote the straight peronista ticket.

In mid-1951, in an attempt to get further labor support, as well as to keep labor in line, the president reportedly formed a private militia from the ranks of the Confederation and was arming it to the teeth. According to a story in a privately-circulated publication, *El Ciudadano* (The Citizen), published occasionally without official sanction by the Radical party, Perón drew up a confidential workers' defense plan to "defend the government in the event of military action against it."

Time Magazine reported that five thousand *descamisados* of "absolute confidence" were enrolled and divided into "shock troop" detachments, "special mission" units, and "reserves." A list was made of strategic zones, including rail and bus stations, ports, communications centers, power plants, food warehouses, water works, public markets, government offices, union headquarters, theaters and stadiums.

The new peronista militia got its first important workout during the September, 1951, abortive military uprising. The Confederation's boss, José Espejo, shouted the radio alarm and workers rushed to the Presidential Palace, jammed their big diesel busses across roads by which troops or tanks might have been moved on the capital, and succeeded in helping snuff out the revolt. Then they rounded up and arrested suspects, ran spot checks for illegal arms and so on. So successful was this first trial run that it was decided to improve the workers' equipment. *El Ciudadano* published the texts of three letters from an arms firm promising delivery of five thousand pistols and two thousand automatic carbines to the Eva Perón Foundation.

How much the average worker has actually received from Perón is questionable. Urban workers have benefited more than rural workers—hence the trek from *estancia* to city. Most workers now have minimum wages, an eight-hour day with special overtime pay, paid vacations, and the *aguinaldo*, a Christmas bonus which equals one-twelfth of a year's pay. Some workers also get severance pay, and are guaranteed certain minimum working standards. The practical effect of all this social legislation varies, Argentines explain, pointing out that their civil service could "hardly be expected to enforce the letter of every law." When workers report a slight violation in a foreign-owned plant, government inspectors often swarm in to look things over and impose heavy fines, but they are not so strict with Argentine firms.

More men and women are working in Argentina today: for every 100 workers in 1943 there were 129 in 1951. Social legislation is estimated to cost 60 per cent of their basic payrolls, and the cost per man hour is nine times what it was in 1943. This was passed along to the consumer and helped create the wage-price spiral and chronic inflation.

Although President Perón claims Argentina's living costs are among the world's lowest, and says that government employees currently get 700 *pesos* a month compared to 280 in 1946, he ignores the fact that the dollar value of his workers' salaries has slipped after two official *peso* devaluations, and even more on the unofficial basis.

Little is printed in the Argentine press about the deteriorating international trade position or the country's falling industrial production. The only economic fact that gained wide circulation was the drought which occurred in 1949–50–51.

But the Argentine wage-earner knows how much more it costs him to live. Milk and butter became increasingly hard to buy in 1951. Meat could be purchased, but often only on payment of a bonus to the butcher and not at the controlled price. Textiles and clothing were getting scarcer and more expensive. Railroad fares were increased up to 50 per cent just after the 1951 presidential elections. Even controlled prices on many foods were raised during the year. And living costs were overtaking, if they had not already passed, the increased wages granted by the government.

In revealing his economic plans for 1952, President Perón told the workers they must keep their demands to a minimum, increase production, and practice the "inflexible austerity" which had been prescribed as the remedy for the nation's economic ills. The newspaper *Democracia* urged men to have their suits turned instead of buying new ones, and women were told to do their own hair and nails because anything else is "waste which jeopardizes the national economy." It was the new clothes and the chance to go to the beauty parlor which poorer Argentines had wanted so much. So *Democracia* dramatized the Argentine housewife as the "Sentinel of the Fatherland's Economy," and "Mistress of the National Destiny." When her neighbor buys a new hat, the ideal housewife deliberately flaunts her old one, keeping her good clothes for special occasions, the paper declared. "Nobody notices a woman who goes marketing in silk and high heels: it is the girl in the housedress who gets the complimentary *piropos*."

In the economic crisis of 1952, many of the workers' advantages seemed to be drying up. Whether or not, like the *estanciero*, the laborer has enough in reserve so that the pinch is not too great no one can tell.

With all the living cost increases, the Argentine worker could still be regarded as better fed, better housed, and more self-satisfied than any similar group in Latin America. But this is based on a fairly low standard. Argentines tell you: "As long as our workers have full stomachs you are not likely to find revolt. But let the pinch come—and then anything can happen."

Chapter XIII

The Family Is Everything

SIT DOWN at dinner with a typical Argentine family, whether the family is poor, middle class, or in the landed *estanciero* group, and several things will probably strike you at once.

Your host's mother will be in the place of honor. Children old enough to sit up by themselves will have chairs. The table itself will be dressed with the finest linens and silver the family can afford. No matter how poor the host, he will probably serve several courses. And in nine cases out of ten you will have wine. Cousins, uncles, aunts, and other in-laws are likely to be present. Dress will be more formal than in the United States. The children will talk, but there will be far less of the easy give-and-take of the *Yanqui* household, for regardless of what they do outside, the children well know—having been taught from birth—that their parents' rule dominates. Papa is head mama is his deputy, and *his* mother, as the oldest and most respected member of the circle, is the queen.

The authority of the father exercises a great influence in Argentine life. Families of Spanish, Italian, and French descent are closest-knit and most conventional. Those o northern European and British background are apt to incline more toward our own standards.

Under the "father rule" set up by the civil code, Papa has long exercised the same kind of unlimited and un questioned authority so often employed by the Presiden of the Republic in running the government. Presiden Perón today uses it in even greater degree and many o his followers call him "Papa Perón." But the point so ofter overlooked by North Americans is that Argentines, who have known such authority all their lives, do not resent i or think it strange and new.

Father rule and command makes the family a kind o dictatorship in miniature. Depending on the personality of Papa, it may at times be benevolent, at others tyranni cal. Papa will speak of his place as "*mi casa*"—my house There is no real word for home in Spanish. *Hogar*, which is employed in writing, actually means hearth, or fire place. Except in reference to the popular magazine of th same name, the word rarely appears in conversation.

In the Argentine home no member can make an impor tant decision without Father's approval. If, as sometime happens, family disputes go to the courts, again and agai Father's rule, albeit arbitrary, has been upheld. True, h can, and often does, make his wife the executive office who handles the actual administration. She receives the freely-offered aid, advice, and sometimes overruling opinion of *his* mother, who is likely to regard her son as still subject to her admonishment irrespective of his age.

Today, as the family becomes more of a mutual council, the Argentine wife is beginning to emerge from her traditionally inferior position. Nevertheless, in most of the older families, especially outside Buenos Aires, the tradition, which is encouraged by both State and Church, changes slowly.

From childhood, Argentine girls are taught that orders must be accepted even from baby brother, because he is a man. Except among progressive city families of means, a young girl of "respectable family" always has a chaperone. Sports, which are becoming more and more popular among many *señoritas*, are tending to minimize the chaperone's role and make informal introductions possible, for, as many a young Argentine woman will point out: "After all, she cannot follow you on a bicycle." Even today, however, girls seldom see young men after dark and they have little time for close friendships with the opposite sex until they are close to the marriageable age.

Argentine boys and girls grow up carefully separated and remain that way. A young man who seeks to come calling in the conventional Argentine family is either welcomed as a prospective bridegroom or simply not received. At the parish or public school a girl is given a thorough training in home economics—sewing, cooking, runnng a household, and managing servants. A girl from middle or upper-income families may study enough music, history, and literature to take part in intelligent conversation, but her most important lessons are designed to make her an attractive and successful wife.

Most Argentine *señoritas* are not supposed to have ideas about careers or social freedom, despite the increasing exceptions to the rule. Although marriage or the convent are no longer the sole alternatives, most girls are engaged at sixteen and married before twenty. Family matchmaking is still common. Argentine law permits boys of fourteen and girls of twelve to marry with parental consent. When parents do not approve, the official minimum is twenty-two for both. While early marriage is encouraged, child weddings are no longer fashionable. Even so, an unmarried girl of twenty-one is a rarity. If she lacks a ring at twenty-five she is considered an old maid.

Not many *señoritas* are specifically ordered to marry the man their parents choose. Yet, among the distinguished old families of Argentina, the young people are likely to meet only those who have been approved by their parents. Thus, mother, father, and grandmother can more or less determine ultimate selection. While a marriage may not be forced if the girl and boy dislike each other, the fact is that generally the parents do manage a compromise.

Intermarriage between upper-class families is part of the Argentine tradition. Those who defy it by eloping or otherwise circumventing parental wishes are few indeed. Generally, love and desirability are reconciled. In such cases the dowry is an important factor.

A little farther down the economic ladder in middle-class families, standards are beginning to inch toward those in the United States. Social ambition motivates

many. When an Argentine family becomes more prosperous, it usually wants to marry its daughters off to young
men with more social or economic prestige than it possesses. Argentines consider it a special mark of distinction
to be connected with an aristocratic family. Any Argentine who is even remotely connected with such a family
always manages to mention his relations in conversation,
so that you will be aware of the fact that he is not simply
a *fulano de tal*—a somebody or other.

Argentines have an enormous interest in society news,
especially as it is glowingly detailed in such publications
as *Atlantida, Saber Vivir* and *El Hogar.* Every important
wedding, engagement, or dinner gets pages of pictures,
plus a full description of who were there and what they
wore. There is no society gossip, however: the Walter
Winchell approach is unknown in Argentina and there are
no Cholly Knickerbockers.

Even poor families like to stage elaborate church weddings. Even though the boy's salary is low and the girl's
family poor, pride demands that appearances be maintained. Sometimes the family may postpone the wedding
a year or more in order to scrape up enough money to
provide a big church ceremony with white tie and tails
for the groom and a wedding dress with a train for the
bride.

Once the honeymoon is over, the husband's family
takes control. In the United States a bride who does not
get along well with her in-laws will usually put up a
good front and cut contacts to a minimum. In the Argentine, the bride's sense of obligation to her husband's clan
above her own is paramount. Many a boy's mother takes
full advantage of her privilege to run her son's household

with an iron hand. She may even rule on the wife's clothes, friends and opinions.

In many larger families several married sons, their wives and children, may live under the same roof. One well-known wealthy family occupies an entire apartment house in Buenos Aires especially built for them. Each son or daughter has a single floor of the large luxurious structure. This exemplifies the Argentines' desire to maintain the family as a unit.

The breaking up of the old houses and the increase in apartment living is, of course, changing this practice. Yet young people in Argentina cannot escape completely. A New York couple can and often does move to Chicago, Detroit, or Los Angeles. A Philadelphia pair can move to San Francisco without completely changing their lives. A young married couple living in Buenos Aires would have to make serious sacrifices if they moved to another city.

The wife has the responsibility of running the house, arranging the formal entertaining, and managing the children. The husband checks and countermands when he feels it necessary. Many Argentine husbands ask for a list of their wife's intimate friends and decide whom they may see and whom they must not see. One sees women smoking only in the cosmopolitan circles in Buenos Aires.

Not until the Argentine wife reaches upper-middle age and heads her own family does she obtain the full rewards of dignity, responsibility, and standing which are regarded as compensating factors in Argentine marriage.

This closeness of the family tie creates a social self-sufficiency that leaves little time for contact with outsiders. So much so, in fact, that most foreigners seldom succeed in establishing an intimate friendship with any Argentine family. The Germans succeeded better than most others because their wives and daughters did not seek the independence enjoyed by American and English women and thus were not likely to spread advanced ideas among Argentine women.

The conservative Argentine believes strongly in the virtue of womanhood and the sanctity of the home. Even in Buenos Aires he disapproves of innocent luncheons of married women with male friends. He believes platonic friendship between men and women is impossible.

Films, fashion magazines, and visitors from North America are encouraging Argentine women to be more daring and audacious. A group of unescorted young Argentine women will today have tea, luncheon, or cocktails together in places where, not many years before, the only women were the mistresses of their fathers and brothers. One also sees two Argentine couples going out together of an evening, the double-date eliminating the need of a chaperone when the families of one couple are known to the families of the other.

Argentine wives who are smarter than their husbands (it does happen there too) rarely demonstrate the fact, at least not if they want to keep harmony. The wife is always expected to think first of her husband, then of herself. Her role, she is taught, is important, but always subordinate. The one thing she is encouraged to exhibit with full approval is how much she loves her lord and master.

Flattering the husband's ego is the prime essential in a successful Argentine marriage. The best way an Argentine wife can demonstrate this is to have plenty of children. Many an Argentine family considers three a minimum: they usually have five or six.

Food at home will be prepared especially for the husband's taste and the house is managed to suit his convenience. The Argentine wife's non-homemaking activities—charity work under the direction of the Church, bridge parties, teas, social calls, or visits from the family —are generally confined to the hours between lunch at home and the customary late dinner.

Until just a few years ago women were not allowed to drive their own cars. Club and civic activities were unknown. Eva Perón succeeded in getting suffrage for Argentine women. They voted for the first time in the November, 1951, presidential elections and elected twenty-nine women to Congress. They were expected to —and many did—vote for Perón. Before the army forced Evita to give up her vice-presidential candidacy, she counted on the women's vote to elect her.

Foreign residents, especially the North Americans, helped bring about this emancipation of women—a fact which caused resentment in many older, more conservative families. They do not like to see Argentine women reading more, having their own ideas, demanding their own rights, and "flaunting their revolt" against old customs.

Most United States women who marry Argentines are astonished and shocked by their husbands' frequent love affairs. One husband defensively explained: "It's the women who marry—we remain single. Our wives are expected to keep their knowledge of such things to themselves. We Argentines are men first, husbands second."

If he is not able to boast of his pre-marital affairs and

if, after a proper period, he does not take a mistress, many an Argentine male thinks he has failed to demonstrate his virility and to be successful. Having a love affair might ruin an American politician, but *not* having one might make a Latin politician suspect. The names of favored mistresses of important Argentines are generally open secrets, and no one regards this as at all unusual. However, the rules governing such affairs are as ironclad as diplomatic protocol.

Ruth and Leonard Greenup give some interesting details on this subject. "A man may take his mistress to a night-club, to dinner, or even the theater. But he must not escort her to an official function or a big party where wives are present. If he has taken his mistress to a dine-and-dance place and there encounters a married couple he knows, he refrains from speaking to them. They also ignore him. Yet, the mistress is not cut off from society. She may act as the man's unofficial hostess when he entertains a group of men friends. If other women are there, none is likely to be the wife of any man present."

The mistress of many an Argentine persuades her man to finance her in a little shop or underwrite her career on the stage. Some of these clandestine alliances last for years, strengthened by bonds of deep affection. To educated Argentines the prevalence of the double-standard does not mean moral decadence. Visiting North Americans are told that it is no worse for an Argentine husband to keep a mistress for twenty years or so than it is for an American to live legally—by means of divorces—with three or four women for an equal length of time. Argentine men insist they honor and respect the home and the family far more than American men.

Since it is legally impossible to get a divorce in Argentina, our high divorce rate and the fantastic stories about it so widely publicized continually shock and astonish the Argentines. They raise eyebrows at Hollywood films in which wives publicly flirt with other men and husbands have affairs with their friends' wives. Moreover, in a Hollywood production, they point out, a man expects his wife to work; if need be she is his partner in crime. In an Argentine film, the heroine is always the bird in the gilded cage, worshipped from afar.

Argentine men are among the world's most jealous. Many Argentines say the main reason they would not want North American wives is because American girls have so many men friends and hear words of love from many men before they marry. "The American husband," an Argentine said, "likes to think he has won his wife against a field of competitors. We demand brides who have never thought of anyone but us. We may be fooling ourselves, it is true. But we like it that way."

Having been brought up in the traditional way, most Argentines wives willingly accept the conventional, unwritten rules. Many an inter-American marriage has been wrecked by the unwillingness of North American brides to conform. Argentines educated in the United States frankly discuss the reasons.

Their chief complaint against North American wives is their independence and their lack of obedience and respect for their husbands. "They want to have their own friends, bank accounts, and outside interests," one Argentine explained. "They want their own cars, and even to use them after dark. We do not like that."

The following characteristic remarks illustrate the Argentine's attitude toward North American wives:

"American women lack fire and passion."

"They have no manners."

"They insist upon drinking and smoking like men."

"They are too frank and easy in their relationships with men."

"They have too much education and do not respect their husbands' opinions sufficiently."

"They do not know how to dress properly."

On one occasion when it was pointed out that visiting girls from the United States certainly draw appreciative and often poetic compliments, one Argentine answered: "True. We like such things in *other* women, but not in our wives!"

The attitude of a growing number of Argentine women toward North American wives and husbands differs sharply. What many Argentine women admire about American husbands is the fact that it is not customary for them to keep mistresses. The *casa chica*, or little house, for a mistress is the exception, not the rule in the United States. Another point repeatedly mentioned is the fact that most American husbands have few secrets from their wives and share their pleasures and interests. One woman said: "When an American plans an evening of dancing, theater, or other entertainment, he invariably includes his wife. The Argentine rarely considers taking her along. He may come home for lunch every day. But often he leaves his wife five nights out of seven while he goes to the café or the club, to sports events, or to a meeting with friends."

"American husbands," one woman explained, "are far

more dependable. They may lack the courtly gesture or the ability to whisper enough well-turned compliments, but they make it up in other ways." "We like the freedom American husbands give us," another said, "freedom to have an opinion and to express it, and to discuss family affairs without fear of being arbitrarily overruled. And mostly, freedom to be men's equals, not their chattels."

Chapter XIV

The Church Is Everywhere

EVERY ARGENTINE, rich, poor, or middle-class, is strongly affected in everything he does and thinks by the Catholic Church. It asserts its power at every important event in his life—birth, baptism, confirmation, marriage, and death. It is also very much a part of his ordinary life. He sees dignitaries of the Church officiating at the opening of Congress and blessing the swords at military and naval academy graduations. When an Argentine completes a new building, he often feels it essential to ask a priest to bless it. Priests are present at the opening of many a new shop in Buenos Aires and of almost any kind of structure in a remote village. Priests offer invocations at festivals and labor meetings.

To the Argentine the Church is more than the center of his religion. It is a culture that molds him and leaves a lasting impression on his mind, body, and soul. The Church's code of ethics sets his standards—whether observed or ignored. It prescribes his favorite madonna and the St. Christopher medal he carries. Visible reminders of the faith are everywhere—the cross on the wall, the tiny figure in a corner niche, the black-robed divinity student on the street, and the church on the plaza of every town. Today the Church and State in Argentina are more closely linked than they have been for generations, and the tie between priest and layman is stronger than ever.

The influence of the Church and its role as the spiritual anchor in the Argentine's daily life begins at christening. Almost before they are able to talk most Argentines begin to absorb the Church's principles and ideas from mother, maid, and grandparents. From them the child learns to cross himself before the madonna, to repeat the proper prayers, and to know his own patron saint. The chances are that the Argentine boy or girl does not go to a parochial school, for Argentina has relatively fewer schools of that kind than the United States.

A *porteño* youngster's first remembered experience may be a visit to the great Cathedral on the Plaza de Mayo. He soon gets to know its quiet interior, hung with richly woven and embroidered banners, its tremendous candlesticks and lanterns, its thousands of candles and crucifixes. He may be taken to see a pontifical high mass attended by the President of the Republic and his Cabinet, who arrive in horse-drawn carriages as thousands look on. The rich vestments, the exquisite copes and mitres are part of a colorful pageantry which is, in its own way, probably the closest thing to some of Britain's traditional ceremonies as anything that exists in the Americas. The Church in Buenos Aires, reflecting *porteño* sophistication, does not stage the primitive processions you see in the Indian countries of Latin America.

Churchgoing has social as well as spiritual significance. In Buenos Aires as well as in the smallest interior communities mothers and sisters go to church far more often than fathers and brothers. A boy may have to attend church, but as he grows older he will probably fall into his father's and older brother's habit of turning up just before services end. The young *caballeros* stand near the church entrance to await the *señoritas*. When they appear there are the usual demure nods, the inquiries about father, mother, uncle, aunt and cousin, and related small talk. Often couples visit the nearby *confitería* for a midday ice and even dance under the watchful eye of the chaperone.

The most memorable personal church event in the eyes of Argentines is their marriage ceremony. By Argentine law, couples must first be married by the local *registrador civil*. However, good Catholics do not accept this as sufficient, and bride and groom rarely leave for their honeymoon until the religious ceremony is performed by the priest, usually the day after the civil act.

The always conservative Church has the strongest interest in preserving the traditions of Argentine family life, for its strength comes from this very source. Church leaders successfully fought divorce laws long before the military regime came into power. Divorce is traditionally anathema to the Church, and it is still banned today primarily because of the Church's influence.

Felix Weil points out that the Church's preponderant

position does not mean that all Argentines are devout or regular churchgoers. However, "on the whole, good Argentines consider it a matter of social esteem and propriety to belong to the Church, and to accept the clergy's 'spiritual guidance.' Not to do so would be tantamount to remaining seated when the National Anthem is played. It is just not done—except by open non-conformists."

Two groups are most loyal to the Church, Hubert Herring notes. First are the top provincial families, who have the best names, the most land, the biggest houses. To them the Church is an instrument of regularity, discipline, and conservatism which they know will help safeguard the nation from intellectual dissent. Second is the group of the inconspicuous faithful, the Church's chief support in every land. These are the women in black on the streets of the provincial towns who lead their docile children into the big edifice on the plaza. These are the dutiful *peons*, strong in faith and simple in mind who have, in the past, accepted the traditional paternalism of the priest and the *estanciero* as natural.

Even those Argentines who follow Church precepts most closely feel their religion is very different from that of most other Latins. They regard the Church in Brazil, Paraguay, Bolivia, and Latin America's west coast countries as a primitive institution; they think it is so corrupted by Indian pageantry and symbolism as to be almost another religion.

Outside Buenos Aires the Church's influence on every individual is even stronger than in the capital. In every block of staunchly-conservative Córdoba, for instance, you are likely to meet a priest, dressed in his long, belted cassock and round bowler hat with a curled brim. Near the Cathedral on the Plaza de San Martín you will see many nuns and scores of children in parochial school uniforms—the boys in dark suits and short trousers with stockings reaching above the knee, the girls in high-necked serge dresses. When the occasion comes they will be dressed in their white first-communion finery and have stiff, formal photographs taken by the itinerant street photographers. The hierarchy in Córdoba even has its own newspaper, *Los Principios*, which in some ways is more conservative than the Buenos Aires Catholic daily, *El Pueblo*.

In many small Argentine towns sacred church relics form an essential part of local tradition. In Catamarca, for example, the heart of Friar Mamerto Esquiu, churchman and orator, is highly revered. His birthplace is enshrined, and his statue stands in the plaza where it is visited by thousands every year. The religion of the mountainous town is saturated with a very personal belief which revolves around the tiny wooden figure of La Virgen de la Valle, the Lady of the Valley. The grotto where she was discovered and the Cathedral of Catamarca are besieged by pilgrims who seek her favor. They bring her jewels, rich clothing, and other gifts.

In rural communities the rich *estancieros* often adopt the local church as part of their feudal pattern. They are likely to have more control over the priest than he has over them. The owner of an *estancia*, with his tremendous economic power, is naturally a dominant force in the region. The Church depends on his gifts and his contributions to its charities more than he depends on the local priest for salvation. The *estanciero* is also likely to have more education and experience than the priest. However, if the priest has a strong personality he may exercise power and entertain important families and be entertained by them as well.

There are relatively few churches in rural Argentina. In all three Patagonian territories in the 1940's there were only ten churches along the coast, only one on the edge of of the mountains, and none in the interior. Although the people are practically churchless, they are not irreligious or pagan, except in the most isolated Indian areas. You see religious books, pictures and images in most homes.

In the United States, all income groups support their church. But in Argentina financial support comes chiefly from the wealthy with token contributions from the middle class and the poor. The Church is usually the only institution to which rich Argentines do contribute; they seldom give money to universities or foundations as do our Fords and Rockefellers.

Argentine landowners have always insisted on separation of Church and State, not because of their democratic principles, but because they considered government policy their prerogative. Argentines have never had a violent clash between Church and State as have Mexicans and to a lesser degree Chileans. Leaders like Mitre, Sarmiento, and Rivadavia opposed Church domination, though they themselves were Catholics. In 1826–27, President Rivadavia limited the powers of the Church and instituted certain reforms. He ended direct state allowances to priests, abolished tithes and ecclesiastical courts, and seized some superfluous monasteries.

In 1884 it was decided—presumably once and for all—that public schools would be secular and would not teach religion, though Church schools would not be forbidden.

After the Pope's representative was expelled for pressing the issue of religious education too vigorously that year, virtually everyone took the solution for granted. Clericalism and anti-clericalism was hardly a serious political issue.

North Americans have a hard time understanding the exact relations between Argentine Church and State. The constitution states that "The Federal government supports the Roman Catholic Apostolic Church," but Argentines insist that does not mean Catholicism is the official religion. "The President must be a Roman Catholic," they explain, "but not his cabinet ministers or other officials." The President names the bishops of the cathedrals from lists submitted by the Senate, approves or rejects papal decrees, and submits to the Pope the names from which he must choose certain chief members of the hierarchy.

Sometimes this caused friction between the Holy See and the government. Often the Papal nuncio enjoyed far greater status with one President than another. The nuncio, as in many other countries, is the dean of the diplomatic corps, whether in the country for a week or for years. The Cardinal outranks every Argentine but the President at all functions.

From the very beginning of the military regime in 1943, General Ramirez and his friends set out to win the Church's support. They declared their government to be a Catholic, corporate state founded on Hispanic tradition based on social precepts of the Church. Ramirez demonstrated his Catholicism by taking a priest, Father James Wilkinson, to the Casa Rosada with him. For a time the "Grey Eminence" appeared behind the scenes, the central figure in many a whispered story. When the tales grew embarrassing, Wilkinson departed, but the alliance between the Catholic and the military hierarchy continued.

It reached its peak when Ramirez decreed that religious instruction be given in every school. This reversal of Argentine tradition fell like a bombshell on the nation. Church leaders who had long assumed the question of religious education was closed could hardly believe it. Luis Cardinal Copello congratulated Ramirez on the decree, but the clergy was divided on the government's attempt to associate itself with official Catholicism.

In general, however, the hierarchy went along with the militarists and later with Perón because they also opposed the Communists and the anti-clerical Radicals and Socialists. Catholics wanted financial aid for their institutions and they believed religious education would save the souls of irreligious Argentines.

During Perón's first election campaign, Cardinal Copello never specifically endorsed him. But a pastoral letter, signed by most of the highest Church authorities, demanded that no Catholic vote for candidates whose programs included legalization of divorce, separation of Church and State, or secular education. This broke the solid Conservative front and won Perón many a vote, especially from poorer Argentines who are inclined to accept most of what the Church recommends.

Soon after the election, Perón's congressmen converted into a law the 1943 decree which imposed religious instruction on public and private primary and secondary schools. The constitutional provision for freedom of religion was by-passed by a clause permitting students whose fathers "manifest opposition" to Catholicism to substitute classes in "moral instruction." The law also provided salaries for the priests who taught these courses.

The day after the Senate passed the law, Cardinal Copello and the bishops of Buenos Aires and Rosario and the archbishops of Santa Fé, Córdoba, Paraná, and San José visited the President. They presented him with a memorial and thanked him for putting the country "once more on the road of its religious tradition." They commended him for having given "a more solid base to social justice, to the unity of the Argentine people, to the true fraternity of the American continent."

Perón appointed "ecclesiastical advisers" to various government institutions, even to the Transport Corporation of Buenos Aires, which runs all the city's trolleys, busses, and subways. Priests attended every kind of Peronista party meeting and rally to give their blessing to the proceedings, thus creating the appearance of Church support for everything the government does.

One of the first leading priests to come out for Perón was Father Virgilio Filippo of Buenos Aires. A strong, often bitter orator, he supported Perón so fervently he caused some of his women parishioners to walk out on his sermon just before the election of 1945. He appeared at political demonstrations and awarded prizes and medals to outstanding factory workers. In a sense Father Filippo resembled our Father Coughlin. In 1948 he was elected a peronista deputy from the City of Buenos Aires, winning by the slate's smallest majority. So far as Argentines know, no attempts to restrain him have ever been made by the Church.

To win church friendship, Perón also encouraged such things as the religious Easter Week parades through the streets of the capital. Before this such parades were virtually unknown in Buenos Aires. Easter Week was the *semana de turismo* (tourist's week) when thousands of *porteños* jammed trains, busses, and cars for visits to the Córdoba Hills or Mar del Plata, and hundreds of Argentines from the interior visited the metropolis.

Democratic Argentines and foreigners have noted that the Church has increased all of its activities. Many of them believe it has more and more influence in the daily lives of the people.

Church leaders point out that the Church established Argentina's first educational institutions, helped set up its earliest communities, and introduced its civilizing influence to the Indians. They insist it has always had a leading role in the country's history and philosophy.

But they admit that the affinity of many priests for the Perón regime stemmed from several immediate reasons. First, many Argentine priests were Spaniards or had been educated in Italy or Spain during the rise of Mussolini and Franco and came to favor military regimes. Second, many of the clergy viewed democracy with skepticism, partly because their chief support came from the wealthy, landowning oligarchs. Third, many of the European-trained priests feared that Freemasonry, which they associated with British and United States opposition to Catholicism, might gain strength under an administration which was overly friendly with Washington.

Argentine Catholics are by no means united in their viewpoints. The most outstanding anti-peronista in the clergy is Monseñor Miguel de Andrea, Bishop of Tenemos. He was the only Argentine bishop who refused to sign the pastoral letter which favored Perón's election in

1946. Later some five hundred Catholic laymen defied their clerical leaders and signed a manifesto denouncing Perón. The bishop's outspoken defense of freedom reputedly cost him a promotion. During the election campaign he warned workers not to sell their freedom for a handful of benefits. He declared that class hatred was "being set on fire dangerously and the fire is being increased by racial hatred. . . . It is urgent that this fever be stopped before the delirium causes irreparable harm." In sermons and pamphlets, he opposed the government's efforts to gain control of the trade unions, which he thought should be autonomous.

For most of his seventy-five years, Bishop de Andrea has worked to help the underprivileged. In 1922 he founded the Federation of Catholic Workers Associations, a women's trade union of Buenos Aires. His home for single working girls is the only private institution of its kind which was not absorbed by Eva Perón's social welfare foundation. His national and international standing was so high the Peróns dared not touch him.

During the latter part of President Perón's first administration, relations between peronistas and the Church cooled. A storm broke when Perón sought to legalize prostitution, which had been outlawed in 1936. The labor unions demanded the red-light houses be reopened and inspected, and the government sponsored the idea "to improve public health." But the Church raised the cry "National shame!" and the militant Acción Catolica Argentina violently opposed the scheme. This time the President backed down.

But the biggest cause of friction came from Perón and Evita's attempts to lift *peronismo* from the status of a political doctrine to an article of faith for all Argentines. "The implication," Robert J. Alexander said, is "that what Perón and the peronistas do is not to be questioned, not even by the Church. . . . If the trend toward a totalitarian form of Peronismo continues, the teaching of that 'one true faith of all Argentines' is likely to come into conflict with the teaching of the faith of the Church."

Fleur Cowles asserts that the Peróns succeeded in hypnotizing not only gullible political followers but many of the "unsuspecting religious." "They have managed, somehow," she says, "to let their subjects continue to cross themselves reverently, to kneel solemnly in their churches, and yet everything is arranged so that, simultaneously, many of the same people have been taught to recognize Perón as a living saint. The cult for the Perón-idol has been developed with brilliant skill, for it 'allows' the church its place and its 'face' while allowing Perón to go beyond the prerogatives of Catholicism."

But Evita's deification of her husband annoyed the priests. Their voting instructions to their parishioners in the November, 1951, election were remarkably noncommittal.

Argentine charity and philanthropy belongs in our consideration of the Church and its effect on the daily lives of Argentines because the Church has long been the most favored recipient of benefactions and the most important of benefactors in the Argentine scheme of things.

As noted previously, relatively few Argentines ever give large sums to local universities, schools, hospitals, or most other institutions. Special drives are held annually for such groups as the Patronato de Leprosos which aids the country's lepers, but appeals such as our Community

Chest, cancer and heart funds, Boy Scout Campaigns and TB stamp sales have never existed. Money is often raised through a lottery which can run into sizable figures.

Most Argentines prefer to handle their own charitable giving. Rarely will they pass a beggar without tossing him some coins, since they feel this brings good luck as well as God's blessing. Unlike other Latin capitals, Buenos Aires had few alms seekers even before the Peróns established their own approach to charity and declared that outright solicitation was beneath Argentine dignity and created an undesirable impression on visitors.

From 1823, when President Rivadavia founded the Sociedad de Beneficencia and turned it over to the "ladies of Buenos Aires," the Society of Charity was Argentina's leading charitable organization. The ladies contributed their money and their time, and except for the period of the Rosas dictatorship they operated it autonomously for the good of the poor and the sick. Traditionally, the President's wife was named its head. When Perón took office, however, the dowagers neglected to offer Evita the honorary presidency. Three months later Perón appointed a government official to take over the venerable group and Senator Diego Molinari denounced the ladies as silly, useless females.

Two years later Evita established her own Social Aid Foundation, with what was announced as a few thousand of her own *pesos*. By 1950 it had become one of the country's biggest businesses. Today the Foundation reportedly collects more than one hundred million dollars a year. Its biggest support comes from the General Confederation of Labor, whose six million members frequently give a day's pay in connection with some benefit received. If employees want a labor conflict satisfactorily solved they give the Foundation a present. They generally get what they want. Congress gave the Foundation the right to collect certain taxes and to take over any private charity. Representatives of the Foundation often call on businessmen for huge contributions. If they demur, government inspectors discover deficiencies in washrooms, lighting, or building construction, fine the owners, and order repairs. This can be very costly. Next time the businessman is more cooperative.

Someone once declared Evita ran the Foundation "as casually as a bride's checking account." When Fleur Cowles asked Evita about her records of the Foundation's funds and spending, the First Lady replied: "Keeping books on charity is capitalist nonsense! I just use the money for the poor. I cannot stop to count it."

The Foundation invaded every possible Argentine activity, including politics. By eliminating almost all other private charity and welfare organizations, Evita managed to go directly to the masses. Every expectant mother and every anaemic child were told that they received medical care and assistance "because Perón and his wife love them and because a regime of social justice rules the country." The victims of any fire, flood, or train wreck get the immediate help of the Foundation. The poor of Paris, Vienna, and the Canary Islands received gifts from Argentina's beautiful Santa Claus. Planes bringing medicine, food, and blankets from the Foundation arrived promptly after such Latin American disasters as the Ecuadorean earthquake and the Bolivian revolution.

There are scores of huge Foundation warehouses in the capital and other cities which bulge with clothes, shoes, and peronista tracts for the needy. The Foundation operates its own clothing factory and distribution stations, its own hospitals, nurse schools, clinics, and drug dispensaries. Not long ago it established a chain of grocery stores where, as noted previously, packaged food sells for lower than prevailing prices. Evita simply told the manufacturers what food she wanted and how much she would pay. The Ciudad de Mexico department store is now run by the Foundation, and there have been reports it plans to acquire Harrod's and Gath y Chaves.

In her office in the Department of Labor, Evita personally gave help to the needy one day a week. A carefully screened lineup awaited her attention. As each person approached the First Lady, an aide handed her a small card stating the problem. After chatting a few minutes, Evita handed out hundred- or fifty-*peso* notes or issued orders to her subordinates to provide a home, food, or job. She did it in the lady-of-the-manor tradition, not unlike the *estancieros* who presented gifts to their workers when they felt the time was ripe. Evita made her Foundation a very personal operation. The President rarely interfered.

On the theory that the poor must have the best, she built luxurious homes for the aged, for unmarried mothers, for working girls. She gave a few of them excellent accomodations and, of necessity, promised the others that their turn would come soon.

An oft-displayed example is the model Children's Town in the suburbs of Buenos Aires. It has tiny houses, shops, banks, a school, a church and jail, luxurious dormitories, dining-rooms and playrooms. In theory, two hundred poor children aged from two to five live there, and eight hundred more come in by the day. After a two-hour tour one visiting diplomat's wife commented: "This is the wish fulfillment of a little girl who never had a doll house of her own."

According to her newspaper, *Democracia*, Evita's last thought was for the poor. The night before she died, it reported, she asked to be alone with her husband to tell him: "No matter what happens, the only thing I ask you is never to abandon the *grasitas*, humble ones." The President announced later that anyone needing help should continue to write to his deceased wife and aid would be given in her name.

Chapter XV

How the Argentines Are Educated

ATTENDING A late show in an Argentine theater one evening, an American visitor spotted a youngster he thought should have been home in bed. Casually he asked his parents why the boy was not resting up for school at that hour.

"*Pero, no, Señor—this* is a most important part of his education . . . he will probably learn more here than he would in any classroom."

Many an Argentine parent believes that education is only partly formal, and that much of the real instruction their children need for daily life must come from outside the school. Yet despite this, the average Argentine is greatly interested in education, and seeks to make it available to his children with all the facilities at his command.

Since the time of President Domingo Faustino Sarmiento, who died in 1888, education has been a powerful force in Argentina. Today, under the military regime, Sarmiento does not get the attention he did when he was honored throughout the hemisphere as one of the most notable teachers any American nation has yet produced. But education continues to receive a major share of the official budget—about $300,000,000 a year.

One of Sarmiento's chief reasons for wanting to develop Argentina's schools was that in his time the country's best schools were all controlled by foreigners. Argentines, then as now, rarely established private institutions of learning. Foreigners established them for their own children. The foreign schools, excellent as some were, helped perpetuate foreign customs through the second and even third generation. Argentina's public schools have since gradually overcome some of this influence, but it has never been completely eradicated. Even today foreign schools are highly important in Argentina. Many a well-to-do family which cannot afford to send its youngsters abroad to study will send them to the United States, French, or English schools in Buenos Aires.

Today, the American schools in Argentina are becoming increasingly popular. There are three principal reasons.

1. In these private schools Argentine youngsters meet other children from well-to-do families.

2. Argentines believe their children can more easily learn other languages where there are small classes and foreign teachers as well as contact with English-speaking classmates. This, they add, is a factor of no small import

in a country where no man is considered educated unless he speaks two or three languages fluently.

3. Many Argentines want their children to graduate from American colleges or universities, and for this they need proper preparation.

Some Argentines like the idea that the American high schools in their country are co-educational and have the same kind of bands, cheerleaders, football games, and dances as they do in the United States. Furthermore, the American schools do not require the white pinafore uniform that Argentine students wear in their schools. Such Argentines see nothing wrong in schoolgirls of twelve using lipstick; others consider this utterly shocking. The government has not interfered with the private schools, but it does require that all pupils in American, British, and other foreign schools pass local official examinations each year.

Education in Argentina is free and compulsory for all children between the ages of six and fourteen. In Buenos Aires and interior cities the law is strictly enforced; but the farther away from the metropolis schools are, the less the law is observed. In some remote areas education is sketchy. There are not enough schools or truant officers.

Official sources say that attendance in all schools through university level is 2,500,000, but the figure may be distorted. There are no certain figures on how many start and complete primary school. All children who have ever attended school are automatically considered literate.

Primary education includes two years of kindergarten. Five years of general primary education are complemented by two years of practical training. Specially-designed programs for adults are offered.

Secondary education at a *colegio* or *liceo* consists of a minimum five-year course; three years of general studies are supplemented by two years of specialized work. The curriculum for both boys and girls is similar, including sciences, languages, music, drawing, mathematics, history, and geography.

In his first five-year plan President Perón provided scholarships for children whose parents cannot afford to pay for their secondary training and for free transportation, meals, and textbooks.

Beyond the primary and secondary schools are specialized schools which offer two-year training courses. These include normal schools for future teachers of primary grades and commercial schools which offer accounting, mechanical drawing and stenography, as well as more general instruction in such fields as history, economics, and mathematics. Technical schools teach theory and practice in all branches of industry.

It is said that only one out of every eleven Argentines goes to secondary school. Still, Argentina's educational system is far more advanced than that of most Latin countries. Most Argentine youngsters, rich or poor, start to school wearing the white coverall pinafore. Argentines know its advantages: it protects the youngster's clothing, it makes the rich boy no better than the poor, and, since it must be clean and fresh every week, even the poorest working mother will have to launder it over the week-end.

From first grade Argentine children pay attention to grooming. They slick their hair back as their fathers and elder brothers do. They take life more seriously and less boisterously than our small fry.

City school textbooks are quite good. Top authorities in history, geography, and other subjects are writing simple children's books, some with many pictures and cartoons. Incidentally such books are not only useful for the youngsters. Many a North American finds studying Argentine children's books is a simpler, more practical method of learning Spanish than taking a course from Berlitz.

Unfortunately, Argentines say, rural education is far behind urban education. Often rural schools are crowded, inadequate, one-room buildings. On many big *estancias* owners often pay for a schoolhouse which the province operates. The major subjects are history, arithmetic, and geography to which are added some elementary hygiene and physical culture. Free bus service has been provided in some remote areas with neither private nor public transport. One third of Argentina's farm homes are three or more miles from the nearest school.

In July, 1952, Governor Carlos Aloe of Buenos Aires Province discovered a "repulsive state of affairs." Argentine textbooks were shot through with excerpts from the works of Benjamin Franklin, Mark Twain, Browning, Grimm, Schiller, and Turgenev—all subversive influences in the peronista view. He formed a committee to revise all the province's textbooks. "The schools," he declared, "must teach the child the mysticism, the soul and the sentiment of Peronism."

Not to be outdone, the Minister of Education banned the third, fourth, fifth, and sixth grade readers published by Estrada. Congress lent a helping hand by making

Evita's *La Razon de Mi Vida* required reading in all schools.

Under the present government more and more teaching has been placed under federal control. Loyalty checks by federal political police are demanded of teachers and students alike. Primary, secondary, or higher school teachers whose allegiance to *peronismo* is the least open to question are quickly ousted. Pictures and slogans of Perón and Evita are hung in every school. Teachers are instructed to inspire their students to super-citizenship and the greatest reverence and respect for authority.

From infancy, Argentine children are now taught that their nation's history virtually begins with President Perón and that anyone disagreeing with his policies, ideas, and institutions is literally a traitor to Argentina and humanity. School children spend a good portion of their time parading in official demonstrations throwing flowers at the day's hero and waving small blue and white flags.

Religious teaching in the schools was introduced by the military government late in 1943. Parents may request that their children be excused from the religious classes, but in practice few do. Parents with any governmental connection would be suspected of disloyalty if they refused to let their children take religious instruction.

Many teachers opposed the introduction of religious classes, even though they personally had strong Catholic convictions. But religious instruction has been official for almost ten years, and it will certainly continue as long as the present government is in power.

The university, or *facultad*, where the Argentine gets his major formal education, has an importance and standing throughout Latin America far greater than we have ever known here. The universities follow the European model. There are no campus life, fraternity houses, or week-end proms. A student may join a sports club like the C.U.B.A. (Club Universitario Buenos Aires) for *futbol* and rowing, but other extra-curricular activities of our schools simply do not exist. Students are predominantly male. They are generally older than our undergraduates in years and in outlook.

One famous Argentine doctor recalls a story of his fellow students' after-class activities. A group of them rented a small apartment for studious and amatory pursuits. They stole a taxi driver's meter and set it up outside the door. When a newcomer found the free flag down, he discreetly retired. If the flag was up, the apartment was his. The honor system called for payment in proportion to usage, but this was no problem. Said the doctor: "Since we Argentines love to boast of our virility, many of the boys frequently overpaid."

In the United States, the student usually takes a general course before proceeding to his specialized field. In Argentina, after he finishes his secondary education, he enters the university division which teaches the subject in which he is most interested.

Some students are from the upper-class families, whose names have long dominated the fields of law, government, and medicine. Others come from the middle class. Most of them represent the ambitious segment of every group of the population.

The Argentine who enters the university at eighteen is already able to vote. And since most enter two to three years later, they are strongly interested in politics. They feel it is their duty to participate actively in national life.

They believe they are part of the small percentage of the people who are destined someday to run the country, just as many Argentines feel that someday their country will run the rest of Latin America. All the political parties have cultivated students' support and counted on it to help in elections, demonstrations, coups, and reform movements.

To some young Argentines being a student is something of a profession, providing an opportunity to live off papa year after year, but the larger proportion work during the day, attending lectures as and when they can. That is one reason why they may go to the university for years.

Law students often get court posts to finance their studies. Similarly, medical students try for hospital orderly jobs, or positions in the Health Department or the Asistencia Publica, the municipally-operated first-aid service maintained in almost every Argentine community. Nepotism is frequent—good jobs often go to the young men with influence who don't need them.

Tuition is free at the national universities, but the student must pay for his books and his board if he lives away from home. Only graduates of secondary schools may enroll as regular university students, but others may attend classes as *oyentes* (auditors) without the right to take examinations or degrees.

Compulsory class attendance was abolished many years ago. Students who don't like a particular professor's politics or teaching methods are free to cut his classes. They can take their own time in deciding when they want to take their examinations. After completing the requirements, they get a degree.

Before Perón most Argentine professors were not full-time teachers. Often they were medical men, lawyers, or scientists who received nominal salaries for the hours they lectured and spent the rest of their time practicing medicine, writing, painting, or engaging in businesses. Many were senators and deputies. It used to be said that one of the surest ways to become Argentina's president was to get to be a college professor—this having applied to Perón's civilian predecessors, Roberto M. Ortiz, elected in 1937, and Ramon S. Castillo who took his place in 1940.

The fact that Argentine professors were, in the past, so often men of affairs sometimes helped students gain a broader viewpoint. Undergraduates had an opportunity to meet successful men in their chosen fields, though often they had little time to devote to students. Since the instructors did not depend on their positions for their livelihood, they were far more independent than either our professors or Argentine teachers in secondary schools. Again and again the Argentine government found it easier to dictate to secondary-school teachers than to university professors who were, and possibly still are, the center of opposition to the military regime.

In 1918 the students of Córdoba University got fed up with the rigorous discipline, incompetent professors, and backward teaching practices common to most Latin American universities. They demanded participation in the direction of school affairs and the selection of the administrators and professors. They wanted to free their schools from partisan politics. The students went on strike and eventually got what they wanted—representation in university councils and a voice in the appointment of professors.

The Córdoba incident spread throughout Argentina and all of Latin America. Chile was particularly affected. Strikes began and reforms followed as far away as Mexico. In the years following, all Argentine students won the right to form their own university governing bodies in conjunction with a majority of faculty members. They discussed and debated every local and international issue. To defy the authorities university students would stage a quick strike, boycott a professor, or march in the streets in mass demonstrations.

The majority of Argentine students have always been strongly pro-democratic. Because most of them were ambitious and filled with an individualistic spirit, they did not feel the appeal of Communism. But some of them became intense nationalists and leaders in the Alianza Nacional.

From the start Argentine students and their professors formed one of the most stubborn and valiant opposition groups to the military government. They neglected classes for political activity and staged numerous strikes and demonstrations. Their fervent disapproval led the government to "intervene" the universities and put their own officials in charge. More than a thousand professors, including some of the finest minds in Argentina, were dismissed or summarily pensioned off. Students who had taken part in strikes and demonstrations were expelled or kept from taking their examinations on one pretext or another. Even those who managed to take them found they never passed.

A good many leading personalities found it impossible to continue as teachers. One of the first to resign was Dr. Alfredo Palacios, rector of the University of La Plata, and the grand old man of Argentine politics. A leading lawyer, statesman, and savant, Palacios was a dramatic figure on the Argentine scene. He dressed conspicuously, favoring a handlebar mustache, huge black sombrero, and long hair.

Dr. Bernardo A. Houssay, the second Argentine to receive a Nobel Prize, was forced to resign from the Physiology Department of the University of Buenos Aires at the age of fifty-nine, though the usual retirement age is sixty and that is not arbitrary. A doctor of sixty-two was called to fill a post in clinical surgery at the same university, but he, needless to say, was a peronista. When Houssay won the Nobel award some months after he retired, almost no attention was given to him in the Argentine press.

In December, 1947, the universities were theoretically returned to their own administrators, but Perón kept the right to appoint each university head. Directly or indirectly, the President appoints twenty of the twenty-five members of the directing committee of each university.

President Perón did establish full-time, adequately salaried teaching staffs. Formerly professors were grossly underpaid and frequently had to get outside jobs if they lacked private incomes. Families who once had to keep promising children out of school because they needed their earnings now receive government subsidies.

Naturally this applies only to those completely sympathetic to the regime. The government's weapon to keep rebellious students in line is its monopoly on higher education. To enter engineering, teaching, law, or medicine, a university degree is necessary and only a national university graduate can get one. To graduate he must receive the government's political stamp of approval. Even to enroll in classes a student must have a "certificate of good conduct" from the Federal Police.

As in all Latin America, Argentine universities have concentrated on cultural and professional studies. They produced so many physicians and lawyers that many graduates could not find employment in these fields. At the same time, while the professions were overcrowded, there was a great shortage of technicians, industrial engineers, etc., especially when the government began to stress industrial advancement. Many businesses have petioned for permission to bring in foreign experts, explaining: "We would like to employ Argentines for these jobs, but we simply cannot find anybody trained for them." American, British, French, and other firms have brought in many foreigners, while Argentine university graduates go jobless or take inferior positions.

In some fields—rubber, automotive, electrical—the Argentine who gets training abroad has no trouble finding a good post when he gets home. In other cases, especially medicine, the Argentine who goes abroad to study on his own initiative and gets a degree in the United States cannot practice unless he also gets a local degree. As a result, most Argentine doctors, dentists, and similar professionals complete their education in Argentina, get their licenses to practice, and then after a few years go to the United States for specialized training in such fields as cancer and heart disease.

Training in the United States has posed another problem. The Argentine government wants to allow only peronista representatives to go to the United States. If, for example, the American Embassy awards scholarships through official sources, the recipient is likely to be a firm believer in Perón. On the other hand, if our Embassy makes its own choice, official Argentine sources are resentful.

Regardless of politics, however, most Argentines who come to the United States are enthusiastic about our country and anxious to learn American techniques and develop them at home. The more who come to see us at first hand, the better our mutual relations are certain to be, because, knowing each other, we come to be friends.

Chapter XVI

What the Argentines Read

OUTSIDE THE downtown Buenos Aires Boston Bank Building where the United States Embassy offices are located is a newsstand operated by an efficient and introspective custodian named José. José is no ordinary newsboy, whipping out papers for customers who are in a hurry. His stand, which covers a good portion of wall space adjacent to the bank's entrance, looks almost like the periodical room of a sizable library.

There are dailies in an amazing array of formats and languages. There are magazines in every category: sports, radio, movies, architecture, housing, the arts and sciences. There is even a sophisticated monthly intriguingly titled *Saber Vivir—Know How To Live*—a subject of no small appeal to Argentines. Customers often leaf through a few magazines, oblivious to the heavy traffic on the Diagonal Norte close by, and then purchase their choice.

Argentines are among the greatest readers in Latin America or anywhere in the world. Reading at least two or three of the twenty-one daily newspapers published in their capital alone, or several of the two hundred magazines, is one of their principal sources of daily education.

Porteños are not only the greatest of Argentina's newspaper and periodical readers, but book buyers and readers too. Between four and six thousand titles are registered annually with the National Register of Intellectual Property which corresponds to our Bureau of Copyright. The Argentine capital boasts some of the world's finest book stores. These range from little second-hand shops to spectacular establishments like the *Ateneo* and *L'Amateur* in the center of town filled with floor after floor of publications in every language. There are several book shops like Mitchell's and Mackern's which feature books in English; others specialize in other languages. All during the day you will find them crowded, not just with students, but with business and professional men who drop in for a look around and a purchase, considering this one of the pleasures of a normal day.

The number of libraries in Argentina also reflects this interest in books. There are several hundred in the city of Buenos Aires alone. The National Library contains more than half a million volumes, the Congressional Library more than two hundred thousand, the Municipal Library of Buenos Aires the same number. All of the private cultural organizations and the various secondary, normal and university schools scattered throughout the capital and elsewhere have their own libraries. There are a thousand more under the direction of the National Commission of Peoples Libraries which supervises the activities and contributes to the support of any library which meets the requirements of the law established by Sarmiento in 1870. The finest private club library in the world was said to have been that of the Jockey Club, which had sixty thousand books on law, Argentine history and literature. This library could be used by students who obtained special permission. They can no longer enjoy this privilege, however, for the library was recently destroyed by mob violence.

The nation was long noted for the independence and high quality of its leading newspapers, which were head and shoulders above other Latin dailies. Editors usually rated *La Prensa* and *La Nación* among the ten top newspapers in the world. However, Argentina's press has suffered greatly under Perón. His government made no attempt to suppress papers. It simply put them out of business by enforcing obscure sanitary and zoning laws, by giving their workers privileges which increased labor costs, and by restricting their newsprint supplies. Gradually peronistas bought control of some papers. By 1950, five of Buenos Aires' chief dailies (*La Razon, Critica, Noticias Graficas, El Mundo,* and *La Democracia*) were properties of the government-directed press trust, ALEA. Three others (*La Epoca, El Laborista, El Lider*) were owned by staunch peronistas. In 1951 the government expropriated *La Prensa,* and turned it over to the General Confederation of Labor.

Before the military regime came into power foreign news often received twice the space devoted to local affairs. *La Prensa's* major news pages carried long dispatches and often full texts of events which a majority of North American papers might cover in a few paragraphs. Local news was secondary, usually grouped in departments—agriculture, journalism, religion, etc. *La Nación* put only very exceptional developments on page one. Editors of both morning papers simply felt that nothing that occurred at home was half as important to Argentines as what happened abroad, and other dailies both in the capital and throughout the country followed their lead.

As a result, during its most flourishing days, *La Prensa* carried more foreign news than any other Latin-American daily. Yet, except in Paris, London, and for a time Washington, it had no correspondents of its own abroad: it used the services of the United Press and was the U. P.'s most important customer. The United Press considered *La Prensa's* patronage so lucrative that it kept a resident vice president in Buenos Aires just to make certain *La Prensa* got the best possible service.

La Prensa achieved its independence of the advertiser by building a tremendous volume of classified advertisements. These, in traditional London *Times* style, filled its first six to twelve pages. Starting in the first years of World War II, readers found a summary of the news in front page headlines; they had to look inside for fuller reports. All advertisements, incidentally, had to be paid for in cash in advance of publication. They produced such excellent results that *La Prensa* never had to solicit advertising.

The conservative *Prensa's* editorial policy never flamboyantly favored democracy—that was left to the less gentlemanly afternoon papers. Instead of attacking the government's anti-press campaign outright, for instance, *La Prensa* might editorially praise Dean Carl W. Ackerman of Columbia University's School of Journalism for a speech on freedom of the press. In this it reflected Argentine temperament—and the Spanish habit of circumlocution to make a point.

As *New York Times* correspondent Milton Bracker put it, *La Prensa*'s editorial technique was always to analyze by documentation, to concentrate on principles rather than personalities, to ask and deplore, not berate or insult. Perón was not *La Prensa*'s first target. In its eighty-two-year history, it applied the same critical approach to virtually every one of his predecessors. It also faced threats from all of them. Perón's immediate predecessor, General Edelmiro Farrell, was the first to close it (for five days) because of a single story exposing inadequacies in a municipal hospital.

La Prensa was more than an outstanding newspaper; it was a national institution. It offered free medical and legal services to all. Besides the newspaper offices, the ornate gray headquarters on the Avenida de Mayo housed clinics, a hospital, operating rooms, a free music conservatory, a public library, an auditorium, a study center, a gymnasium, and consulting services for farmers, cattle breeders, and housewives.

Perón's war against *La Prensa* began with minor attacks. The daily was fined for disturbing the peace with the noise of its presses, for parking its trucks improperly, for sanitary violations. When the government seized control of all newsprint, including *La Prensa*'s privately purchased supply, the paper had to apply for its share each day. Still *La Prensa*'s editorials stuck to the argument that Perón had violated the constitution, but it did not attack him personally. And Perón kept to the pretense of legality, finding tiny infractions of laws.

In January, 1951, the news vendors' union called a strike, making such extreme demands as a 20 per cent cut of *La Prensa's* classified advertising income, cancellation of all subscriptions, and closing of the branch offices where less than 400 of the paper's 485,000 copies were sold. The printers followed the vendors out on strike. The remaining employees who tried to get the paper out were forced out of the building. Publisher Alberto Gainza Paz was charged with endangering the security of the state. In March he escaped a jail sentence by fleeing to his mother's *estancia* in Uruguay.

A Congressional committee examined *La Prensa's* books minutely and decided the paper owed several million dollars for evading newsprint duties. Congress ordered its expropriation and Perón assigned it to the General Confederation of Labor.

On November 19, 1951, after a ten-month absence, *La Prensa* reappeared. Its twelve-page format was the same. The single difference was that the auction ads on the back page were all for real estate: the cattlemen who had previously used that page to sell as much as one hundred thousand head in one series of auctions had apparently forgotten *La Prensa* as a medium. The masthead listed the issue as "Volume 1, Number 1." The lead editorial reported that the paper had now "chosen the path of honesty," and a two-column story, wrapped around messages from and photographs of Perón and Evita, summarized the official version of how the paper came to die and was reborn as a worker's organ.

While protesting its promotion of good neighborliness, the new *La Prensa* openly featured slanted, bitter news stories and editorials. Most of the despatches come from Agencia Latina, another official news service which tries to cover South America. AL finds that almost every story gives an opportunity to present the United States as an imperialistic and dollar-hungry colonial power.

As a rule, *La Prensa* usually leaves AL's more colored stories to other papers. It likes to pose as the "serious section" of the peronista press. It features news of "Bolivia's gallant battle to win a fair tin price from American buyers," of Chile's "great need to nationalize its copper mines," and of Brazil's "determination to follow the Argentine example of refusing to send its sons to Korean battlefields."

The *Christian Science Monitor* reports that the broad "good neighbor" policy of the new *Prensa* is to deal with the other nations of South America as though they were "backward" or "underdeveloped" and to try to convince them Argentina can give them better help and guidance than any other country. First emphasis is, however, on Argentina's kind of nationalization.

"Other peronista dailies have their own special rules," the *Monitor* adds. "*Democracia*, for example, which is now six years old, concentrates its stories on '*justicalismo*,' the special brand of peronista social justice. It also has exclusives from the columnist Descartes, generally regarded as the pseudonym of President Perón. *Epoca*, the evening paper, has adhered to its role as the outspoken supporter on the home front of an isolationist foreign policy and a critic of attempted imperialism within Argentina's own borders. It is the organ of the extreme nationalists. The majority of the remaining newspapers merely print what they are told."

By the end of 1951 it was almost impossible to find newsstand copies of *La Nación*, the only remaining big independent paper in Buenos Aires. Under government rationing of newsprint, it was forced to cut its press run by about half to some 125,000 copies a day. Those who secured copies loaned them to friends, and crowds of *porteños* read the issues posted in glass showcases in downtown offices. The shortage of exchange with which to buy newsprint cut all newspapers to six or eight pages and restricted circulation.

The dissipation of foreign exchange and soaring labor costs also made old and venerable book publishing houses despair. Argentine book publishing had received a tremendous impetus during the Spanish Civil War when many publishers with experience and excellent taste moved to Buenos Aires. More than one hundred publishing houses, not including universities and government institutions, published the best of the world's literature, technical encyclopedias, textbooks, etc., for readers at home and abroad. In 1944 an estimated seventeen million books were exported. Argentine books could be found even in Mexico, where the Spanish publishing business was almost as large as in Buenos Aires.

Spanish and Spanish-American writers like José Ortega y Gasset and Americo Castro sent their manuscripts to Buenos Aires to be published. The *Colección Austral,* a Spanish forerunner of English pocket-books, published 630 titles in 1947. The Club *El Libro del Mes* (Book-of-the-Month) was established to help the Argentine choose from the mass of literature before him: it selected one outstanding Argentine book and one translation each month. There were no "book dividends," but club members could buy at a discount.

Most popular were melodramatic romances and inaccurate historical novels, but there was a growing vogue for mysteries. In 1950, Virginia Lee Warren reported the old favorites—Hemingway, Cronin, Maugham, Steinbeck, Caldwell, dos Passos, and Faulkner—were still much in demand, but George Orwell, Graham Greene, and Tennessee Williams were also popular. Among contemporary Argentine writers Eduardo Mallea is probably the best-selling author. He is best known in the United States for the translation of his novel, *La Bahía de Silencio, The Bay of Silence.*

But the cost of paper and printing materials has increased by 90 per cent in the last few years, and publishers are forced to operate on a day-to-day basis. They are also menaced by a law which allowed Perón to tax up to 50 per cent all income from foreign books, which included about 80 per cent of all those published, other than technical studies. Book-reading is still an upper-and middle-class pastime—except for the outstanding bestseller of 1951, Eva Perón's *La Razon de Mi Vida.*

There is little direct censorship of books, but publishers know better than to translate books which might be criticized. "The smart thing to do," one publisher confessed, "is to pretend that unfriendly works do not exist."

Spain is a subject to be treated gently, but other books which attempt to show up totalitarianism are acceptable, if they make no reference, direct or indirect, to Argentina. Kravchenko's *I Chose Freedom* was a tremendous success.

How Argentines find time to read the mass of news-papers, magazines, and books offered them no one knows. New publications constantly appear. A favorite story in Buenos Aires declares that while it might not always be true that when two Greeks get together a new restaurant comes into being, it is certain that when two Argentines meet a new publication is definitely in the wind.

Chapter XVII

How Argentines Amuse Themselves

WHEN THE football championship games between Argentina and Uruguay were played, the excitement in Buenos Aires was so intense that newspapers brought out special editions.

Futbol—which is closer to soccer than our collegiate Saturday afternoon game—is Argentina's and Latin America's most popular sport. Scores of magazines in almost every Latin country publicize its professional stars, describing their home life and their activities with all the idolatrous details we customarily reserve for our Hollywood stars. Sports pages feature *futbol* news; radio stations put *futbol* scores before all else.

When the Argentine-Uruguayan championship was scheduled, the press was full of hands-across-the-border editorials, optimistically proclaiming how the series of games would help cement relationships between the two countries, bring about better understanding, and make for brotherly affection.

The championship contest ended disastrously. The umpire was accused of making an unfair decision. Fighting broke out, and in a few minutes the stadium was a shambles. There have been few international matches since.

Even in purely domestic championship matches, rivalry has reached such heights that guards search the spectators entering stadiums and politely confiscate any knives and revolvers until after the event.

Damage inflicted on an offending referee is not confined to profanity and libel. On more than one occasion officials have been hustled out of the stadium in ambulances because they were so badly hurt. At other times the ambulance, hastily summoned by the riot squad, was the only vehicle in which the umpire could escape.

Futbol is exclusively a masculine sport. No women play and few attend the matches which Sunday after Sunday brings crowds of up to one hundred thousand to Buenos Aires' River Plate, Hurican, and other stadiums. The turnouts in secondary cities are only slightly smaller. Argentines play *futbol* in every town in the land, and every newspaper, except obscure political organs, carries full play-by-play accounts of the big games in Sunday afternoon and Monday morning extras.

The reasons why Argentines like their sports and amusements offer a clue to their character. If you want really to know a people, seek out what they do to enjoy themselves. Consider *futbol*.

Argentines love the game because of its unique drama

and the opportunity it gives them to witness personal heroism and individual improvisation. The top-rank *futbol* player must possess the abilities of a sprinter, a ballet dancer, and a juggler. He deftly catches the ball with foot or body, and he can kick it with either foot almost as far—and just as accurately—as our players throw a baseball. Argentines play the game with a unique brilliance not found elsewhere. Scientific teamwork patterns are intricately developed, yet the individual has the greatest opportunity to star.

Argentines take the utmost pride in winning international championships. At the Pan-American games held in Buenos Aires in February and March, 1951, the host nations swept up a triumphant total of 1,071½ points, to our second-place 734½. But for Argentine fans, it was hard to abide by the counsel of Evita ("sports and games teach us to be good losers") and her husband ("Lose a hundred times but . . . make a hundred new friends"). The last big prize of the meet, the basketball championship, was one that Argentina dearly wanted, after winning the world amateur title in 1950. When the United States and Argentina met in the Pan-American championship final, 25,000 highly emotional spectators inside the arena and 5,000 who listened outside did what they could to help the home team's cause.

Every time an Argentine took aim for a foul shot, the crowd was silent. Every American foul shot was made amid a screaming din. When the United States captured the title with a 57–51 victory, two hundred police immediately surrounded the Americans to get them safely off the court. Outside, where mounted cops were at work, a street was cleared for an American getaway.

Sportsmanship in the British or American tradition, while much talked about, is still a rather vague practice in Argentina. The handshake before the game, the outward sign of courtesy, even the terminology used in many sports, comes directly from the British. When the game gets really serious, however, such niceties are likely to be quickly forgotten.

Baseball and cricket have never caught on in Argentina. Polo, however, is a highly popular sport, witnessed by many thousands. The fleet-footed Argentine ponies have won international fame for their owner-players who, in lusher days, thought nothing of taking a string of a dozen ponies on a trip up to Old Westbury, Long Island, just to compete in a few important games.

Horse racing is, next to *futbol*, probably the Argentine's most popular sport. Argentina boasts about a dozen tracks, the two largest in Buenos Aires. The great Hipodromo Argentino, in Parque Palermo, oldest and most traditional, has races on Saturday afternoon; newer, even larger, San Isidro, the following day. At the height of the season, September–October, the races are great social events at which the smart set gathers. The Jockey Club manages both the racing and the pari-mutuel gambling. Large sums of money are bet there—you can start at two *pesos*—but Argentines do not wager away from the track.

While gambling is undoubtedly a major factor in the great enthusiasm for *futbol* and horse racing, perhaps the reason it does not occur away from the events is that the Argentine has unlimited opportunities to gamble in other ways. The lottery goes on endlessly, both in the city of Buenos Aires and in the provinces. There are weekly drawings with substantial prizes; there are other drawings during major holiday seasons.

Most Argentines try their luck on the lottery on a fairly regular basis, and tobacco shops everywhere display lottery tickets in their windows. Youngsters get the gambling habit early. An Argentine schoolboy won't spend his twenty *centavos* for a piece of candy; he will probably use it to play the wheel of fortune at the school gate. Because the lottery is so important in the Argentines' lives, they watch the way it is operated more closely than they watch any other government activity. They demand complete honesty. The government of former President Castillo was able to shrug off all kinds of official scandals, but when a fixed-number conspiracy was discovered in the Federal Lottery it proved disastrous.

The greatest gambling stakes, however, are wagered at the great summer resorts. Buenos Aires itself has no gambling casino, but Mar del Plata is only two hundred and fifty miles to the south—five hours by car, an hour by plane. The vast, many-storied casino at Mar del Plata is one of the few places an Argentine lady can visit unescorted in the evening, and generally she feels as safe as if she were in a government bank. In effect that is just where she is, for the Casino was built by the government of the Province of Buenos Aires with profits from previous less ornate casinos.

The Argentines' realistic assumption is that gambling is an ineradicable characteristic of the Argentine people. The government believes it is better to get the biggest share of the profits for its own social welfare programs and other purposes than to try to limit the urge to gamble.

The Church, incidentally, keeps mum on the subject, save for an occasional editorial in the daily *El Pueblo*.

Argentines crowd the gaming boards at Mar del Plata as we crowd Coney Island on a sunny Fourth of July. There are fifty-six roulette tables going full blast in season, far more than Monte Carlo ever had. To get to the Casino, you pass through a series of gardens manicured to the hilt, like everything else in Mar del Plata, and enter a vast red brick palace. Uniformed aides—the Casino requires 4,500 employees—are available to run errands, fetch drinks, and show you around. The place is so big a newcomer often requires a guide. The Casino not only has its own beach and luxury hotel, but swimming pools and Roman-style baths, underground parking spaces, a big night club, plus a group of sports arenas whose total capacity equals that of Madison Square Garden.

Its theater regularly imports full-scale opera companies and the Ballet Russe de Monte Carlo. A big movie palace features Argentine productions and a few carefully-censored imported pictures.

Before and after gambling, you can attend a lecture on poetry, see an art exhibition, or look at jewelry shops, where winners can buy at least one pin or ring to keep their luck. There is even a place to park the baby, complete with puppet shows and sitters.

In the Casino's main public halls, decorated in quiet shades of gray and gold, are row after row of green baize-covered tables. Here you can start with *peso* chips and go up into the thousands. If you want to bid higher—and the sky is the limit—there are a series of other smaller rooms. Most elegant is the Mother of Pearl Salon. Even before the current inflation it was customary for a dozen visitors to win or lose sums of $25,000 and more. Baccarat and *chemin de fer* are played in these smaller rooms, which are favored by unescorted but highly respectable elderly and bejeweled ladies with large bankrolls.

Apparently there are no amateur gamblers among the Argentines. Most of them, especially the *porteños*, carefully work out their own systems before the season at Mar del Plata. When the infallible method goes wrong Mar del Plata's rocks may be the scene of a suicide as melodramatic as the lyrics of a tango. More numerous are the players who abandon their baggage at smart hotels, turn in their crack train or plane tickets, and take the bus back to Buenos Aires to plan furiously for another try at the earliest opportunity.

The formality and ceremony of Argentine amusement is well illustrated by the daily life at Mar del Plata in the mid-December through February season. The Duke of Windsor, in his Prince of Wales touring days, reportedly called Mar del Plata the only place where he felt inadequately outfitted. He declared: "Even the beachcombers wear white tie and tails." The Prince was exaggerating— but not much.

The beaches at Mar del Plata are set between rocky promontories. Each has its own social standing, customs, and unwritten rules of etiquette. Playa Popular is the least formal. A few of its bathers even dare to change to swim suits at home and bring along hampers filled with food for midday eating. Some carry little tins of canned heat to boil water for their *maté*. But it is obvious that this is not society.

The ultra-modern Argentines who have gone into hock

rather than miss the season would not dream of sunning themselves at any other place than Playa Grande. Here, even the location of your rented beach cabaña, replete with little wicker chairs, brass name-plate and dressing-room, is as much a symbol of acceptance as a listing in the *Social Register*. Placement, in fact, is in the hands of a director who has charge of the same protocol for the swank Opera Colon in Buenos Aires.

At the top of the list are the old families whose *estancias* provide their incomes. Even the diplomatic set has no special entree. One knowledgeable ambassador once remarked: "My cabaña locale is a better barometer of the true state of relations between the Foreign Office and my government than any Palacio San Martín spokesman. And with all the pressure in the world, I can't better it if *they* say no."

At Mar del Plata a fashionable Argentine goes to the beach at 11 A.M., never with less than two retainers to handle the offspring and accessories. He sits poised and unblinking on a chair or hammock, never on the sand, until 1 P.M., never later. The vendors on the Playa Grande who sell *empanadas*, little raisin-filled meat pies, and *alfajores*, sweet cakes, have signs identifying them as "The Duchess," "The Princess," or "The Queen." Prices reflect the degree of royalty. Among older Argentines, dodging a tan is as elaborate a process as acquiring one is for Miami and Asbury Park sun lovers. These Argentines consider persons with dark skins inferiors from lesser Latin-American countries, so they avoid the sun. For many years, society-conscious Mar del Plata authorities prohibited the building of stucco and tile houses. Everything, they insisted, had to be constructed of solid red brick or massive brownish stone to ensure the dignity which characterizes the town today. Even movies with bullfights were banned, lest anybody think such things went on in Argentina.

The younger people in fashionable circles have in recent years become dissatisfied with this time-honored fustiness. Young Argentines buy as many lotions and creams as North Americans to cultivate assiduously enough tan to impress less fortunate stay-at-homes. They strip to outfits as brief as those worn by the Hollywood stars whose magazine photos set the mode.

Golf and tennis, a stroll on the Rambla, which is Mar del Plata's equivalent of our boardwalk, a stop for tea, are other events of seaside life. Everybody changes clothes at least half a dozen times a day. Since Mar del Plata's visitors generally come as family groups, uncles, cousins, aunts, and in-laws are likely to fill the same hotel or chalet. The men, who fuss even more than the women, rarely unbend to the extent of wearing the kind of sportswear we fancy. Even so, they make their *señoras*, who often as not are wearing mourning black, seem pale in comparison.

Vacationing Argentines are more likely to forget formality in the hills near Córdoba which are dotted with scores of hotels and cottages, or in the south, near Bariloche where a chain of beautiful lakes extends through to Chile. The Bariloche area, locale of the Nahuel Huapí National Park is popular both in summer for the superb scenery and mountain air and in the winter for skiing.

In summer those Argentines who cannot afford to go far away from the capital visit places like Tigre, a green-grown Venice twenty-one miles north of the capital on the

delta of the Paraná River. A favorite week-end spot, it is
a yachting and rowing center. Dozens of clubs and restaurants provide easy, inexpensive pleasures. Even the
poorest can row and build a little fire to roast meat and
sausages.

Argentines are fond of clubs. The Club Gimnasia y
Esgrima (Fencing), in Parque Palermo, some twenty-five
minutes by subway and bus from downtown Buenos
Aires, is said to be the world's largest. It has more than
fifteen thousand members, who pay an extremely modest
yearly fee for the use of swimming pools and fields for
futbol, hockey, tennis, basketball, and handball. Each
week-end, *porteño* families jam the Club's three-story
building, roam the landscaped grounds, dance on the terrace, and dine at lower prices than prevail in town restaurants. They also have the use of the Club's big downtown
headquarters, equipped for swimming, bowling, basketball, handball, and fencing, plus its library, ballrooms and
roof garden. Gimnasia y Esgrima was started by an Argentine lawyer who persuaded the municipal authorities
to give him a portion of the unclaimed lottery prizes.

At the other social extreme from the popular Gimnasia
y Esgrima is the Jockey Club of Buenos Aires. Its members are the *estancia* families and others of social prestige.
Few outsiders ever crash its charmed circle, except for
members of the diplomatic corps who almost automatically receive honorary memberships. That applies even
to Perón who has not even been granted the customary
deference accorded the President of the Republic.

The Jockey Club's elaborate headquarters were destroyed by a mob in April, 1953. It possessed an amazing
library and a beautiful collection of paintings. Its wine

cellars were superb, its elaborate dining-rooms of regal magnificance, its Turkish baths like the dream of a Roman emperor.

The Club owns the race tracks at Palermo and San Isidro. It boasts two eighteen-hole golf courses, polo fields and many other properties. In those luxurious days before the Jockey Club was destroyed the profits made from these holdings enabled it to charge its members less for the use of its palatial home and its meals and other services than expensive hotels and restaurants.

Another unusual club, but with a large membership, is the Automobile Club. It operates a chain of tastefully decorated service and rest stations throughout the country. They service your car, give travel information, and sell gasoline at a slight discount. The Club's headquarters, located in the most exclusive part of Buenos Aires' residential district, are in a modernistic skyscraper topped by a huge restaurant with excellent food and a superb view of the entire capital. The Club fosters road-building, facilitates imports of visitors' and members' cars, and sponsors automobile races—another popular Argentine sport.

There are hundreds of other clubs throughout the area stretching north and south of Buenos Aires, and there are other clubs around every one of Argentina's smaller cities and towns. Almost every large commercial institution has its own club from the National Sanitary Works to the London Bank. So do nationality groups. Every school, university, department store, and shipping house has its own club.

Many believe that the overcrowding and monotony of the single rooms and smaller apartments where the lower

middle-class and poor Argentines live have been responsible for the growth of these clubs. But many of the first
clubs were started by the British and the Hurlingham and
Olivos are still considered among the smartest. For a time
they limited the percentage of Argentines they would
admit. This caused resentment which led to the formation
of rival organizations. Today no such restrictions apply.

Some Argentines feel their numerous clubs contradict
the frequently-repeated criticism that Argentines are unwilling to join together and cooperate in a mutual effort.
Others believe the club in a sense represents an extension
of the family. "When you are a member," we recall hearing one Argentine say, "you become part of a family with
a strong sense of loyalty to those within the fold. Your
club is opposed to all others."

An incident illustrates this. An American correspondent was invited to a foreign club on the banks of one of
the Tigre canals, and asked a question about the club of
another nationality group just over the high bush fence.
"But I have never been over there," said the host, "even
though I've been coming here to our own club for the last
twenty-five years. We have our group and they have
theirs."

It is in their clubs—and in their cafés and *confiterías*—
that Argentines do most of their social drinking. But
never does it equal the amount we drink. Most Argentines prefer wine and certain mild mixed drinks. Scotch
is the most popular liquor, but because its price is high
you rarely see an Argentine drinking it unless he is with
foreigners or wishes to create an impression of affluence
by ordering a "whiskey *con* soda."

Argentina's wines, which come mostly from Mendoza,

are first class and imported by nearby republics. At the clubs, the cafés, and the *confiterías* you see wine served at lunch or dinner. Children often get theirs with water or soda. Workers who cook steaks for lunch on the job usually bring along a good-sized bottle of red wine, which is so cheap that everyone can afford it. Poorer families generally buy their wine in large glass wicker-encased five and ten liter sizes.

Their most popular cocktail is the San Martín which is similar to our Martini. It is made of local vermouth and gin, usually of equal proportions, and often served before dinner. But just as many Argentines prefer vermouth with soda for sociability.

In most cafés the free lunch (plates of peanuts, sliced meats, biscuits, etc.) served with even the simplest drink is so abundant that a visitor often feels he has consumed an entire meal while supposedly developing an appetite for lunch or dinner. As in Paris, the law in Buenos Aires makes it a misdemeanor for a waiter who has served a patron to hover expectantly near him unless he is called.

Next to their clubs and the cafés, Argentines enjoy the movies most. Argentines prefer Hollywood films, their own movies, and Mexican pictures, in about that order. Italian and English films have also been popular. Spanish films have rarely done well.

Our films are popular, not only because of technical superiority, but because their plots have more action than others and are comparatively easy to follow despite the English dialogue. City-dwelling Argentines do not like our pictures with dubbed-in Spanish voices. They were tried for a time, but the *porteños* were so startled to hear Greer Garson and Clark Gable speak Spanish that they sent up indignant howls. The Argentines' favorite movies are our big technicolor epics like *Blood and Sand* and *Gone with the Wind.*

Every American star and many secondary players are known to Argentine filmgoers. Local film magazines feature Hollywood articles about them as much as articles about Argentine stars. Even when American films were banned in order to conserve the dwindling dollar supply and to aid the local industry, Argentine fan publications continued to write about American stars.

A succession of ambassadors from the United States have fought to have the restrictions on our films lifted. Finally, in 1951, arrangements were made whereby the eight major United States film companies operating in Argentina were granted permission to remit a portion of their earnings.

Since the Argentines started making their own films, they have changed their minds about the significance of our pictures. Many an Argentine, though he considered himself reasonably sophisticated, once believed that our films fairly accurately reflected life in the United States. Now he sees that his own mystery thrillers, comedies, and tragedies are as remote from Argentine actuality as many of ours, and he realizes scenario writers are the same the hemisphere over. But it has not stopped him from wanting to go to the movies.

Now more and more Argentine movie fans like their own movies and are less likely to pooh-pooh them as second-rate imitations of Hollywood. Argentina produces about fifty to sixty features a year, plus a large number of shorts. Studios are located in and around Buenos Aires.

Argentine film makers do not deal with any theme that is likely to disturb the government. Since Evita Perón had been on the inside of Argentine film-making, first as an extra, then as a top featured actress (when she became Perón's favorite) she knew a good deal about the industry and kept a sharp eye on the film moguls to make sure her favorites were properly recognized. Opponents were controlled in many ways. Only the government can import film, and any producing firm which strays from the line finds its negative supply cut off. Actress Nini Marshall, who made the mistake of being too chummy with the opposition when Perón's fortunes were low, still finds no theater or film company will take her.

According to law, 40 per cent of all films shown in the nation's two thousand theaters must be local products. Until recently, there was no attempt to decree subject matter. But in 1952 Undersecretary of Information Raul Apold summoned producers to his office. What he told them was echoed the next day in a peronista daily: "We feel it timely to remind producers, directors, and writers of the film industry that it was not created to glorify the body of this or that actress . . . but to work intelligently to bring culture to all members of the national community."

Almost all movie theaters have reserved seats. Argentines are especially fond of the Sunday afternoon "vermouth" showing, which begins about 5:30. Often they buy tickets to it two or three weeks in advance. Saturday night and holiday evenings are, as everywhere, also highly popular.

Perhaps the best-liked American films of the last decade were the Andy Hardy series starring Mickey Rooney.

These gave a warm friendly picture of our family life. Andy's father for the first time convinced many an Argentine that North Americans were not quite as wild as depicted in some of our other films. The easy give-and-take of this screen family had a far stronger effect in selling Argentines on the United States than most of our war films.

It is an interesting commentary that despite all their propaganda efforts during World War II German and Italian films never made much progress with the Argentines. Only the postwar Italian pictures have been successful in Argentina. German films never caught on.

Few Argentine films are shown in the United States outside of the special Spanish-language theaters. This seriously annoys Argentine producers. At one time it caused the government to insist, unsuccessfully, that our films would be screened only to the extent that Argentine films were played in the United States.

Argentines are great theater-goers, but only Buenos Aires has a really thriving theater. Argentines usually have to wait until they go to the metropolis to see the latest productions.

Buenos Aires has twenty-eight legitimate theaters running in season. Many are centered on or around Corrientes, the Broadway of Buenos Aires. According to a compilation by *Variety*, the theatrical weekly, some 115 productions were put on during the first nine months of 1951. Twenty-four were translations of foreign dramas. Translators, by the way, often get the same billing as authors, and rate just as highly.

Argentine audience reaction is as unpredictable as ours. Successes are sometimes unexpected, as were *Our*

Town, and *Arsenic and Old Lace*, both of which had extensive runs. In 1951, *The Heiress* had a short run, while André Roussin's *Nina*, seen briefly on Broadway the same season, ran for 103 performances.

Argentina's theatrical world is not as tense nor as highly competitive as Broadway, probably because the returns cannot compare with what can be earned in the United States. Standards of presentation and staging admittedly do not equal ours, although they are far above those found elsewhere in Latin America. Most musicals are poor because the casts lack speed and polish.

For a long time one of the most popular musicals was at Buenos Aires' Maipo Theater which burlesqued current affairs and political developments. Today, poking fun at anything official is not permitted. The "disrespect" law actually makes it a criminal offense. To bring action a politician need only indicate that he is offended. Theatrical people who have dared oppose the government have in some cases actually had to exile themselves to find jobs.

The municipality of the Federal District of Buenos Aires rates movies and plays, judging some suitable "for families," others as "inconvenient for children." The theater or film house is subsequently expected to refuse to sell tickets—and deny admittance—to youngsters.

Argentines are great music patrons. Buenos Aires' Teatro Colón is one of the great opera houses of the world. Built in Greco-Roman style and proportioned in the grand manner, the magnificent plush, gold, and crystal house fills a complete city block. Since it was inaugurated in 1908, it has played a leading part in the city's life.

The French architect who designed the Colón was told
to make it "bigger than the Paris Opera so we can show
France that Buenos Aires is a real metropolis."

Seating 3,500, more than that of any other opera house
in the Americas, including the Metropolitan, the Colón
is used for opera, concerts, and recitals. Its revolving
stages accommodate six hundred people. Argentines say
the Colón surpasses both its Parisian model and the
Vienna Opera House, and can only be compared to
Milan's La Scala. There are eight balconies—the first
four for evening dress.

Argentines like to recall that it was at the Colón that
Arturo Toscanini began his rise to musical immortality
when he was called from his violin to take the baton in
1910. The same red curtains have gone up on Caruso,
Pavlova, Chaliapin, Lily Pons, Heifetz, and Rubinstein.
On his trips to the Argentine Rubinstein plays a solid two-
week season of ten concerts, afternoons and evenings.

An official school trains both chorus and ballet, but
local voices for leading roles lag behind top standards for
varied reasons. Some Argentines tell you it's the very lack
of discipline or the unwillingness to submit to it that has
prevented the development of first-rate artists.

The Colón has always been the prize showcase for
Argentina's top society. Family boxes and memberships
were always handed down from generation to generation.
Wealthy Argentines made grand entrances and exits on
such gala nights as the 25th of May and the 9th of July.
The entire diplomatic corps and government officials also
attended, as well as local politicians, would-be social
leaders, and ordinary citizens who wished to shine in
their reflected glory.

Though the Colón never made money, the capital and municipality of Buenos Aires always paid the deficit. When the military government took over, its leaders anticipated that families of wealth and position would snub the opening gala performance. So on the first big holiday all seats were called in and redistributed to important men in the Perón regime. They came to the gala in their most resplendent uniforms; their wives wore their most brilliant jewels, dresses, and furs. The tradition was maintained. They proved, to themselves at least, that they were fully as good as the socialites who had previously graced the Colón.

Aside from the Colón, there are many musical societies which sponsor concerts in Buenos Aires and secondary cities. The season begins in May and continues through the winter until September. The Asociación Wagneriana secures the most gifted singers. The Asociación Filarmonica Argentina sometimes gives its concerts in leading movie theaters, and at the Luna Park Boxing Arena when wrestlers and prize fighters have a night off.

Argentina's outstanding musical figure is the composer-conductor, Juan José Castro, who for many years conducted the Colón orchestra. He has conducted extensively in other American capitals, and he has composed symphonic poems, the Biblical Symphony for chorus and orchestra, chamber and ballet music, and various works for piano and violin.

Argentina's popular music reflects the national character. Almost every restaurant of any size has a small orchestra to play at dinner and even at lunch. Practically every *confitería* has live—not wired—music. Only a half dozen places have actually installed American-style juke boxes. One of these is, of all places, in the subway at the Presidente Perón railroad station.

Many native Argentine orchestra players have assumed foreign names. Argentines have the notion that foreigners are better musicians than they are. At the Confitería Rex in Buenos Aires, one of the most popular places to drop in for a coffee or a snack, the orchestra is led by Istaban Weishaus. The mixed group of men and women musicians sit on a little balcony overlooking rows of tables and chairs and play furiously if sadly to cover the sound of endless conversation.

Argentina's inability to produce important music of its own has been a source of considerable distress. Many an Argentine will tell you his country's national anthem sounds like the overture to an Italian opera.

The music for which Argentina is best known is the tango. An Argentine once said the tango does not reflect Argentine life; Argentine life tries to reflect the tango. It was first heard in the last years of the nineteenth century, in a form very different from the tango of today. Some say it was at first a hybrid mixture of the Andalusian tango, the Cuban *habanera*, and the Argentine *milonga*. Others insist its elements are African, Brazilian, and cheap Italian.

John White points out that when the twentieth century dawned, no one would have dared play a tango in an Argentine ballroom because it was considered a rather shameful inheritance from the city-despised gaucho. It was spurned by respectable society. When the *nouveau riche* families began going to Paris to spend their money their sons introduced the tango to the French and it immediately became popular. Women found it exciting.

After becoming the rage in Paris, the tango became refined and it was perfectly proper for any young Argentine
lady to dance it in public. Imported back from Europe it
immediately replaced the waltz, the polka, and other old-
fashioned dances—a striking example of Argentina's preference for anything that came from abroad rather than
something produced at home.

However different their viewpoints on the tango's deri-
vation, all authorities agree that though the form is now
distinct, it is in no sense final. The tango, as the Argentines know it, continues its constant evolution, absorbing
all sorts of elements. Though not as popular as in the past,
it has now become a part of Argentine life. To a stranger
all tangos sound alike. The rhythmic pattern hardly
changes, yet new tangos are introduced week after week,
while old ones are played and replayed again. It has a
kind of monotonous charm and nostalgia in keeping with
its origin.

In the smartest of Argentine night clubs the tango takes
a secondary role to the imported fox trot. But go to a
real Argentine spot and you find the tango playing endlessly. Even when the musicians occasionally switch to an
American tune they play the double beat to the end of the
phrase as if it were a tango. The contrast of Argentine
music with that of other Latin-American countries is very
distinct. Argentina's music is no more like the Mexican
miariachi band than Dixieland jazz is like an old-time
Strauss waltz. Nor is it like the Chilean *huaso* or the
Cuban *mambo*. Argentines do not serenade their *señoritas*
with tangos: it would hardly be appropriate.

Argentina's favorite tango singer is Carlos Gardel, who
died many years ago. One radio station devotes an hour

of its day just to playing Cardel's recordings. His film revivals are invariably sellouts. His photo, seen in many a bar and café, shows a profile like that of Rudolph Valentino. Hugo del Carril, who has appeared in New York, is currently a favorite tango singer. Libertad Lamarque, another outstanding star, now sings her *Pampa Mia* outside Perónland only.

Even before Perón decreed that half of all musical programs must consist of Argentine music, the tango was the predominant rhythm heard on the radio. But more and more serious music from the United States is broadcast in recorded concerts.

Before World War II the favored recorded orchestras were the Berlin, London, and Vienna State Symphony. Many Argentines felt that the only good music came from Europe. But today they hear the orchestras of Stokowski, Toscanini, the Boston Symphony, the New York Philharmonic, and many others. This has convinced many that we are not complete barbarians. If we can play good music so well we cannot be such an uncultured people after all. Our jazz rather contradicts this opinion, but most Argentines feel jazz is primarily for the younger generation. The youngsters love it and they talk knowingly of Tommy Dorsey, Xavier Cugat, and other popular North American musical figures.

Television came to Buenos Aires just in time to help peronistas campaign for the November 11, 1951, Presidential elections. The first program was devoted to the "sacrificial" gesture of Evita in renouncing the Vice Presidential candidacy; it was telecast on October 17, the sixth anniversary of the day the *descamisados* returned Perón to power. The official announcement that Argentine video would be "the best in the world, far clearer than that in the United States, because of the competence of Argentine technicians," undoubtedly puzzled American firms. The sole transmitter, studio equipment, and receivers were all made in the United States, and American technicians helped install them.

Radio Belgrano promised to televise all the big *futbol* games, auto races, horse races, and other spectacles, but for a long time every home would continue to be dominated by the radio, blaring away all day with the music of a tango.

Chapter XVIII

Meat and Wheat Make Argentina

ONCE ANNUALLY each ambassador in Argentina gets out his top hat, has his striped trousers pressed to razor sharpness, and sets forth with his aides for the biggest social event of the year. It is not a state dinner or the opening of the Opera Colón. It is the cattle show.

As you approach Parque Palermo in the smart northern section of Buenos Aires, you find all traffic headed in the same direction. Everyone is going, from the President of the Republic and his ministers to the factory worker and the *peon*. No one wants to miss the opening of the Sociedad Rural exhibition.

This is the one time of the year when the Argentine *estanciero* feels he comes into his own. He may be denounced, as he frequently is, as the "decadent representative of the *oligarquía*, who has bled the country of its money so that he can waste it in Paris." However, when he displays his Blue Ribbon winner, the *estanciero* knows that he and his products have been responsible for Argentina's wealth and greatest fame.

The attention lavished on one of the Shorthorn or Aberdeen Angus champions provides a clue to the Argentine sense of values. A champion bull listed in the Breeder's Book, bred and crossbred in the endless quest for perfection, will be accorded more care than a Hollywood star. He gets his baths and treatments of olive oil. His long curly coat is brushed, and the thick hair above his eyes is specially arranged. His short, perfectly-formed horns are polished, his hoofs carefully manicured.

Many champions are not even grazed on the grassland. Instead, they are confined to small pens, provided with cows to give them milk, then brought to the big barn and installed in private quarters for feeding, grooming, and watering in special luxury. Skilled veterinarians watch them constantly. They are fed bland mash dashed with molasses. Everything possible is done to produce the kind of animal whose progeny will also be meat-bearing champions.

The members of the Sociedad Rural—an organization founded in 1866 and, Argentines will tell you, outranked only by the Catholic Church—long influenced legislation, political power, and to a lesser degree public opinion. They knew that as members of the most exclusive and important farmers' association in the Americas, they were responsible for developing Argentina's cattle economy. They imported the first shorthorns, started the cattle shows, introduced the experimentation which advanced the breeds. They brought into one solidly-organized group men with such wealth and power that they themselves could not fully understand their responsibilities and privileges.

At first Argentina's *estancias* were rough, sometimes primitive places where cattle were raised for hides and tallow. Some meat was salted and shipped overseas. Five steps paved the way for the *estancia* of today.

First, the invention of barbed wire, which enabled the *estancieros* to divide off their grazing areas and keep their animals from straying or being rustled away.

Second, the arrival of immigrants who came to work on the land, providing a vast source of low-cost labor.

Third, the railroads, built by foreign capital to carry the products of the *estancia* to deep-water ports for shipment overseas.

Fourth, refrigeration. Developed first by the French, then by the British, it enabled the Argentines to halt overseas shipment of salt meat or live cattle and freeze meat for shipment overseas to arrive in the most perfect state.

Fifth, improvement of breeds. Many Argentine *estancia* owners were little interested in the quality of their cattle. But when they saw how their own Merino sheep, averaging only thirty-nine pounds, brought two and three *pesos* a pound in the London market while British Lincolns far outweighed and outsold them, Argentines got interested and began importing. "Pedigree," a word the British introduced, is now an accepted Argentine term.

With improvement of the breed came an increasing interest in the quality and nature of Argentine grasses to fatten the cattle. Some *estancia* owners refused to break their rich sod, feeling the plow somehow befouled their pasture. But members of the Sociedad Rural experimented with fields of alfalfa, which often thrived seven or eight years without replanting. Others grew clover, barley, and foxtail to replace the wild grasses.

Nature's contribution, however, was the greatest. The *estancieros'* herds never needed indoor feeding because, in most cases, they could graze all year round. There were, of course, winters when loads of hay had to be brought in and grain was buried in silos for droughts. Occasionally there were locust and grasshopper plagues, and sometimes hailstorms. Generally however, until the last few years, weather has been almost uniformly kind.

The *estancieros* developed a system whereby they did not feed their cattle on corn, as we do in the United States, but rather bred them on one *estancia*, fed and fattened them on another, and then sent them off to market in the size that would fetch the best price. Generally, this was around 800 pounds, compared to our customary 1,100. Argentines prefer beef from young cattle, explaining it is more tender. The small steer gets a very substantial premium per pound over the larger one.

Since 1883, when the first British refrigerating plant was opened in Argentina, big foreign meat-packing plants have dominated the slaughtering and shipment. Some years ago some of the smaller *estancieros* felt that these concerns were a monopoly which established quotas and fixed prices so as to give only certain influential *estancieros* and themselves the highest profits. The Confederation of Rural Societies, made up mostly of farm-dwelling *estancieros* who often criticized the older and better established Sociedad Rural as a group of absentee owners, helped establish the Argentine Corporation of Meat Producers (C.A.P.) in which they insured their own prices and which in a sesnse served as an extension of their *estancias*.

When the Perón regime came into power, C.A.P. was linked with the government. As politics and economics became more closely meshed than in almost any other country, Argentina began to face difficulties and actually experience meat shortages, something which previously would have been considered impossible.

At the end of 1951 Argentina was estimated to have about forty-three million cattle, well below the forty-five million head estimated for 1949. And it appeared likely that Argentina would not be able to supply both the British market and her own. *Estancieros*—and everybody else in Argentina—had plenty of explanations of what had happened. The most likely explanation lies in a combination of several points.

For much of their country's economic trouble, the government is entirely responsible. Conception of a new and greater Argentina which could make its own machines as well as grow its own food made it embark on a program of industrialization at the expense of agriculture. The Argentine Institute for the Promotion of Exchange was established to handle all exports. I.A.P.I. paid farmers and stockmen low prices for their products and sold them abroad for high prices, using the profits to build up industry. Seeing their own profits decline, the farmers balked, cut down their production, and kept their cattle from the markets. In 1951, for instance, Argentine farmers on a sit-down strike planted less than twelve million acres of wheat as compared with seventeen million in 1943. In February, 1952, cattlemen were offered 21 per cent more for cattle on the hoof in an effort to get more beef off the *pampa*.

Argentines were eating more themselves. Before the war they ate about 60 per cent of the nation's produce; now they consume more than 80 per cent. In 1950 the per capita meat consumption in Argentina was the world's highest—247 pounds per year. Australia and New Zealand were next highest at 147, the United States was fourth. Meat is the favorite Argentine food because it has always been tasty, cheap, and abundant, especially as compared with such foods as eggs, fish, and vegetables. Even in 1952 a pound of onions cost as much as a medium cut of meat. "If you only have so much to spend," one Argentine queried, "which dish would you choose?" The nation's health authorities have worried about the carnivorous tastes of Argentines for years, but not until recently did Perón begin urging his countrymen to eat more vegetables and less meat.

The 1952 economic crisis was due partly to the weather. For two years severe droughts parched the *pampas*. Land once rich with corn, wheat, and cattle cracked and blew away in clouds of dust. Droughts also depleted herds and lengthened fattening time.

Perón's industrialization program lured workers from farm to city. His labor laws made *estancia* management as intricate as running a factory. Both large and small landowners complained that figuring their workers' overtime, days off, hours worked, etc., took so much time they had little opportunity to see to cattle and crops. They complained even more about the extra pay they were forced to give *peons*.

Mechanization on the farm did not keep pace with

mechanization in the city. In fact, since 1941, Argentines themselves point out, the country had not made much agricultural mechanization progress, having only one tractor for each 1,863 acres. In 1951, I.A.P.I. offered credit for machinery purchases, but there was little machinery to be had.

Estancia-owners also feared the government's effort to break up their estates would mean cattle-raising in the Argentine manner would cease, for, they pointed out, on their large estates cattle are grazed by moving them from field to field, something impossible in a limited area.

The government's answer was that breaking up the estates would probably do little harm. It pointed out that this free movement of cattle had encouraged the foot-and-mouth disease, a subject, incidentally, which is worth a brief note since it has long been a highly disputed point between the United States and Argentina.

Aftosa, foot-and-mouth disease, first appeared among Argentine cattle in 1870. Though seldom fatal, it causes painful sores on animals' mouths and hoofs. Because the cattle are unable to walk far or eat much, they become scrawny and unmarketable. In Argentina the disease occurs in a mild form, and it is not considered as seriously as in the United States or in Britain, where it is endemic.

Aftosa does not affect humans, but because the virus spreads so rapidly and is so hard to stamp out, the United States refused, in 1927, to allow imports of meat from *aftosa*-infected areas. Then an outbreak of foot-and-mouth disease in southern California in 1929 was traced to trimmings of fresh meat brought by a ship from Buenos Aires. The following year, the Smoot-Hawley Tariff Act extended the ban to cover meat from all parts of Argentina.

Argentines refuse to understand it is primarily a medical problem, and have considered it almost entirely a political and economic issue. They feel that the embargo was a protectionist measure, and should be lifted.

To ease the situation, the State Department tried to conclude a sanitary agreement with Argentina to permit importation of meat from non-infected areas, but the Senate refused to ratify it. Some Americans felt that if the Argentines had a chance at our market they might take more forceful methods to prevent *aftosa*. Currently, since Argentina no longer has a surplus of beef to export, the question is academic.

By 1952 the once great breadbasket and meat market of the world was obviously in short supply. Argentina had the greatest trade deficit in her history and the export outlook for the future looked grim. No wheat at all was expected to be available for foreign trade. Prospects for rye, barley, and oats were little better. The only pastoral product of which Argentina had a surplus was wool, and despite lower price offers, there were few takers.

To save enough meat to fulfill the British beef contract, President Perón proclaimed Argentina's first meatless day on February 1. The Plaza Hotel in Buenos Aires offered *bacalao vizcainay*, codfish in rich Spanish sauce, instead of its regular Châteaubriand. Restaurant La Cabaña, home of "baby beef," featured chicken pie in place of the succulent mixed grill. One meatless day a week was a shock to most Argentines.

Another shock was the "inflexible austerity" program President Perón announced later in February. He decreed a second meatless day per week and ordered slaughterhouses to close one day and slaughter only for export a second day each week. He curtailed immigration, except for agricultural workers and a few skilled technicians, and announced that government expenditures would be kept to a minimum. He appealed to the nation to save food, pleading that it was the first time in five years he had asked any sacrifice. The President called for a 20 per cent increase in production, and said that with it, the national problems of inflation and lack of foreign exchange would be solved. And he promised that farmers would receive 33 per cent more for their crops.

In May his promise that all of the nation's resources would be used to counteract the devastating drought and other factors which had diminished agricultural production was put into action: some eight thousand troops were ordered into the fields to help harvest the corn crop. Perón had also promised to double agricultural production by irrigating 2,500,000 acres of arid land and by stimulating production by mechanization and other means.

By then the rich black earth of the River Plate area showed signs of returning to its customary life and wealth. But unless the President could make the farmers more enthusiastic supporters, Argentina's agricultural problems could not fully be solved.

Chapter XIX

Industries of Argentina

STEP INTO a car outside the entrance to the United States Embassy offices on the Diagonal Norte in Buenos Aires. Tell your chauffeur to skirt the Plaza de Mayo and head southward along the Paseo Colon. Within a half-hour's drive, you will get a synthesized view of Argentina's commerce and industry—the two things which so many Argentines hope will change their country from what they consider a colonial economy to a modern, independent leader of Latin America.

Along busy Leandro Alem are arcaded office buildings and some of the great warehouses of the biggest importing firms—Singer Sewing Machine, duPont and Duperial, Peabody. Here are the old foreign companies who have long imported the goods made in Detroit and Liverpool, Zurich and Rotterdam. Since their country's birth, Argentines have imported the manufactured products from the world's industrial centers.

A mile or two south, and along the oily stream of the Rio Riachuelo, heralded by an odor which at times hangs over the entire area like a dense cloud, are the big *frigorificos*: Swift, Armour, Anglo, and Wilson. Argentines know them well, for to these slaughterhouses and meat-packing establishments have come the cattle from their *estancias*—large and small—to be processed for use at home and for shipment to the markets of the world.

It was from the sale of her meat plus her wheat and agricultural products, her mutton and wool, her quebracho and hides, that Argentines got the foreign exchange to buy their Fords and Frigidaires, the flannels and the furnishings for their everyday use, comfort, and luxury.

But continue your southward journey beyond the limits of Buenos Aires toward the provincial capital of La Plata where the rich *pampa* comes up almost to the edge of town. Here, rising on the flat, grassy land, you see the full turn of the cycle: new plants and warehouses, many of glass-brick with sharp, clean lines and towering chimneys. "All this," Argentines tell you proudly, "has come in only a few years. These factories are making products which will someday free us from our economic subjugation of the past."

The drone of spinning factory wheels often floats over the herds of grazing cattle. Some of the factories here on the road to La Plata, elsewhere in Buenos Aires and in some of the other cities, still bear names which indicate either foreign establishment, partnership, or the use of rights, patents, and trademarks. Yet to many Argentines this is unimportant. Even if raw materials are agricultural rather than mineral, or if, as in many cases, they have to be imported from abroad, the factories prove to the Argentines that their country is coming of age industrially.

"Today," one man tells you, "more than half our country's national income comes from industrial sources. Is not that evidence of what we have accomplished?" The answer you gather is yes—for to deny it or to cite contradictory facts is considered the worst possible taste by many Argentines.

"*Industrializacion*" is a word Argentines love to use. Workers throw it into their conversations. Up-and-coming businessmen and professionals, reading more and more technical journals, use it with familiar intimacy. Classes on the exact sciences boom. Even the *estancieros* whose interests have always been in their short-horned cattle or Aberdeen Angus, and who opposed the mill and factory, now talk knowingly of percentages, increasing production, rise in consumer goods, hard and soft lines, and replacement markets.

Argentines, like many other Latin Americans, feel that only through industrialization can they gain their independence and raise their living standards.

The most important manufacturing fields today are meat-packing, machinery and vehicles, metal goods, and flour and milling. Contrary to general opinion, the lack of available coal and iron has not dampened the industrial spirit, though it has hampered development of heavy industry.

Though many Argentine *estancieros* fear the industrialization which is held out so brightly as a new way of life to Argentines, we feel that some of the more alert landowners are going into the manufacturing business. Some of them think it is just good sense. They sometimes get special tax advantages if they set up certain essential operations. Moreover, the *estancieros* have capital to invest and know that much of Argentina's industrialization must use agricultural products, hence is eventually bound to benefit them.

For a long time wealthy Argentines preferred to use profits to add to their already extensive land holdings. They improved the breed of their animals and the methods of cultivating their herds. Other funds were invested abroad and used for travel and luxury living. With certain exceptions, which will be noted later, comparatively few of them were interested in the early days in reinvesting in industry in their own country.

Since Argentina presented almost unlimited opportunities, foreigners were eager to provide funds to construct utilities, transport, meat packing plants, import and export businesses. Foreigners first began to develop Argentina's textile mills and other light manufacturing. Until the late 30's most foreign companies operating in Argentina made little pretense of being Argentine. In the United States, Shell has always hidden its foreign ownership. Firms operating in Argentina, however, spelled their names in their own languages. An Argentine who went into a Belgian utility would find most of the officials, and often the lesser employes, Belgian. The same thing was true in perhaps even greater measure in British-owned railroads.

Foreign owners sometimes said they needed their own nationals in positions of trust. Occasionally they would privately explain they felt Argentines were "lazy" or "indifferent." Although many an Argentine performed the work of a foreigner with the same efficiency, he received lower salary and rank. United States firms, more often than the British, gave their employees special living allowances enabling them to rent better houses, dress more smartly, and own a car or two which they could import more cheaply from home.

In many cases, dollar salaries were not large by the standards at home. However, translated into *pesos* and measured against the generally lower Argentine living costs, they gave the *Yanqui* a better house or apartment, more servants (who were generally overpaid by Argentine standards), and a much greater opportunity to enjoy life. Moreover, the relatively few years most North American officials spent in Argentina before moving on made Argentines feel that all of them were unstable, temporary visitors.

Often those young Argentines who were denied equality, or others who felt slighted in their dealings with foreign firms, became the most active members of Argentina's nationalist organizations, and launched the bitterest attacks against the United States and Great Britain.

"You only came here to get as much money as you can and then go home," many said. "You have no intention of making your career in Argentina."

The military government's nationalization program has, in recent years, changed this feeling. By law, foreign companies are now required to limit the number of their nationals to a small percentage of the total employed. Usually these are persons in key executive posts—accountants, operating vice presidents, etc. Formerly, many British, French, Dutch and other foreign employees acquired Argentine citizenship as an expedient to cover them until they eventually returned home. Now officials check with great care.

Rare is the man who gives up United States citizenship even though planning to stay in Argentina permanently. People of other nationalities, however, who first came on a brief assignment, have become Argentine citizens.

Foreign investors were attracted to Argentina in large measure for two reasons. First, the country offered great opportunities for development and growth. Second, until not long ago there were few restrictions or even binding regulations.

Before 1932, for example, no one in Argentina paid an income tax. The Argentine businessman with a successful company might earn from 30 to 50 per cent profit a year. Branch offices in Argentina could send home almost unlimited remittances.

Until 1935, foreign banks had a leading role in Argentine commercial operations. In that year the Banco Central de la Republica, in a move that foreshadowed many subsequent nationalist steps, took over all banking control functions from other governmental agencies. National and foreign banks were able to buy stock in the new agency. But it was non-negotiable without Central's consent and the influence of each stockholding bank was limited.

A group of young, previously untried Argentine financiers brilliantly built up operations during this time and helped speed development of local business and industry. When the military government took over in 1943, most of them were forced out. Some resigned directly; some just read about their "resignations" in the papers. The pace of financial nationalization was further stepped up in 1946. Today the Central Bank completely controls the entire banking system. All individual bank deposits are held for its accounts. It fixes loan policies, operates parts of the government's stake in the insurance business, runs the stock exchange and other major financial activities.

Yet despite this Argentinization, the average citizen probably has some money on deposit in a foreign bank. Thousands of Argentines in Buenos Aires and in other cities where it has branches deal with the First National Bank of Boston, largest United States branch bank in the Argentine. Thousands of others keep accounts in the National City Bank of New York, the London Bank, the Royal Bank of Canada, and with French, Italian, Spanish, Dutch, and even Syrian banks. In the United States many foreign banks also have branches or representatives, but they usually stick close to Wall Street, and do little business with the average American. Though foreign banks in Argentina have lost much of their prestige, Argentines still do business with them on a day-to-day basis, and find that their way of operation has influenced —and continues to influence—their daily life and outlook.

The situation was similar with Argentina's railroads, until their recent nationalization. The British owned and operated at least three-fourths of the country's railroad mileage. The French owned one road. The rest, chiefly in areas where private foreign companies did not care to invest, were Argentine.

The British, in effect, divided the territory between southern, western, and northern lines. The railroads dominated transport and the owners developed political

influence to retain their hold. Most Argentines believe
that railroad representatives helped put through the
Mitre law which gave them the right to import goods for
their own needs duty free. It provided liberal tax exemp-
tions and permitted the roads to pay only 3 per cent of
their net annual receipts. Net annual profits were officially
limited to 6.8 per cent of the invested amounts averaged
on a three-year basis.

Everything was done to keep official earnings within
the legal limit. The railroads set up their own British subsidiary construction companies whose charges siphoned
off the profits. Sometimes they paid with special bonds
whose high interest and amortization had to be met before profits could be acknowledged. Or they issued vast
blocs of stock against established values.

Moreover, though the railroads always denied it, if
they took the trouble to answer at all, many Argentines
gradually came to feel that rail executives did everything
possible to hamper construction of highways because
they did not want competition from trucks and trailers.
Over the railroads' opposition a special gasoline tax for
road building was passed in 1932. Argentina's roads are
still poor for a country so advanced in other ways.

Argentines gradually learned these facts, although
they were little publicized. During World War II Argentines urged nationalization, which was finally achieved
under President Perón.

At the beginning of the war, British investments in
Argentina totalled about two billion dollars. Much of this
was held by independent firms whose London home
offices often existed primarily to handle stocks listed on
the London Exchange. Stocks and bonds in firms operat-

ing in Argentina were bought and sold by Britons and others who knew little of the country except what they read in an occasional dispatch, an annual report, or perhaps such financial publications as the *Review of the River Plate*. In the early forties the British had to liquidate many of their foreign holdings to pay for arms and to purchase goods in other world markets, and their investments began dropping drastically.

When the Argentine government decided to expropriate the railroads, local managers and home offices protested. Just what a fair price for the properties would be of course depended on one's viewpoint. The British complained that investors many of whom were poor widows and orphans who had invested in the shares were being defrauded by expropriation prices which they hardly considered equal to the true value of the property. A barter was finally made for meat, wheat, and other cereals which seemed reasonably fair to both sides.

President Perón in February, 1952, told how many of the deals for foreign investments had been completed: "When we purchased the railroads, they asked eight billion *pesos* ($568 million at the then-current rate of exchange). We didn't pay that amount, and we didn't pay with money—we paid with wheat. We issued currency in an amount corresponding to the wheat we purchased from the farmers at twenty *pesos*, and they were satisfied because they used to get six. We sold to the British at sixty."

He said the deal also gave Argentina 23,000 properties that were not railroad facilities. He added that these had been sold by the government producing enough to pay back the original issue of currency. "In this way the railroads did not cost us a single penny," he declared. "We purchased telephone networks and gas utilities in the same manner."

Today the railroads are obviously not as well run as before. During the war and the long period of purchase negotiations, no new trains, locomotives, or other equipment were put in and both rails and rolling stock wore out. The Perón regime has not reinvested its money in new equipment. Trains are often brightly repainted to make them look slick and streamlined but this does not fool anyone very long—especially if one rides them.

The trolley systems, also purchased from the British, were in the same condition. Some new Mack trolley busses have appeared in Buenos Aires. But the town's ancient tram cars are still jammed beyond belief during rush hours. Scores of men hang on to the rear platforms, held, *porteños* say, only by hope and charity.

To the surprise of many visitors to Argentina, the nation's most vital industry, the big meat-packing plants, was also long dominated by Britons and North Americans. It often suited the interest of the *estancia* owners to go along with this arrangement. For one thing, they were not interested in the physically dirty business of slaughtering their steers, dividing them up into the appropriate parts, and then carrying on the highly diverse job of overseas shipping and distribution. Also, the big packing plants worked closely with influential families.

Most of the large packers were United States concerns, Swift, Wilson, and Armour among others. They were operated profitably for many years by very high-grade executives from the United States. However, they became victims of an economic squeeze play that was almost of deadly proportions. They were told the price to pay for cattle; they were allowed no control over their labor either as regards wages, hours, or the number of employees to be retained on their payrolls. In addition they were told at what price to sell their finished product. The consequence was that profits disappeared and deficits resulted. After months of negotiation, while I was ambassador, the government finally agreed to take up the losses and pay them 6 per cent on their capital investment. This was, of course, unsound as a permanent solution but was helpful as a temporary expedient.

The Argentines have very little experience with investments in corporate securities. They have a somewhat distorted idea of capitalism, especially the foreign variety. To most of them, a capitalist was often a well-fed foreigner unable to speak Spanish who had designs on Argentine land, cattle, or possessions. Capital was rarely visualized as a tool for production. "Capitalist" was hardly ever used in an approving sense. Perón's own dim view of capitalism and the anti-capitalist notions stressed by his party reflect this.

Because foreigner investors often sought to get their investments out quickly and were unwilling to stay for a long-term pull, many Argentines who did go into capitalistic operations decided in true Argentine fashion to go him one or two better. Profits were rarely limited by any concept of public responsibility. No anti-trust laws prevented competition-killing price agreements. Profits, as noted, ran as high as 50 per cent—and even if paid in full the taxes were small.

When the military government came into power, it quickly put the nationalization effort into high gear. The railways were among the first to become 100 per cent Argentine. A national Merchant Marine, established by President Castillo in 1940, was expanded. One British-Argentine newspaper ran slighting editorials about "the gaucho at the wheel," but Argentines made their original hodge-podge of ships into a thriving operation.

In May, 1949, the Argentine State Line, with great cheering from the press, formally acquired the vast Dodero transportation empire which held virtual monopoly of Rio de la Plata shipping, sent liners and freighters all over the world, and owned several airlines. In 1951 it became Latin America's new tonnage leader. Argentines boasted theirs were the only Latin-American passenger liners with regular services. Three new 116-passenger ships maintained a regular schedule between New York and Buenos Aires in direct competition with long-established United States lines and drew record crowds of well-wishers every time they arrived and left port.

After Perón bought Argentina's telephone system from the Americans, one of his first steps was to cut rates, low as they were. The idea was apparently to prove that the United States, via International Telephone & Telegraph, had been overcharging. The nationalists, of course, applauded—overlooking the fact that the quality of service soon began deteriorating despite the fact that the I.T.&T. retained a long-term management consultant and supplier contract. Before long rates began to climb too. To Argentines the most shocking thing was that drugstores, tobacconists, and other shops in Argentina which had offered customers free telephones for as long as anyone could remember had to put in pay telephones.

This time, however, Argentines were reminded that it

applauded the idea—or at least did not violently disapprove. The government bought machinery and equipment abroad with the huge foreign exchange supply built up during the war. Sometimes it purchased things that were not needed. Graft in some cases was beyond belief, yet Argentina bought nevertheless. By taking possession of important industries formerly under foreign membership, Argentina significantly reduced her service payments abroad. How much she lost on current operations at home no one has as yet indicated.

The government also took a special interest either as an outright owner or as a partner in important new sectors of industry. The preferred legal method—and there are still many methods highly doubtful, if not downright illegal by our standards—is the semi-official or mixed company. In such set-ups the government invites itself to join private capital "in the ownership and management of such public utilities, transportation companies, industrial and commercial ventures, as it feels essential."

Many an Argentine worker will cite figures to prove that Argentina's industrialization has proceeded at a faster pace than industrialization in the United States during recent years. He will point with pride to his country's foodstuffs, her wondrous wines, her cigarettes and tobacco, her cement, soap, glassware, and clothing.

Not unnaturally, he will gloss over the fact that Argentina lacks coal, iron, sufficient petroleum; and that it has little cheap electric power or the fast-flowing rivers from which it could be developed. Instead, reflecting what's fed to him daily by the controlled press, he will insist that despite the lack of large-scale mills, Argentina is now reportedly producing one-third her steel requirements, some 60 per cent of her ceramics, and 10 per cent of her machinery. "More and more," he will say, "we are becoming a buyer of capital goods, not a market for consumer goods. We ourselves are exporting to other Latin-American countries."

Even before the war, Argentine industry had begun rapid expansion. As hostilities drew near, several large international firms withdrew funds from Europe and invested them in Argentine cotton ginning, vegetable oil production, dairy produce, and textile mills. Some got great reserves of materials, machinery, equipment, and tools into the country which they turned to production, and of course tremendous profits. Others began making a wide range of drug items, first-class furniture, and perhaps best known to North Americans, the famed Argentine alligator bags and leather goods.

Many Argentine industrialists traded with both the Axis and Allies long after Pearl Harbor. Some stopped after the United States and Britain issued almost identical black lists of several thousand Axis or pro-Axis firms, since Argentines trading with black-listed companies or individuals, directly or indirectly, were denied any United States or Allied goods or services.

Perhaps one of the greatest industrial growths was in construction and the pipes and radiators, stoves and bathroom fixtures, fittings and the boilers necessary for the multitude of apartment houses, factories, office buildings, homes and other structures throughout the country.

Among those who expanded most were Bunge and Born. Its founders, E. A. Bunge and J. Born, were Belgian-Jewish financiers of world-wide connections. Leading figures in the firm in this generation were Alfredo Hirsch, a Jew, and Jorge Oster, a Catholic. The Bunges in the group, as well as members of the Hirsch family, both married into Argentina's aristocracy. Though the Jewish surname caused the latter to be singled out by anti-Semites, they had become Catholics. Bunge and Born controlled more than fifty companies, including flour mills, *estancias*, quebracho concessions, chemical and industrial firms, and loan associations. At one time they exported 30 per cent of all cereals in Argentina and were middle men for so many other products that they had most of the foreign exchange available. It was from them that the government bought its pounds and dollars rather than from banks.

The Bemberg industrial-financial empire was the largest family fortune in Argentina. It was headed in the third generation by Otto and Federico, two gentlemen of high ability and character. They produced most of the beer in Argentina, including Quilmes and Palermo and also had interests in Rheingold Beer in the United States. Stock of their Quilmes Company was listed on the Paris Bourse and actively traded in. They owned malt companies, industrial credits, factories, *estancias*, cotton companies, winter resorts, mortgages and banks.

Their fortune was so vast and their ability in business and astuteness so well recognized that jealousies were created among both government officials and business people of lesser caliber.

When Otto Sebastian Bemberg, father of Otto and Federico, died in Paris in 1934, and the Bembergs declared and paid inheritance taxes in France, of which country the elder Bemberg was a citizen, political rumblings were inevitable. A story current in Buenos Aires is that the military regime might have ignored this fact— save for one incident. When Señora de Perón was in Paris one of her aides suggested to Otto's widow that it would be a gracious gesture to invite Evita to tea or perhaps to dinner, since after all she was the First Lady of Argentina.

She refused. The story goes that Evita de Perón then called the President on the long-distance phone and urged him to move full speed ahead in levying a higher settlement than that contemplated against the Bembergs. Later in Buenos Aires the wits pointed out that failure to give this tea party was probably one of the most expensive acts on record—costing about twenty million dollars.

As the government moved to industrialize Argentina, its policy became one of state socialism, though it never admits such a term. Private capital is neither sufficient nor interested enough to carry out the vast projects Argentina wants and possibly needs. What President Perón has done in some ways goes far beyond what the British Labor Party tried during its term of power.

Strange to North Americans—yet in a way inevitable in the Latin pattern—those Argentines who believe the government must finance industrialization are often themselves very conservative. Yet, they do not realize the kind of labyrinth created when every state-dominated economy is actually a will-o'-the-wisp. At first it seems an easy way of eliminating all the risks, worries, and iniquities of free enterprise. Every nation that has tried such short cuts has found that government is no substitute for private initiative. The regime in power is forced on and on by its momentum to more rigorous authoritarian rule.

Over and over it is proven that there is no man or group of men wise enough to oversee all the details of the national economy. The problems that arise are countless and all seem to interlock. An attempted solution, more often than not, raises more serious problems.

When Perón became President, gold and hard-currency reserves had risen to 6,032,000,000 *pesos*, while monetary inflation had begun. The *peso* was still converted at four to the dollar and reserves were 175 per cent of currency, 41 per cent of all Argentine money outstanding. If prices had risen, so had wages.

By April 30, 1952, net gold and exchange reserves had fallen to 1,354,000,000 *pesos*. Currency in circulation had risen to 17,260,000,000, money in public hands to 45,038,-000,000 *pesos*. This tremendous loss in reserves coupled with the increase in the supply of *pesos* left far too little in reserve to back all the *pesos* then in existence. And after successive devaluations ("readjustments" in the multiple-exchange rates) in 1949 and 1950, those *pesos* were worth no more than 20 cents at official exchange, 4 cents on the black market, 7 cents on the average. The national debt, 7.1 billion *pesos* at the end of 1943, had risen to over 34 billions.

In the first four months of 1952 the government pumped 1,330,000,000 new *pesos* into the top-heavy financial structure, and made available an additional 1,-845,000,000 *pesos* in new bank credits; the total of loans stood at 44,158,000,000 *pesos*, a staggering 163 per cent of deposits.

For all the cash and credit, businesses and businessmen

were strapped. Stock quotations normally keep pace with inflation, but on the Buenos Aires stock market a list of ten blue chip issues worth an average of 220 *pesos* a share at the start of 1952 sold on May 22 for 157, more than a 25 per cent loss in 22 weeks.

The most solid firms were offering promissory notes in payment of current bills, and one for 420,000 *pesos* from a conservative metal-working establishment was discounted at 8 per cent a month. The few individuals with cash available for private loans were collecting up to 15 per cent, a level at which the fee is no longer interest but participation.

Commercial failures in May, 1952, totaled 250,488,503 *pesos*, nearly double in one month the total figure for 1951, when the year's total was 127,000,000. At that, they were being held down by executive order: that same month a bankrupt cement block firm, Fortalit, began firing workers preparatory to going out of business, but was ordered by the Ministry of Economy to revoke dismissals and resume production within ten days, lose money or not. This was one of several examples which made observers believe the government was motivated primarily by fear of mass unemployment.

Chapter XX

The Argentine and His Government

THEY TELL a story in Buenos Aires about a new Ambassador who, on the day after his arrival, paid a series of courtesy calls on the President and other high-ranking Cabinet and Congressional officials. Returning to his residence, he telephoned his downtown office.

Believing his line was tapped, he talked deliberately with glowing comments on the brilliance, personality, and intelligence of each man that he met. Within a week, the smiles and the warmth of the greetings he received from various officials made his future activities smooth and effortless. Only then did he send back a frank, honest, untapped report.

An Ambassador wanting to carry out his assignment in Argentina has to make a point of saying, over the outside telephone, only what he would be willing to have printed on the front pages of the afternoon papers. He also has to make sure that no confidential matter is ever discussed where it could possibly be overheard.

Many Argentines consider the Perón government's interference in their private lives annoying and stifling, but it is unique only in degree. Even observers who compare the Perón regime with that of Rosas would hesitate to describe the intervening governments as flaming democracies. In Argentina, the government has always run the citizen more than the citizen has run the government. The average Argentine has always been in more intimate daily contact with his rulers than we have, even with all our new agencies, rules, and regulations.

Historically-minded Argentines will tell you that they, like most of their Latin neighbors, have suffered from *caudillismo*—bossism—the tendency to follow a strong leader rather than a set of principles. Despite Argentina's experiments with democracy, its predominately literate, stable population, and its sound economy, it has never completely gotten away from the *caudillo* tradition. This was brought from Spain by the *conquistadores* and it flourished on the *pampa*. The *gaucho caudillo* fought Indians, local rivals, and finally national leaders. As Argentina advanced economically and politically, the Argentines lost some of their zest for fighting—prosperity always tends to build a more conservative, less venturesome people. But the *caudillo* idea lost little of its hold.

European immigrants easily transplanted their old Mediterranean political tradition of personalism to the *pampa*. The Argentines made few attempts to interest the newcomers in local affairs, and often the immigrant did not care who ruled, so long as the government was reasonably efficient and maintained order.

All Argentines were brought up by Church and family to respect the rule of leadership from above. They never really developed a sense of participation in and responsibility for self-government. They did discuss and argue politics fiercely and still do today. Argentines have always talked more than they have acted—a characteristic common to many people.

The President of Argentina has vast authority. He not only proposes laws to Congress and has power to veto legislation: he can issue decrees that have the effect of law. He makes the policies that govern the nation, and can put them into effect without consulting Congress.

The President's control of national finances extends far beyond our concept of executive authority. Not only may he submit budget estimates to Congress but he may spend money that Congress has not appropriated, and for purposes that it has not been specifically authorized. He may appoint and remove almost all of his administration without consulting Congress. And he may expel from the country any aliens convicted of a crime by a foreign court, or whose presence compromises the public security or perturbs the public order.

By declaring a state of siege, a Latin American President may toss out all constitutional guarantees and make himself an absolute dictator. Both old and new Argentine constitutions provide that the President may declare, with the consent of the Senate, one or several districts of the nation in a state of siege for a limited time in case of foreign attack. In case of internal disturbance, he has the power only when Congress is in recess. The Constitution of 1949, which increased the powers of the President, provides that he may also declare a state of precaution or alarm in case "of a disturbance of public order which threatens to disrupt normal developments in the life or essential activities of the population."

Alexander W. Weddell, a former United States Ambassador to Argentina, once pointed out that the Anglo-Saxon mind is essentially legislative while the Latin is essentially executive. Argentina, he explained, inherited from Spain traditions of a vigorous executive, accustomed to act without consulting any other authority and overriding the legislature whenever it conflicted with his desires. The idea of an executive subordinate to the legislator was completely foreign to Spanish ideas. All during Argentine history, executive supremacy has been the rule.

Many Latin American constitutions read much like ours, but the citizens take a different view of them. Instead of recognizing the constitution as a fundamental, superior law, Latin Americans regard it as an ideal toward which they are striving. Many Argentines admit their legislation, constitutional and otherwise, was never expected to work as it reads. Give a group of Argentines a chance to draw up a law, and they will do it extremely well. But asking them to make it practical is something else again. "Practicality, practicality, that is all you *Yanquis* think about," they will probably tell you.

Some Argentines feel this is due to their inability to take positive action in order to move ahead rapidly to accomplish a task. Others confess that so many Argentines are accustomed to thinking selfishly of their own needs and desires that they are unable to cooperate, despite their high-sounding principles.

The founding fathers of most Latin American countries

tried to avoid *continuismo* by providing that the President could not be re-elected immediately. Argentina's Constitution of 1853 set the executive's term at six years, with no re-election for another six-year period. That constitution had only been amended a few times before Perón became President: he decided it needed to be modernized. In 1949 a Perón-dominated Constitutional Assembly met in the blazing summer heat and voted to abandon the traditional prohibition on immediate re-election of the President. This cleared the way for Perón's second election. When North Americans pointed out that Perón was the first Argentine President to succeed himself, Argentines protested: "If Franklin D. Roosevelt could be elected for four terms, why should you complain about Perón being President for two?"

The assemblymen made only one change in the brief preamble to the Constitution, the 150 words or so every Argentine school boy and girl learned to recite in the past one hundred years. The brief addition epitomized Perón's philosophy: The nation is "constituted socially just, economically free, and politically sovereign." But within the body of the document were more important changes, expanding the powers of government and President, and embodying major points affecting every citizen. The State is empowered to take a far more active role in every phase of activity concerning every phase of the Argentine's daily life—political, economic, social.

Workers, says the Constitution, have the right to work for a fair reward, to acquire skill, to worthy working conditions, to the preservation of health, to their well-being, to social security, to protection of their families, to economic improvement and to the defense of their occupational interests. Nothing is said about their right to strike.

Old people are, according to the new Constitution, given the right to assistance, lodging, sustenance, clothing, care of physical and moral health, recreation, work, tranquility, and respect. The State is pledged to support marriage and family property and to aid mothers. Children are to have the "special and privileged consideration of the State." Primary and advanced schooling are to be provided. The universities must set up obligatory courses for students' political formation "so that each pupil may know the essence of what is Argentine; the spiritual, economic, social and political reality of his country, the evolution and historical mission of the Argentine Republic and so that he may acquire a consciousness of the responsibility he should assume in the undertaking of achieving and consolidating the aims recognized and established in this Constitution."

Businessmen found the Constitution gave the State control of all foreign trade. It also ruled minerals, waterfalls, petroleum fields, coal fields, gas deposits, and other sources of energy—with the exception of vegetable resources—were the "imprescriptible and inalienable property of the Nation." Public services in private possession should be transferred to the State by purchase or expropriation with prior indemnity.

The Argentines found that their new Constitution enabled Congress to draw up a budget to cover as many as three years and gave the President authority to coin money and regulate its value. It allowed the President to veto part of a bill submitted to him by Congress rather than having to accept or reject the whole measure. The power of Congress was restricted by a provision that only the President can determine subjects to be discussed by special sessions.

The new Constitution also made the judiciary branch of the government more or less subservient to the executive. In 1946 Perón had declared war on the Supreme Court, which had ruled many of his decrees unconstitutional. The Argentines revered their Supreme Court as highly as we and most were furious when peronista senators impeached four distinguished justices and the Attorney General. Perón then staffed the high court with his supporters who had direct supervision over judges of lesser federal courts, telling our newsmen: "Well, did not your Franklin D. Roosevelt try to pack the Supreme Court when it did not do what he wanted?"

Some idea of where President Perón is heading became clear in December, 1951. Without inviting or even informing opposition parties, his government staged a Constituent Assembly in the remote Chaco Territory along the Paraguayan border, 450 miles northwest of Buenos Aires. Acting quickly, the territory was made Argentina's fifteenth province and named Presidente Perón Province.

The Constitution of the new province opens with the words "This is a worker state." It establishes favored trade unionists, that is, members of Perón's General Confederation of Labor as a new aristocracy of the land. They will enjoy a heavily weighted vote in elections. Of the provincial Chamber's 30 deputies, 15 will be chosen by the province's estimated 200,000 ordinary voters; 15 by its estimated 30,000 union members. There will be two types of polling booths—one for the public, including independent union members, the other for CGT members only.

The new Constitution also provides that only members of selected "professional organizations," that is, Confederation unions, may serve on the province's juries.

The angry Radical and Social parties said they would boycott future elections. They also pointed out that the trade union's double voting privilege violates all the national Constitution's provisions that all inhabitants of the State are equal before the law. But there is little they can do about it.

Most Argentines are passionately addicted to legalism, partly because so many professors, legislators, and other prominent men were trained as lawyers and keep a legalistic viewpoint all their lives. Although the President never went to law school, he shares this feeling. He has sometimes gone to extremes to accomplish his ends in a legal way. As a result, his regime has been marked by relatively little violence.

Perón maintains the forms of democratic republicanism. He gets Congress to authorize what he wants to do—like expropriate *La Prensa*. Congress is his rubber stamp in which the opposition is repeatedly brushed aside. There has been no move to abolish the opposition's seats in the Senate and Chamber of Deputies completely. Yet the opposition's arguments simply do not appear in the press except in rare instances. But to throw them out completely would not be in keeping with Argentine character.

The President reportedly feels that since he took all the proper legal steps to remake the Constitution he now can do anything he wishes under it. Argentines appreciate this official correctness, for most Argentines would no more think of skirting it than they would dream of going out with mussed hair or an ill-pressed suit.

On the other hand, their emphasis on legal correctness does not mean that most Argentines want strictly to obey the law.

Argentines, says writer Ernesto Sabato, "never take a law or an ordinance at its face value—they interpret it. Every Argentine is an expert in the theory of the law. But the truth of the matter is that he never limits himself to interpreting the law. He interprets it in his favor, that is to say, he violates it. He adduces this or that reason, but the real one is because (as the old Spanish saying goes) 'It is his royal pleasure' a concept which makes every subject the king's equal."

Sabato points out that Buenos Aires has the worst traffic conditions of any Latin city because the pedestrian invariably does his royal pleasure. Every mayor of Buenos Aires who has attempted to regulate traffic has come the most ignominious cropper. One decided to proceed slowly, a street at a time, part of a street, one corner. He stationed four policemen at this corner to supervise the observance of the traffic ordinance. It was such an entertaining sight that the *porteños* gathered by the hundreds as though it were a sideshow. The result was that the intersection turned into the worst traffic snarl in the city. This had to be returned to normal with the pedestrian as fractious as before, crossing the streets whenever and however he pleases.

The most sought-after privilege an Argentine can acquire is some form of *fuero*, the old Spanish privilege which exempted its holder from compliance with regulations. Argentines do not think it is peculiar that the first *derecho,* or right, granted to all lawmakers from Congressmen down to City Councilmen is the legal right to break laws. Often when an Argentine community secured control of an expropriated electrical plant or waterworks, all officials immediately put themselves on the free list. "Why not?" many will ask you. "Don't we deserve it? Besides, we who have the privilege know how to use it."

President Perón often proclaims that there are no more specially privileged Argentines, but many say that today the number is far greater than ever. After the government bought the railroads from Britain in 1948, one of its biggest headaches was collecting fares from passengers. Ardent peronistas would declare: "But the railroads are ours now!" Most people seldom bothered to buy tickets before boarding a train—there was always the chance your stop would come before the conductor appeared, or perhaps you could tip him to let you ride free. To stop this the government slapped a flat twenty-*peso* fine on all passengers who did not buy their tickets in the station. Some Argentines were so angry at this attempt to make them pay that they tossed a conductor off the train. Another protesting passenger pulled a gun. Crowds gathered at the stations to shout "Death to the fine!" Eventually the incidents decreased, but riding without a ticket was still the thing to do, since it was only the government that was not collecting.

Argentines say the *fuero* is so deeply a part of Argentine thinking it tends to create general disrespect for laws and law enforcement. Stemming directly from Spain and Italy, this tradition has been part of Argentine life so long no one can remember when it did not exist. Rarely, however, is it publicized in Argentina. Even the mention here will undoubtedly draw protests from Argentines who insist "But why talk about such things?" or "But it's so much worse in other Latin countries, why pick on us?"

Depending on his political viewpoint, the average Argentine blames most of this corruption on the opposition. Even if the party he supports is "in," somehow he will hold its enemies responsible for any governmental graft. For example, most of those who opposed Perón felt that the greatest corruption of recent times occurred during the years Miguel Miranda headed the Argentine Institute for the Promotion of Exchange (I.A.P.I.). Peronistas charge that long before this the Banco de la Nación followed a policy of lending money to *politicos* with influence, a "courtesy" often repaid with needed legislation or ministerial action. The German banks were also extremely liberal in extending credits, especially to Argentine Army officers whose favor they sought.

Some Argentines feel that when well-to-do *estancieros* and businessmen served in government there was less graft and corruption. Yet others say that in a number of cases where top-ranking Argentines acted as lawyers for foreign concerns and later became cabinet ministers or Congressmen, they helped put through laws which gave their former clients what they wanted on a silver platter. Not until long afterwards was any hue and cry raised, and even then there were few indictments or convictions.

On a lesser level, Argentine businessmen who require an import or export permit, a construction license, or anything at all from the government, always expect they will have to grease someone's palm. The amount of necessary greasing depends on the warmth of one's relationship with the proper authority, and on the value of the favor.

This again is significant—for personal friendship can mean as much as money. Often as not the favor, or *gauchado*, is extended above or behind the law on political differences in return for what might be an expected favor at a later date.

Many large Argentine business firms keep a full-time employee or two whose job it is simply to maintain good relations with those in power. The company head himself generally considers it his task to watch the top level. The second, third, fourth, and fifth layers of bureaucrats are just as important, however. They can see that licenses and other papers are not buried or lost for months or even years.

The custom was followed even in foreign embassies which had what might be called an "expediter" familiar with the back doors of customs, immigration, and other key departments. He could achieve in a day what might otherwise take an infinitude of time, red tape, and protocol.

Private citizens needing such useful papers as the permanent identification *cedula* which all Argentines are obliged to carry, or a police good-conduct certificate necessary for a passport or a visa, know how many things can go wrong if a proper aide cannot be obtained. Naturally Argentines who can not afford such help wait in line outside the doors of the official offices, day after day. The others get speedy action.

The low salaries paid public employees make this extensive operation of small grafts almost inevitable. Unable to live on what he earns, the civil servant keeps his palm out for gratuities. It is interesting that rarely is the issue of eliminating graft raised in Argentine political campaigns. Few political leaders have ever pledged clean-up drives. Apparently they feel graft is part of an established system bigger than any one man.

It is frequently said that nobody in Argentina keeps a completely honest set of books for the government tax collectors. "If such books were kept," one Argentine explained, "the collector probably would not believe them."

President Perón was once asked: "Why not decrease duties on imports and exports so as to encourage trade and instead broaden income taxes to include more people? The United States has long found this a far better method. It would seem so much better to tax profits than to put all sorts of restrictions on business and then try to get taxes out of losses."

"You do not understand the Argentines," he replied. "It would never work here. Our people are simply not temperamentally able to do this. If I were to try collecting such income taxes as you suggest, I would need as many tax collectors as taxpayers."

Chapter XXI

Politics and the Spoils System

THE SPOILS system is at the heart of Argentine and Latin-American public administration. But whereas our parties in power take some conciliatory steps to give important positions to the opposition, in the Argentine the group in power—long before Perón—was expected to take all the jobs—not just the big ones.

Fully as important as party service for the Argentine who wanted to climb the political ladder was the partisan aid rendered the boss just ahead, the district leader to his superior, he in turn to the next man a rung higher. It is true that in the past some outstanding men have been appointed to important ministries and ambassadorial posts because they were worthy citizens. But in general the spoils system has always applied a hundred per cent.

Moreover, while our politicians have used the spoils

of their own political victories to organize followers and build a tight, efficient political machine, before Perón there was little compact party organization in Argentina. Argentina's political parties have often changed structure and even names with great rapidity. They have rarely built up organizations able to maintain their vitality despite years of power.

Today most of President Perón's opponents are pretty sure they will never regain control at the polls. For one thing, the President controls all means of influencing voters. Opposition parties need permission even for a *churrasco*, barbecue—the equivalent of our clambake. They are forbidden to invite the people to wine festivals, where prospective voters used to soak up all the wine they could drink as they listened to candidates' golden promises of the future. Perón denies the press, radio, and most other means of publicity to his opponents.

And the President counts the ballots. In Argentina, as in many places where political parties seize and hold power for a long time, the controlling group usually wins. In the past, elections in Buenos Aires were fairly accurate, chiefly because everything could be watched by representatives of all parties. Outside the capital the party in power manipulated the election machinery so that the opposition got only a token vote.

In essence, those who oppose Perón feel their only hope lies in obtaining greater support from those groups who have the force to bring about a change. This means the Army, labor, and other organizations. Most people feel that only the Army could succeed by itself. Other groups would have to team up to force the regime out of power.

A peronista leader, on the other hand, expressed it this way: "If we voluntarily stepped down we could never again gain control except by another coup. Besides, we can hardly expect any forgiveness. Our fate would undoubtedly be imprisonment, exile, or worse. And that we are by no means willing to face."

As he took the oath of office for his unprecedented second term as President on June 4, Juan Domingo Perón epitomized the successful *caudillo*, 1952 style, an adroit and resourceful politician.

He uses the velvet glove rather than the iron hand. He employs roundabout methods to create a way of getting what he wants without appearing to move directly. A man of great personal magnetism, he can turn the charm on or off at will. He flatters the visitors he wants to impress with an attractive smile and makes them feel everything they say is tremendously important. Frequently he can take a completely different approach to each of half a dozen or so visitors—a practice which can, and does, often cause confusion.

His early-to-rise habits horrified more leisurely Argentines at first; now they are accustomed to his long hours in the Casa Rosada.

Like many other Latin politicians he is tremendously sensitive to criticism. He is frequently outraged by what he considers unfair personal criticism in the press, and especially in periodicals printed in North America, which his people erroneously tell him represent the views of the State Department.

President Perón admires many of the things we believe in, is indifferent to others, dislikes many more. He does not fear us. His anti-United States campaign is mostly for domestic consumption: he does not take it too literally and is, or was, friendly to us. Privately he may say that his actions are "just like some of your American politicians—Big Bill Thompson of Chicago, for instance, fighting the King of England in his election campaign." But he does stir up many Argentines to be anti-Yankee.

The President does not want direct loans from the United States. He has built himself up as Argentina's Economic Liberator, asserting his country's sovereignty and financial independence. Like any dictator, he must preserve face in his own country, and when we emphasize the fact that we have granted him a credit all good will evaporates and he becomes resentful.

President Perón is utterly convinced of the justice of his own cause, and in this he had tremendous encouragement from his wife. Blonde, diminutive, brown-eyed Evita had a highly vivacious nature which covered a cool and calculating personality. She, far more than the President, was driven by the desire to dominate those who once rejected her. In many cases she forced her husband to make shrewd decisions, to resolve problems over which he worried and hesitated. Through her efforts in the Labor Ministry, the General Confederation of Labor, the Peronista Women's Party, her social welfare foundation, the press, radio, and newsreels, she directly intervened in almost every phase of Argentine life except the Army, where her following among the enlisted men and non-commissioned officers was not thought well of in higher military circles.

Her self-portrait, *La Razon de Mi Vida*, turned out to be more a paean to her husband than an autobiography. Expressing her mystic fanaticism and lack of proper perspective, she declared she truly felt she was the mother of her people.

One of her last statements promised: "Living or dead I will lead the women and the workers in defense of President Perón, leaving no brick standing that is not a peronista brick." As political and labor leaders vied in proposing new honors for her after her death, members of the Peronista Party were ordered to wear black ties to party functions for the rest of their lives.

Evita was always the center of attention in Argentina. The bitterness and adoration she aroused made her career so dazzling as to have been matched by few women in history. She was so set on achieving her ambitions that she could not compromise. Frequently she told friends: "Without fanaticism one cannot accomplish anything." And always she sought the center of attention, for, as much as anything else, she was dominated by a desire to make clear to those who at first ignored her that she was not merely their equal but their superior.

In fact, in conversations with members of Argentina's top economic group the point was frequently made that if, instead of snubbing her, they had somehow won her over to their side the whole course of Argentine history might have changed.

Evita's desire to assert herself was matched by seemingly boundless energy. Her ambition was like a motor without a governor, reaching incredible speed before racking itself to bits. It forced her to follow the rigorous diet that undermined her health. She wanted to have one of the loveliest figures in the world and to be the world's most expensively dressed woman. Constantly and astutely she told her *descamisados*, or shirtless followers, that she wore her elaborate wardrobe only in trust for them . . . and that someday they would have similar luxuries.

The diet begun several years before her death gave her the svelte, glamorous figure that a crew of personal photographers snapped in literally thousands of costumes. But her diet sapped her youth and energy, weakened her already overworked body, and paved the way for the ravages first of pernicious anemia and later of cancer.

As a final resting place she wanted a memorial not unlike the Taj Mahal where her body would be permanently preserved and sanctified for future generations.

"Long after I am physically gone," she reportedly told friends, "I will, through this monument, continue as a dominant force in Argentina." The monument, as she conceived it, would keep her spirit alive for the Argentine people to whom she publicly described her "exalted body as a bridge over which the masses can carry their troubles to Perón."

The desire for self-perpetuation was always strong in her life. Her name was carved on so many buildings and was associated with so many organizations that a mere listing would fill a page. These included the Argentine benevolent organization which spends millions, homes for the aged and working girls, schools, streets and plazas, super-highways and bridges, the country's largest steamship, gas works, Buenos Aires' subway stations and even a newly discovered planet.

Her memorial tomb as Evita conceived it before her death was to depict all these. And here, according to her plans, were to come peronistas as to the shrine of a favorite saint. On the sixth anniversary of President Perón's return to power, her husband decorated her for services and proclaimed the following day a national *fiesta* "in honor of Saint Evita." After her death, moves were made to give this beatification churchly authority. At the time of the anniversary Evita, in a choked, emotional speech, significantly called the title given her by her husband her greatest honor, adding: "I have left my bed to pay a debt of gratitude to Perón and to the workers. I do not care if I have to part with pieces of my life to pay for it."

The speech had an unexpected sincerity, for long before she reached the height of her power, Evita's vanity had a special obsession with immortality and permanent greatness. The clouded circumstances of her birth, crushing poverty, youthful lack of culture and education and the insults and humiliations suffered on the way up, gave her a drive she was determined would not be stopped even by death.

When Evita met Perón he was a brilliant young officer whose wife had died in 1939 just before he had returned from trips to Italy and Germany. They became friends, and Evita used her knowledge of the theater to aid Perón in his personal rise to military leadership. One example is typical. An earthquake had killed thousands in the remote province of San Juan. Perón, who then headed the Welfare Ministry, wanted some way of dramatizing the need for aid.

Evita suggested that he walk down Calle Florida, a bevy of beautiful actresses on each arm, theatrically "begging for the poor victims." Newspapers and newsreels, advised in advance, carried Perón's name to millions. And while other officers made purely technical speeches, Evita gave Perón's talks on the radio all the rabble-rousing appeal she had learned in years of broadcasting. When, in October, 1945, he was temporarily toppled from power, Evita arranged to have him spirited from his hospital room to address a howling workers' mass meeting that swept him back into control.

A few months later, just before Perón ran for Argentina's Presidency, they married. Perón walked away with the election. Evita, sure Argentina's cattle barons who had so often rebuffed her ambitions would have to accept her as First Lady, entered what was perhaps her happiest period. She ordered herself a trousseau comprising furs, jewelry, and costly evening gowns. Buenos Aires' finest shops would be ordered to send over everything she fancied. When some had the "impertinence" to send bills she told them: "Are you not honored enough that I wear your things?"

But the parties at the big mansions did not materialize. Those of wealth and position gave a unanimous cold shoulder. Her only social invitations were official. Often even Perón's militarists were unable to make their wives and daughters take the hand of the wife of the President. To Evita, womanlike, this was the worst snub of all. She determined to show everybody—on her own terms. Again, eternally feminine, she was convinced the snubs had been due to two causes. One, her clothes and figure. Two, the fact that her family was unknown and lacking in traditional name or titles. She determined to show them quickly, as was her wont.

As with everything else she had ever done, Evita plunged ahead. She was an attractive woman with a lovely profile and perfect teeth, but she had inherited a tendency to take on fat rapidly. This tendency probably came from her mother, Juana Ibarguran, a plump, jolly woman and mother of five. So Evita began dieting, no easy or usual task in a country such as Argentina. Ruthlessly she eliminated the fancy teas, the lush luncheons and the heavy late dinners standard among so many Argentines. Often she skipped meals, and she had herself repeatedly massaged. She completely eliminated drinking and smoking, in contrast to the President who is a chain smoker. In less time than seemed possible she trimmed a third off her former weight. To further emphasize slimness, all of her outfits were made almost skintight.

Then she left for Europe. Her aim there was to impress doubters at home by the reception she got abroad. Secondly, she expected to be made a papal marquise in Rome, a title which would force Argentine society to accept her.

Her sixty-four costumes, two personal maids, her Czarina's collection of jewels dazzled Europeans. So did her figure. But her clothes struck them as tricky and in poor taste. One, a black, clinging costume which she donned to be received by His Holiness the Pope, may have cost her the papal honor she desired. Arriving twenty minutes late for her audience, she was given a routine half-hour interview and no honors at all.

Bitter, disappointed, but too good an actress ever to show it, Evita partially relieved her anger in typically womanly fashion. She changed her hair color to pale blond and had it upswept continental-style. Then she threw out rooms full of her inelegant, multi-hued clothes, bought $40,000 worth of new clothes from Paris' Dior,

Fath, Balmain, and Marcel Rochas. As if to augment her dignity, she even dropped the name Evita and insisted on the formal Señora Maria Eva Duarte de Perón.

Next, she arranged to give herself a monster welcoming celebration in Buenos Aires. Immediately thereafter she plunged into a frenzy of activities which for almost three years left Argentines, and the rest of the world, dazzled. All the time she was burning herself up under the same rigorous diet.

Originally the President had given her a desk in the Ministry of Labor and Social Welfare, a key agency which made labor support his principal power prop. Primarily he sought to keep his wife occupied by taking her mind off her lack of women friends and social activity. Evita, however, wanted other activities. Her ambition was boundless.

She took over Perón's propaganda, labor relations, and scores of other activities. She rose at 7:00 A.M., and began holding daily sessions with hundreds of "deserving poor." One incident is typical. A group of representatives of a suburban utility company was meeting in the Ministry with labor representatives seeking an increase in wages. As was her custom, she suddenly swept into the room and asked: "What are you boys and girls discussing?" The utility people explained the request for the pay increase and said that if they granted it they would be bankrupt within a month or two.

"Give the boys and girls what they want, I'll arrange things," she said. The firm agreed to the increases. Evita did not keep her promise, and so a week later the firm sent its representatives to call and remind her of what she had said.

"How much will it cost you a month?" she asked. They cited the amount.

"I will give you an order on the Central Bank—they will pay you the difference every month," Evita said. Later an official of the Central Bank was asked how the bookkeeping procedures were handled on such an operation. Shrugging his shoulders he smiled and said: "Well, we have many ways of doing things, and we do not believe too much in accounting anyway."

Señora Perón not only granted financial help but she dispensed medical advice to many of those who came to ask for aid. Frequently she would order three grams of aureomycin or two of streptomycin.

Her own health continued to decline. In January, 1950, her illness was first publicly revealed. Dr. Oscar Ivanissevich, Argentine Minister of Education and a well-regarded surgeon, operated for what was described as appendicitis. Though announcements reported no complications, she never completely recovered. For this and other reasons, Dr. Ivanissevich lost favor and secretly Evita began receiving treatment for her growing illness from another physician, Dr. Helen Zawarski of Buenos Aires' National Central Hospital.

Though warned that the red corpuscles in her blood were only a third of normal, she kept driving herself harder. She had one more goal—to secure voting rights for Argentine women and have Perón re-elected President and herself the country's first woman Vice-President.

Here, at last, would be official recognition, the thing she had always been denied. Again, with dramatic showmanship, the stage was ready. There would be a monster demonstration with two million fanatical supporters demanding that she accept. Society would be shown. So would the Army—the group which makes and unmakes presidents and which had been increasingly restive at her growing power. During the two-day demonstration, August 22 and 23, 1951, peddlers sold flags, banners, and *empanedas*—the little meat pies so favored by Argentines. Evita got her acclamation—on schedule. The President made a speech, and a clamor arose for her. Suitably flustered, Evita appeared expressing amazed surprise. But instead of millions there were, contrary to what was said in the controlled press, scarcely three hundred thousand persons. She was like a hostess whose guests did not appear. Her undeniable beauty had taken on a glacial quality, giving her face a masklike appearance. In place of her once almost girlish laughter there was a vocal intensity like that of a woman consumed.

A few days later the Army officials gave President Perón an ultimatum. Either Evita would restrain her ambition or they would act—and nothing would change them. The shock further aggravated her condition. Almost simultaneously with news of an abortive military revolt against the President in September, 1951, Perón's propaganda ministry announced that she was suffering from influenza. A few days later the ministry reported that she had pernicious anemia "of regular intensity, being treated with transfusions, absolute rest and general medication." Less than three weeks later—after one public appearance at the Loyalty Day rally where she was termed a saint—word was given that treatment would be accepted from a North American surgeon.

Dr. Abel Carcano, noted Argentine cancer specialist,

flew to New York on a passport issued on President Perón's direct order. He persuaded Dr. George Pack, famous cancer surgeon and radiologist of New York's Memorial Hospital, to fly back with him to Buenos Aires on October 22, 1951. On November 4, Evita was admitted to the Polyclinico Presidente Perón, one of Argentina's most modern and best equipped hospitals. Its entire second floor had been expectantly cleared for a week. Two days later, official bulletins reported surgery recommended by the attending doctors was carried out. There was no indication whether Dr. Pack or Dr. Ricardo Finocchieto, an Argentine surgeon in attendance, performed.

On Saturday, July 16, 1952, the crowds keeping vigil outside the Presidential residence saw the dim light on the second floor bedroom snap out and a moment later Perón himself announced to waiting cabinet ministers: "Evita is dead."

For days the normal life of the country was paralyzed. A national demonstration of grief over the loss of their First Lady was staged by the workers. Most observers felt the emotion genuine, proof that Evita, who had led her people into totalitarianism and toward bankruptcy, had also won their love.

The powerful Partido Peronista advocates peronism and *justicialismo*, though few party members could tell you just exactly what those terms mean. In 1952 the Association of Argentine Writers asked academicians of Argentina and Spain to introduce officially the two isms into the Spanish language. The government newspaper *Clarin* declared that since such terms as Communism, Socialism, Conservatism, and Liberalism had infiltrated into the language, the peronistas' request was quite reasonable.

Official definitions were forthcoming: Peronism is a "movement striving for national unity and using *justicialismo* as its political, economic, and social doctrine." *Justicialismo* is "a new philosophy of living—simple, practical, popular, profoundly Christian, and profoundly human." True peronistas felt that a more down-to-earth meaning was that expressed by the daily actions of Perón and Evita.

Even if an Argentine reads no newspapers, listens to no radio, avoids the theater and movies, he finds ample evidences of *El Lider* everywhere. On every new structure built by the government, on every road improvement, on every park beautification project are the tremendous *Perón Cumple* and *Evita Dignifica* signs. Everywhere throughout Argentina are tremendous pictures of Perón and the "martyred" Evita—on the walls of buildings, in every office and schoolroom, in shop windows, on the fronts of tram cars and busses.

If you ask an anti-peronista what party he belongs to, he will probably reply Radical, Conservative, or Socialist. He may warn you not to translate the names literally— except for the Socialists, the terms mean little more than our party designations. Your Argentine friend will tell you his party rarely unites with another—each one wants to be leader, and hates to give up its independence. Now there is another reason for non-cooperation: Perón made it legally impossible for parties to form a coalition.

In the last century the Conservatives pretty much ruled the country body and soul. They believed Argentina should remain a semi-colonial state, sell her meat and wheat for high prices, and not think of industrializing. Regaining power in 1930, they held it by sheer audacity until 1943.

One outstanding exception to the usual Conservative ruler was President Roberto M. Ortiz, who was elected in 1937. Immediately after his inauguration President Ortiz repudiated election frauds and pledged himself to restore democratic government and honest election. Since this spelled doom for the anti-democratic Conservatives, they became his implacable enemies. When President Roosevelt sent his famous message to Hitler and Mussolini in 1938, urging them not to plunge the world into another war, President Ortiz was the first chief of state to express hearty approval. His pro-American speeches and his democratic acts made him an idol of the common people.

But in 1940, approaching blindness forced him to turn the government over to his Vice President, Ramón Castillo. Many Argentines point out that the change was similar to what might have happened if Franklin D. Roosevelt had had to turn over the Presidency to conservative John Garner during his first term. The New Deal might never have come about. "This shows," Argentines say, "that even in your country one man can change the course of events."

Castillo had made no secret of his sympathy for the Nazis and Fascists. One week after Pearl Harbor he imposed a state of siege and maintained it for nearly eighteen months, until he was finally and forcibly removed from office in June, 1943.

Many Argentines feel the recent unimaginative leadership and inner-party squabbling of the Union Civica Radical are responsible for the undemocratic governments they have had since 1930. The Radical Party was formed in 1890 to represent the growing liberal element in Argentina. It is not radical, but just about dead center politically. Its announced aim was honest government, and it represented the new middle class.

Today the Radical Party advocates many of Perón's aims: controlled economy, liberal labor laws, and increased industrialization. In some ways its leaders seek to outdo Perón by urging the nationalization of even more industries than he, for instance the meat-packing plants. Radicals are less anti-American than peronistas, and favor freedom of speech and press. "We want to allow every group the right to say what it pleases," they explain. "This is in sharp contrast with the peronistas, who believe that only the government has that privilege and personal rights are secondary."

In 1894, a leftist Radical founded the Socialist Party on Marxist principles. Ten years later it elected its first deputy to Congress from Buenos Aires, the aforementioned mustacioed Dr. Alfredo L. Palacios. The party won a sizable membership among the workers in the capital and its suburbs, attracting many intellectuals and middle-class Argentines. It advocated a new and balanced economy between the capital and the interior and an improved relationship between industry and agriculture. Organized along democratic lines, its leaders consulted the rank and file on all major matters of elections and policies, while the other parties followed the old-line political committee control.

For many years before Perón the Socialists won a majority in Buenos Aires elections. But the party rarely

took a strong position on issues within the labor movement, and the membership of trade union leaders in the
Socialist Party became largely formal and traditional.
The Socialists lost ground when President Perón made
his big play for the workers. In many cases union officials
went over to Perón's Party, leaving old-time Socialist
leaders completely stranded.

By the late 1940's the Socialist Party had become the
party of the intelligentsia par excellence, with particular
strength among the anti-Perón students. Before they
were suppressed, the Socialist publications, especially
the weekly, *La Vanguardia*, were among the widest read,
the most sprightly and biting of all opposed to Perón.

Although the 77,318 Communist votes in the 1952 election topped the Socialist total, the Reds actually have less
influence in Argentina. The Argentine Communist Party
got its start in 1919 because of a rift in the Socialist
Party. The going was rough until the depression of the
1930's, when, despite persecution, the Communists began to recruit hundreds of members.

In November, 1951, Frank Kelly, Foreign Editor of the
New York Herald Tribune, found the Communists well
entrenched in the General Confederation of Labor and
its textile, construction, light and power, maritime and
railroad unions, as well as those of the cooks, waiters and
bakers. Many were shop stewards and committeemen,
active and forceful in promoting their party's aims.

Latin American Communists get a great deal of their
strength from the intellectuals—writers, teachers, artists,
etc. In early 1952, estimates put the number of card-
carrying Argentine Reds at between 35,000 and 50,000.

Most of them were in Buenos Aires, city and province, and others in Rosario, Córdoba, Mendoza, and parts of Santa Fé. No one knows the number of Red sympathizers.

Perhaps the best way to judge the likelihood of Communist success in Argentina is to consider some of their appeals and note why some have drawn followers and others failed because of the very nature of the Argentines themselves.

The Marxist theory that a dominant class has always exploited the masses and that the class struggle has always been the main agency of historical change has helped win over some of Argentina's leading labor groups. But the milder Socialist interpretation always had a greater appeal. Generally, Communist success in unions depended on specific individual leadership in certain groups—another instance of Argentines following a *caudillo* rather than a set of principles. Naturally, the Argentine workers who suffered most from the low living and working standards were most anxious for the kind of Utopia promised by the Communists.

Nationalization of foreign-owned utilities "essential to the good of the State" has always had a strong appeal. As noted in the new Constitution, this is Perón's policy and also the ideal of a great many Argentines, pro- and anti-Perón. Those Argentines who resented United States, British, and other foreign influence were sold on the idea that foreigners had no such hold in the Soviet Union.

The strongest Communist appeals have been to those Argentines who sought neutrality in international relations. The Communists now articulate this as opposition to the United States program for arms standardization in Latin America.

Soviet cultural achievements have also been stressed, generally via special institutes established in Argentina by the Soviet Embassy and legations. During the war and immediately after, Soviet propaganda emphasized Russia's wartime economy and power. The U.S.S.R. sponsored a few exhibitions of their tanks, guns, and planes. Much more was accomplished by the United States press services and films which carried stories that indirectly sold the idea of Moscow strength.

Of course this was during the period when Washington was all for Russia's winning friends in Latin America. The United States conducted most of the negotiations which led to the resumption of Argentine diplomatic relations with Moscow on June 6, 1946. At the time, our viewpoint was that Latin America, and especially Argentina, had to export to live. Since we could not absorb what Argentina produced, getting Russia to exchange Argentine meat, wheat, and agricultural products for cars, tractors, and farm machinery which the U.S.S.R. was expected to supply was regarded as sound thinking. The Russians exported little. But the promise did have an immediate political and propaganda repercussion.

When the Kremlin line supported the United States, Argentine Communists, of course, went along. They even heaped praise on pro-Allied dictators whose jails were full of Reds. Winston Churchill became a noteworthy subject for some Communist dailies during the first Big Three meetings.

Since then, Uncle Sam has become the favorite Soviet whipping boy. At times the Communists have moved ahead on their own, hitting at our alleged failure to give Argentina the machinery she needed for industrialization.

Most Argentines fear leftist extremism far more than Naziism or Fascism. During the war, both of the latter groups had far stronger support than did the Communists, and Perón's setup was more or less molded in their image.

The Argentines' sense of individuality makes them oppose a too-rigid Moscow doctrine. The Communists, realizing this, have sought to claim that they are a hundred per cent Argentines. The pro-Nazi nationalists made similar protestations in their days of ascendancy, with considerably more success. One reason, perhaps, is that as Catholics the Argentines have always known of the Church's opposition to Communism.

The Russian Embassy in Buenos Aires has had a sizable staff. However, there is virtually no trade between Russia and the Argentines and it stands to reason that the employees of the Russian Embassy are mostly used for purposes of propaganda for which millions of dollars are spent each year. About half the money is estimated to come from Russia, the other half being subscribed by local Communists. Schools were established for the teaching of methods of street fighting and the handling of mobs, and small arms for distribution were run up the river as far as Rosario. The employees of the satellite ministries were all paid through the Russian Embassy so that it could maintain the control of their activities.

In Argentina the Communists work whenever they find an opening—with labor, with liberal and intellectual groups, and with the Peronists. The Reds have pretty well abandoned their separatist tendencies to concentrate on infiltration. They have sought to win over the strongly nationalistic young Argentines who have been disillusioned and disgruntled by the years of Conservative government. Since these men and women already hated foreign capital and democracy, the Communists have tried to convert them to revolutionaries.

Argentine Communists denounced the Ramirez regime as fascistic. They cooperated with Radicals, Conservatives, and Socialists in exile in Uruguay to fight the military government. The Reds violently opposed Perón's first election, made frequent use of the word "Peronazi" to describe his followers, and sometimes clashed with them in the streets.

Early in 1946 the Communists suddenly began to make distinctions between "good" and "bad" Peronists. The change occurred shortly after the arrival of a Soviet trade mission to Buenos Aires. In June, two days after his first inauguration, Perón announced the re-establishment of diplomatic relations with Russia. The Communist daily, *La Hora*, reciprocated by declaring Perón's election triumph was "the result of popular unity against imperialism and the oligarchy." The party's chief leader, Victor Codovilla, announced: "We shall support the Perón government with reservations."

President Perón was quite aware of the Communists' change in line. He said the party "has adopted a more skillful tactic, although a quite obvious one of infiltrating the ranks of labor. It acts as a wolf in sheep's clothing."

Yet for three years the President showed the Reds a surprisingly large degree of toleration. The Communist press was virtually untouched. He allowed the Communists to have two deputies in the Mendoza provincial legislature, and about half a dozen city councilmen. But he set up three federal agencies to keep meticulous track of the Reds. Later he purged suspected members and fellow travelers from schools, universities, and public posts.

President Perón may believe he has gained a good deal from his system of permitting the Reds to operate under his strict surveillance. His extensive espionage system knows what every Communist, and every other Perón opponent, is doing and planning.

In 1949, the Communist newspaper was closed by the police, and now Communists have the same trouble publishing propaganda, showing their movies, and calling public meetings that other opposition parties have. The Communist candidate for President in 1951, Rodolfo Ghioldi, was critically shot in the lung at a campaign rally in Paraná.

But early in 1952, Argentine delegates attended the highly-touted International Economic Conference in Moscow. President Perón is said to have approved the meeting by declaring it would afford a defense of European interests against the harmful steps of the United States.

Ofttimes the Argentine Communists claim that the only trouble with Perón is that he has not carried out his own program as effectively as he might. "We are better peronistas than Perón," they assert. "And we were first to attack the United States as a stronghold of the malefactors of great wealth and as a plutocratic imperialistic nation."

The true extent of Communist success may not be known for a long time. But this much is obvious: Wherever there is widespread poverty accompanied by rising living costs, increasing economic difficulties, and growing class hatred, Communists find a fertile breeding ground. This condition is more true of some other nations in Latin America than of the Argentines.

Chapter XXII

The Argentines and Their Army

A CAFÉ story, currently popular in Buenos Aires, concerns the mother of three sons. One was a genius, the second average, the third an idiot. Asked what she wanted them to be when they grew up, she replied: "The first will be a judge. The next will run the family *estancia*. And the third has but one choice: he must become an Army officer."

While the tale illustrates the attitude of many Argentines toward the military force which, since 1943, has dominated their government, it fails to throw much light on a more important question: How can an Army which has steadily lost favor with an increasing number of Argentines remain in power after nine years?

In the eyes of many an Argentine their Army is an Army of Occupation. A non-militaristic people who

300

avoid conscription like the plague, they sometimes feel their Army's maneuvering, posturing, and bickering is either opera bouffe, or the scrapping of a group of robber barons disputing their take. Sometimes Army leaders have appeared brutally terroristic. At other times they keep themselves very much in the background.

Many an Argentine is convinced the Army runs Perón. Others insist Perón runs the Army. All agree the Army's role as the nation's defender is secondary. Argentina's Army has not fought a real war since shortly after our Civil War. It sent no troops to fight in World Wars I and II; not even a token force to Korea. Essentially, the Army must be considered a part of government, for the Army makes the government and not the government the Army. No administration has ever stayed in power in Argentina when it lacked Army support. And, most believe no government can stay in power long if the Army does not back it.

The term "Army" can mean many things, but the control is in the hands of the top-ranking officers. Most foreign observers concede their power is not nearly as great as it was in the time of the *coup d'état*. Since then Perón has twice been elected President, moved into every phase of Argentine life and, as we have seen, developed labor as a strong and vital force. Perón, moreover, has succeeded in neutralizing many other ambitious officers who might have moved to force him out.

Many Argentines believe that without Army backing no one but an assassin could push Perón out if he does not want to retire. Such moves, of course, cannot be forecast. But some things about the Army's collective personality, which is stronger than that of any of its leaders, can be described and may in themselves provide a clue.

What kind of Army has Argentina? What gives the Army its influence and power? And how did it get that way?

There are four prime reasons for its present stature: (1) training and influence, (2) discipline and organization, (3) flaming faith in its own patriotism and program and (4) ruthless determination for power and the force of arms to back it up.

Added to this is another motive increasingly more important—fear. Army officers are afraid of what might happen to them if they let go the reins and allow a truly democratic government to take over. Most officers think they would not only lose their benefits and promotions if they left the ministries for the barracks, but that they might also face strong public reprisals.

Despite Perón's role and its traditional place in Argentine activities, the Army itself is neither a *caudillo*-led force nor a personal dictatorship. Rather, it is a group in which a careerist military clique dominates; a clique which at times appears to give orders to Perón and at other times to take his command. The clique is like the secret police in that it survives upsets and at all times remains in power, despite changes of names and official forces in the halls of government.

Army officers like to believe Argentines hold them in the highest regard and that this gives them a kind of continuous mandate permitting them to act as the highest court on political and other issues. They also believe they have the right and the duty to take over when they feel the civilian administration has failed.

Up until June, 1943, Argentina's Army had usually been content to reflect the thinking of a handful of rich *estancieros*. Upsets occurred only when they thought it convenient. But in 1943, the younger officers became exasperated and decided to take over themselves.

Most were members of a secret lodge known as the G.O.U. (Grupo Oficiales Unidos) which included an important majority of the 6,000 officers who commanded an Army of approximately 100,000. Members of the G.O.U. were strongly and militantly nationalist, though scorning extremist organizations such as the Alianza Libertadora Nacional, which in those days had strong Nazi and Spanish Falangist support. Both G.O.U. and officers' cadre were in many ways the product of Prussian training and influence which made them a kind of permanent caste in the body politic.

The Argentine Navy, numbering some 40,000 men with an officer corps of about 4,500, was also an important force. But it has never been as political as the Army. For a long time the Navy had only one officer in the military cabinet. Even now, naval officers frequently give the impression that they wish they had never entered into the business of running the state. One high-ranking Navy man explained: "We have gained little but ill will and the reputation of being subservient to the Army."

Many Air Force men were strongly pro-Perón. They felt that something was needed to arouse the more traditional ground Army officers and believed Perón was the one to do it.

Very few of Argentina's smartly uniformed, sword-wearing Army officers come from the wealthiest class. There is a sprinkling of old *estancia* family names in the

Army rosters, but it has never been a rich man's career. Most leaders are from the ambitious middle-class families —Spanish, Italian, German, Irish. This is the same strata from which the democratic opposition also stems, a unique factor in more ways than one.

The intensity with which they pursue their careers has long distinguished the thinking, action, and tradition of Argentina's Army officer group. This characteristic can be noted among the cadets entering the Colegio Militar, Argentina's West Point, and in the officers who have spent their whole lives in service.

The cadet or officer who is unwilling to subjugate all else to his career rarely lasts long. Argentina's militarists have felt a pride in staying apart from the civilian population.

No outsider, reservist, or non-career man has ever risen to a top rank in Argentina. There is no Argentine officer comparable to General George C. Marshall, who went to Virginia Military Institute instead of West Point. Moreover, since the permanent officers corps, not Congressmen, pass on cadet admissions to the Colegio, the type has become almost self-perpetuating.

Cadets have no soft training. The discipline is especially rigid when contrasted with university laxity. The four-year course and the years which follow leave an imprint far deeper than that of West Point, Sandhurst, or St. Cyr. Right from the start, cadets are taught such rules as assuming a poker face while on duty, the strict code of honor for every detail of an officer's life, and the right of an officer to command unquestioning respect from the conscripts who make up the force. Cadets have conscript orderlies. Friendly yet respectful relationships between officers and G.I.'s such as have recently been encouraged by our top brass would never be permitted in Argentina.

Even the history taught at the Colegio was different from that previously studied at the universities. Army men, in fact, felt the civilian version so far out of line that one of the first things they did on obtaining power was to order many textbooks rewritten. They also banned certain radio programs including one sponsored by a United States businessman's group, which re-created dialogue to dramatize historic events not in strictest accord with the Army's version.

Emphasis at the Colegio has always been on campaigns, tactics, field maneuvers. The first heel-clicking Prussian instructor came to Argentina in 1912 to reorganize the army: he was followed by a number of others who taught German methods. The Nazis, who aimed to create a powerful Argentine military group in their own image, invited many young officers to Berlin to observe their new tanks and planes. One of their guests was Juan D. Perón.

Their efforts did much to develop the officers' cadre that moved, not on orders of Berlin, as some melodramatic observers reported, but on the basis of a shared philosophy, tradition, and belief; a lack of faith in democracy and its "trappings,"—freedom of speech, press, and elections. Army officers would act just as the Germans wanted without requiring anything as direct as an order.

This basic philosophy helped bring on Argentina's 1930 military coup, first since 1890. Quickly organized by General Uriburu, it was first cheered, then booed, by Argentines who found promises to rout out corruption as meaningless then as they did a decade later.

The G.O.U. was born not long afterwards. Its chief force came from the colonels' level. Under Argentina's Army organization, these were the men in the most strategic positions, the highest ranking officers in direct contact with the troops. They taught the conscripts the principle of respect for authority, personal loyalty, belief in the duty of the military to act as guardians of the people, and the need to "give Argentina her place in the sun."

Argentina's conscripts have always come from the poorest, least-educated class. In the past every able-bodied male had to report with his age class. About one name in every ten was drawn to fill the ranks. In practice, however, young men of wealth or education rarely entered as privates. Students were exempted if they took a three-month, part-time marksmanship course. University students, as a result, became the Army's traditional enemies because they had rarely served, or served reluctantly.

In the first months of military rule in 1943, Argentines were left breathless with the succession of decrees designed to repair errors of speech, morals, finance, agriculture, and political opinion. Army officers ran the nation as they had their corps, attending to every detail of national life. When they saw food costs were high, for example, they simply "solved" the inflation problem by ordering grocers to slash prices. Argentines noted how, when public problems refused to be so easily solved by military regulations, their Army officers were upset, uneasy, and uncertain what to do next.

Ambitious Colonel Perón sold himself to his fellow officers as the man with the answers. He saw from the beginning that he needed the help of many other Army officers. As President, he gave provincial governorships to colonels and generals.

Many obscure officers named to head departments put families on the payroll and spent money in unlimited quantities. Figures, of course, were never made public, and no one in Argentina dreams of a congressional probe. In addition, Perón sought to win Army favor by having Congress grant pay increases. He also had Congress give non-commissioned officers the right to vote, a privilege the Army had traditionally denied itself to "make sure it would be a disinterested party in all national conflicts."

Aside from the feeling that they had a mandate to take over from the "unscrupulous politicians" and provide the "discipline which the people obviously needed," Argentina's Army officers had other reasons for wanting to remove the civilian government of Ramón S. Castillo.

Some were anxious to repair their own damaged professional prestige. They also sought to give the Army arms equality with their biggest neighbor, Brazil, who had received strengthening Lend-Lease aid from the United States.

Not that they expected war. Argentina's seventy-five-year record of peace and her settlement of at least three thorny boundary disputes by arbitration pretty well precluded this. Argentina had even ceded territory to which it had a good claim and served as an arbitrator for others in boundary differences to avoid armed conflicts.

But Argentine Army officers said they did not want to have to depend on the United States to defend them in the event of a U.S.–Russian war which they definitely expected. The desire to be self-sufficient in the event of war provided the basic thinking beneath the five-year plan and the industrialization of the nation. Like the Nationalists, their slogan was, "Sovereignty above all else." Other militarists also dreamed of creating a country in which the individual served the State—not the State the individual. Their program was one of social justice somewhat related to the social approach Perón later developed.

Argentina's Army has been on a war basis, or its equivalent, since June, 1943. The Armed Forces have received at least a quarter of the national budget, perhaps more. Only part is published. Not listed is atomic research in which Perón has recently claimed important advances, some of which he said were based on discovery of a vein of uranium-bearing ore near Mendoza. Experiments are reportedly made at the super-secret atomic "pilot plant" on an island in Lake Nahuel Huapí.

Perón has also stated that war is an "inevitable social phenomenon, requiring long conscientious years of preparation, and accomplishable only through the combined efforts of Government, private institutions, and all the people." The problems, he has added, "are so diverse and require such technical skills that no capacity or intellect can be dispensed with."

In an attempt to develop public interest in the Army, Perón often wears his general's uniform, appears at parades and demonstrations, speaks in favor of many Army ideals. Though hardly a popular Army, it must be admitted that many Argentines love the polished show of strength put on by their armed forces.

Another step in Perón's aim to develop a public consciousness in the Armed Forces has been the drive to deify Argentina's Washington, General José de San Martín, as the country's outstanding national hero. San Martín's military record is stressed and his name has become a rallying cry for chauvinism. There are many reasons. For one, it helps keep down factionalism, especially important at this time. It spurs greater efforts at a moment when Argentina must produce more, as imports are reduced and exports cut. And it brings Argentines closer together in the face of economic difficulties and criticisms from abroad.

In *Latin American Politics and Government*, Austin F. MacDonald answers the questions of many North Americans who overlook the importance of Latin American armies. "'Why,' they ask, 'do the Latins permit their dictators to continue in power? Why don't they do something about it?' To 'do something' about a machine gun when you happen to be on the wrong end, is not easy. It takes a special brand of courage and perhaps a large degree of foolhardiness. So the dictators continue to dictate with Army support. Even Latin presidents who are confirmed democrats have no illusions as to their sources of power." In the past, Argentina's Army officers always knew that a couple of regiments marching from the city's outskirts to the downtown Plazo de Mayo were enough to bring about a change in government, the removal of a cabinet minister, a new bill. Since this could be done within a matter of hours, the threat was often more implied than real. So every Argentine President, as well as the leaders of other Latin countries, have tried to keep the Army united in their behalf.

Perón, as an Army man himself, has been especially

aware of this. His device, and skill, has been to make the Army subservient to him, rather than the other way round.

No one can say with certainty just how much of the Argentine Army currently supports Perón at any given time. Rumors—and in no other Latin capital do they spread as quickly as in Buenos Aires—constantly tell of dissatisfaction and planned counter-moves. "Wait around," old timers tell a newcomer, "you will see something big next week." The big event may be postponed for months or years, and the insiders are often as surprised as anyone at what finally happens. The situation in Argentina always appears to be touch-and-go, for, as disagreement develops, Army loyalty makes officers think of their quarrel as a family affair and decide that they have to stick together and hold on by force if necessary.

President Perón's greatest military interest has, not unnaturally, been in the Army's seat of power, the Campo de Mayo barracks on the outskirts of the federal capital. Here, sitting like a giant cannon aimed at the heart of Buenos Aires, are not only the leading infantry, artillery, anti-aircraft and cavalry groups, but the School of Arms, Communications and Non-Commissioned Officers. Some ten thousand men are permanently based here and the shifting population is always large.

It was from Campo de Mayo that the Army marched to take over the government in 1943. In 1945, Campo de Mayo officers turned against Perón, and forced him to resign for several days. While they wrangled over what to do next, Perón came back. On September 28, 1951, Campo de Mayo was the center of a brief military revolt against Perón. It was later described as one of the least successful attempts ever made.

To make sure that his own followers are in this and other strategic bases, Perón and those closest to him have constantly moved men and officers. They have established garrisons in every province and territory instead of the six or seven previously covered. Divisions of these officers in whom Perón has confidence get weapons and arms. Others whose loyalty is in the slightest doubt get one or two bullets per rifle and no heavy arms.

The Army's two principal bones of contention with Perón were his wife and his one-time economic czar Miguel Miranda. Miranda is now dead and hence is no longer an active issue. And Señora Perón's star dimmed beginning with the fatal illness which developed in the fall of 1951.

The officers' opposition to her was strong from the start. Most of them had never been able to stand the idea of a woman having so much influence in running the country. Army officials shuddered in August, 1951, when the cheering *descamisados* begged Evita to run for the Vice Presidency. "If anything ever happened to Perón," they said, "she would be our Commander-in-Chief!" Their rumblings echoed in the Casa Rosada, and Evita tearfully told her people she could not run for the office.

To develop his own strength Perón has encouraged the natural rivalry of the Army, Navy, and Air Force. "So long as their surplus energies are used up in fighting one another," he reportedly has said, "they won't have the strength to bother me much."

As an overgrown police force with a reactionary outlook, the Army was long disliked by organized labor. Workers also heartily disliked the Federal Police of Buenos Aires, who at one time were per capita almost twice as numerous as those of New York City. With Perón in power the Federal Police have been militarized more and more and have in effect become an army in themselves, a possible adjunct or rival, to the regular forces.

Army officers, moreover, have been pleased at the reflected glory they received from those who favored Perón's policy. They also realized that while labor was not an armed force, it was well organized. Labor leaders have been able to summon up tremendous numbers of fanatical followers and, by stopping work, paralyze all activity for indefinite periods. Army officers still feel that no one else in Argentina has the President's strength, so it might be best to string along for a while longer.

Most observers believe if the Army ever revolts against Perón, the leaders will be young officers who have the most to gain and the least to lose. The question of whether or not Argentina's Army conscripts would battle against organized labor in the event of a real showdown is often debated. Some believe the resultant bloodshed could plunge the country into such chaos that it would be difficult to continue any kind of normal activity. Army officers, like most other Argentines, are in no great hurry to force a physical battle and prefer a more comfortable method of waiting it out.

For his part Perón is known to count on the support of the Ministry of National Defense, headed by General Humberto Sosa Molina, a very fine Army officer dedicated to the interests of his country. The Ministry, created in

1949, has jurisdiction over key civilian defense agencies as well as the Army, Air Force, and Navy. Some observers believe it lacks strength and have likened it to the fourth side of a triangle.

General Molina, a good friend of President Perón, has had many contacts with the United States and its representatives. In late 1947 he was host to Lieutenant General Willis D. Crittenberger, the first top-rank United States officer to see Argentina's military installations and training establishments since the end of the war. In May, 1948, General Molina journeyed to the United States where he was a White House guest and received many attentions. He returned to Argentina with a very friendly attitude toward Washington.

Our own government has not neglected to seek friendship with the Argentine military. Since 1939 we have sent ground and air missions to the country to help to instruct Argentines in our military organization and tactics. During the war and until 1947 we refused to sell arms to Argentina because of Axis influence there. Since then there have been many friendly military visits, and Argentine officers have added the study of English to their curriculum.

Chapter XXIII

The Argentines and Their Neighbors

To SEAL the friendship pact signed by Chile and Argentina after the settlement of a bitter border dispute in 1902, a massive statue was erected in the Uspallata Pass —a Christ of the Andes with arms outstretched in blessing. According to the favorite Latin story, a stranger, sighting the monumental figure high in the mountains between the two countries, asked why it faced Argentina rather than Chile.

"That's easy," a Chilean replied. "Not even the Lord could trust turning his back on the Argentines."

The tale sharply illustrates the underlying uneasiness existing between the people of Argentina and one of her five closest "good neighbors." To a greater or lesser degree, a similar attitude persists toward the others— Uruguay, Paraguay, Bolivia, and Brazil. Despite official

Good Neighbor talk and an unwritten rule against discussion in print, most Latin countries are jumpy about the powerful republic next door, and fearful of some incident which might turn a border encounter into a more serious matter.

One of the greatest mistakes North Americans make about Argentina is to assume that peronistas are the only Argentines who want to dominate the rest of Latin America. Argentina's Army officers have made the most of it, hence, attention centers on them. But the fact is that most Argentines firmly believe their country is Latin America's natural leader, and whether they discuss it or not, they are apt to look down on other Latins and feel they should be leading what they consider the more backward republics. This is true of both *porteños* and provincials who may have rarely encountered a Paraguayan or a Brazilian. The *porteños*, perhaps, feel this superiority most: the citizens of Mendoza, closest to the Chilean border, next. The feeling diminishes up in the Bolivian and Paraguayan regions where poorer Argentines are less power-conscious. Like the Argentines' pride, the desire for leadership, however, generally applies to all classes.

Because of this widespread and deep-seated feeling most Argentines have cheered the frequent speeches of Perón and government officials which stress the role they must play in leading Latin America. Some of these pronouncements are mild; others, saber-rattling. The latter get a great press play. Several officials have stated that Argentina must eventually absorb not only parts of Chile, but Uruguay, Paraguay, Bolivia, and Southern Brazil. This is an extension of a well-worn dream of an Austral

Bloc, based on the old viceroyalty of the Rio de La Plata which included Uruguay, Paraguay, Bolivia, and Argentina. Other Latins became aware of it about 1889 when Argentines demonstrated their pride in their growing population and power at the first International Conference of the American States in Washington. In the days before World War II, Nazi leaders echoed the same idea to Argentine Army officers—promising that, when the Germans won, Argentina would be permitted to dominate all of Southern South America, and thus circumvent United States aspirations. When aggressive speeches voicing this Pan Argentine idea cause an upheaval in neighboring capitals, Argentine officials quickly explain they are "purely for local consumption," just as they do with anti-United States pronouncements.

For a time, many Argentines themselves felt that Perón had inspired a number of the military coups in other South American countries. He was credited—or blamed—for new military governments whether or not he had anything to do with them. Though facts on which to base conclusions are slim there is little doubt that many such reports have been greatly exaggerated. To many Argentines, the idea of their aggressive designs on their neighbors is as ridiculous as our planning action against Canada. Yet many Chileans and Uruguayans feared that Perón's attitude, particularly in the days when he was rising rapidly, might someday mean their end—even though they did not know exactly how, or why, he might want to take them over.

On the other hand, many Argentines who approve of their country's leadership resented only the fact that Perón was the one taking the lead.

Argentina's interest in its neighbors has been intensified since the initiation of the Good Neighbor Policy. When war cut off European and Far Eastern trade, Argentina and other Latin countries were more or less forced to cooperate with one another. As a result, Buenos Aires in recent years increased rail contacts with her nearest neighbors and set up and extended inter-continental steamship and air routes.

To implement these she also sought a series of economic treaties with Chile, Paraguay, Bolivia, and other Latin countries. News that these broad agreements would abolish customs barriers, provide trade, and bring about investments of considerable Argentine funds for the development of mineral and other resources required for their country's new industrial program at first delighted most Argentines. It sounded good. It gave them the feeling that their country was growing and finding her place in the sun.

Peronistas conveniently ignored the fact that such agreements would form an Argentine-dominated economic bloc much like those Argentina had always accused the British and the United States of creating to keep smaller countries as their colonial affiliates and raw-material-producing satellites.

In 1951 and 1952, Argentina, faced by her own economic difficulties, began to change the approach. In the column he purportedly writes under the name of "Descartes" in the newspaper *Democracia* Perón suggested the prompt establishment of a confederation of Latin American states. His viewpoint, which appealed to many Argentines, was that the Third World War already was a fact, that the final decision "will be a long and painful matter for Russia as well as the United States—most probably decided more by progressive destruction and exhaustion rather than through violent military action."

President Perón declared that though Argentina could not avert this, she could "be able to offer to the peoples, innocent victims of the madness of their own rulers, timely aid when the disappointed and hungry decide to seek a better life in a less selfish, freer and happier mankind." Reduced to more practical terms this developed into a program to induce other Latin American countries to form their own pool of strategic materials and fix their own price for these so that they would not have to deal in scarce dollars or through the United States.

The President in effect threatened to use his country's food exports—when these materialized again—as "critical materials," a classification already given to meat. What he was most interested in, it became clear, was getting what his country needed, like steel, tin plate, war equipment, and machinery. For example, one deal was made with neighboring Chile whereby Argentina sent one hundred thousand cattle on the hoof through the Andean passes in return for fifteen thousand tons of copper.

The British were also warned that sterling prices, no matter how high, would not be deemed sufficient in the next beef contract. The British were told, in effect, that they would have to deliver oil, steel, coal, and tin plate whether these items were in trans-Atlantic short supply or not.

President Perón hoped through this program to win the results he had not been able to obtain by earlier treaties. The fact is that in most of the previous treaties little was said of the fact that they were generally opera-

tive only under certain conditions and many of the glowing promises simply never materialized.

Moreover, currently Argentina cannot afford to help
her neighbors develop their resources as she suggested
just after World War II.

Despite their desire to dominate the hemisphere, most
Argentines are not tremendously interested in the day-
to-day affairs of the republics across their borders. Most
newspapers carry comparatively little news about what
is going on in Bolivia, Paraguay, Chile, and Uruguay,
especially in contrast to the columns they print about the
United States and the rest of the world.

What are relations with the other South American
countries as most Argentines see them?

Chile shares with Argentina her longest border—some
2,600 miles strung from peak to peak in the high Andes.
Unlike the U.S.-Canadian border, which is roughly twice
its length, the Argentine-Chilean boundary is by no
means unguarded. Chileans are painfully conscious of
Argentine armed camps extending south down to Patagonia. They know they are not as strong as they were in
the late nineteenth century when they served an ultimatum on Argentina, demanding boundary concessions.
They were then ready to fight, but peace was achieved
and the Christ of the Andes statue erected and eloquently
inscribed: "These great mountains will crumble before
our two nations ever make war upon each other."

The average Argentine is likely to think of Chile in
mixed terms. He gallantly professes admiration for the
beauty of her *señoritas* who, he reluctantly admits, are
more attractive than most other Latin-American women.
He is aware Chile's population—5,537,000 by the coun-

try's own 1947 official count—has not grown as fast as Argentina's. He is familiar with the superiority of Chilean wine, which sells at a premium in Argentina. He knows personally, or from friends, of the *simpatico* atmosphere of Viña del Mar, the lovely Pacific seaside resort which was especially popular with Argentines during those years when their money could be favorably exchanged with the Chilean.

Official relations, however, hardly reflect these notions. In fact, they have cooled considerably since Perón's early days in the Casa Rosada. After *La Prensa* became an official government organ, it began a series of attacks on Chile as a "backward nation." Her President, Gabriel González Videla, was described as a "tool in the hands of Washington and Wall Street." He was warned against "making deals with foreign economic imperialists," negotiations displeasing to Perón's Foreign Ministry.

Argentines, always short of minerals, want regular supplies of Chilean coal, copper, and steel. Once Chile was ready to make these available. Now she wants to use them for her own ambitious industrial program.

Democratic Chileans have also been annoyed by the favorable attitude of the official Argentine press for General Carlos Ibáñez, the former dictator-president reelected in 1952. During Perón's visit in February, 1953, they gave him an extremely cool reception.

Ibáñez supporters denied charges that their candidate was hand-picked by Perón, but in Buenos Aires a labor group formed a pro-Ibáñez organization and gave it headquarters in a building formerly owned by *La Prensa*. In July, 1952, Santiago formally accused Argentina of engaging in an "excessively offensive" propaganda campaign against Chile.

In the disputed land of the Antarctic, Chileans have twitted Argentine ambitions. They insist that their territorial rights include a pie-slice segment of the region below both their own and Argentina's border. Britain, Argentina, and Chile have claimed various islands and land in Antarctica for years. In 1947, Argentina set up a weather post on Deception Island in the South Shetlands. Chile set up posts on Greenwich Island nearby, and on Graham Land, which they call O'Higgins Land in honor of their national hero. In March, 1948, González Videla dashed down to the Antarctic region to take possession of the territory. In recent years, Chile and Argentina have put aside their differences in Antarctica to present a united front against Britain. Though frozen wasteland does not seem terribly important, Chileans make much of their claim because, as many Chileans explain: "It was our way of showing some kind of superiority over Argentina." It is important to keep in mind that there is a definite Argentine-Chilean rivalry for the oil in southern Tierra del Fuego.

For years, Argentine official policy was predicated on a possible Chilean-Bolivian combination and on the fact that Chile dominated Bolivia before Argentina herself became the chief foreign influence in that mountain-ringed, landlocked country.

Argentines recognize Bolivia's wealth of tin, silver, and petroleum. They sympathize with their government's efforts to get Bolivia to ship her products through Argentina, rather than over the Andes to the port of Arica in

Chile. This would put Bolivia's major export trade under Argentine control—and ensure Argentina's first claim to their usage.

Bolivia's illiterate population, her weak leadership, and great economic promise have long interested succeeding Argentine governments. In 1951, the peronista press began playing up the strenuous, if not overly successful, diplomatic moves toward implementing old agreements which would bring more Bolivian oil, tin, and other products to Argentina. As part of the drive, Argentine papers have also sought to make a big play of Bolivia's "gallant battle to obtain a fair price for her tin" from buyers in the United States.

One Argentine railroad connects with La Paz. Years ago the Argentine government undertook to finance another to Santa Cruz, but ran into difficulties. It is still abuilding, but their Brazilian rivals are going to beat them. Santa Cruz is also the goal of a new rail line from Santos and São Paulo, Brazil, which will stretch all the way across the continent to Arica, Chile.

Argentine oil men were keenly interested when, in 1937, Bolivia expropriated Standard Oil's fields in their country. Ever since then Argentines have been active in Bolivia's oil development, particularly through their Y.P.F. state oil trust.

President Perón has brought pressure on some unfriendly Bolivian governments though Argentines often jokingly wonder why. They say: "Since the regimes change so rapidly, you only have to wait a little while before the 'outs' themselves oust the 'ins.'" But since Bolivia imports 85 per cent of her wheat and half her meat from the Argentines, the government in La Paz finds it difficult to resist Argentina. At one time Bolivians appealed to the United States to provide food in case Argentina should try to force acceptance of her terms by stopping all shipments. A partial agreement was subsequently reached, adopted by Bolivia's Congress, and the pressure lessened.

In April, 1952, stories circulated that Perón had armed the rebels who helped the Bolivian Nationalist Revolutionary Movement stage its successful *coup d'état*. Both the M.N.R. and Perón denied it. Victor Paz Estensoro flew back to La Paz from a six-year exile in Argentina to become President, and Evita's Foundation rushed planeloads of foods and medicines to the stricken Bolivians. Buenos Aires recognized the new Paz Estensoro government, and during the six-week period before Washington did the same, the Buenos Aires press shouted that we were refusing to recognize Paz Estensoro as a reprisal for Bolivia's demand for a higher tin price—another example of our "imperialism."

Most Argentines know little and care less about Paraguay though their government completely dominates the little land-locked nation. Many Argentines consider it a primitive, remote land where 1,500,000 poor illiterate Guaraní Indians fight each other in constant civil wars. Those who have sailed up the Paraguay River have smiled smugly to see the clean towns, progressive farms, and white people on their own side of the river contrasted with the squalid primitive homes of the *mestizos* and Indians on the Paraguayan side.

Paraguay's main avenue of commerce is the Paraguay-Paraná river system, which flows for hundreds of miles through Argentine territory. Argentines own and operate the steamship companies that connect Paraguay with the outside world.

The Argentine government also owns 75 per cent of the Paraguayan Central Railroad—the only railroad worth mentioning. And of course the rail outlet for Paraguay is through Argentina.

Much of Paraguay's wheat comes from Argentina as do almost all manufactured articles. Argentines own most of Paraguay's bakeries. They control the quebracho industry, and have a considerable stake in *yerba maté*. The Paraguayan *guaraní*, which is the unit of currency, is tied to the Argentine *peso*, and foreign exchange is obtained through Buenos Aires. The average Paraguayan regards Buenos Aires as the center of the universe. Their usually unstable governments are necessarily so amenable to every Argentine suggestion that, as Willard and Verna Smith explain in *Paraguayan Interlude,* Asunción has been described as "a branch office of Buenos Aires."

Paraguayans have long had to be content with this for there was little else they could do. As a debtor nation, owing Argentina on the $16 millions or more she's invested (U.S. investment is supposed to be no more than $5 millions; the British $10 millions) Paraguay interests Argentina not only as a restraining wall against her bigger neighbor, Brazil, but as a fruitful field for her own economic expansion.

Though Argentines consider Paraguay economically weak, politically inept, and ruled by little cliques of braggart heroes who have constantly kept their masses ignorant, ill-fed, and sick, officially the Argentines have long been Paraguay's zealous friend. Their governments faithfully supported her in the long bloody Chaco War with Bolivia and helped her seize the major gains from the Chaco peace. With British backing, the Argentines have built most of Paraguay's railroads and helped improve Paraguayan agriculture.

The major news Argentines get from Paraguay, however, is the not infrequent reports of political revolts. Rarely does a newspaper or a magazine attempt to provide any background or interpretation of the country. Few Argentine tourists ever travel here.

Brazil touches Argentina only in the narrow span between Uruguay and Paraguay. Yet the rivalry between the two countries is great—though it is essentially more psychological than economic.

The Argentines often look down on the Brazilians as occupants of a tropical land filled with palm trees, vast jungles, and strange snakes and multicolored birds. Brazilian Portuguese is close enough to Argentine Spanish so that an Argentine visitor can generally make himself understood with little difficulty.

Porteños say the Brazilian *samba* was never popular in Argentina until it was introduced by Carmen Miranda in Hollywood movies. The average Argentine admires the beauties of Rio. He knows the beaches at Copacabana are a charming place to go in the season, but he thinks Brazil's now closed casinos "could never compare" with his own Mar del Plata.

Brazilians profess to find the Argentines rude and uncultured. They often speak of what they call their "crude emphasis on material possessions" since most Argentines will unfavorably compare Brazil's smaller number of telephones, bathtubs, cars, and refrigerators, much in the same way that we do in our appraisal of other countries.

Incidentally, as Argentines dislike most of the other Latin Americans, so most of them dislike her. The terms they employ in speaking of Argentines are likely to include "conceited" and "arrogant." They tell you they can spot an Argentine miles away, that when he leaves his country he brings Argentina with him.

Though there is often great official cordiality, Brazilians and Argentines have had many differences. Argentines feel superior because, they say, they are more advanced in both culture and material things.

This, however, has not interfered with Brazilian-Argentine commerce. In fact, trade with Brazil could be even greater if Argentina had more wheat to supply. Argentines buy considerable Brazilian coffee, fruits, and tropical products.

Many Brazilians resented Perón's supposedly undercover activity against their President, Gaspar Dutra (1945–51) despite the fact that Dutra was a military man. The methods Perón used to cut off wheat shipments during one crisis caused bread prices to rise and produced considerable worker unrest, and they have not quite been forgotten. Argentine-Brazilian relations warmed after Getulio Vargas, Dictator-President for fourteen years, resumed the Presidency in 1951.

Perón still has ideas of better relations with both Brazil and Chile. On December 20, 1951, writing as "Descartes," he called for a union of Argentina, Brazil, and Chile as "a means of survival in a third World War." The three countries individually could not reach economic greatness, he said. Federation would be the best means of "living out the most colossal clash of our times between a united Asia and Europe and the United States."

He added that the Latin American countries were threatened by "new colonial forms of domination either by Communist assault or by economic penetration," and said it would be suicide not to work for confederation. Having expressed the idea, his article concluded: "Argentina is prepared, ready and willing."

Most significant, aside from the proposal itself, was the fact that it omitted Argentina's closest neighbor, Uruguay, for here is one country which many hundreds of thousands of Argentines really know and like. To *porteños*, seeing a friend off for Montevideo, Uruguay's capital, was no more exciting than watching a Staten Island ferry pull out, or seeing the Oakland boat heading for the trip across San Francisco Bay.

Every night at 10 P.M., down on their Dock Sud in Buenos Aires, whistles would blow, the gangplank go up, and the old-fashioned many-decked river boat tugged out to the muddy Rio de la Plata for the overnight journey.

The Montevideo boats still run, but the journey is not the same any more. The lights strung out along the river embankment as one leaves Buenos Aires, and the traditional *toastados* and coffee served just before arrival the next morning, haven't changed in all the years. But the contrast between state-controlled Buenos Aires and free Montevideo is now sharp and dramatic.

Newspapers in Uruguay are far closer to ours in the way they tell the news. *La Mañana* is pro-government; *El Pais* is in opposition. But both say exactly what they please. You step into a Montevideo telephone booth, dial a number, talk and hang up. Then, if you have just left Buenos Aires, you realize that there was no danger of the wire's being tapped. Baggage is inspected by customs authorities, but no books or magazines are seized as seditious, no letters scrutinized as dangerous, and no questions asked about family, friends, or religion.

Since 1943, hundreds of Argentines have found it expedient to take the night boat or the forty-five-minute plane ride to Montevideo to escape the police. Argentine exiles in the Uruguayan capital own an appropriately named bar, El Refugio, which is the first stop of many political fugitives. The most famous exile of 1951, Alberto Gainza Paz, publisher of *La Prensa*, went to his mother's *estancia* in Uruguay, when he had to flee.

For many years the only thing Argentines needed to travel to Uruguay was a *cedula*, or identification card. Many Argentines habitually spent their vacations at one of the many Uruguayan beaches which stretch eastward from Montevideo. Thousands of them owned chalets at lovely Punta del Este, the most famous resort. Many wealthy Argentine families invested in Uruguayan land and business—it is close to home, but out of reach of the Argentine government.

Argentines find a vacation in Uruguay as pleasant as we do a trip to Canada, even though the geographical differences between the two countries are hardly visible. The men and women in Montevideo and Buenos Aires look, dress, and outwardly behave pretty much the same. Out on the *estancias* life is similar to that on the other side of the Rio de la Plata. Even the gaucho tradition is similar.

But there is a great difference in attitudes. Argentines

aspire to dominance. Uruguayans know their country is small and make no effort to be more than they are. Some observers believe that because Argentina has always overshadowed her neighbor, Uruguayans have self-consciously declared their independence and expressed it in their individualism and democracy.

Uruguay owes its independence largely to the fact that neither Argentina nor Brazil is willing to see it become a part of the other. Perhaps because it has neither the men nor the resources to defend itself in a long struggle, it has always been a leader in plans for mutual defense within the hemisphere.

Unlike Argentina, Uruguay did not stay neutral during the war or later try to establish a "third position" between communism and capitalism. Uruguayan democrats speak up for their beliefs—and know they can count on our help if necessary. When Perón cut off wheat shipments to make Uruguayans vote for his favorite candidate in their election of 1946, the United States shipped thousands of tons of wheat to its spunky little South American friend. Perón's candidate lost.

Argentines know Uruguay as one of the few South American republics without racial or religious problems and with little clerical influence. It even renamed Christmas *Dia de la Familia* (Family Day) so as not to offend anyone. Church and State have been kept strictly apart. "We feel both are vital to democracy, but only when each follows its own course," Uruguayans say.

Some Argentines think their nationalization program resembles the Uruguayans'. The Uruguayan government has a virtual monopoly of banking and insurance. It owns and operates the light and power plants and the telephones. A government agency controls the state monopoly of cement, alcohol, and fuel. A national refrigeration plant has a monopoly on domestic meat, though several foreign companies maintain their own plants for export trade. The government owns and operates a number of hotels and casinos, and even one night club. It runs about a fourth of the country's railroad mileage.

But, Uruguayans point out, "The government does not run us, we run it." Businessmen and technicians, not politicians, administer the state services on orders to make them pay while giving cheap and efficient service. The state agencies use their profits for public benefit— Uruguay was a "welfare state" long before the term was invented. Its economy, based on meat, wool, and hides, is sturdy, and its currency strong. Uruguayans are secretly pleased as they watch visitors from rich, mighty Argentina struggle to stretch their shrinking Argentine *pesos* in Montevideo shops.

In December, 1951, *Newsweek* reported that Uruguay's only major foreign problem is Argentina. The purest democracy in the Western Hemisphere is temperamentally incompatible with the strong-arm rule of Perón. The scores of Argentine exiles who frequent Montevideo irritate the Argentine President, but Uruguayans are not afraid of their big, blustering neighbor. The peoples of the two countries are much alike, although the Italian influence is stronger in Argentina.

Though there have been many protests, Uruguayan newspapers continue to carry articles by Argentines who oppose the Perón government. Uruguayan radio stations broadcast these charges, and sometimes beam them back into Buenos Aires where they can easily be received on regular wave lengths. The Uruguayan government has never interfered with the activities of Argentine exiles.

Elsewhere in the hemisphere, peronista diplomacy is active. After General Manuel Odria came into power in Peru, relations with Argentina grew stronger. Perón also has friends among the military rulers of Venezuela. Argentine embassies in every Latin capital circulate peronista propaganda under the diplomatic frank.

In almost every country Argentine labor representatives offer scholarships or trips to Argentina, distribute literature, speak before various groups, and constantly seek to sell the viewpoint that Perón is labor's friend and that labor will benefit by following his lead.

In February, 1952, peronistas organized a new Latin American Labor Confederation in Asuncion, Paraguay. It was patterned on Perón's "third position" between Communism and capitalism. Other hemisphere labor organizations had not unanimously welcomed Argentina's government-controlled unions so they formed their own international group.

Chapter XXIV

The United States and the Argentine

A GROUP of well-dressed Argentine businessmen called on the head of a United States film company some years ago with a request. "It may seem ridiculous," they explained, "and you may want to turn us down. But we are in the men's furnishings business here in Buenos Aires, and the new Clark Gable film, *It Happened One Night*, is ruining our trade."

"How?" asked the movie man.

"Well, in one scene Gable takes off his shirt to go to bed—and he wears no undershirt. Now our young Argentines are refusing to buy undershirts and our business is being seriously affected!"

The movie man was first amused—then astonished. If one Made-In-Hollywood film could set such a trend, what might a whole series of pictures do?

His wondering was no idle musing, for films from the United States as well as our increasingly numerous books and magazines, cars and bathtubs, recordings and radio broadcasts, introduce Argentines to more than just notions about undershirts. Argentine morals and manners, ambitions and aspirations, outlook and perspective have all been affected by the strong winds from the North.

In the last two decades the influence of the United States in Argentina has increased tremendously. By this we mean influence in the widest sense. In part it is due to the decreasing role of Europe. Today, fewer well-to-do Argentines are visiting the Continent; fewer European books, films, and theatrical companies are coming to the Argentine. British influence has declined with the number of its investments. As the world grows smaller and Uncle Sam's role larger, every Latin-American country, even those which want to remain neutral, has become involved in foreign affairs.

Many Argentines do not relish our increasing influence, but more and more are beginning to realize it is an inescapable fact of life.

The influence of the United States is most obvious in the things Argentines use and do every day. Argentine women began to notice it when they bought products by Elizabeth Arden and Helena Rubinstein, and talked about them at home, at tea, at bridge, and at canasta, which, incidentally, came from the Rio de la Plata countries. At first only the wealthy ladies bought imported products. Today, these two firms alone do so much business in Argentina that both have established their own local manufacturing facilities. Almost every Argentine woman, no matter how poor or remote from the big city, prefers United States lipsticks and lotions, make-up and eye shadow, thinking they give her added glamour.

Both soap and soap opera in Argentina have been conspicuously influenced by the United States. Palmolive manufactures both soap and cologne in Argentina. The firm's daily serial gave Evita Perón one of her early radio jobs. Pond's finds that Argentine society girls, who once would have avoided such publicity, are now just as happy as any of our debutantes to explain, in full-page advertisements, how they became lovely and engaged through using the well-known product.

The number of other products from the United States Argentines use every day is tremendous. Every Argentine knows the Ford, the "Cad-ill-jack" and the "Boo-icke," even though it is often hard for newcomers to discover that the latter mean Cadillac and Buick. Ford, General Motors, and Chrysler have their own assembly plants in Argentina, turning out the most popular models as well as trucks and busses. Since the end of the war such production has decreased and some plants diverted entirely to official production, but our cars are still far more popular than the less expensive British, Italian, and French makes.

The strange usage to which our trade names are sometimes put is another never-ending source of delight to North Americans and an unspoken indication of Argentine regard. A leading baggage house is called Pullman, a word which does not exist in Spanish. A smart shoe shop is named Larry, not the Spanish equivalent, which would be Lorenzo. A dress house is called Daisy, not Margarita. R.C.A.-Victor is known under its own name, but pronounced in Argentine Spanish it sounds something like "Erra Sa Ah Veek-tor." Many homes, even in remote areas, boast their own "Sing-air" since so many Argentine women sew or have their clothes especially sewed for them.

Nylon has become a standard word to describe anything new, different, slightly miraculous—and probably made in the United States. Importation of nylon stockings, incidentally, was officially halted in 1951. They have become an important under-the-counter item and are constantly requested by every Argentine woman lucky enough to have friends in the United States.

Our influence, however, goes deeper than our washing machines and refrigerators, both of which are now coming to be accepted as a mark of a modern well-established Argentine urban family.

This influence shows in the desires, ambitions, and outlook of many Argentines, especially the younger generation. Their increasing informality of manners and customs stems in no small measure from the United States.

Our influence shows in the movies the Argentines prefer, the effect such films have on their daily lives, and their own desire to emulate the Hollywood model at least to some degree. It shows in the news and features they read, those from both the news services and syndicates— most of which are edited in the United States. It shows in the books, translated or original, in their shop windows and in their homes, in their advertisements, and the clothes and accessories they wear. Mostly, however, it appears in the realization on the part of more and more Argentines that this is the age of business and industrialization, of science and technology, of chemistry and medicine, in all of which the United States is the leader.

The most direct United States influence possibly arises from the news which Argentines read every day. For many years no Argentine paper or popular magazine has been really pro-United States. *La Prensa*, when it was free, and *El Mundo* before it became an official organ of the government, were not unfriendly. Neither was *La Nacion*. At the same time, these papers could hardly be regarded as strongly pro-United States in the same sense that the British-controlled *Mundo* was pro-British. Yet Argentines could hardly ignore the very bulk of news dispatches from the United States.

For many years Argentina's leading news services were the United Press, Associated Press, and the International News Service. They appeared in scores of papers throughout the country, even those which were anti-United States. In the early days of World War II, for instance, the Nazi *Deutsche La Plata Zeitung* carried a United States wire service, with carbon copies filed to Berlin, until the paper was black-listed and the agency got an opportunity to break its contract. The United States press services were popular with editors and readers because their stories were less prejudiced. Our press services had extensive news-gathering and handling facilities, and too many new stories that could not be ignored originated in the United States.

United States wire service reports from Europe often beat French, British, and German services. They went beyond politics to record news of economics, science, art, music, and personalities. Editors Press Service, headed by Joshua Powers, provided *La Prensa* and other dailies with all kinds of syndicated columns, special features, and cartoon strips. You could find advice to the lovelorn and health and beauty hints in many Argentine papers. "Jiggs and Maggie," "Winnie Winkle," "Flash Gordon," "Terry and the Pirates," in translation, were as familiar to Argentines as to fans here. Argentines have their own strips, like the mythical Indian "Patarazu," which was once syndicated in the United States, but it never had the following of "Donald Duck" or "Popeye," which in Argentina was called *Espinaca*, spinach. When *Espinaca* swallows a can of spinach to restore his strength, the howls of glee, Argentines say, can be heard in Patagonia.

The American correspondents working in Argentina represent such news agencies as United Press, Associated Press, and International News Service as well as individual newspapers including the New York *Times*, the *Herald Tribune*, the *Christian Science Monitor*, the New York *Daily News*, *Time*, *Newsweek* and others.

Censorship imposed by Argentine authorities has varied widely. At times anything filed for dispatch from Buenos Aires is blue-penciled to the extreme and at other times material could go out untouched. Everything depends on the situation prevailing at the moment. Sometimes stories are mailed to Montevideo to be wirelessed to home offices without censorship. Sometimes the mail is censored, sometimes it is not. Sometimes the correspondent's dispatch is seen in the United States by the Argentine Embassy in Washington and a protest is made. At other times even those stories most unfavorable to Argentina are ignored. In addition to the regular correspondents many visiting writers and editors came through Buenos Aires to observe and study conditions in Argentina. Some of them had long experience and their own sources of information. Others, much to the annoyance of the Argentines, made hasty visits and wrote inaccurate and superficial articles.

Magazines from the United States used to be popular in Argentina, but censorship and the shortage of exchange have cut down the list to a few "technical" publications. *Time* has been banned off and on during recent years as have *Newsweek, U.S. News and World Report, Life, Look, Business Week,* the *Saturday Evening Post, Cosmopolitan, Vision,* and others.

In view of the trouble United States news services and magazines have had in getting into the country, the material supplied by our Embassy Information Service has become increasingly important. It supplies Argentine papers with objective stories and texts of important speeches and State Department policy statements free of charge. Small daily and weekly papers often use the Service to supplement commercial sources.

The Information Service was preceded early in the war by the Asociación de Difusión Interamericana. Established by a number of United States businessmen, when Argentina was officially "neutral," the A.D.I. had to insist it was purely cultural. Now the Information Service functions as a regular Embassy department, though it operates from separate headquarters.

The Service maintains an extensive 16-mm and 35-mm motion picture distribution system both in Buenos Aires and interior cities. Operators take mobile truck units into rural areas for showings, frequently in schools and institutions. Boastful, extravagant, overly dramatic films are no longer used. Instead, programs include pictures of our industry and schools, our cities and towns, our industrial and social developments.

Argentines especially like a film which tells of a trip on a Greyhound bus. They say such a film gives them a much better idea of the United States than a straight Hollywood epic offering little background or explanation. "We see ourselves in the role of travelers," they say. They also like March of Time movies, narrated in Spanish. These appear not only in commercial theaters but in re-runs by the Information Services.

The Lincoln Library, another Information Service function, has also taken several unusual steps to make the United States better known to Argentines. Instead of locating on an obscure side street in Buenos Aires, it occupies a large first floor shop near Plaza San Martín right in the heart of Calle Florida's most exclusive shopping section. The Library's large plate glass show window displays posters about news and information pictures as well as the latest books in English.

Argentine crowds not only look at the window displays, but come in by the score to browse, study, and borrow books. Most lending libraries with new foreign books charge regular fees like our renting libraries. By making books available without charge or deposit, the Lincoln Library attracts not only secondary-school and university students who can read English and are interested in a wide variety of subjects, but older Argentines as well. The Library carries publications both friendly and unfriendly to the United States.

Early in the morning of July 9, 1952, a bomb shattered the front of the Library. Next day, despite hammering repairmen, hundreds of Argentines visited the building to use its services.

Some Argentine friends of the United States are interested in us because of their desire to trade and carry on business. Argentine industrialists admire our machines, our motors, and our marketing methods. They want more of them. They are the people who come in contact with the suppliers of such items. They may have made trips to the United States. Generally they like our way of operating. This group feels the pinch whenever export and import controls are imposed and constantly seek better official relations.

Some idea of their current commercial stake is shown in Argentina's exports to the United States, which in 1951 was $216.2 million dollars or 1,183,000,000 *pesos*, of which wool sales comprised half. Argentina's imports from the States during that year came to $230.8 millions of dollars.

Argentine commercial agents, who import and distribute United States products and sell Argentine products to us, are also likely to be pro-United States. So are the students who read and hear a great deal about us, and the Argentines who come to the States for visits or for medical treatment. At the Panagra offices, fares to Rochester, Minnesota, have been computed and posted because Argentines ask how much it costs to go to the Mayo Clinic almost as frequently as they want to know the fares to New York and Washington.

These Argentines who know the United States Chamber of Commerce in Argentina and its operations, who patronize the United States banks, and who have lunched at the American Club in Buenos Aires have become most friendly to Americans. It was Argentines such as these who put on warm demonstrations of welcome to our sailors during the visits of United States vessels.

In fact, pro-United States Argentines sometimes get so enthusiastic about our country as a miracle land that they embarrass patriotic but realistic North Americans.

Said one observer: "If I could bring eighteen million Argentines to the States, I'm sure fifteen million would return home enchanted with us. The most successful selling job we can do in Argentina, therefore, is to offer substitutes for this hard-to-arrange, expensive trip to our country. It does pay off."

The Instituto Cultural Argentino-Norteamericano, with headquarters in Buenos Aires and several interior branches, is one of the agencies which also tries to provide Argentines with an accurate picture of the United States. Many Argentines study English at the privately-supported, unofficial Instituto, participate in its plays for language practice, or stop in to listen to records, hear an occasional visiting speaker, or attend a special party on an American holiday.

Another pro-United States rallying point is the Club Universitaria Argentina Norteamericano. Its members include some 823 of the 1,500-odd Argentines who have spent four years in universities in the United States. They come from all political groups. Some were government-sponsored students, now official technical advisors. Others are sons and daughters of well-to-do Argentine families who chose American schools because of their interest in the United States or because it is now difficult to send their children to Europe and they want to give them the best education available.

A leader of the Club Universitaria is an unusual chemist, Casimir Lanas Sarrata. He left his native Spain because of opposition to Franco. Later he started a business of his own, Dana Perfumes, now highly successful both in the United States and Argentina. He has developed an enthusiasm for the United States more vital—and effective—than that of any *Yanqui*.

Some Argentines dislike us for purely personal reasons. Others nurse strong political bias. Still more follow the varying official attitude. Some government people told us we should not become alarmed by the President's anti-*Yanqui* speeches because "Perón's campaigns to whip up hatred are intended for domestic consumption." Yet the very fact that they are stirred up means that they must affect at least some Argentines or they would not continue to be so essential a part of the official program.

More and more North Americans who go to the Argentine are genuinely interested in the country. They are disturbed about political conditions, partly because unrest affects their own business, partly because they hate to see democracy losing ground. However, most of them have learned to hold their tongues in front of Argentines. More and more Americans are being invited into Argentine homes. They have come to understand what first appears to be Argentine coldness and keep trying even if rebuffed.

The personal reasons why so many individual Argentines dislike us are important, but the organized opposition to the United States is far more significant and far more serious. It finds its most vehement expression in the nationalist groups. From 1950 on attacks on the United States have been growing more and more bitter.

By the spring of 1952 all newspapers—they were, of course, all official organs—were engaged in a concerted attack on the United States. One of the most venomous examples of the official condemnation of our country was carried on posters used during the 1951 election campaign. These posters made the statement that the citizens of the United States were "thieves and robbers whose only national interest is domination, and who should leave the country."

I went to the Argentine in August, 1947. I had no prejudices, and I was under instructions from President Truman and Secretary of State Marshall to be as friendly as possible with the Argentines. Although I was familiar with a number of Latin-American countries, it was my first trip to the Rio de la Plata. I had no preconceived ideas about what I expected the Argentines to do or what kind of people they would be.

Because the journey was hurried, I could only take hand baggage. The first calls on the President are always made in formal clothes. I did not have formal clothes, but Guy Ray, the Embassy's Chargé d'Affaires, was easily able to secure them for me. Argentina is extremely protocol-conscious, so the Embassy had its own favorite rental agency for borrowing exactly the correct clothes. Thanks to this agency I was able to appear properly dressed. It is customary for an Ambassador presenting his credentials to make some formal remarks written, of course, by Embassy people trained in exactly the proper formal thing to say. After presenting my credentials and shaking hands with the Cabinet members, I said to President Perón: "You and I are both practical fellows. I think you have heard everything in my speech before. So, perhaps instead of reading it to Your Excellency and keeping your Cabinet standing, you might like to have me just give it to you so that we will have time to talk about more important things."

He smiled. "That's good. Let's go into my private office and talk." We did, for more than an hour. We covered a score of issues and established an atmosphere of friendly association and mutual confidence.

Subsequently, I traveled to every part of the country —north to the Chaco, and south to the tip of Tierra del Fuego. Often I flew in a small Embassy plane with General Caldwell, our Military Attaché, and Colonel Donovan. Our trips ranged far into the interior. I had unlimited opportunity to get to know Argentines who did not live in the capital—and, in turn, to let them know a United States ambassador.

Travel is one part of an ambassador's assignment, but he has other tasks as well. He has to conduct official business with as little inconvenience or disturbance as possible. He has to keep Washington informed and to carry out Presidential and State Department instructions. He should also strengthen contacts with government officials and with local leaders of art, literature, and science.

Our government keeps a sharp watch of Argentina's economic activities. The agricultural attaché, or one of his assistants, visits every part of the country to obtain information on cattle production, grains, cereals, and a host of related products. Obviously, this is no mere idle curiosity. This information enables us to determine how our own products will fare on world markets. The planting schedules for thousands of our farmers and the food requirements of European countries are dependent on both the the United States and Argentina.

If our agricultural attaché were to base his reports on statistical information alone, he certainly would not get the most accurate results possible. He must be friendly with the heads of agricultural societies, and with key *estancieros*, and officials in government agencies who are willing to talk privately about things that do not always go into official reports. He also needs to keep in contact with all kinds of people to get accurate, up-to-the-minute information. Grain figures, for example, were often late or overly optimistic. However, watching rail shipments provided a measuring rod much like the index of commercial activity supplied by our own boxcar loading figures.

Our military, minerals, oil, political, and other attachés all operate in their own individual ways, some methodically, some with the kind of rare insight and understanding which makes them real authorities and invaluable to the ambassador.

The system is extremely businesslike, but with a necessary diplomatic touch. A businessman who becomes an ambassador, therefore, does not find himself in a completely strange world. Often, in fact, an ambassador from outside the diplomatic orbit is able to cut through conventional patterns, while still utilizing to the fullest the experience of the career men who form his staff.

Official Embassy reports are drafted by specialists, then they go through regular routines established by the State Department to insure uniformity in its activities around the world. Some are coded for cables and radiograms, others sent by diplomatic pouch. Couriers carry the most vital pouches strapped to their wrists as they fly across the hemisphere. Contents of the pouches are considered untouchable because if opened by foreigners they might cause a break in diplomatic relations.

Another vital phase of an ambassador's assignment is to make certain he does everything possible to facilitate the work of the press correspondents from his own country. Only then can they do the best job possible in keeping readers at home informed. I no sooner arrived in Buenos Aires than several American correspondents came to see me asking what my attitude would be toward their activities. I told them they were assured of fullest cooperation. After several days, they returned. They said that they had met and had drawn up a plan for a weekly press conference. I limited this conference to American citizens representing recognized publications. Throughout my stay in the Argentine, my relations with the American press corps was most cordial. I found the correspondents did a truly admirable job in reporting the facts as they saw them.

Relations with American businessmen resident in the country are also a vital part of an ambassador's assignment. When I first came down many of these men, numbering four thousand with their families, were uncertain where they stood regarding imports, exports, labor, financial, and other problems. Explaining that I lacked their familiarity with local conditions, I urged them to get together and draw up a program that would further United States-Argentine commercial relations. "If I can accept it without reservation," I said, "I will do everything possible to put it through." Such a plan was developed and cooperation was improved, even though obviously every objective we sought to accomplish could not be realized.

In addition to reporting and analyzing for Washington what goes on in the country to which he is accredited, the job of an ambassador is to promote his own country's interests and to present its point of view as effectively as possible. In order to deal with such agencies as the Foreign Ministry and the important government offices it is necessary to follow a special kind of official routine. Many Argentine officials, for example, do not even appear in their offices until 11 A.M. They stay until 1:00. Then they go to a large lunch followed by a *siesta*. The hardest work of the day often begins around 4:30 in the afternoon. Appointments with high government officials are usually made between 5:00 and 7:00 P.M., a time when most North American men would like to be finishing a game of golf, returning from the office, or winding up their day's activities.

There are so many mistaken ideas about an Ambassador's social life that some details may be of interest. Almost every one of our Embassy luncheons, teas, or dinners, no matter how small, was designed to bring together some Argentines and Americans. Because differences between peronistas and their opponents were so great, care had to be taken about invitations. Nevertheless, during this period, the United States Embassy was about the only place where opponents and members of the regime were able to meet under one roof amicably.

An ambassador who dislikes too much protocol and red tape has definite advantages. My experience in business and in cattle-raising helped establish an immediate community of interest with many Argentines, so much so, in fact, that the days were never long enough to meet all the people it would have been interesting to know.

Members of the Embassy staff were encouraged to get to know Argentines in government, business, and in private circles. An unusual step was to permit Embassy staff members to entertain Argentines in our official home. The Embassy Residence with its staff of seventeen men and five women, all living in the building, had to be paid for anyway, and our Embassy was saved both the higher rentals and the higher prices charged by hotels and clubs. This made their extremely small entertainment allowances go much farther.

Entertaining at the Embassy naturally brought a volume of return invitations to all kinds of Argentine functions. These ranged from high teas to invitations to the *estancias* where a whole steer or sheep was often roasted over the fire. Unfortunately, it was necessary to decline a good many invitations. Not only was there insufficient time but eating the quantity of food put away by many an Argentine was an utter impossibility for any visitors desirous of keeping their health.

We gave important receptions at the Embassy for two visiting United States fleets, one under the command of Admiral McCormick and the other under the command of Admiral Foskett, each with twelve hundred enlisted men. My wife and the wives of the Embassy officials invited a number of young Argentine, American, British and other young ladies to come to the dances. Considering the number of letters we received from the boys and their families when they got home, all had just as good a time being entertained as we had in entertaining them. With this extraordinary number of unattached young men on leave in one of the world's largest capitals, some feared an unfortunate incident might occur. However, the late General Bertollo, Chief of Police at Buenos Aires, told me afterward: "Never once during the visit of either fleet had I any reason for concern. Your boys conducted themselves with great credit not only to the American Naval service but to their Argentine hosts."

At various times Argentines interested in sports, literature, law, and science were Embassy guests. And we also followed an open door policy at the Embassy offices, receiving practically any Argentine who had business to discuss.

The press of duties was sometimes so great that the only place an Ambassador could find relief was in the Turkish bath near the Embassy offices. Here, sitting in the steam room at midday, I sometimes had an opportunity to talk to all kinds of Argentine businessmen and officials. I recall one particular midday session not long before my departure which has particular significance today.

"You know," one of my Argentine friends said, "wouldn't it be a great idea if in a broader sense the people of our own two countries could come to know one another on the same intimate, friendly basis as we men who gather here. Here we can be completely natural. Here we've come to know, to like, to get along with each other. If we could do the same in our other relations maybe the hemisphere and the world would be a happier place. And the things which perplex both of us might soon disappear."

On reflection, I think my Argentine *amigo* could not have been more right.

Index

P9-ARV-236

The Brain Book

By the same author
The TM Technique

The Brain Book

Peter Russell

HAWTHORN BOOKS, INC.
Publishers / New York

A HOWARD & WYNDHAM COMPANY

THE BRAIN BOOK

Copyright © 1979 by Peter Russell. Copyright under International and Pan-American Copyright Conventions. All rights reserved, including the right to reproduce this book or portions thereof in any form, except for the inclusion of brief quotations in a review. All inquiries should be addressed to Hawthorn Books, Inc., 260 Madison Avenue, New York, New York 10016. This book was manufactured in the United States of America.

Library of Congress Catalog Card Number: 78–65399

ISBN: 0–8015–0886–X

1 2 3 4 5 6 7 8 9 10

Contents

Preface

Within our own heads lies one of the most complex systems in the known universe. Its power and versatility far surpass that of any man-made computer, and, as the late Professor Anokhin of Russia remarked, no human being has ever come anywhere near to using its full potential. There are two principal reasons for this underuse. First, most people's brains are to some degree hampered by fatigue and stress. We cannot get as much from a brain that is tired and dull as we can from a fully alert, stress-free nervous system. The growing realization of the need to free ourselves from deep-rooted stresses and negative conditioning is reflected in the continually expanding interest in meditation, relaxation, stress reduction, psychotherapy, Gestalt, bioenergetics, biofeedback, counseling, rolfing, massage, yoga, etc.

Yet freeing ourselves from accumulated tensions is not in itself enough. We also need to know how to use the enormous potential that is thereby being made available to us. Unfortunately no handbook came with the brain and no one told us how to get the most out of it: Instead we have learned to use it very much through "trial and error." Over the last two decades research into the function of the human brain has given us a much clearer idea of how it works. By applying these findings to everyday tasks all of us can begin to benefit from the brain's natural way of functioning and so begin to use our incredible potential that much more fully.

It is toward this second aspect of self-improvement that the present book is directed, and as such is complementary to my earlier book on meditation and the reduction of stress. My own interest in this particular aspect of mental development owes much to Tony Buzan, who has already done considerable work in this area. I first met Tony through one of those synchronistic chains of events in which everything seems to fit into place. (More and more nothing appears to happen by chance.) The day that I finished the final typescript for my book *The TM Technique* I sat back in an armchair, and deciding to switch off for a while, switched on the television—a rare indulgence. On came a program called "The Enchanted Loom," about the brain's vast untapped potential and the many ways in which people were now beginning to use it more fully, particularly through a deeper understanding of the roles of the left and right sides of the brain. I immediately recognized that the approaches being discussed complemented my studies and interest in meditation—they were the relative, or particular, side of mental development, as opposed to the absolute approach of meditation. The two were obviously not in conflict but very complementary; each approach had a lot to offer to the other. I resolved somehow to get in touch with the originator, and one of the key figures in the program, Tony Buzan.

Three days later a Mr. Mark Brown visited me with an interest in meditation. During our conversation it came out that he was involved with a certain Mr. Buzan! He duly gave me Tony's telephone number, and being in London a week later I took the opportunity to get in touch. Meanwhile Tony had already heard through Mark of my own work, and on the evening that I telephoned had been discussing with an American colleague, who also wanted to meet with me regarding meditation, how they should get in touch. So when I introduced myself saying "You don't know me but. . . ." I was greeted with "Oh yes, but I do. I was just talking about you. Come on over." We talked into the night and into most of the next week; both of us sharing with each other as much as possible of our respective work and skills.

Since that meeting in 1974 many creative sparks have flown between us and we have worked together on a number of projects, including the writing of this book. One of the aims of the book is to present and supplement the theoretical background used by Buzan to support the practical methods suggested in his book *Use Your Head* (based on the BBC TV series of the same name, published in America under the title *Use Both Sides of Your Brain*), and to relate many findings from experimental psychology to the everyday use of the brain.

APPROACHING THE BOOK

The book has been divided into two sections. The first part gives some basic information about the human brain, its development and structure. It is impossible to deal adequately with such a large and expanding field in less than a hundred pages—one could hardly do it justice in a thousand pages. The purpose of this section is to provide a general background to the second part in which specific brain functions and ways of improving them will be discussed. Aspects of brain research not relevant to this have had to be omitted.

Any book that selects some avenues of research and ignores others is going to be biased, and this book is no exception. By far the greater part of brain research to date has been hell-bent on trying to measure present levels of ability—to see how well or how badly the brain performs in the suboptimum conditions in which we all live and the grossly suboptimum conditions of the experimental laboratory. Very little research has been directed toward how we can maximize our abilities.

In this book I have argued for a much greater optimism with regard to brain potential. I am more interested in the amazing things the human brain *can* accomplish and the ways in which we can help it do so than I am in the ways at which we are at present using it. So I have been selective. But the fact that a book can be filled with optimistic news about the brain is for me a source of optimism in itself.

As with many books, you do not necessarily have to start with the first chapter and plod through in sequence. You might like to turn first to the short section that deals with this very point (pp. 202–07), or to the last chapter, which gives an overview of the whole book, or anything else that takes your fancy or seems relevant. Flipping through also gives a good overview of what to expect and helps comprehension when it comes to looking at the book in depth. In the second part of the book much of the advice on using your brain is given at the end of each chapter; you might like to take this in first and come back to the theoretical side later. Whatever your approach, make sure you enjoy the reading.

The summaries at the end of each chapter are in the form of mind maps. (The development and use of these is explained in chapter 13.)

The main points are better organized if one starts with a general concept at the center of the page and branches out using lines, arrows, boxes, and colors to represent the more detailed points and the ways in which they are related to each other. Such maps can take a variety of forms, but they all share the attribute of breaking away from the restrictions imposed by ordinary linear prose.

Going over the map provided will serve as a good review of the chapter and has been shown to improve memory of the material significantly. Even better is to make your own maps. Guidelines on this are given on pages 176–82.

Regular courses are run on most of the topics covered here. For details of courses offered in North America, Europe, and elsewhere, please contact:

The Learning Methods Group
BCM Box 606
London WCIV 6XX
England

Telephone: 01–455–8266

Telex: 923229

In addition I welcome feedback and discussion and can always be contacted through the publisher.

Acknowledgments

Special thanks to Tony Buzan for the many discussions that led to this book and for his valuable criticism during its writing. Thanks to Mark Brown and Brian Helweg-Larsen for comments and feedback and for several ideas which have innocently percolated the text. Thanks also to Fru Segal and Ruth Walmsley for their flexibility when it came to typing large chunks of the book in "no time."

Part One
DEVELOPMENT AND STRUCTURE

1.
The Spearhead
of Evolution

What are the brain's limits?
Is the brain like a computer?
Why don't we use our brains fully?
What makes a genius?
Does early environment affect a child?

There are brains that can detect the minutest changes in light, sound, smell, and touch; delicately and accurately integrate the actions of many muscles; regulate the functioning of the body's many organs so as to preserve the optimum conditions for life. Such brains learn from experience, and they have found ways to communicate with each other through simple "languages" and so share their knowledge. They are also sensitive to magnetic and electric fields and ultraviolet light. They can analyze the polarization of sunlight and use it to tell directions. They keep a constant track of time, even through the night. These brains function as accurate guidance systems; compensating for wind direction, they correlate the rapid beating of four tiny wings, landing their encapsulating little bodies delicately at the center of a waving flower. Such brains are the size of a grain of salt, contain a mere nine

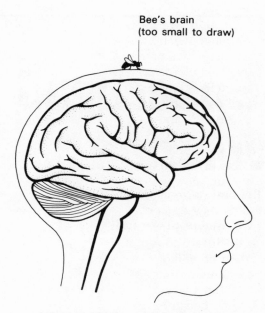

Bee's brain
(too small to draw)

Figure 1 The bee and the human brain.

hundred neurons, and can be found inside a bee's head. What then can we expect from our own brains, ten million times the size, and many billion times as complex?

Clearly the human brain has to control a much larger body. This, however, is only part of the answer; a much smaller brain could carry out all the necessary functions quite satisfactorily. A shark, for example, has a large body and very accurate senses, but its brain is very much smaller than ours.

Where we differ most radically from bees and sharks—and from virtually every other creature—is in our highly developed use of language, our capacity to learn not only from our own experience but from that of others, and our ability to adapt the environment to our own needs.

A human being has the faculty of self-consciousness, in the sense of being aware of his own experiences and of himself as a conscious being.* With this awareness of his own conscious processes comes free-

*Because I find the alternatives unwieldy, I use "he" throughout in its everyday androgynous sense of "he or she" except where "he" is obviously intended.

dom of choice and the ability to make deliberate actions. He is also an intelligent being. Intelligence, in its broadest sense, may be defined as the ability to modify instinctive behavior in the light of previous experience; to abstract common elements from situations that may appear to have nothing in common and to apply these insights to future activities. Intelligence and self-consciousness together give human beings the unique capacity to progress and evolve within their own lifetimes.

The smallest development in physical evolution takes thousands of generations. Mental evolution is many times faster. An individual's nervous system is continually changing and adapting to the environment throughout his life. Our knowledge of ourselves and the world around us is growing at a fantastic rate. The number of new books and scientific papers, for example, is doubling every eight years.[1] The more we apply this knowledge to our own betterment, the faster we will progress and evolve, both as individuals and as a race.

The culmination of millions of years of evolution has been the development of the human brain. Not only is the human brain aware of its own existence, but through it the universe has begun to know itself. Our minds have become the spearhead of evolution, and the degree to which we progress depends upon the degree to which we make use of this most incredible product of nature—the degree to which we use our intelligence and our consciousness to the full.

UNLIMITED POTENTIAL

The intricate web of nerves that constitutes the human nervous system weighs only three and a half pounds yet is probably the most complex system known in the universe. And, by the awe and wonderment it produces, it is for some the most beautiful.

The more that is learned about the human brain, the more its capacities and potentials are found to go far beyond earlier speculations. The storage capacity of the brain, for example, is sufficient to record a thousand new bits of information every second from birth to old age, and still have room to spare. Recent experiments suggest we may in fact remember everything that happens to us.

As a processor of information the brain is extraordinarily fast. It can, for instance, receive the visual image of a person's face in a few hundredths of a second; analyze its many details in a quarter of a second; and synthesize all the information into a single whole, create a conscious three-dimensional full-color experience of the face, recognize this face out of thousands of others recorded in memory—even though the face may never before have been seen in this position, this light, these surroundings, or with this expression on it—and recall from memory details about the person and numerous ideas, associations, and images connected with the person, all in less than a second. At the same time it will be interpreting the expression on the face, generating emotional feelings toward the person, deciding on courses of action, possibly starting intricate combinations of muscle processes throughout the body, resulting in an outstretched hand, a smile, and complex vibrations of the vocal cords (full of subtle intonations), saying "Hi, Sam." While all the foregoing transpires, the brain will be analyzing and digesting other visual data and data from the other senses, using some of them, such as sounds and smells, to help identify the face. It will also be monitoring and adjusting the body's position, keeping it in balance or moving smoothly; and it will continually be checking on several hundred internal physiological parameters, such as the temperature and chemical constituents of the blood, and compensating for any deviations from normal so as to maintain the body in its optimum state of functioning. The brain continues in this way, perceiving, remembering, monitoring, and integrating a myriad different functions every second of every day of our lives.

Human perception is extremely acute. The nose, for example, can detect one molecule of gas, while a cell in the retina of the eye is sensitive to a single photon of light, and if the ear were any more sensitive, it would pick up the sound of the random vibrations of its own molecules. The brain is sensitive to magnetic and electric fields, to the phases of the moon, and possibly to the positions of the planets as well.[2] There is now increasing evidence that we are also sensitive to the mental activities of other people, being directly affected by their moods and thoughts.[3]

In order to cope with the problems of day-to-day survival the normal brain appears to limit its awareness, filtering out a large part of its sensory input. However, the brain's full sensitivity is sometimes revealed in pathological cases. Physicist Leonid Vasiliev reported on a man who could suddenly make out tiny objects from great distances. He died within twenty-four hours, and a blood clot was found on the right side of his optic prominence. Schizophrenics show abnormal sensory acuity. Addison's disease (a shortage of adrenal cortical hormones) enhances taste *150 times* and sharpens smell and hearing.[4]

It is frequently stated that we use only 10 percent of our full mental potential. This, it now appears, is rather an overestimate. We probably do not use even 1 percent—more likely 0.1 percent or less. The apparent limits of the human brain are only the limits of the uses to which we put it, and the limits of what we believe is possible.

In terms of its complexity and versatility, the human brain far surpasses any computer on earth. Computers, it is true, are very fast at mathematical calculations and step-by-step logical processes, but these represent only a small part of the brain's many abilities.

The most important difference between the brain and a computer is that the brain not only works in a linear step-by-step fashion, but also performs parallel processing, integrating and synthesizing information, and abstracting from it generalities. Whereas the human brain can recognize a face in less than a second, there is no computer in the world that could do the same. Computers have been developed which can recognize a simple object such as a cup from a collection of ten or so other objects, but they will take several minutes to do this. Moreover, they cannot recognize individual objects—only general classes of objects.

A transistorized computer capable of all the human brain can do would not fit inside Carnegie Hall. Recent advances in electronic miniaturization allow the circuitry for a sophisticated pocket calculator to be put on a small chip only a few millimeters square. Yet even using such tiny circuits, a computer containing the same potential as your brain would weigh more than ten tons. Conversely, the whole of the world's telephone system is equivalent to only about one gram of your brain— a piece the size of a pea!

Despite the vast amount being discovered about the brain's fantastic capacity and the ways in which it works, few people know how to make the best use of their brains. A major reason for this is that as children few of us were taught about mental functions themselves. We were probably told to remember various facts but not taught about how memory works and how best to remember, told to study and digest books but not taught how to approach a book in order to get the most out of it, told to read but not taught how the eye and brain work during reading, told to observe but not taught about the processes of attention, told to make notes but not taught in what form information is most easily assimilated by the brain. It is little wonder then that people continually complain of poor memory, slow reading, and lack of concentration.

There are numerous handbooks on gardening, building, television repair, travel, car maintenance, solar generators, and windmills; and many handbooks on the body, health, diet, and sex. But there is almost nothing on how the brain works and how to get the most out of it. In this book recent research on the brain and its potential will be brought together to show how your brain can be used more efficiently and how to take the best care of it.

A BORN GENIUS?

Until recently, it was thought that a chimpanzee could not learn language. Studies in the United States, however, have now shown this to be false. The chimp's deficiency lies not in its brain but in its larynx. It has no proper voice box. So researchers have concentrated on using various forms of sign language rather than speech to investigate the chimp's linguistic abilities.

In the late 1960s Allen and Beatrice Gardner, at the University of Nevada, taught a female chimp the sign language used by deaf-mutes, and within three years she had a vocabulary of over eighty words and was making up combinations of words on her own.[5] Following this, David Premack, at the University of Los Angeles at Santa Barbara, taught a chimp a language using simple plastic shapes of various colors. In this case, the chimp not only readily mastered a vocabulary of 120 words but began to make abstractions and form concepts from them.[6] Even more impressive work has been done at the Stanford Research Institute, where a gorilla has learned a vocabulary of over one thousand words.[7] And a thousand words is the working vocabulary of the average American. If a "dumb" gorilla can do this, what can a human brain do given a real chance?

Numerous studies on geniuses and gifted children suggest that our mental abilities are not genetically inherited in the same way as are red hair, blue eyes, or ear lobes. Our mental aptitudes seem to be determined more by the quality of our early environment, especially the periods immediately before and after birth. A common feature of nearly all gifted children is that they were brought up in a rich and varied environment with plenty of opportunities to learn.

In 1800 a German doctor called Witte decided to give his child Karl as rich an environment as possible. Although slow initially, Karl

Witte quickly caught up. By the age of six he was described as a "precocious lad"; at nine he entered the University of Leipzig; at fourteen he gained his Ph.D., and at sixteen his Doctor of Law.[8]

Dr. Witte's program became the model for many aspiring parents in the nineteenth century. Professor Berle, at Tufts University near Boston, gave all four of his children a rich and varied environment during their early years, and all four developed the most remarkable minds. The odds against all four being so-called "natural" geniuses are many millions to one.

In England a Mr. Thompson applied the principle to his two sons, and both grew up to lead most successful lives. The second entered Glasgow University when only ten years old and went on to become one of the greatest physicists of the nineteenth century, Lord Kelvin. He continued to lead a full and healthy life right up to the age of eighty-three, contradicting the popular notion that such people burn themselves out early in life.

John Stuart Mill, probably one of the greatest nineteenth-century philosophers, had a similar early education and by the age of three was learning Greek. Mozart, born into a family of musicians, heard his father's music and had instruments around him from a very early age. By five he was playing and composing for the violin and at eight had written his first symphony. Many centuries before him, Julius Caesar first started acquiring his tactical skills when he rode into battle at the age of three, seated behind his uncle. Similarly with Alexander the Great. Time and again we find that the great names of history had benefited from a full and stimulating environment during the earliest years of life.

Georges Gurdgieff, the mystical teacher, once wrote that a person needs three forms of nourishment: air, food, and experience. Deprive him of any of these and he will die. That air and food are essential has long been obvious, but only recently have we recognized the value of experience. Deprived of sight, hearing, touch, taste, and smell, a person starts hallucinating, may lose touch with normal reality, and become extremely frightened. Few people have withstood such conditions of total deprivation of experience for more than a few hours.[9]

The newborn child is in a particularly sensitive state and even a slight restriction of nourishment can have lasting effects on its development. We now recognize the need to ensure that a child has plenty of air and the most suitable foods, but as far as experience goes, most babies are half-starved. Little wonder then that geniuses are such a rarity.

THE EARLY ENVIRONMENT

At birth most babies, when held up with their feet on the floor, will begin to behave as if they were trying to walk. We in the West have tended to belittle this, believing that a child should not start walking until the age of fourteen months or so. In Uganda, however, where mothers encourage this walking reflex, babies are found walking at seven to ten months. This is not a special characteristic of the race, for if a Ugandan baby is brought up in England, he generally does not walk until fourteen months.

At six weeks the Ugandan child is sitting up on his own with no support and participates actively with the world around him. And at one year he is talking as well, with a large vocabulary. The mother follows the infant in helping him with whatever he tries to do: Playing, grasping, and talking are all positively encouraged.[10] Unfortunately, though, the Ugandan child is virtually abandoned by his mother at the age of four, and this rapid early development is largely wasted.

A child is born with a natural insatiable curiosity to explore and find out more about the world he is inhabiting. He is born thirsting for experience and knowledge. Yet too often in trying to help children we hinder them. We don't give them problems to solve so much as answers to remember, and if this intense curiosity is not exploited, it may be wasted forever.

Babies who are spoken to as human beings rather than just cooed at have a much greater opportunity to pick up the basics of human language. They start speaking earlier and generally stay ahead in their development. It is found, for example, that children in professional families, who have a rich verbal environment, develop speech faster than those in families of blue-collar workers.

Generally, though, we still impose severe handicaps on the young child trying to learn language. At the time when his brain is soaking up language, we teach him that a certain four-legged creature is called a "woof-woof." A little later he has to relearn that it is a "doggie," and later still that it is really a "dog." By the time the second or third relearning is taking place a lot of time, energy, and potential learning capacity have been wasted. Treat a baby as a simpleton, and he will behave like one. Treat him as a conscious, learning, evolving center of creative intelligence, and he will show that he is just that.

Winifred Stoner tried putting these theories into practice, treating her daughter as an adult and encouraging her natural inquisitiveness from birth onward. By the age of three she could use a typewriter and was composing poetry, and by five she could speak eight languages fluently, including Esperanto.[11]

In New York, in 1952, Aaron Stern, a survivor from a Nazi concentration camp, decided to start giving his newborn daughter, Edith, a rich environment from the moment she was born. The radio was tuned to classical music all day. He talked to her as much as possible, though baby talk was forbidden, and showed her flash cards with numbers and animals on them. At one year she spoke simple sentences; at two she knew the alphabet; and by the age of four and a half she had read volume one of the *Encyclopaedia Britannica* from beginning to end. At six she read two books and the *New York Times* every day. She skipped alternate years in elementary school, skipped secondary school entirely, and enrolled in college at the age of twelve. At fifteen she was teaching higher mathematics at Michigan State University and working on her Ph.D. Her IQ score is a consistent 200, on a scale where 150 represents "genius."[12] Edith's education was not an all-around education but was very biased toward intellectual learning and was also very dry and not the sort that we would not necessarily wish upon our children. Nevertheless, it does bring out the sort of remarkable development that can take place when a child is given intensive stimulation and encouragement from an early age.

What is interesting about such children is that generally they are not just gifted in one particular field; they are not just brilliant mathematicians with no ability in literature or art; they are natural all-rounders, showing equal abilities in a diversity of studies, in sports, in art, in leadership, or in whatever else they turn their attention to. Nor are they social misfits; providing the training is not forced, they are very much the opposite.

This should be the normal pattern of mental development.

A rich early environment explains why the eldest child of a family is often found to be the brighter and more successful one. A survey of top scientists reveals that 70 percent of them were the first child in a family.[13] Parents generally tend to devote more of their attention to the first child; by the time the second and third come along, their attention is divided and the novelty has begun to wear a little.

Interestingly, this trend is sometimes reversed in very large families—the later children showing increased intellectual growth. The theory is that a large number of elder brothers and sisters enriches the later child's early environment, compensating for the lack of parental attention—what is called the big-brother effect.[14]

EARLY EDUCATIONAL PROGRAMS

Maria Montessori established a broad network of schools based on the idea of encouraging the child's own natural learning ability—his insatiable curiosity and unending questioning. Believing there to be no practical limits to the child's ability to assimilate his environment, she provided a rich diversity of experience for the child. Most children in her schools were reading effortlessly by the age of three or four. Over the years she looked after six mongoloid children, who would ordinarily have grown up mentally retarded. Montessori treated them just like other children at her school. By the time they had finished, they were equal in intellectual abilities to "normal" children in conventional schools.

In 1965 the United States set up Head Start, a diverse program designed to increase the development of socially deprived children. It was not as intensive as some of the individual programs just described. In a typical program children would be given just two hours a week of increased attention, and facilities not available at home. Yet even this small enrichment had positive and lasting effects. Ninety-six studies have now been completed and all show some beneficial changes. Far fewer Head Start children need to attend special schools. In one study only 1 percent needed special education, compared with 30 percent of similar children not participating. IQ scores rose significantly from an average of 92 to 100, and remained at this higher level. Mathematical and linguistic abilities increased, and Head Start children also showed greater confidence and social competence than control groups.[15]

In another study forty babies, all of whom had mothers with an IQ of 70 or less, were divided into two groups. One group received personal, highly intensive enrichment treatment on a daily basis. By the time they were four years old, they showed an IQ of 130—which is gifted by normal criteria. The other group, who had no special attention, had an IQ of 80 on the same tests (there is usually a tendency to shift toward the mean of 100 from parent to child).[16] Similar enrichment programs in England and Europe have been equally revealing.

Another remarkable innovation in early education has been the television series "Sesame Street." Much of theory has here been applied to millions of children at a time and with profound results. Their later performance at school in reading, writing, spelling, mathematics, and general education has startled many of their teachers.

Education in many other countries has likewise begun to recognize the value of early learning. Public education in Russia, for example, begins at the age of three rather than at five, and it is claimed that as a result Russian children are, on average, up to two years ahead of those in the West.

A rich early environment can, though, be wasted if not properly followed through. Our present educational system is not well equipped to deal with prodigious rates of mental development, and it is an unfortunate fact that the gifted child is sometimes held back by traditional ideas of what should be normal.

A typical case is the girl whose mother gave her a rich and varied environment from the very beginning and always treated her and spoke to her as another adult. The little girl began to show the rapid development characteristic of such children. By the age of three she had mastered the basis of arithmetic, doing the mental calculations of a nine-year-old; she could hold a fluent, coherent conversation with adults; and she was continually questioning everything that happened, soaking up her environment and learning at an accelerated rate.

At the age of five she went to the local school along with other children of her age. But the educational system was simply not geared to deal with such a bright child. Becoming embarrassed, the poor child began to pretend she did not know as much as she did. Within a few months she had begun to become "normal," and began to lose her abilities. She found it much easier to get on at school if she did not know the meanings of long words, if she could not do her sums, and if she could only count as far as ten, like all the other children. The worrisome thing is that when prodigious children begin to perform this way, they are very clever at it; they can hide their abilities so well that often the teachers themselves are completely deceived by it and have no idea of their real abilities.

A recent study by the Social Sciences Research Council in England has measured just how much such children can be held back by the educational system. It was found that, on the average, gifted children were two and a half years behind their mental age. Though only around eight and a half years old, the children studied had a mental age of

fourteen, as measured by their IQ. But they were found to be performing only as well as children of eleven and a half.[17] Compared with others
of their age, they were still gifted, but in terms of their true capacity
they were backward.

Yet even were he not held back, the most gifted child would
probably still be functioning at only a fraction of his full potential. The
possibilities that await us once we fully understand how to educate our
brains are truly fantastic.

Figure 2

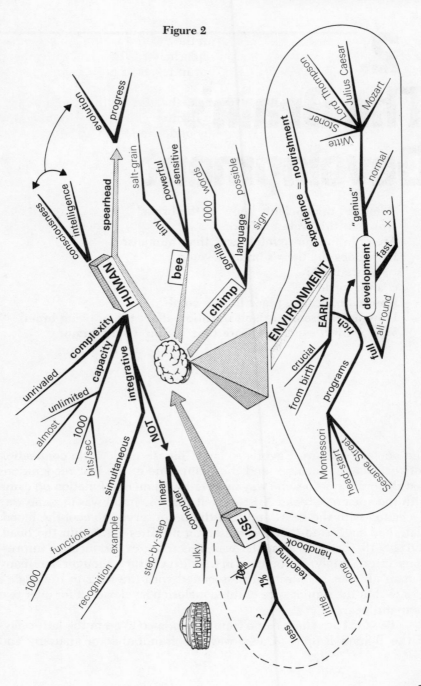

2.
The Brain's
Development

What did the ancients know of the brain?
How has the brain evolved?
Are dolphins more intelligent than humans?
How does the baby's brain develop
   before birth?
   after birth?
Can learning take place in the womb?
How do environment and nutrition affect the growing brain?
Why is birth such a delicate time for the young brain?

The ancient Indians, Egyptians, and Chinese made little connection between mental faculties and the brain. One of the first recognitions that the brain was in some way involved with mental functioning came with the ancient Greeks. Aristotle felt that the mind was in some way associated with the heart and that the brain served to cool the blood. Plato had suggested that the reasoning faculties lay within the head, and saw the brain as a mental wax, recording experiences as impressions. Interestingly, Herophilus, in the next century, thought that many of man's higher abilities were associated with the folds in the brain's surface, but the significance of this conclusion lay dormant for over two thousand years.

    The next advances came from Galen, who lived in the latter days of the Roman Empire. Galen was the grandfather of anatomy and performed some of the first dissections of the brain. He too felt that the seat of the soul was in the brain and believed that the ventricles, the open spaces in the brain usually filled with cerebrospinal fluid, were very important. This emphasis on the ventricles continued through the Middle Ages, both Saint Augustine and many of the Arab anatomists of the time believing them to be involved in man's higher faculties. There were still many, though, who associated the mind with the heart. And in India it was thought that the mind could not be localized anywhere in the body, but was a function of the whole organism—a theory still held by some Indian teachings.

For fifteen hundred years little progress was made, practical research often being hampered by the feeling that to examine the brain was to violate the seat of the soul. It was not until the eighteenth century that it became clearer that the whole of the brain was involved in mental functioning. By this time many of the major nerves were being traced and the general electrical activity of the brain had been discovered.

By the early nineteenth century it had become apparent that if certain areas of the brain were damaged, this could result in the loss of specific functions. By studying different types of damage, researchers such as Franz Gall, the German anatomist and physiologist, built up careful maps of the brain's surface allocating specific functions to each area of the brain. From this grew the science of phrenology, which held that by studying the shape of a person's skull, in particular the bumps upon the skull, it was possible to assess his or her mental aptitudes.

By the beginning of the twentieth century, however, it had become apparent that mental functions could not be so neatly localized. Hughlings Jackson, the famous English neurologist, had suggested that complex mental processes involved the whole of the brain's activity, and Sir Charles Sherrington, a pioneer in neurophysiology, made the now famous remark that the brain resembles "an enchanted loom, where millions of flashing shuttles weave a dissolving pattern, always a meaningful pattern though never an abiding one, a shifting harmony of sub patterns. It is as if the Milky Way entered upon some cosmic dance."

Over the last fifty years our knowledge of the human brain has grown at a prodigious rate. Psychology itself has become one of the most rapidly expanding fields of knowledge. It now draws on subjects as diverse as biochemistry, microtechnology, and cybernetics and has itself specialized into disciplines such as neuropsychology, physiological

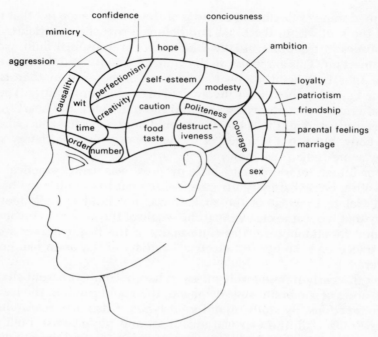

Figure 3 Phrenologists' map of the brain.

psychology, developmental psychology, and clinical psychology.

The human brain has become the most challenging frontier of science, and brain research now generates more than half a million scientific papers each year. Psychologists and neurophysiologists are no longer the only people seeking to understand the brain and its potentials. Chemists are looking at the 100,000 different chemical reactions occurring each second in the brain; molecular biologists are marveling at the highly sophisticated transformations taking place in each nerve cell; cyberneticists are applying information theory in an attempt to understand the brain and its almost limitless potential for memory; mathematicians are having to use computers to investigate their own relatively simple models of brain processes; and quantum physicists are investigating the possibility that brain activity may even involve superconductivity and "electron tunneling."

Yet still we seem hardly to have begun. The old saying that "the more you know of a subject, the more you discover what you do not know" seems particularly true as far as the brain is concerned. We know that functions are not well localized, and we know that the brain does not work like a simple telephone exchange, passing on messages from one call to another, nor does it behave like an electronic computer responding in fixed ways to the stimuli it encounters. As to how it does work we are still very much in ignorance. We know far more about what happens in the rest of the world around us than we do about what happens within that intricate web of nerves within our own heads.

THE EVOLUTION OF THE BRAIN

The first nervous systems grew out of simple sensory receptors located at the surface of primitive multicellular organisms. The receptors passed information about heat, light, acidity, etc., to the interior of the organism. Over the eons other cells developed that passed messages back from the interior to the surface, and on this basis simple nervous systems evolved. In the first jellyfish-like creatures the elementary nervous system had become a loose network of nerve cells extending throughout the organism, and with the evolution of simple molluscs the nerve cells began to clump together into a number of small groups called ganglia. Segmented worms were the first creatures to develop specific front and back ends, and in them the sense organs and associated ganglia are found gathering together toward the front, that is, the head. Over the ensuing millennia the ganglia grew more intricate and interwoven until, in the early fishes, the first simple brains appeared. From that time all vertebrates—that is, all animals with a backbone—have possessed a well-developed brain and spinal cord, with nerves radiating to all parts of the body.

In many respects the lower parts of our brain and spinal cord have not changed significantly since the time of the early fishes, 100 million years ago. The major changes that have taken place have entailed the massive extension and enlargement of the top end of the primitive brain. In reptiles came the first signs of a cerebral cortex, though it was still very tiny and only one cell layer thick. By the time the first mammals had appeared, some 50 million years ago, this simple cortex had expanded to take up half of the brain volume and was largely concerned with the sense of smell. On top of this a new layer of cells, the neocortex, began to grow. In man the neocortex consists of six cellular layers covering the whole surface of the brain. In fact it is several times larger than the surface of the brain and has become folded in upon itself many

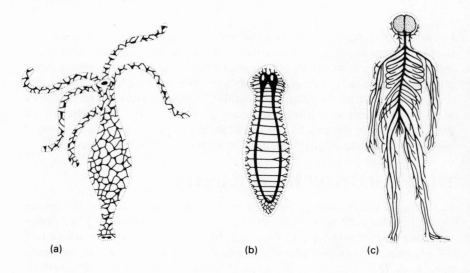

Figure 4 Evolution of the nervous system. (a) Simple net, (b) worm, (c) man.

times—if spread out flat it would cover an area of four hundred square inches. Although only three millimeters thick, our highly developed neocortex is responsible for many of our higher capacities, such as language, the development of skills, a virtually unlimited storage capacity, and our higher thought processes.

There are several animals with larger brains than ours—elephants (and elephants, it is said, never forget), whales, and dolphins. Whales and dolphins also have larger and more convoluted cortices, it being generally thought that the degree of convolution is significant as far as overall intelligence is concerned. Few experiments have been conducted on whales, but a large number have been performed with dolphins, and it appears that in several respects the mind of a dolphin is superior to that of man. The left and right halves of the brain appear to be even more specialized than our own. They can speak in stereo, by controlling the left and right air passages separately, and hold two or possibly three conversations at once using different frequency bands. In one experiment that set out to study dolphin language, the dolphins had begun to put their noses out of the water and make humanlike noises in the air—a very strange behavior for dolphins in the wild—as if they were attempting to communicate with the experimenters. This started happening long before the experimenters had succeeded in gaining the slightest inkling about dolphin languages.[1] In another experiment dolphins were found teaching other dolphins to count to ten in English and teaching them far more effectively than the human experimenters could. It is also of interest that a dolphin's life is based upon love more than competition—they seem to have learned to live in harmony, both with one another and with their environment. When John Lilly, one of the pioneers in dolphin research, realized that he was probably dealing with very advanced beings, he closed down his laboratories, feeling that his research could not be ethically justified.

THE GROWING BRAIN

The brain is by far the most complex organ in the human body. It takes longer than any other organ to reach its full development, and its pattern of growth is markedly different. In most other organs the basic structural development is completed during a relatively short period while in the womb. Any further growth in size is through cellular division as the organism grows. With the brain the opposite occurs. The brain has its full complement of cells long before birth—that is why the heads of babies seem out of proportion to the rest of their bodies. But its structural development continues throughout life, as the nerve cells become more and more intricately interconnected.

The human child is born into the world in a relatively helpless

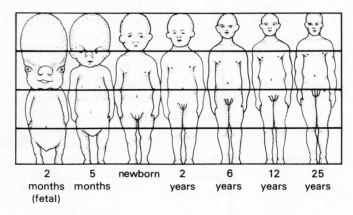

| 2 months (fetal) | 5 months | newborn | 2 years | 6 years | 12 years | 25 years |

Figure 5 Relative sizes of the brain and body at different ages.

state. Unlike many other animals that can fend for themselves within minutes or hours of birth, the human infant needs the care of its parents for many years. This gives it a major advantage over other animals. It is no longer reliant upon instinct for its survival: Instead it is flexible and can learn from experience, adapt to its environment, develop skills, and learn language.

The growing fetus passes through very similar stages in its development from single cell to human being, as did the species over its four billion years of evolution. As with the first primitive organisms, the brain of the early embryo starts from the surface. A small plate appears on the top side and then curls up to form a groove. The sides of the groove meet, forming a tube that then becomes sealed at one end. This is a rudimentary spinal column, and from the sealed end of this tube the rest of the brain grows—one second of development in the fetus corresponding to a thousand years of evolution. Five weeks after conception the top part of the tube has become enlarged and bent over in the shape of a question mark. And at eight weeks the first of the two brain spurts begins.

The term *brain spurt* is given to those periods in which there is a very rapid development of the brain. The first such growth occurs from eight to thirteen weeks after conception and entails the proliferation of billions of cells called neuroblasts. It is from these neuroblasts that the neurons themselves develop, each neuroblast developing into one neuron. Thus the number of neuroblasts formed at this stage determines the total complement of nerve cells.

Nutrition is very important at this stage. It has been found that if the mother is undernourished, particularly if she lacks certain amino acids, the total number of neuroblasts, and hence the total number of neurons, is significantly reduced. Studies of children in the Third World whose mothers were undernourished, have shown that many are born with only 40 percent of the neurons found in Western children.[2] It has also been suggested that one of the reasons why Western children born in January, February, and March show a higher incidence of mental retardation is that the crucial period in brain growth would have occurred during the summer months of June, July, and August, when mothers were more likely to be eating salads than steaks.

Though significant, the number of neurons in the brain is not the most important factor in determining mental abilities. Of far greater consequence is their degree of interconnectedness. The wiring up of the neurons occurs during the second brain spurt, starting some ten weeks before birth and continuing for about two years after birth. It is during this period that much of our basic learning takes place.

During the second brain spurt each neuron starts sending out numerous fine feathery fibers in all directions, making connections with thousands of other neurons, sometimes as far away as the other side of the brain. The cell bodies themselves grow larger and the cortex becomes much thicker. Also at this stage many of the longer fibers traversing the brain are coated with an insulating material called myelin, which speeds the conduction of neural impulses.

This prolific increase in connectivity results in a rapid growth of the brain. At birth the brain weighs 350 grams, 25 percent of its adult weight, but it is growing at the rate of 1 milligram a minute. At six months it is 50 percent of its adult weight; at two and a half years 75 percent; and at five years 90 percent. At this stage the major part of the child's intellectual development has already been completed.

It is during the second brain spurt, when the neurons are making their trillions of interconnections, that much of our basic learning and

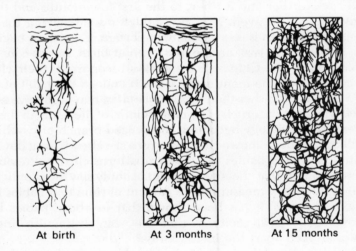

| At birth | At 3 months | At 15 months |

Figure 6 Sections from the cerebral cortex of children at birth, at 3 months, and at 15 months old, showing increased number of fibers and a thickening of fibers. Pictures such as these are produced by first staining the tissue with a dye that is taken up by only about 1 percent of the cells. There are therefore about one hundred times as many cells in each picture as those shown here. (From R. H. Lindsay and D. A. Norman, *Human Information Processing*, New York; Academic Press, 1972. Reprinted with permission.)

mental development takes place. But even before this, the growing fetus is responding to and learning from its environment in the womb. Simple reflex conditioning has been shown to take place in the spinal cord after only eight weeks, long before the cortex has begun to develop. Doctors have inserted a thin optical fiber into the womb and observed the embyro at ten weeks reacting to changes in its environment. At five months the electroencephalogram (EEG) shows that the fetal brain responds to light in much the same way that an adult brain does. And later it responds to specific sounds coming in from the outside through the mother's abdomen.

PRENATAL PSYCHOLOGY

There has in this century been a growing awareness that the first years of life are crucial to a person's development. We realize that what happens to a child when it is one or two years old can affect the rest of its life. More recently it has become apparent that the time could be pushed back further and further, to the first few months and the first few days after birth even. Now psychologists are realizing that what happens before birth is also crucially important. Education begins not at five, not at three, two, or one, nor even at birth, but at conception —a point which the Chinese have always recognized, their children being considered nine months old at birth. Indeed the habit of dating our age from birth rather than from conception may well have encouraged us to neglect the crucial first nine months of life. Only in the 1970s has prenatal psychology become a recognized branch of psychology.

It has now been shown that the senses are already well developed at birth, that young babies can discern patterns clearly. Previously it had been thought that the newborn child simply saw areas of light and dark. But, by simply measuring the amount of time that babies looked at various patterns, it has been shown that newborn babies have a well-developed visual acuity in that they can distinguish lines one eighth of an inch apart ten inches away.[3]

Tom Bower, who has done considerable research on infant perception at the University of Edinburgh, took this work further and showed that right from birth the child experiences a three-dimensional world. Using polarizing goggles so that the left and right eye see different images, he created the visual illusion that there was a solid object in front of the baby. He found that even newborn babies stretched out their hands to touch the apparent object, but as soon as their hand closed upon empty air instead of a solid object the baby started crying. This showed that at birth the child expects visual objects to be tangible and indicates a simple unity of the visual and tactile senses.[4]

Other experiments at Edinburgh have shown that sound and sight are similarly integrated, the newborn baby turning its head in the direction of a sound to see what is there. They have shown that a baby is also born with the ability to recognize smells as pleasant or unpleas-

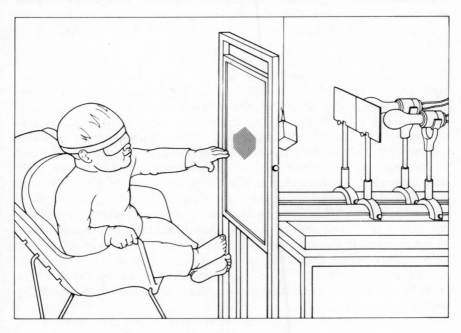

Figure 7 Intangible object is produced by a shadow caster, in which two oppositely polarized beams of light cast a double shadow of an object on a rear-projection screen. An infant views the double shadows through polarizing goggles that make a different shadow visible to each eye. The innate processes of stereopsis fuse the two images to make the infant think he is seeing a solid object in front of the screen. When the infant tries to grasp the virtual image, he is startled when his hand closes on empty air; within a fraction of a second he cries and his face expresses surprise. When a real object is placed in front of the screen, none of the infants shows any sign of surprise when he touches it. These results indicate that the infants expect a seen object to be solid and tangible. © 1971 by *Scientific American*, Inc. All rights reserved. Reproduced with permission of *Scientific American*.

ant, turning its head away from unpleasant smells.[5] Thus at birth the sensory system is already sufficiently developed to localize objects by sight, touch, sound, and smell.

The newborn child can also recognize a human face. Robert Fantz, a researcher at Western Reserve University in Cleveland, presented day-old children with the choice of looking at a picture of a face, a bull's-eye, newsprint, and circles of various colors. He found a distinct preference for the human face, most of the babies looking at it far more than the other objects.[6] During the next two weeks of life the child learns to recognize those particular faces that it sees the most.

Much of this complex perceptual organization takes place during the last two months in the womb. Then after birth the basic perceptual frameworks are refined and developed according to the types of experience that the infant encounters. Studies with newborn kittens have demonstrated the crucial role of early experience in the development of perception. A kitten brought up in an environment containing only horizontal lines, was, as an adult, found not to have the ability to see vertical lines clearly, stumbling into chair legs as though they were not there, though happily jumping onto the horizontal seat of the chair.[7] An analysis of the visual cortex of the brain showed that the corresponding cells for vertical lines were far less well developed than those for horizontal-line recognition. Whether this is because the relevant systems never developed or because they were there but atrophied through disuse is still a matter of debate, but either way, it is clear that the newborn brain modifies itself after birth in a way that best suits the environment in which it finds itself.

To assess the effect of a rich environment on brain growth, Mark Rosenzweig and colleagues, at the University of California at Berkeley, allowed a group of baby rats to grow up in a cage full of ramps, ladders, wheels, tunnels, trapezes, and other stimuli, while a second group was left in ordinary barren cages. They were actually looking for changes in enzyme levels, but when, after 105 days, the brains of the rats were examined, it was found that the cortices of those rats raised in the rich environment were larger than the "impoverished" rats. There were 15 percent more glia cells (see chapter 3), and although the number of neurons had not increased, the neuron bodies were 15 percent larger, the fibers were more prolific, and most importantly, they were making more interconnections with other neurons.[8]

CAN LEARNING OCCUR IN THE WOMB?

A field in which there has been a lot of interest recently is the acquisition of language. "Normal" children—that is, those who have not had a particularly rich early environment—usually begin talking after the first year of their life. By eighteen months they have a vocabulary of about half a dozen words and at two years a vocabulary of more than a hundred words. The traditional view has been that during the first year of life, babies are not mature enough to learn languages. Talking, however, is only the outer manifestation of the development of language; long before he first utters a meaningful word a baby can be observed responding to the language of others.

Studies have shown that *even at birth* the child responds positively and specifically to the tones of the human voice. A high-speed film of a newborn baby when slowed down many times and examined frame by frame shows that tiny gestures on the part of the child are synchronized with specific tones and syllables from the parents. Sounds other than the human voice, however, produce no such response.[9] The fact that this is happening at birth implies that some simple linguistic skills are learned while in the womb, presumably by the fetus hearing speech from the outside world and using it to acquire the basic sounds and rhythms of language.

While he's in the womb, a child learns the sound of his mother's heartbeat, and after birth the sound of a human heart will have a very soothing effect on the baby. It has been suggested that this also accounts for the universal appeal of rhythmic music to adults. The pace of the rhythm is usually within the range of the human heart, and the faster the rhythm the more "exciting" the music. An unusual example of learning in the womb comes from a mother who used to sing in a Bach choir while pregnant. With the birth of her child, she gave up the singing yet found that whenever there was a Bach choir on the radio, her baby daughter would become totally absorbed in the music, losing interest in everything else, even food.

THE VULNERABILITY OF THE YOUNG BRAIN

Although the second brain spurt is from ten weeks before birth until two years after birth, it is greatest during the first few months after birth. It is at this stage that the brain is said to be most plastic—plastic in the sense of being most easily modified by its environment. The recent research on the newborn child suggests the height of plasticity occurs around the time of birth itself. But not only is the brain's learning ability greatest at this stage, the brain is also at its most vulnerable.

There is now accumulating physiological evidence for the psychoanalysts' common claim that many problems in later life can be traced back to traumas in early childhood, particularly birth traumas. Sigmund Freud showed how early childhood experiences could affect our attitudes and behavior for the rest of our lives. Melanie Klein, the distinguished child psychologist, took the idea further showing how much the first months of life were important. Arthur Janov, the originator of primal therapy suggested that our experiences of birth itself can have profound psychological effects. Now R. D. Laing has argued that we are conditioned by our fetal life and even by conception itself, reenacting these periods throughout our adult life.[10]

Similar ideas are at the basis of several modern approaches to birth. Frederick Leboyer, for example, recommends that the newborn child not be greeted with harsh light, a slap on the back, and separation from his mother, but be given a gentle, loving transition from life in the womb to life in the outside world. Such babies seldom start howling immediately after birth, and their mortality is reduced by half. A follow-up study on 120 "Leboyer babies" found that, on average, the babies began to walk two months earlier and generally developed faster. In addition, the babies were happier, with few sleeping problems, and none of their mothers reported difficulties with toilet training.[11]

There has recently been a lot of concern about the effects of smoking during pregnancy. Smoking reduces the oxygen supply to the fetus, and it has been found that the reading scores of children whose mothers smoked during pregnancy were significantly lower than those of children whose mothers did not. There are many other factors that have been found to have equally damaging repercussions on the growing fetus. Alcohol, lead in the air and water supplies, certain food dyes, the emotional stability of the mother, the father's behavior, fatigue, noise, and the mother's social habits all have measurable effects.

At birth the child is particularly vulnerable, and yet this is very often the time at which the mother is most heavily drugged. Babies born to mothers who have been given drugs to reduce labor pains are often measurably "stoned" when they are born—and even one month later.

There is evidence that the amino acid taurine is important for brain development. The young child has only a limited ability to synthesize taurine but has a high uptake of the amino acid during the most active growth phase, deriving his main supply from milk. Human milk has twice as much taurine as cow's milk, which suggests that breast feeding may have important benefits for the brain's physiological development as well as for the child's psychological development.[12]

Malnutrition is a factor to which the growing brain is particularly susceptible. Normally the brain is protected from any undernourishment by what is called brain sparing. If there is any lack of essential vitamins, proteins, amino acids, oxygen, etc., then it is the other organs of the body that suffer first—the organism makes sure that the brain receives its essential supplies as long as possible. Far more of the individual's energy, time, and resources have been put into the development of the brain than have gone into any other organ. It is our most valuable organ and one that should be protected above all else. During the first two years, however, undernourishment can have severe effects on the developing brain, despite natural brain sparing.

When undernourishment occurs over the first two years of life, brain development is severely impaired. The brain is smaller, the number of glia cells (see pages 40–41) is reduced, there is less myelination of fibers (see page 23), and enzyme levels are lowered.[13] It is also found that the cerebellum suffers more than the rest of the brain in size reduction (probably because the cerebellum is the last part of the brain to form, beginning to develop only three months before birth and finishing about one year after birth). Among other things, the cerebellum is responsible for the integration of limb movements, which explains why early undernourishment has often been found to result in poor body coordination.

The most significant effect of poor nutrition is the reduction of the number of connections made between nerve cells. To study this effect researchers fostered a group of baby rats onto a mother who already had nine pups of her own, thus reducing the amount of food available for each rat in the litter. After weaning, they were fed on a similarly restrictive diet. When the brain cortex was later examined under an electron microscope, it was found that the total brain mass had been reduced by 23 percent and, even more significantly, the number of connections between neurons had been reduced by an average of 41 percent. It is the number of interconnections between neurons that is important, and it is likely that all aspects of nervous and mental development had been severly damaged by the poor nutrition.[14]

The situation is further compounded by the damaging effects of a poor environment. Two studies, one of children in Mexico City and the other of Jamaican infants, have shown that children who were not only undernourished but also came from homes that provided a poor environmental background, suffered far more than those who were simply undernourished.[15] Conversely, severely undernourished children who, at about the age of eighteen months, were adopted into middle-class American homes showed remarkable recoveries, both in physical and in intellectual terms. Many factors are important in the overall development of the brain. In this case the richer environment was sufficient to compensate for the earlier poor nutrition.[16]

NATURE OR NURTURE?

So far the emphasis has been on the crucial effects of early environment, including those vitally important first nine months. There is also the question of the extent to which mental skills are genetically inherited, and which is the more important—*environment* or *inheritance.* The widespread debate over this question is often called the "nature-nurture" controversy.

The "nature" camp would say that Mozart's musical talent, for example, was largely inherited from his parents, being encoded in the genes. The "nurture" lobby on the other hand, would claim that being born into a musical family, he had a rich musical environment very early on—even in the womb—and it was this that led to his great musical talent.

A third factor in individual differences could come from small variations in chemicals within cells. If a chemical was only present in minute quantities and was not being constantly synthesized, then it could become unevenly distributed between the daughter cells at the time of cell division, and so possibly lead to different behaviors at a later date. Such an effect would be neither genetic nor environmental. Supporting evidence for this third factor comes from the finding that genetically identical bacteria reared under identical conditions can show individual variations in behavior.[17] It is quite possible that similar factors play a part in the development of the growing human embryo, all the body's cells having descended originally from one cell.

The principal debate, though, is still one of nature or nurture. Much of the research in this field has centered on studies of twins. Monozygotic twins—that is, twins that have split from the same egg—

have the same genetic makeup, whereas dizygotic twins—coming from separate eggs—have different sets of genes. The extent to which inheritance plays a part can be evaluated by the extent to which monozygotic twins are more alike than dizygotic twins.

The early studies suggested that inheritance played a significant part in mental faculties. More recent work, however, suggests that the environment is far more important than hitherto supposed.

The issue is, however, still far from settled, and it is one that is guaranteed to bring out the emotional side of objective psychologists. Perhaps the most interesting study in this field is the one that showed a significant correlation between the attitudes and backgrounds of the researchers and the results of their research.[18] Researchers who had been brought up in a rural environment, for example, tended to find that differences were innate, as did also the younger researchers.

It is only since the late 1960s that psychologists have begun to realize the extent to which the very young brain can absorb and adapt to its environment. Many factors that were previously thought to have little or no effect on the young child are now being shown to play a considerable part in his development. With these findings has come a general shift toward nurture as playing a very large role in individual differences, and is the principal factor behind genius.

Figure 8

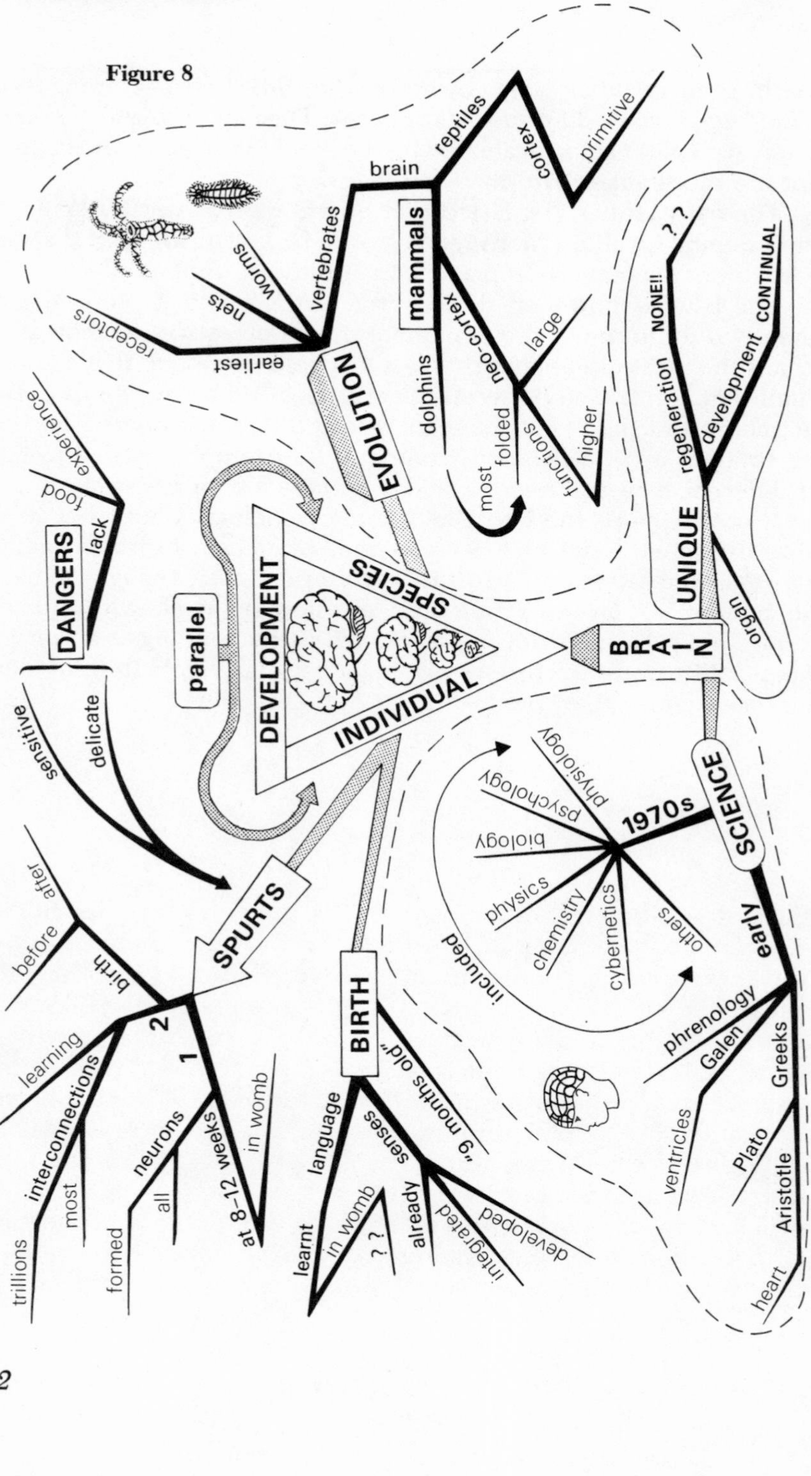
BRAIN
EVOLUTION
earliest
receptors
nets
worms
vertebrates
brain
reptiles
cortex
primitive
mammals
neo-cortex
large
dolphins
most
folded
functions
higher
UNIQUE
regeneration
NONE!!
? ?
development
CONTINUAL
organ
SCIENCE
1970s
physiology
psychology
biology
physics
chemistry
cybernetics
others
included
early
phrenology
Galen
ventricles
Greeks
Plato
Aristotle
heart
DEVELOPMENT
SPECIES
INDIVIDUAL
parallel
DANGERS
lack
food
experience
sensitive
delicate
SPURTS
birth
before
after
2
1
learning
interconnections
trillions
most
neurons
all
formed
at 8–12 weeks
in womb
BIRTH
"6 months old"
language
learnt
in womb
? ?
senses
already
integrated
developed

3.
Ten Billion Neurons

What is a neuron?
Do neurons die?
How do they work?
What are dendrites and axons?
What do they do?
What is a synapse?
Why is it so important?
What do the glia cells do?
How is the brain structured?
What is the brainstem? the midbrain? the cortex?

The most well known of the brain's cells are the neurons. The human brain contains something on the order of ten billion neurons—that's about three times as many neurons as there are people inhabiting this planet, or about as many neurons as there are stars in the Milky Way. This vast number immediately suggests that the cells themselves are minute, and also that the brain is immensely complex. A typical neuron in the cortex of the brain may make over ten thousand connections with other cells, and the total number of synapses in the brain is probably on the order of ten trillion at least—10,000,000,000,000. The mind boggles at its own complexity.

There is little hope that we can analyze all the interconnections in a single brain. Research workers at Cambridge University have spent three years analyzing the nervous system of a very simple worm. This creature has only twenty-three neurons, yet it took a team of scientists and a computing system three years just to analyze the interconnections of these few neurons. To try to analyze the interconnections of the neurons in a human brain by this method would take longer than the projected life of the universe.

DO NEURONS DIE?

Neurons are unlike nearly every other type of cell found in the human body in that they do not usually reproduce themselves. In every other organ of the body there is a continual turnover of cells, some being replaced every few hours, some every few weeks, and some every few years. But the neurons you are born with, or rather the neurons you have three months after conception, are the same neurons you will have when you are eighty.

It is often said that although neurons do not usually regenerate, they are nevertheless constantly dying, at the rate of about a thousand a day. There is, however, very little evidence to support this claim. In the last hundred years there have been only twenty studies on the decrease of neurons with age; ten of these studies were with humans, and ten with animals. Generally the results are far from conclusive: Half the human studies show there is a decrease in the number of neurons with age, half show there is not. Even the studies that show there is a decrease are highly contestable. Two of the principal ones were done in 1919 and 1928 and the brain tissue examined came from just a few museum specimens.[1] Nor was this a representative sample—two of the patients had in fact died in hospitals for the insane. From this very limited study extrapolations were made applying to the whole human race. With regard to the animal studies, in those cases that showed a loss of neurons with age the animals were left alone in isolation. When the animals lived together and had a normal level of stimulation, no loss was found.[2]

Even if neurons were to die at the rate of at least several thousand a day, by the time you were eighty, you would have lost $1,000 \times 365 \times 80$ neurons, in other words, a mere 29.2 million or so neurons. I say "mere" because the total number of neurons is approximately ten billion, so you would have lost less than 1 percent of the total. Since there is an enormous redundancy in the nervous system, even this minute loss would be very unlikely to have any effect whatsoever on mental functioning. Indeed, since the number of connections between neurons is increasing throughout life, we should expect to see a continual growth in mental abilities, rather than any deterioration and, as we shall see in chapter 5, there is mounting evidence that this is the case.

AXONS AND DENDRITES

The typical neuron consists of a central cell body a few thousandths of an inch across. Its principal fiber, called the axon, usually one

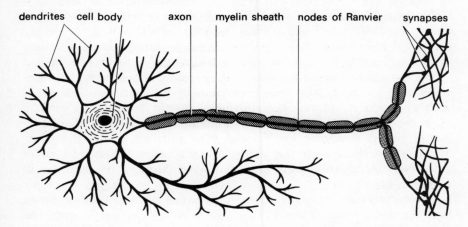

dendrites   cell body   axon   myelin sheath   nodes of Ranvier   synapses

Figure 9 Simplified diagram of typical neuron. Electrical charges are received from other cells by the dendrites. Their overall effect on the cell body governs the rate at which impulses are sent out via the axon and transmitted to the dendrites of other cells at the synapses.

Figure 10 Photograph of a neuron from the cortex of the brain (magnified 1,000 times). The thin line running downward from the cell body in the center is the axon. The thousands of small knobbly projections on the dendrites are the dendritic spines, where connections are made.

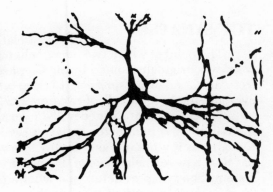

of the longest, carries outgoing information from the cell body to other neurons. There is normally only one axon per neuron, though it may divide along its length into many collaterals going off in different directions. For most of its length the axon is covered in a thin fatty coating of myelin, which both serves as an insulator and speeds conduction of electrical impulses. Toward its end the axon becomes thinner, branching out into fine fibers that terminate on other neurons. They may terminate directly on the cell body of another neuron, or they may make connections with a second type of fiber called dendrites. (The Greek word *dendron* means "tree," and the dendrites of a neuron are so named because of their treelike qualities—hundreds may radiate from a single cell, each one branching off into many fine feathery fibers.)

Whereas the axons transmit pulses from the cell body, the dendrites are generally the receptive part of the neuron, though, as with all brain structures, the distinction is not always so clear-cut. Most dendrites are covered with thousands or even millions of tiny bumps called dendritic spines, and it is at these points that they make connections with the axon, or sometimes the dendrites, of other cells. Altogether there are some 100,000 miles of dendrites in a human brain.

Neurons vary widely from one part of the brain to another. Some have hundreds of dendrites on them, some have only few. In some the fibers are only a millimeter or less in length; in others they may be up to two feet in length, stretching from the brain to the base of the spinal cord. Some make tens of thousands of connections with other neurons; some one or two. Yet despite such wide variations, their basic structure is generally the same.

THE SYNAPSE

The point at which two nerve cells meet is called the *synapse.* The word was originally coined by Sir Charles Sherrington, who derived it from the Greek word *synapto* "to clasp tightly." Strictly speaking, however, it is incorrect to talk of two nerve cells meeting, let alone clasping tightly, because there is generally a very small gap of about one five-thousandth of a millimeter between the two sides of the junction. Although this is a minute gap—many times thinner than the ink on this page—it is nevertheless one of the most important points in the nervous system. The synapses determine whether or not a pulse is transmitted from one cell to another; they are therefore the essential modulators of

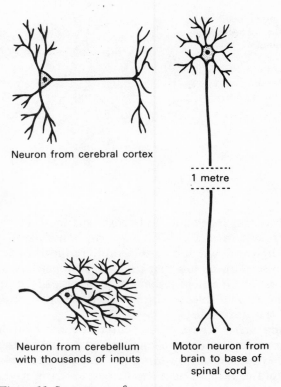

Neuron from cerebral cortex

1 metre

Neuron from cerebellum
with thousands of inputs

Motor neuron from
brain to base of
spinal cord

Figure 11 Some types of neurons.

brain activity and are currently thought to be closely involved in the encoding of memory.

Synapses usually occur at the junctions of axons and dendrites, but several other types of synapses are found in the brain. Axons may synapse directly with other axons, or with the cell body itself. Or dendrites may synapse directly with other dendrites. Synapses have also been discovered in which there is no gap between the two cells. In this case, there appears to be direct electrical transmission between neurons. There are also junctions that do not involve synapses at all. These are called ephatic junctions and occur where very fine unmyelinated dendrites interconnect with each other like the fibers in matted felt, and in this case the transmission is again direct.

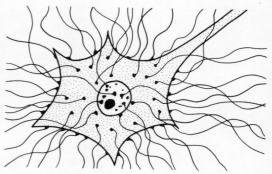

Figure 12 Drawing of a cell body with a large number of axons from other cells terminating upon it. Note the small size of the synaptic knob compared with the cell body — the cell itself being only a few thousandths of an inch across.

The ends of the axons tend to become much smaller in diameter as they branch out toward other cells, and consequently the nerve impulses are slowed down and considerably reduced in amplitude toward the synapse. This means that the electrical activity in one cell is insufficient to set off electrical activity in the next cell. Instead it causes various chemicals to be released into the synaptic gap, and these cross over to affect the next cell.

Before the pulse arrives, these chemicals are contained in tiny vesicles in the synaptic terminal of the first cell, and there may be several hundred such vesicles waiting to be released. When the pulse arrives, a few of the vesicles near the surface are ruptured and distribute their contents into the gap. One of the chemicals released, called the transmitter substance, flows across the gap and produces a depolarization of the membrane of the second cell. If this membrane is sufficiently depolarized, a new impulse is triggered and starts flowing down the second fiber. One interesting point about this transmission is that it is a one-way process; the vesicles containing the transmitter substance are only on the axon side of the synapse and electrical changes in the dendritic spine cannot set off changes in the axon.

The pulses in the axons and dendrites obey what is called the all-or-none law—each pulse is of the same intensity; there are no half-measures. The electrical changes across the synapse, however, are variable, being proportional to the amount of chemical released into the gap. Thus the greater the frequency of the incoming pulses, the greater the number of vesicles released and the greater the amplitude of the potential change on the other side. Whether or not this potential change results in an impulse being transmitted down the second fiber

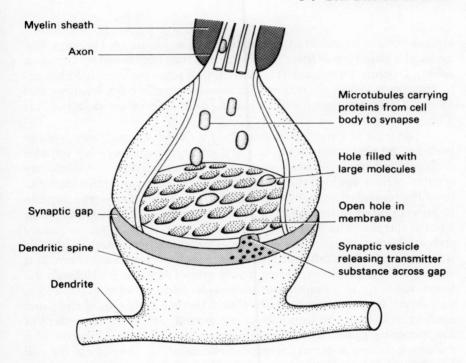

Myelin sheath

Axon

Microtubules carrying
proteins from cell
body to synapse

Hole filled with
large molecules

Synaptic gap

Open hole in
membrane

Dendritic spine

Synaptic vesicle
releasing transmitter
substance across gap

Dendrite

Figure 13 Simplified diagram of fine structure of synapse. The vesicles fit into a vacant hole at the synaptic membrane and on the arrival of a pulse down the axon release their contents into the synaptic gap. The net amount of transmitter substance received by the second membrane determines whether or not the pulse is propagated in the dendrite of the second neuron.

depends on whether the induced potential change is high enough.

Recent explorations of the synapse under the electron microscope have revealed that the surface is not a simple membrane; rather it is a regular latticework. The points of intersection of the framework form little bumps, and in between are hollows about one-twentieth of a micron across (a micron is one-thousandth of a millimeter).[3] This is just the size of the vesicles containing the transmitter substance, and it is thought that a vesicle can only release its contents into the gap once it is resting snugly inside one of these hollows. A typical synapse contains about 150 hollows, but many may already be filled with large molecules and so not be accessible to the vesicles. Thus the number of vesicles available when an impulse arrives, and hence the likelihood of the impulse being transmitted across the gap, depends on the very fine molecular structure of this grid, which is in turn controlled by chemical changes within the neuron. It is thought that some such minute changes in chemicals at the synaptic surface are responsible for learning and memory—something we will be looking at in much more detail in Part Two.

The type of synapse just described is called an excitatory synapse because the nerve impulse in the first neuron excites a nerve impulse in the second one. There is a second kind of synapse called an inhibitory synapse, which works in the opposite manner. It decreases the excitability of the second membrane making it more difficult for a nerve impulse to be generated in the dendrite. Whether or not a pulse is created at a particular dendritic spine depends on the net effect of the excitatory and inhibitory synapses made there. The inhibitory synapses play an important part in moderating the activity of the nervous system. If it were not for them, an excitation would spread like wildfire through the brain, resulting in a continuous state of convulsive activity.

Most, if not all, neurons are spontaneously active all of the time, sending out about ten impulses every second. The collective effect of the incoming pulses from thousands, or in some cases a quarter of a million, synapses does not therefore determine whether or not the cell fires but modulates the pattern of its incessant activity. Thus in any one second there are hundreds of billions of impulses flashing through the brain producing unbelievably intricate waves of shimmering activity, always changing and far beyond our imagination, "as if the Milky Way had entered upon some cosmic dance."

GLIA CELLS

From what has been said, it might be expected that the brain was packed full, with 10 billion neurons and all their fibers. As well as the neurons, however, there are billions of other cells called glia cells. In fact it is estimated that there are some 100 billion glia cells in the human brain—that is, about ten times as many glia cells as there are neurons. Unlike neurons, the glia cells do not have axons or dendrites; they are rounder in shape. The glia are packed between the neurons and cover all their bodies, axons, and dendrites. The only part of a neuron that is not so covered is the gap at the synapse. Indeed, *glia* is the Greek word for "glue"; they glue the brain together.

Glia cells appear to be involved in nearly every aspect of neuronal activity. They look after the nourishment of neurons and are an inter-face between the blood vessels and the neurons themselves. They act as scavengers, consuming waste products, especially the transmitters and other chemicals released into the synaptic gap between neurons. They insulate neurons from one another, both chemically and electri-cally, and are the source of the myelin coating that covers the longer fibers. Unlike neurons themselves, the glia can divide and reproduce. This is important not only for maintaining the population of glia, but because where they divide there is an opportunity for an axon to push through and make connections to other cells. Thus the dividing of glia cells may be part of the learning process.

Glia are also electrically sensitive, and it has been suggested that they may act as liquid crystals in resonance with the surrounding elec-trical fields. That is to say they may have the characteristics of semicon-ductors. If so, they could pick up very faint electrical changes in the nervous system and amplify them several thousand times in much the same way transistors amplify faint signals in electronic circuits.[4] Just imagine 100 billion transistors inside your head!

AXONAL TRANSPORT

It is also becoming apparent that the neurons themselves perform many other functions than just the simple transmission of electrical impulses. In 1963 it was observed that where an axon had been con-stricted for some reason, there was a swelling on the axon on the side near the cell body, rather as if matter passing down the axon was being dammed up by the constriction. Six years and 100,000 fibers later this hypothesis was confirmed.[5] Using techniques of cinematography, it was observed that the entire contents of the axon appeared to be moving down toward the tip. Among the particles moving down the axon were mitochondria, commonly described as the powerhouses of the living cell, and the vesicles containing proteins, enzymes, and the transmitter substances released at the synaptic gap. It would seem that much of the material used at the synapse is manufactured in the body of the cell and is then moved down the axon to the synapse itself.

Other experiments, involving the injection of minute amounts of a special amino acid containing silver molecules that show up under the microscope after staining, have allowed neurologists to measure the rate of transport more accurately. Most of the materials seem to be traveling at the rate of a few millimeters a day. This may not seem very fast at first, but when we remember the minute size of the cell, it is a relatively rapid motion. In terms of the mitochondria it represents about one thousand per day passing down the axon, and when we take all the other particles and vesicles into account, we find that the total amount of material transported per day is three times the volume of the cell itself. Each neuron is therefore having to produce three times its own weight each day! Moreover, since the axon does not grow any longer, all the material passing along its length must be consumed in one way or another at the synapses.

This main flow is rapid enough, but it has also been found that some proteins are moved down the axon very much more rapidly still, at the rate of some 2.8 meters per day. This means that proteins generated in the cell body can be at the synapses within an hour or two, or, if the axon is very short, within minutes. This has important implications on memory, for it provides a mechanism by which the cell body can modify the synapses at the end of its axons.[6] Proteins, which on their arrival filled vacant holes in the synaptic grid, would directly affect the amount of transmitter substance that could be released across the gap, and hence the transmission characteristics of the junction.

THE REGIONS OF THE BRAIN

We have looked briefly at the fine structure of the brain, at the neurons and at some of the incredible processes taking place within them, now let us get an overall picture of how the brain is organized. Neuroanatomy is the most complex of the biological sciences, there being thousands upon thousands of different groups of nerve cells performing various specific functions. For our purposes, however, we can consider the brain in terms of just a few basic regions.

Spinal Cord. The oldest part of the brain is the spinal cord, stretching from the neck down the center of the vertebrae to the bottom of the back. As was seen earlier, the spinal cord first forms as a tube, and this is still apparent in the adult spinal cord, there being a thin hollow down its length that is filled with cerebrospinal fluid. There are two principal functions associated with the spinal cord: It performs very simple reflexes, such as the knee jerk reflex, and it acts as the principal communication channel between the head and the rest of the body. The control of the body is conveyed via the spinal cord, and all bodily sensations reach the brain through the spinal cord. All, that is, except those relating to the head itself, which enter and leave through the brain stem.

The Brain Stem. This is situated on top of the spinal cord. It still possesses the tubular structure of the spinal cord, and in some respects can be thought of as an extension of it. In the brain stem is a very intricate network of nerves about the size of your little finger called the reticular formation. It receives nerves from all areas of the brain and likewise sends out nerves in every direction. The reticular formation plays an important role in maintaining wakefulness, and if it is isolated from the rest of the brain, the organism goes into permanent sleep. It also monitors and filters the information coming in through the senses. If, for example, you are in a room with a clock that is ticking quietly, you will quickly habituate to the sound so that after a short while you will no longer hear it. But the sound is still being continually monitored by the brain, and if the clock were suddenly to stop, or to change speed or volume, you would immediately notice it. The reticular formation would have alerted you.

Cerebellum. Connected to the brain stem is the cerebellum, which somewhat resembles the cortex in terms of its neuronal structure,

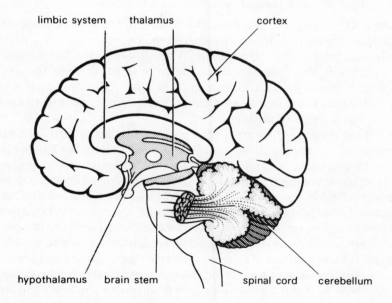

Figure 14 The main regions of the brain.

though it is very much older than the cortex. Although it is undoubtedly involved in a variety of functions, it is primarily concerned with coordination of movements. It seems to integrate the information coming from all the senses with all the muscles so as to produce smooth, finely tuned movements, rather than jerky uncoordinated movements.

Midbrain. On top of the brain stem is the thalamus, a large region containing many nuclei, some relaying information from the sensory organs to the cortex, others relaying information from one area of the cortex to another and interacting with the reticular formation and the limbic system. The limbic system is a group of structures in the middle of the brain that play an important role in emotion and motivation.

Just below the thalamus is the hypothalamus, a tiny structure about the size of a pea, yet a crucial part of the brain. This little organ is largely responsible for the maintenance of homeostasis, ensuring that all the various parameters of bodily function are in balance and function at their optimum. The hypothalamus continually monitors the blood. If there is too little or too much carbon dioxide, it reduces or increases breathing; if blood sugar is low, it makes you feel hungry; if your temperature is too low or too high, it initiates shivering or sweating; if the blood is too salty, it makes you feel thirsty. It also plays a major role in the control of sleep, sexual behavior, and the emotions.

Cortex. Covering the whole of the midbrain is the neocortex, or the cortex, as it is more commonly referred to. Though only one quarter of the brain's total volume, it contains 75 percent of its ten billion neurons. The cortex is also referred to as the gray matter, since the greater density of blood cells gives it a grayish color. The rest of the brain contains many more myelinated fibers passing from one area to another and so has a more whitish color.

Some areas of the cortex play particular roles in sensory activity. The rear of the cortex, for example, is associated with the processing of visual information, a small area on the side with auditory information, and a strip extending from the top center of the cortex down each side is concerned with the sense of touch and also with the control of the muscles. Large parts of the cortex, though, do not appear to be so specific in their function, rather they seem to be concerned with the integration of information from several different senses, in other words, with building up a total worldview. These areas are called the association areas.

As an example of how the different areas interact, let us consider briefly how a visual signal is analyzed. Information from the eye is

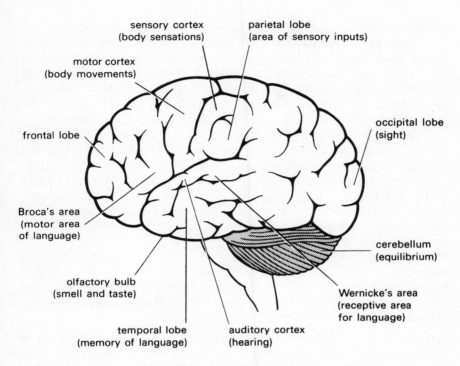

Figure 15 Areas of the cortex.

passed first to the lateral geniculate body, a small group of cells in the thalamus, and from there is relayed to the visual cortex of the brain, though some of it is sent down to the reticular formation. The visual cortex proceeds to analyze the signal: first by picking out lines and boundaries in the information; then picking out lines of specific orientation; then picking out lines not only of a specific orientation but those moving with particular speed, each cell responding to a different combination of line length, angle, and speed; and the next level puts these units together to produce angles and corners moving at specific speeds. This information is then sent forward to what are called the visual association areas, where further analysis seems to take place, and it is probably at this stage that we recognize a handshape as a hand—indeed experiments on monkeys have found cells that do respond to just this shape in the visual field. This information is then sent forward to association areas where it is integrated with other information coming from hearing, touch, smell, taste, and memory.

One of the most striking facts about the human cortex is the large size of the regions commonly referred to as the frontal lobes. Attempts have been made to attribute just about every conceivable function to the frontal cortex—particularly the higher functions, such as emotions, intelligence, memory, and even the will itself. Yet despite the attention paid to these areas, we still have very little idea of their function.

In the 1940s and 1950s, frontal lobotomy (the severing of the fibers to the frontal lobe of the brain) was used in an effort to restore the mental health of psychiatric patients, and with no obvious deterioration in intellectual ability, creativity, problem solving, etc. The only consistent effect was a lack of responsiveness to chronic pain. Patients reported that they still felt the pain but that it no longer bothered them. For this reason the operation is still sometimes used for the relief of incurable pain in terminal cancer.

That the frontal lobes still remain something of an enigma does not mean we should in any way underestimate their value. Remember that it was only a few hundred years ago that the whole of the brain was considered to be of little importance as far as thought processes were concerned.

Meninges. Covering the whole of the brain are a series of membranes called meninges. The outer ones serve a protective function, while the inner ones contain a profusion of arteries and veins carrying blood to the brain. The brain has one of the largest turnovers of chemicals in the whole body. The neurons are continually synthesizing protein, and the more mentally active a person is, the faster is the synthesis. This all requires energy, and the brain has one of the richest blood supplies of any organ in the body. There are literally millions of tiny blood vessels in the brain supplying the cells with nourishment and oxygen. And the brain, though only 3 percent of the body's total weight, consumes 25 percent of its oxygen intake.

The human brain is a highly complex, intricately interconnected web of billions of neurons. Millions of fibers connect each of the different regions with other regions, and in the final analysis the simplified view portrayed here cannot do justice to its true complexity. Most of the different areas are probably involved in almost everything that happens in the brain, the whole forming a dynamic neurological balance, of which science has at present had only the faintest glimpse.

Figure 16

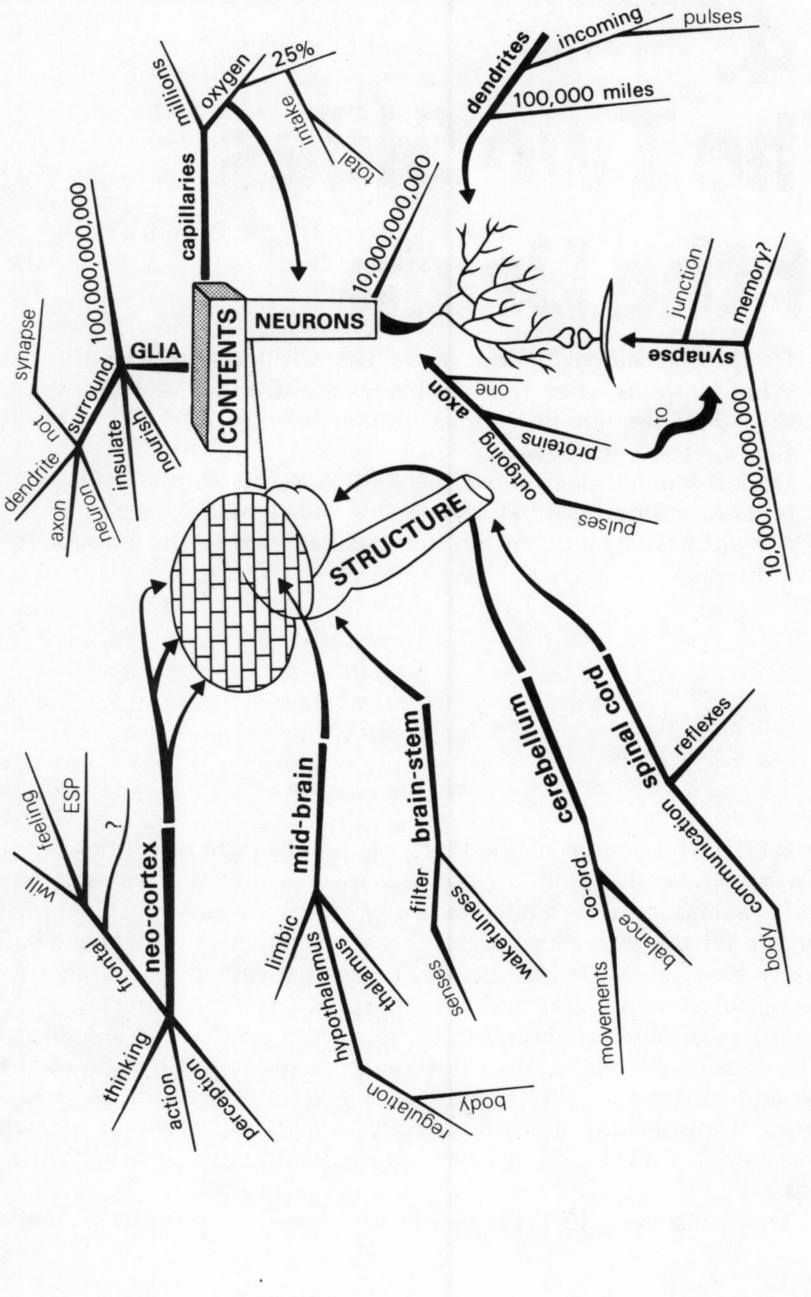
CONTENTS
NEURONS
GLIA
100,000,000,000
surround
synapse
not
dendrite
axon
neuron
insulate
nourish
capillaries
millions
oxygen
25%
intake
total
10,000,000,000
dendrites
incoming
pulses
100,000 miles
synapse
junction
memory?
10,000,000,000,000
to
axon
one
proteins
outgoing
pulses
STRUCTURE
neo-cortex
frontal
will
feeling
ESP
?
thinking
action
perception
mid-brain
limbic
hypothalamus
thalamus
regulation
body
brain-stem
filter
senses
wakefulness
cerebellum
co-ord.
movements
balance
spinal cord
reflexes
communication
body

4.
The Two Sides of the Brain

Do the left and right sides of the brain function differently?
What happens when the two halves are divided?
Why does the left side appear dominant?
Can we use both equally?
Do left-handed people use the right side more?
Is there a difference between males and females?
Are cultural symbols of left and right related to the sides of the
    brain?

The fact that the brain is divided into a left and a right half is not a new discovery. Once the skull is removed, the division is obvious to the naked eye, and it is a common feature of brains throughout the animal kingdom. What is interesting about this division in man is that each half seems to have developed specialized functions, the left side appearing to be better at some tasks and the right side better at others.

The most obvious difference in functioning is that the left side of the brain receives sensations from and controls the right side of the body, and vice versa. The reasons for this are still unclear. Despite a number of interesting theories, there is no obvious advantage in such a crossover. Yet it is found in most mammals and in many other vertebrates.

This crossover effect was one of the first discoveries to be made

48

about the brain, the ancient Egyptians having noticed that injuries to one side of the brain caused a corresponding paralysis to the opposite side of the body. By the beginning of this century it was known that damage to certain areas of the left hemisphere results in the loss of speech, poor reading, and a general deterioration in logical thinking, whereas damage to the corresponding regions of the right hemisphere produces a deterioration in visual and spatial functions, such as the recognition of faces and the ability to dress oneself.

The fact that damage to the left hemisphere produces far more serious defects gave rise to the widespread view that the left hemisphere was dominant. Often the left was referred to as the major hemisphere and the right as the minor one. Recent research, however, has forced psychologists to modify this view on two accounts. First, the right hemisphere has been found to be just as active and just as important as the left hemisphere. And second, each hemisphere partakes to some extent in the functions associated with the other hemisphere, making it more difficult to draw a rigid functional distinction.

THE SPLIT-BRAIN EXPERIMENTS

The left and right halves of the cortex, though separate structures, are connected by a massive bundle of nerves, called the corpus callosum, containing some 200 million fibers. In 1940 two doctors decided to try cutting the corpus callosum in patients with severe epilepsy. They reasoned that if they could confine the seizure to one half of the brain, then the other half could carry on functioning normally, enabling the person to take some medicine or summon assistance. As far as treating the epilepsy was concerned, it seemed to work, and at first there were no observable side effects or disturbances in behavior.[1] This led some psychologists to the view that the corpus callosum played no greater role than physically supporting the two halves of the brain!

Further work on animals, however, suggested that there may be some functional disorders resulting from the operation after all, and this led to a renewed examination of its effects in humans. In the 1960s Roger Sperry, at the California Institute of Technology, began extensive studies on a number of epileptic patients whose corpus callosum had been severed and began uncovering some interesting anomalies. If a patient was given something to hold in his right hand, he could say what he was holding, since the information was going to the left side of the brain. But if the object was in his left hand, he could not describe it, he could only make a guess—though he could later point to the object again with his left hand, showing that the right half had both recognized and remembered the object.[2]

The crossover in the visual system is slightly more complex than in the rest of the body. The eyes themselves are not directly crossed, but the left side of the retina of each eye connects to the left side of the brain, and the right side of the retina of each eye connects to the right side of the brain. Thus, since the retinal image is inverted, the left side of the visual field connects to the right side of the brain and the right side of the visual field connects to the left side. This gave rise to some interesting phenomena in the split-brain patients. If the word *Herman* were flashed to a patient in such a way that his focus lay between the *r* and the *m*, the first three letters would go to the right hemisphere and the last three letters to the left hemisphere. When asked to *say* what he had seen, he would reply "man"; but when asked to point with his left hand to what he had seen, he would point to the word *her*.[3]

The reason that such differences had not been found in the earlier studies was that the two halves of the brain had been able to communicate in other ways. In one of Sperry's experiments a light was flashed in the left visual field so that it arrived in the right hemisphere, and the patient had to say whether the light was red or green. At first the replies were purely guesswork, the left hemisphere having no idea what the right side was seeing, but after a few trials the patient began correcting his mistakes. The left hemisphere might wrongly guess "red" for a green light, but the right hemisphere, on hearing the wrong answer, would start shaking the head and making frowns. The left hemisphere, responding to this information, would immediately say, "Oh no, I meant green."[4] Once such additional sources of information were controlled, the different functions of the two hemispheres began to become more apparent.

One interesting finding was that although the right hand still maintained the ability to write—as we would expect if linguistic abilities are located in the left hemisphere—it lost the ability to draw pictures. With the left hand, however, the opposite was the case. It could not write at all, but it could still draw cubes and simple shapes. The left hand was also better than the right at arranging colored blocks to form a pattern, though it may never have attempted this before.[5]

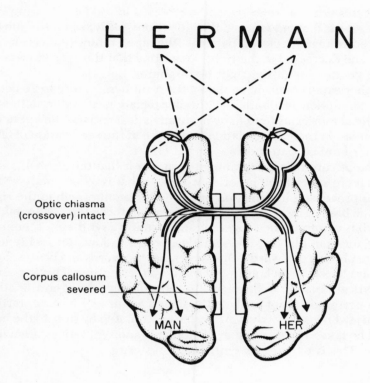

Figure 17 Crossover of visual fields in the brain. The left side of the retina of each eye goes to the right side of the brain, and vice versa. Thus the right visual field goes to the left side of the brain, and vice versa, no matter which eye is being used.

SPECIALIZATION OF FUNCTION

The different functions of the two hemispheres have been confirmed by comparing the electrical activity from the left and right sides of the brain. When the brain is in a fairly relaxed state, it tends to show alpha rhythms—that is, waves of about eight to ten cycles per second. Robert Ornstein in San Francisco compared the relative levels of alpha from the left and right sides of the brain for different mental activities. He found that when he gave his subject a mathematical problem to solve, the alpha increased in the right hemisphere, suggesting that this side was relaxing, and decreased in the left, showing that awareness was focused more in this side. Conversely, when the subject was asked to match colored patterns, the alpha intensity increased in the left and decreased in the right, suggesting that the subject was now making greater use of the right hemisphere.[6]

Other experiments have shown the right hemisphere to be better in the perception of depth,[7] in the appreciation of music (although professional musicians tend to be more analytical and use the left hemisphere more in their appreciation),[8] and also in the recognition of faces and other familiar patterns.[9]

The picture that is beginning to emerge is that the left half of the brain is more specialized in serial processes, that is to say, analysis that involves processing information one bit after another; while the right half of the brain is more specialized in parallel processing, that is, taking several bits of information together and forming a synthesis of them. In writing, for example, one takes an idea, breaks it down into sentences, then into phrases and words. One then takes the words and breaks them down into letters, which are written one after another. This is a serial or analytical process. With regard to recognizing a face, on the other hand, a person does not analyze the image feature by feature starting with the jawline and slowly working his way up, step by step, to the hair. Instead he takes a large number of elements and synthesizes them into a whole. This is parallel, or synthetic, processing.

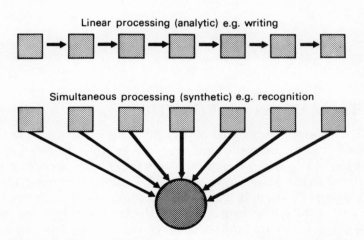

Figure 18 Distinction between linear and simultaneous processing.

Further evidence on this distinction comes from studies of perceptual discrimination. A person generally takes longer to judge whether ten letters are all the same than he does to judge whether two are. This implies that the letters are being evaluated one after another, that is, serially. Conversely, when the items to be matched are shapes, the time taken by the subject is independent of the number of comparisons, suggesting that with nonverbal material the processing is in parallel. When, however, the letters are processed by just one hemisphere (by presenting them in the opposite visual field), the time taken to judge whether or not they are identical increases with the number of letters when they are presented to the left hemisphere, yet stays the same when they are presented to the right. This supports the contention that the left is processing in a serial mode while the right is processing in parallel. But this only occurs for verbal material. When the items are shapes, both hemispheres appear to work in a parallel mode.[10] Presumably the left is now forced to work in a parallel mode, since its verbal abilities are no longer of any use in distinguishing abstract shapes.

While supporting the hypothesis that the left prefers to function in a serial mode and the right a parallel mode, this experiment also shows that this distinction is not absolute—it is only a preference, and, when obliged to, either hemisphere can function in either mode.

The value of specialization of function is that it effectively increases our mental capacity. Each hemisphere tends to analyze its own input first, only swapping information with the other side once a considerable degree of processing has already taken place. Thus we can process two streams of information at once and then compare and integrate them in order to obtain a broader and more sophisticated impression.[11] Specialization of function also divides the load of each hemisphere. It is a very natural course of action to take. We can see it in any organic system—different cells and organs specializing in different tasks—and in any social organization—different groups of people taking on different responsibilities in order to share the load and increase the overall efficiency of the system.

THE QUESTION OF DOMINANCE

Although speech and linguistic abilities in general have for long been associated with a specific area in the left hemisphere (Broca's area in the temporal cortex behind the ear), recent experiments suggest that the right side of the brain also has some well-developed verbal abilities.

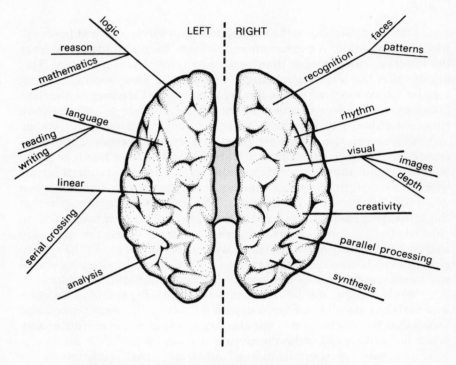

Figure 19 Specializations of the left and right hemispheres.

Damage to the right hemisphere does not usually produce a complete block in linguistic abilities, although it can impede them. A number of patients with right-side-of-brain damage have experienced difficulties in copying and writing, and many have shown difficulties in grammar as well; but they did not show a complete loss of language.[12]

By injecting sodium amytal into the arteries in the left side of the neck, it is possible to anesthetize completely the left hemisphere but leave the right functioning normally. When this is done, it is found that the subject can still understand language, being able to pick out objects that have been described and to follow simple instructions.[13] Other experiments on the right hemisphere have shown that it does seem to possess a moderate degree of syntax, about that of a five-year-old, and the vocabulary of a fourteen-year-old.

The left hemisphere may not be dominant in the sense that it is any more important than the right, but in Western culture at least, the faculties associated with the left do take a more dominant position in our lives. We tend to lay greater emphasis on rational thinking, the ability to express oneself verbally, read well, and generally excel in analytic thinking. We place less emphasis on spatial ability, artistic appreciation, creative processes, and intuitive thought—the faculties more often associated with the right hemisphere.

It is generally much easier for an accountant or a lawyer, say, to be successful than it is for the artist. The highest material rewards go to the logical, rational thinkers, and for them the paths to success are well laid out. For the artist, musician, and the poet the path is much harder. For most it is a question of survival rather than success. Our society, it is true, does support a number of artists, but this is generally regarded as something of a luxury. Providing all the necessities (as judged by our logical minds) have been taken care of, we can afford ourselves a little artistic indulgence. Yet it may well be that art and creativity are as necessary to the survival of our society as science and logic are.

The emphasis on left-hemisphere processes goes back to early school days. When most of us went to school, education was still based largely around the three R's—reading, 'riting, and 'rithmetic—all essentially left-hemisphere functions. There were, of course, art classes, music lessons, and the occasional dance or drama class, but in most cases these were seen as an extra. They were a special treat for Friday afternoons—providing, that is, you had got all your sums right and had corrected all your spelling mistakes.

This type of education, combined with society's emphasis on analytic rather than synthetic thinking, has led to the left hemisphere's becoming dominant in usage. It also has had the unfortunate side effect that children who are better at using their right hemisphere may have been wrongly classed as subnormal or retarded. Indeed, a study at the University of Houston showed that a number of children classified as "mentally retarded" actually showed normal or superior development in artistic ability.[14]

Some schools have tried increasing the proportion of the curriculum devoted to the arts, and with encouraging results. At the Mead School, in Bryam, Connecticut, children spend half their time in art classes of one form or another and the other half in "regular" subjects. As a result their performance in mathematics, science, and a variety of other subjects actually increased. Indeed, the school's performance was above average in nearly every subject.[15] Other schools in both Europe and America that have tried similar projects have found the same: The extra time spent on developing the faculties of the right brain also helps those associated with the left brain. This is because the two do not work in isolation—each supports and complements the activity of the other.

A complete education should give equal emphasis to both verbal-analytic thinking and to aesthetic-synthetic thinking. If only the verbal-analytic side is being educated, the student is effectively being cut off from many ways in which he could directly experience the world around him. And without direct experience education can become dry, meaningless, and boring. As one worker in this field put it, "His brain is being systematically damaged. In many ways he is being de-educated."[16]

Yet, tragically, whenever there is any cutback in the public funding of education, it is the arts program that is hit first. This may seem a good short-term saving, but in the long run it is a grave loss to society.

If we look at the great minds throughout history, we find that time and again they were people who used the faculties of both the left and the right sides. Albert Einstein is a classic example. As soon as you see his name, you probably think of a great scientist, the supreme rational thinker, the great mathematician surrounded by figures and equations, a logical left-hemisphere thinker. Yet Einstein's ideas initially came to him as pictures and images, and only subsequently did he put them into words and mathematical symbols. When Einstein hit upon the theory of relativity, it was not through rational analysis. He did not sit down with pen and paper and step by step work out the theory, eventually arriving at the logical conclusion. The theory was born when Einstein was lying on a grassy hillside one summer's afternoon. He was gazing up at the sun through half-closed eyelids, playing with the light that came through his eyelashes, when he began to wonder what it would be like to travel down a light beam. He lay there in a dream state letting his mind wander freely, imagining himself traveling down a light beam, when suddenly he realized (one almost has to say in a flash) just what it would be like. This realization was the essence of the theory of relativity, and it had come to him not as a logical deduction, but as a creative, intuitive insight, the result of synthetic rather than analytic thinking.

There must have been thousands of people who have had similar deep insights as to the nature of reality but had no ability to express their realizations, and were simply ignored as babbling idiots. What made Einstein so great was the fact that he was also a good rational thinker. He could take his insight and, using a mathematical frame-work, give it a logical symbolic formulation, and so communicate it to others.

This combined use of both the right and left hemispheres is a common characteristic of the creative process, whether in science or in art. Leonardo da Vinci was as much scientist as artist, an engineer and architect as well as sculptor and painter. His science notebooks contain exquisite drawings of nature and of the human anatomy that were artistically superior to any others of that time, whereas his art notebooks were full of precise analyses of visual perception that were not fully appreciated for several centuries. The notebooks of many other artists similarly reveal concise analytic thinking linked with deep insight and aesthetic appreciation.

LEFT- AND RIGHT-HANDEDNESS

Since the right hand is connected to the left side of the brain, could there be a connection between right-handedness and a greater use of the left hemisphere? The answer is, probably not. Left-handed people are generally left-hemisphere thinkers as much as are right-handed people. And conversely in people who show a much higher use of right-hemisphere faculties there is no strong correlation with left-hand-edness.[17]

Alternatively, could left-handedness reflect a reversal of the func-tions of the left and right hemispheres? In a few people the functions of the left and right hemispheres are reversed, linguistic abilities resid-ing more in the right hemisphere, but such people are still mainly right-handed. Conversely the majority of left-handers still have their speech areas in the left hemisphere, and the same is true with ambidex-trous people.[18] Just why some people find it easier and better to use their left hand is not yet clear, but it certainly does not usually imply a shift in dominance or a reversal of the functions of the left and right hemispheres.

MALE–FEMALE DIFFERENCES

The specialized functions of the two hemispheres are a little differ-ent in males and females. At school boys are generally better at spatial tasks, whereas girls are better at linguistic ones. Newborn girls utter sounds more often than newborn boys, and during the first few years they utter a larger variety of sounds than do boys. On average they say their first words and first sentences earlier, and at the age of two they have larger vocabularies. There also seems to be less specialization in visual-spatial skills in females, there being a much broader overlap between the two hemispheres. This is apparent up to the age of thirteen and possibly continues later. Boys, on the other hand, have visual-spatial skills localized in the right hemisphere by the age of six.[19] Whether or not this is an inborn difference is not clear; it could be a cultural effect stemming from slight differences in approach to baby boys and baby girls.

The female brain appears to retain its plasticity longer. Being more versatile, it is better able to compensate for damage to other areas. This probably explains why girls have only one-sixth of the reading problems that boys do. These differences continue throughout life. It has been observed that in men, damage to the left hemisphere results in more serious deterioration in language function than it does in women, and damage to the right hemisphere results in a more serious deterioration to visual-spatial functions. In women, on the other hand, the relationship between the functions lost and the areas damaged is less specific.[20]

The electrical activity of the brain reveals that men tend to have lower evoked potentials—a measure of the brain's electrical response to stimuli such as light and sound. Men also have better daylight vision than women.

They are, in general, less sensitive to extreme heat and more sensitive to extreme cold. Men have faster reaction times from mid-childhood on; even as infants, they tend to be more interested in objects than in people, and are more skilled at gross motor movements. Boys engage in tough-and-tumble play more than girls [helping the eye and brain learn to adjust to sudden major shifts in the visual environment]; as infants, they spend more time playing with objects other than toys, and invent novel uses for them. Men excel in a wide range of skills involving the perception of depth in space, an ability that gives them an edge in mechanical tasks. Boys' greater ability in math could also be a spatial skill, since it shows strongest when geometry and trigonometry are included. Finally, the fact that boys are more easily distracted by novel objects, combined with their greater exploratory behavior, suggests a kind of curiosity that leads to success in problem-solving tasks that require manipulation.

Women, by contrast, have more sensitive taste, are more sensitive to touch in all parts of the body, have better hearing (particularly in the higher ranges), are less tolerant of loud volumes (at 85 decibels and above, any sound seems twice as loud to them as it does to males), are less tolerant of repetitive sounds, and have better night vision. From infancy on, women excel in many verbal skills, are better in manual dexterity and fine coordination, and process information faster, particularly in tasks (like neurosurgery) that require rapid choices. Women are more interested in people, as infants are more attentive to sounds and their emotional meaning, and are more socially responsive and empathic. They are less distracted by sights while listening, more accurately perceive "subliminal" messages, and are better at remembering the names and faces of old high-school classmates. Women's greater interest in people also shows up in better empathy.[21]

WHAT UNDERLIES THE SPECIALIZATION?

The distinction between left and right functions may well be more fundamental than "verbal" versus "nonverbal" and may exist even at birth. Studies of the electrical activity of the brains of newborn babies have shown that they process the sound of a click in the left hemisphere and a flash of light in the right.[22] This has led to the hypothesis that the left deals with the "recognition of relationship" or "association with previous experience." A click is highly structured auditory information and can be related to past experiences and hence labeled; a visual flash, on the other hand, is unstructured information and is not so easily labeled. If so, then it is the labeling, or referential tendency of the left, that would lead to the processing of language by the left hemisphere. The left brain would not therefore be just analytic and sequential, but also comparative, relational, and referential. And the right brain not only synthetic, but also nonreferential and integrative.

It has also been suggested that the functions associated with the left and right hemispheres parallel what have been called the "active mode" and the "receptive mode."[23] The "active mode," as its name implies, is concerned with activity, with manipulation, and with directly influencing the environment. Thinking in the active mode is more logical, and attention is more focused with a heightened awareness of boundaries. It is the mode for *doing,* for making things happen.

The "receptive mode," on the other hand, is more concerned with intake from the environment. Thinking in the receptive mode tends to be synthetic rather than analytic, and the attention is more diffuse. This mode is more concerned with letting things happen. It should not, however, be confused with passivity: It is merely a different way of engaging the world. It is probably our emphasis on rationality and the left hemisphere that has led to a predominance of the "active mode" —we in the West are continually making the world respond to our needs. The opposite of this is the Taoist concept of *Wui-Wei*, of letting things be, a surrendering to Nature and flowing with change rather than continually pitting oneself against it.

LEFT–RIGHT ASSOCIATIONS

Psychologist Robert Ornstein has taken this polarity further, suggesting that Western thinking is left-hemisphere dominant, whereas Eastern thinking is right-hemisphere dominant.[24] The evidence for this is, however, very meager. Ornstein also believes that many of our so-called unconscious mental processes reside in the right hemisphere, and he points out that in many societies the left side of the body is associated with unconscious processes and with other functions attributed to the right hemisphere. This is probably a gross oversimplification of the division. As we have seen, mental functions do not seem to fall into such a neat separation between the left and right. Nevertheless, the parallels with the right–left symbolism found in nearly every culture of the world is fascinating.

The right side of the body, or the right hand (corresponding to the left side of the brain, remember), is generally associated with the good, the sacred, the pure; with life, joy, medicine, and health; with heaven and progress. The left is associated with evil, the profane and the impure, with death, sorrow, poison, and illness; with hell and with regression. The right symbolizes masculinity, lucidity, and adaptability; the sun, daytime, and light. The left symbolizes femininity, obscurity, and passivity, the moon, nighttime, and darkness. In China the right is yang, the creative and the firm; the left is yin, the receptive and the yielding. Yang is summer, the time of life and growth; yin is the winter, the time of hibernation and recession. In most cultures the right hand is used for religious offerings and for taking food, and it is the right hand that is shaken in greeting. Christ sat at God's right hand and the *good* thief was crucified on Christ's right. In alchemy the right is associated with the king and with Mars; the left with the queen and with Venus.

In many languages, the words for right and left have other meanings. In English *right* also means "correct." *Sinister* comes from the Latin *sinistra*, "left." In French the word *droit*, "right," also means "straight, not twisted or perverse"; similarly with the Armenian for "right," *adj.* In Italian *destro*, as well as signifying the right hand, also means "the right moment" and is sometimes used in the sense of being clever. The Arabic *yamine* has the second meaning of "prosperity," and also "oath." In many of the Bantu languages of West Africa (Swahili, Nyanja, Lomwe, and Suto, for example) the word for "right" is also the word for "male" (*mkono wa kuume*, "the male hand" in Swahili), and the word for "left" is also the word for "female."[25]

Probably the most detailed left-right symbolism is found in the Tantric writings of northern India. These are fascinating in that although they were written many hundreds of years ago, they foreshadow much of what we are now discovering about the left and right

Figure 20 Cross-cultural associations with left and right, paralleling some of the attributes of right and left hemispheres.

RIGHT (Left brain)	LEFT (Right brain)
Male	Female
West	East
Conscious	Unconscious
Good	Evil
Sacred	Profane
Pure	Impure
Life	Death
Joy	Sorrow
Medicine	Poison
Health	Sickness
Progress	Regress
Heaven	Hell
Light	Dark
Sun	Moon
Day	Night
Yang	Yin
Active	Passive

hemispheres of the brain. Tantric writings associate the left nostril with the moon and with feminine qualities, and the right nostril with the sun and masculinity. They maintain that the breath rarely flows through both nostrils equally, for a while it flows predominantly through the left and then for a while through the right, the changeover taking place once every twenty minutes or so in the healthy person. When the sun breath is flowing—that is, when the right nostril is dominant—one is advised to undertake the actions involving speech and instruction, as well as combat and physical exertion. These correspond to the linguistic functions associated with the left hemisphere, and the "active," competitive mode. When, on the other hand, the moon breath is dominant, one is advised to engage in painting, composing, listening to music, and other creative and artistic activities—that is, with functions associated more with the right hemisphere. The Tantrists also claim that when a person gains enlightenment, that is to say, when he is fully aware both inwardly and outwardly, the breath is found flowing equally in both nostrils. This presumably reflects the fact that such a person would be using both hemispheres of the brain in balance, rather than temporarily suppressing one in order to make full use of the other.

In terms of brain functioning a synthesis of the qualities associated with the left and right hemispheres implies a greater communication between the two hemispheres via the corpus callosum. Over its evolution the human brain has undergone a steady thickening of the corpus callosum. As a species we seem to be moving in the direction of greater communication between the two halves. A similar phenomenon seems to be happening at the level of individual evolution, personal development of awareness resulting in an increased communication between the hemispheres. There has over the past decade or so been widespread growth of interest in techniques of meditation and personal development. One such technique, which has attracted considerable attention from the scientific world, largely as a result of the wide availability of subjects, is the Transcendental Meditation technique. Much of the research has concentrated on changes taking place in the brain itself, and in 1975, Dr. Bernard Glueck, working at the Institute of Living in Hartford, Connecticut, found that the electroencephalogram (EEG) patterns of subjects practicing this technique showed an increased synchrony between the left and right sides of the brain—in other words, both sides appeared to be functioning together—which he suggested showed a much greater communication through the corpus callosum.[26]

This effect has since been borne out in a number of other laboratories in Europe and America.[27]

There are thus two principal ways in which the functioning of the right side of the brain can be brought into balance with that of the left. The meditation approach quiets the brain's activity and increases the communication between the two halves, permitting the right to function along with the left. The educational approach focuses more on developing the actual skills associated with the right. This latter approach is the one that will underlie most of the advice given in Part Two on how to make the most of your brain. The two approaches are not, however, in conflict: They are in fact complementary, the best results being achieved by following up both approaches. The one increases the brain's efficiency. The other helps you use that increased efficiency more fully still.

Figure 21

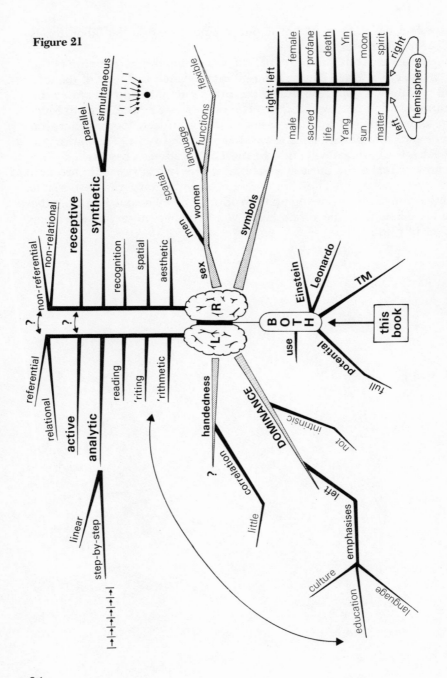

5.
The Ever-
Adaptable Brain

Do mental abilities decrease with age?
Do older people lose memory for recent events?
Can the adult brain compensate for serious damage?
Can the brain be reeducated after an accident?
Can neurons reproduce after all?
How can you make the most of your brain?

It is a common misconception that mental faculties begin to decline after about the age of twenty. Charts of mental abilities are often drawn to look like line *a* in Figure 22. There is said to be a steady increase in ability throughout childhood and youth, followed by a gradual falling off during adulthood. Several lines of research, however, show that this is not the case; one's mental potential continues to increase steadily throughout life, only beginning to tail off after about the age of sixty—and even this tailing off may not be necessary.

One reason sometimes cited for this supposed decline is that neurons are steadily dying off and never being replaced. This is itself a doubtful statement, but even if it were true, it is extremely unlikely that it would have any effect on mental abilities for the following reasons:

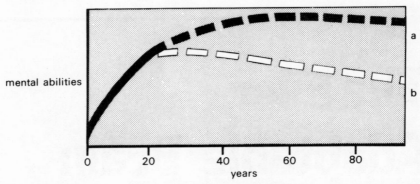

Figure 22 Growth of mental ability with age. (a) Potential continued growth with age. (b) Common misconception of mental ability decreasing after about 20 years.

1. The brain contains some ten to twelve billion neurons, and even if neurons did die at the rate of a thousand a day less than 1 percent would be lost over an entire lifetime. In this respect the human brain deteriorates more slowly than any other organ in the body!

2. When brain damage is very gradual, the loss of function is considerably reduced. To remove less than 1 percent of the brain's material cell by cell over a lifetime would have a negligible effect, if any, on mental abilities. Each time one cell died, the brain would be able to recover from the loss immediately.

3. Since the cells that die would be distributed fairly evenly throughout the brain, their loss is unlikely to affect any specific function. Indeed, since there is already a very large degree of redundancy in the nervous system, it is most unlikely that the loss of this small number of cells would be noticed at all, whether it occurred slowly over a lifetime or in one instant.

Researchers have often been misled into assuming that mental abilities decrease with age because they failed to take into account the development of education over the years. A twenty-year-old person will probably have received a better education than a person of seventy. Thus a straight comparison of the current mental abilities of the two age groups would be measuring the difference in educational backgrounds as well as any intrinsic deterioration. When psychologists began to perform longitudinal studies—that is, studies that followed specific individuals throughout their lives—they found that as far as IQ was concerned there was no deterioration with age. Their scores on intelligence tests appeared to remain stable until the age of seventy. The only noticeable decrease in abilities was that after sixty, people were slower at tasks that involved physical movement as well as mental functioning.[1] In cases where intelligence and other mental abilities have been found to be declining, it was usually because of some sickness or physiological malfunction: It was not a deterioration of the brain itself.

Oxygen is essential to brain function. Although the brain amounts to only about 2 percent of the body's weight, it consumes 25 percent of the body's oxygen intake. If the oxygen supply is reduced, brain function suffers. If the supply is completely cut off for more than two or three minutes, the brain begins to deteriorate irreversibly.

As a person grows older, the arteries to the head, as well as those to the heart, may become clogged by arteriosclerosis as fats begin to build up inside the artery walls. In one study it was found that in people between fifty and eighty years old there was, on average, a 50-percent blockage of the arteries feeding the brain. This can seriously affect mental function. When the arteries of elderly patients were cleaned out, it was found that their IQ scores increased significantly—by 4.6 points on verbal comprehension, and by 12 points on perceptual organization. Measurements of their personality revealed a significant reduction in anxiety, suspicion, distress, disorientation, and feelings of nervousness.[2] Thus a major factor in mental deterioration may be simply the restriction of the oxygen supply to the brain.

Another factor that can decrease the oxygen available to the brain and so lead to a decrease in intellectual ability is high blood pressure. At Duke University a group of eighty-seven people in their sixties were studied over a period of ten years. Every two and a half years they were given a collection of psychological and physiological tests, including a measurement of blood pressure. It was found that those people who had very high blood pressure suffered a marked loss in mental abilities, whereas those with normal blood pressure showed no decline.[3]

Deliberately enriching the brain's supply of oxygen can also reverse any apparent deterioration of function in old people. Brief periods spent in an oxygen chamber can lead to a remarkable intellectual revitalization. Patients given short treatments twice a day for just fifteen days have been found to become more active, ask for reading material, and generally begin to become much more alert. Many were so improved that they were sent home.[4]

Expectancy and belief are confounding factors in any study of the effects of aging. If people are given to believe that mental potential is going to decrease after twenty, then it is very likely that it will. And if they are then told that they are doing as well as can be expected, and to take it easy, the decline will be reinforced. The human mind is remarkably adept at materializing its own beliefs, and graphs such as line *a* in Figure 22, if publicized in the national press as true (as they have been), soon appear to substantiate their own false conclusions.

Conversely, the realization that there is an enormous latent potential in the human brain that can be continually unfolded throughout adult life and even through old age can lead to the pattern of continued development shown in line *b* in Figure 22.

The choice is yours.

AGING AND MEMORY

Older people often claim that their memory for recent events is getting poorer, although they may be able to remember clearly events from their childhood.

Long-term memory is based largely on minute chemical changes in the brain and, chemically speaking, the brain is still very much prepared for learning through most of adulthood. RNA, a complex molecule intimately involved in the process of learning, does not decrease with age. In fact the RNA content in the brain is generally *increasing* throughout life: It usually does not show signs of decreasing until the sixties or seventies.[5] So chemically there is no reason why learning abilities should decrease after the age of twenty.

In fact there is little experimental evidence to suggest that memory does decrease with age in the manner claimed. Many of the studies show the opposite. People of various ages have been tested on recall and recognition of prominent newspaper events that occurred during a period of about forty years preceding the study, and of photographs of well-known faces over a thirty-year span. In these cases no evidence has been found of the older people showing increased forgetting for recent events compared with earlier ones.[6]

Other studies have investigated whether there is any evidence of "living in the past" as far as *personal* memories are concerned. People were asked to name personal associations to common words and then estimate the original date of that association. It was found that the average age of remembered events tends to keep pace with chronological age. There is a slowly increasing lag such that the memories of a person aged one hundred would tend to cluster around the age of eighty. But this hardly constitutes living in the past: It is simply due to the fact that their long span of memory lowers the average age for remembered events. The fact that it is lowered to eighty rather than fifty or lower implies that the recalled episodes were coming more from the latter part of their lives.[7]

A possible reason why memory for recent events may appear to deteriorate in older people is that the brain remembers better those things that are especially outstanding. In childhood there are many more new, remarkable, and outstanding experiences than there are later in life, and these more "special" events are better remembered. Thus a person in a routine situation who does not encounter so much novel material may well find that things are not being remembered as well. In this case deliberately paying attention to what is going on and maintaining an interest in it can lead to a great improvement of memory. Every situation is unique. Be fully conscious of its uniqueness and your memory will not fail you.

RECOVERY OF FUNCTION

In chapter 2 it was shown that the human brain appears to be remarkably adaptable during the first two years of life. If some area of the young brain is damaged, or even removed, other areas of the brain will take over the functions of the damaged area and the child will usually grow up without any noticeable impairment.

There have been many instances of young children who were born with only one hemisphere, or who have had one side removed for medical reasons soon after birth. In such cases the remaining half of the brain has been found to take on the functions of the missing half as well as its own functions.[8] Children are occasionally born with no corpus callosum connecting the two hemispheres—a phenomenon known as agenesis. Yet most of these children grow up normally with no deterioration in function.[9] It appears that the brain compensates for the missing nerve fibers by rerouting the communications between the left and right hemispheres through other pathways lower down in the brain.

Such effects have been known for a long time and have usually been explained by the fact that the brain is still growing and therefore able to adjust to damage to any of its structures. But it has generally been assumed that when the adult brain, or even that of a child over three or four years old, receives similar damage, there cannot be a full recovery of function, although the undamaged areas of the brain may compensate to some extent for the damaged parts. It is, however, now being realized that the adult brain can also show considerable plasticity. It appears to be capable of remarkable readjustment and compensation, and, given suitable rich and varied stimulation, will continue growing and developing right through life.

There are many instances of people who have had large parts of their brain damaged or destroyed, and who were at first seriously incapacitated, but who over time recovered many of the functions lost at the time of injury. A typical case is of the American soldier who received a massive brain wound in the Korean War. He lost all of the area in the left hemisphere normally associated with speech. When examined three months after the injury, he could speak only very laboriously, in two-word sentences. When asked to read the phrase "New York University College of Medicine," all that he could produce was "doctors—little doctors." Yet when he was reexamined eight years later and shown the same phrase he said, without the slightest difficulty, "Is there a catch? It says 'New York University College of Medicine.' "[10] The latent linguistic abilities of the right hemisphere, which normally are suppressed by the stronger language faculty of the left, appeared to take over and develop to such an extent that the right hemisphere could carry on most of the functions previously governed by the left.

In the foregoing case the recovery happened without any specific program of retraining. When a brain-injured person is given special retraining immediately after the injury, the spontaneous recovery of function is greatly enhanced. A young sailor in World War II suffered a severe injury to the verbal cortex in the left hemisphere and as a result was only able to utter a few grunts. Instead of being left to fend for himself, he was given an intensive retraining program. After only one month the sailor had begun to speak again. But he spoke his first few words in his original hillbilly dialect, whereas the lady therapist spoke in a Yankee accent. At this point the trainer wanted to resign because, she asserted, he was evidently faking his condition.[11] She had, however misinterpreted his recovery, which in this case would appear to be not a complete relearning of language so much as a fuller development of language areas, which had, up till then, been dormant.

In another case, examined at length by the Russian psychologist Aleksandr Luria, a young soldier who had received a severe head wound suffered impairment of vision, loss of memory and the ability to speak, read, or write. Reduced almost to infancy, the man resolved to reeducate himself all over again. Through continual perserverance he taught himself to recall and understand, to speak, then to read, and finally to write.[12] And he did all this without large parts of his brain and at a time in life when it had generally been thought that the brain was very set in its functions.

The more immediately the retraining follows the injury, the more effective it is. In cases where the retraining had to be delayed for several months the patients did not make such a quick nor such a successful recovery.[13]

A large number of small injuries have been found to be much less damaging than one major injury, even though the total effect of tiny injuries may destroy more brain tissue than the one sudden injury. Damage to the left hemisphere, for example, does not disrupt linguistic functions so seriously if the damage develops very slowly.[14] This fascinating aspect of gradual damage was demonstrated by removing the motor cortex of a monkey in small increments. After each small piece was removed, the monkey was given intensive exercise and training in walking, and even when hardly any of its motor cortex remained, the animal could still stand and walk.

Some of these findings have been applied with good effect to people who have had a stroke. After a stroke a person may be paralyzed to the extent that he is confined to a wheelchair and is often unable to speak coherently. In the past, very little was done in the way of retraining, and recovery was slow. Today, however, stroke patients are given maximum encouragement to exercise their limbs, taught to walk again, and given intensive speech therapy to help them regain their verbal abilities. Again, the sooner the retraining, the more effective it is.

These principles have also been used in helping young children overcome brain damage. Two American psychologists, Glen Doman and Carl Delecato, established the Institute for the Achievement of Human Potential in Philadelphia to help children who were physically handicapped as a result of some brain injury. Previously it was thought that such children rarely, if ever, overcame their defects. Doman and Delecato's approach concentrated on training the parents in how best to help their handicapped child cope with and surmount their problems. The parents of a partially paralyzed child would be shown how to manipulate his limbs so as to help the brain learn better how to control them. As a result many, though not all, such children started crawling and walking. Others who were mute began to speak, and in many cases IQ scores increased dramatically. In one case a child with a whole hemisphere missing was brought up to the level of the normal child of his age.[16]

Doman realized that if such recoveries were possible with brain-damaged children, even more should be possible with normal children. So he went on to apply his methods to ordinary children, and with equally astounding results. Many children have learned to read by the age of two and showed a greater general emotional development than other children of the same age.[17]

A similar approach has been taken by Moshe Feldenkreis from Israel. He believes in reeducating the motor areas of the brain by manipulating the muscles, thus giving the brain direct experience of how it should control them. At a demonstration of his technique in London, he took a fifty-year-old man who had been a spastic all his life and, by very gently moving the limbs this way and that, taught the brain a much smoother control of the muscles. After just one hour of such treatment the man stood up and walked smoothly just like a normal person, tears of joy running down his face. A miracle? No. Simply the combination of a very sensitive therapist and an awareness of the possibilities open to the adult human brain given the correct retraining.[18]

Another interesting example of recovery of function concerns the split-brain patients discussed in the previous chapter. At the time of the operation there appeared to be a distinct localization of function—verbal skills, for example, residing predominantly in the left hemisphere and visual-spatial skills in the right. Ten years after the original operations, however, each side of the brain had largely recovered from the loss of the other half. The left side had developed visual-spatial skills and other faculties associated with the right hemisphere, whereas the right had developed linguistic abilities. This recovery occurred without any retraining. When suitable reeducation *is* given, the right hemisphere can learn to read and write much faster—in less than six months.[19]

NEURON REGENERATION

The brain's ability to recover from serious injury raises the question of whether or not neurons can regenerate themselves. Until recently this possibility was not generally accepted, it being thought that recovery of function was due principally to the development of innate potentials in other areas of the brain and to gradual recovery from shock caused by the injury. Recent findings, however, suggest that after damage neurons may well be capable of growing new fibers and even of reproducing themselves.

Studies of the effects of brain damage in rats show that the damaged areas do not remain empty but that nearby neurons move into the damaged area, filling up the vacancy.[20] Damage to the visual system of hamsters has been found to lead to a positive redirection of nerve fibers and with them the formation of many new synapses, all of which functioned competently.[21] Other studies have shown that when axons in certain areas of the brain are cut, the end that is still attached to the cell body rapidly starts growing large numbers of tiny sprouts. These sprouts spread out through the nervous system reestablishing contacts with the stranded synapses until all the original connections are restored.[22] Although it was known that such regeneration could occur in the peripheral nerves running from the muscles and sensory organs to the brain, this was the first time it had been found in the brain itself.

There is also the possibility that neurons may actually reproduce themselves after damage. Although neurons do not normally multiply, they do, nevertheless, have the genetic potential for reproduction. In some way this potential is being inhibited in the normal nervous system. Experiments suggest this inhibiting factor may be connected with the electrical state of the cell. Neurons subjected to electrical depolarization (i.e., reduction of the electrical potential across the cell wall) will sometimes begin to divide and reproduce just as other cells do.[23] Neurons can also be induced to reproduce themselves if placed in a medium enriched in potassium ions.[24] This change in ion concentration affects the cellular membranes in the same way as direct electrical depolarization.

These are exciting findings and ones that may revolutionize our thinking about neurons. It has not yet been ascertained whether or not such regeneration can occur in the normal nervous system, but the brain always appears to make the maximum use of the possibilities open to it and one of the most likely places to find such changes in nerve cell membranes would be in damaged tissue.

MAKING THE MOST OF YOUR BRAIN

The research on recovery of function gives a most instructive insight into the adult brain's latent potentials for continued development. If the seriously injured brain is capable of such remarkable recoveries, new areas developing the damaged faculties and neurons growing to regenerate damaged connections, what is the normal intact brain capable of? Can the adult brain draw upon these latent faculties of growth and development without having to go through the traumas of brain injury?

The answer is almost certainly yes.

Moreover, since the healthy intact brain is not handicapped by injured areas and missing connections, its potential for further development is considerably greater than that of the damaged brain. In order to help this natural potential unfold, there are two things you should do:

1. Use your brain

2. Care for your brain

Using Your Brain. The adult brain, like the young child's, thrives on experience. If we are to make the fullest use of its innate potential and continue to grow in mental abilities throughout life, it is essential we give our brains as rich, as varied, and as stimulating an environment as possible. One of the principal reasons that mental faculties appear to drop off after about the age of twenty is that formal education ceases around this age and we do not provide the brain with so many challenges and exercise. After leaving school, or college, many people stop using their brains as much, and with this comes an apparent decline of the brain's potential. Like any other organ, the brain atrophies if not in constant use.

Education, coming from the Latin *e-ducare,* means literally "to lead out," to bring out one's full potential. If the full potential has not been developed by the age of twenty—and it never has—then education should continue. There should be continued learning, continued mental challenges, and continued mental exercise.

The extent to which enriched stimulation can affect the structure of rat brains has been demonstrated by the work of Mark Rosenzweig's team at the University of California. They put groups of rats in environments full of such playthings as ladders, wheels, ramps, rungs, etc., and found that the richer surroundings led to an increase in both the weight and the thickness of the cerebral cortex. Further work at the University of California showed that fully mature rats gained as great an increase in the weight of their cortex as did young rats.[25]

Rosenzweig and his team have since investigated whether the increased growth in the brain came merely from seeing an enriched surrounding or from actively interacting with the environment. They divided their rats into three groups: "enriched" rats, who were allowed to play freely in their complex environment; "observer" rats, who were able to see the enriched environment but not interact with it; and a control group, who lived in an impoverished environment. After one month of this treatment the animals' brains were examined. It was found that the "observer" rats, who had merely perceived the enriched environment but not interacted with it, did not show the same significant increase in brain weight as did the "enriched" rats—in fact, they did not differ significantly from the impoverished group.[26]

One reason rats are often used as experimental animals is that their nervous system is in many basic ways similar to the human nervous system. Applying Rosenzweig's work to the human situation, we might infer that just living in an enriched environment is not enough—we need to interact with it actively in as many ways as possible if our brains are to benefit from it. Watching television may, if you watch the right channels, provide diverse stimulation, but it is generally passive stimulation and is not going to be of great benefit to the brain's development. Much better is directly interacting with the world, with other good minds, investigating new fields (and integrating them with the old), exercising your mind whenever possible, drawing on your resources, setting yourself challenges, and enjoying it all.

The truth of this is borne out by people who have continued with their education throughout life. Research scientists, university lecturers, and polymaths who have applied themselves to numerous problems and continually drawn upon their resources and their knowledge of many different fields of study show no apparent deterioration in mental abilities. They show thriving alert minds right through into old age. Albert Einstein, one of the most creative intellects of human history, pursued his theoretical work right up until his death at the age of seventy-seven. Bertrand Russell, the philosopher, mathematician, historian, politician, and polemic, displayed an outstanding memory, was still writing at a prodigious pace and playing a major role in world affairs at the age of ninety-five. Similarly Carl Jung's mind was very alert and productive in his old age. Michelangelo was still creating masterpieces at the age of eighty—and at a time when the average life expectancy was only thirty-five. Rembrandt was at his apex in the final years of his life. Cezanne, Turner, and Picasso likewise maintained their talents in old age. Gauguin did not begin painting till he was thirty-five but continued for the rest of his life. Bach, Brahms, Haydn, Tchaikovsky, and Britten were all composing excellent work in their last years. George Bernard Shaw's mind was as acute and penetrating at the age of ninety-four as it was at thirty. Similarly, Wordsworth, Tennyson, and D. H. Lawrence showed little if any deterioration of mental abilities in their later years.

The moral is: If you want to get the most from your brain, use it; make the most of it!

Some of the ways in which this can be done will be discussed in Part Two.

Caring for Your Brain.   Regular exercise is invaluable to the brain. In the short term it increases the oxygen supply, and in the long term helps keep the arteries clear. In a six-year-long Canadian study of three hundred school children it was found that those who did additional physical exercise each day and were fitter physically also received higher grades in their academic work.[27] Exercise can also directly affect personality. Regular jogging and physical training lead not only to physical fitness but also to increased emotional stability, increased imagination, and increased self-sufficiency.[28]

Regular rest is also vital for mental functioning. The human nervous system works on a regular alternation of action and rest and is accurately attuned to this cycle. Disrupting the cycle disrupts the brain's natural daily rhythms. During sleep, particularly during dreaming periods, proteins and other chemicals in the brain used up during the day are being replenished. The body also grows during sleep. As adults we may cease growing taller, but the cells in the body are continually being replaced, and most of this growth takes place during the night.

Rest is valuable during the day as well. Taking regular breaks during reading or study improves both comprehension and memory. In addition, such techniques of deep relaxation as Transcendental Meditation, when practiced as a regular part of the daily routine, have been shown to lead to fuller use of mental abilities.

In a simple measure of reaction time, people were asked to press a button as soon as a light came on, and it was found that those practicing TM had reacted faster—0.3 seconds as compared with 0.5 seconds for the control group.[29] Another study measured meditators' ability to guide a metal ball through a complex maze by tilting the board on which the ball rolls. This game requires accurate perception as well as quick and accurate motor responses. Subjects who had been practicing TM performed much better at the task than other people, and their performance increased after a meditation period.[30] Other work has shown that the intelligence growth rate of young children increases with TM. Learning ability, memory, problem solving, and creativity also improve.[31]

As far as food is concerned, a regular, well-balanced diet is good for brain functioning in general. In particular, vitamin E, which increases cell oxygenization, helps nerve cells to make better use of the oxygen available. (The best sources of vitamin E are whole wheat, whole grains and cold-pressed vegetable oils made from seeds—e.g., sunflower seed oil.) Vitamin B and vitamin C can increase mental alertness, and vitamin D helps the assimilation of minerals such as calcium, magnesium, and iodine, which in turn increase alertness. Most vitamins can be obtained from fresh vegetables and fruit. Vegetables should be eaten raw sometimes, as part of a salad, say, since some of the vitamins are decomposed by cooking, especially by stewing.

Natural foods are generally more nourishing than preprocessed goods. Moreover artificial preservatives and dyes have in several cases been shown to be harmful to the brain. Other things to avoid are too much sugar and starch, which can lead to mental dullness, and excess caffeine, alcohol, and other unnecessary drugs.

Food requires thought as much as thought requires food. So think before you eat, and you will eat and think better.

Figure 23

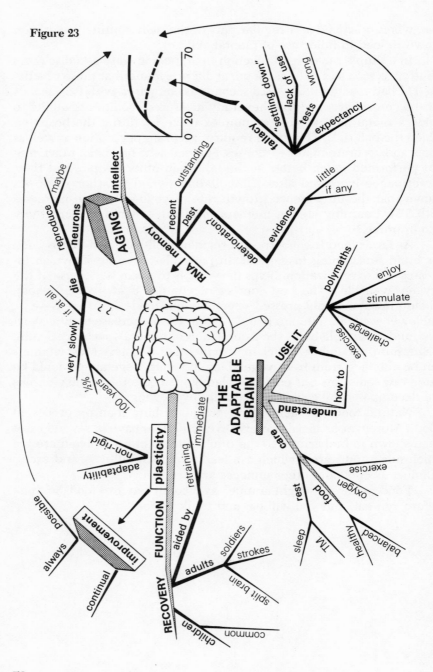

Part Two
FUNCTION AND POTENTIAL

6.
The Psychology
of Memory

Are there different types of memory?
How quickly do we forget?
Can unforgetting occur?
What do we remember best?
Is it good to break study with rest periods?
Does warming up first help?
Why are outstanding things remembered best?
Does "chunking" help?

Memory is undoubtedly one of the most important human faculties. Without it there would be no learning from experience, no intellectual functioning, no development of language, nor any of the qualities that are generally associated with being human. Yet, with the possible exception of consciousness itself, memory remains the most mysterious of the mind's faculties. Despite the fact that more research has been devoted to the study of memory than to any other mental function, comparatively little is known about how the mind remembers things, and why it also appears to forget.

Memory is often thought of as the ability to recall past events. If someone were asked to remember what he ate for lunch yesterday, he would probably be able to give a brief description, and if we were to check back with what he had actually eaten, it would be possible to see how well he had "remembered" it.

Memory, however, is more than just the ability to recall. If the same person were asked what he ate for lunch a year ago, he would probably be very unlikely to recall it. Yet if we could remind him of what he actually ate, he might well say, "Ah yes, now I remember." He would recognize the items and could still be said to have retained some memory of the event. Thus retention does not necessarily imply recall.

If, after reminding one of an event or situation—in this case a luncheon—he still failed to recognize it, this would not necessarily mean that he had no memory of it. It might well happen that under hypnosis he would be able to recall details of the meal perfectly. There may be many events and experiences that are recorded in memory but that cannot immediately be recalled or recognized. Indeed, as will be shown in chapter 12, there is growing evidence that the brain may record everything that is ever experienced.

THE VARIETIES OF MEMORABLE EXPERIENCES

Memory can be divided into several different types:

Episodic Memory. The memory for past episodes and events in one's life, such as tripping over the cat.

Factual Memory. The memory for facts, such as that the Battle of Hastings took place in 1066, or that Einstein formulated the theory of relativity. These are not actual episodes in one's life, though they will have been learned as the result of numerous little episodes at school, in reading, and at other times.

Semantic Memory. The memory for meaning. We remember that a "butterfly" is an insect with four large brightly colored wings, and that "smooth" describes a certain tactile sensation, as well as having several other meanings. The average person remembers several hundred thousand words and meanings.

Sensory Memory. Most people have a strong visual memory, being able, whether they believe it or not, to remember several thousand faces, probably seeing most of them clearly "in the mind's eye." Many will also be able to remember the sound of favorite pieces of music, or the smell of some tasty dish.

Skills. Skills also involve memory. A person remembers how to get dressed, drive a car, or throw a ball. Even walking and speaking are skills learned early on in life.

Instinctive Memory.   The newborn baby "remembers" to suck at its mother's breast, and the adult brain "remembers" how to breathe, sleep, digest, etc. The bases of many such memories are inherited and stored in the genes. This genetic memory also specifies many individual characteristics, both physical and mental.

Collective Memory.   Psychologists such as Carl Jung have suggested that we may also have access to collective race memories. These appear, mainly in dreams, as archetypal symbols that are very similar for large numbers of people, though outside their normal experience of life. '

Past-Life Memory.   Some people appear to be able to "remember" events from before their birth, sometimes from many centuries before. Under hypnosis it is possible to examine this phenomenon more fully, and it is often found that the "memories" do correlate with actual happenings in the life of an individual in the past—though the subject may have no knowledge of that individual's existence.

There is hardly a moment in our lives when memory is not playing a crucial role, and the more we understand how it functions, the more we can help ourselves at work, at home, in play, and in study, both with others and on our own.

THE EBBINGHAUS EXPERIMENTS

The first experimental investigations of memory were carried out by Hermann Ebbinghaus in Germany from 1879 to 1885. Ebbinghaus realized that memory is powerfully affected by meaning and association, and in order to control for these factors, he decided to use words that had no meaning or association. So he made up lists of nonsense syllables. Using himself as a subject, he spent six years in arduous experiments learning and relearning thousands of such lists.

His method was to take a list of nonsense syllables (e.g., TAJ, ZIN, DEC, RAX, DAK, JAF, HUQ) and set about remembering it by what he called the anticipation method. He would first read the list through to himself at a steady rate. Then, going back to the beginning, he would try to anticipate the first word, check whether his anticipation was correct, then try to anticipate the second word, and then the third, and so on until the end of the list. Having gone through the list once, he would go back to the beginning and start again. He repeated this procedure until he could go through the whole list anticipating each syllable correctly, recording how long the whole process took.

In a typical experiment he learned eight lists of thirteen nonsense syllables. After a given lapse of time he learned one of the lists again. By comparing the relearning time with the original learning time, he was able to estimate how much of the original had been retained. By relearning different lists after differing intervals of time, he was able to trace how retention decayed. In order to analyze the results statistically, he collected many sets of results, subjecting himself to the lengthy learning procedure no less than 163 times!

Ebbinghaus's results are summarized in Figure 25. They show a rapid initial decrease in memory followed by a gradual tailing off over the following days and nights. Most forgetting occurs immediately after learning. It will be seen that even one hour afterward more than half the original had been forgotten. Nine hours afterward about 60 percent of the original had been lost, and one month afterward 80 percent had gone.[1]

Ebbinghaus also investigated how the amount of time spent in learning affected retention. In some cases he stopped going through the lists before learning was complete; in others he kept on going through them even after having learned them perfectly. When he retested himself twenty-four hours later, he found that the more trials there were in the original learning, the less trials were needed to relearn the lists. Even when he had continued going through the lists after the

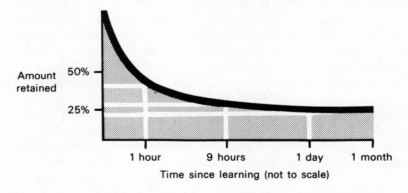

Figure 24 Curve of forgetting, after Ebbinghaus.

learning was complete, he found that relearning was still easier and that the extra trials had not been wasted.

One of Ebbinghaus's major contributions to psychology was to show that a seemingly insoluble problem could be approached experimentally, provided the situation was reduced to a few measurable essentials. In using nonsense syllables he had attempted to eliminate the effect of meaning and association, which are difficult factors to evaluate. Yet in this also lies a clue for the further development of memory. By stripping away meaning and association Ebbinghaus had effectively stripped away all that was most valuable to memory.

Numerous other experimenters since Ebbinghaus have found the same general curve of forgetting; but they have also found that the more meaning, organization, and association there is in the material, the less steep is the curve. And shortly we shall see that, by taking the opposite approach to Ebbinghaus and making the maximum use of these other factors, it is possible to produce a "forgetting" curve that does not decay with time but remains a straight line near the 100-percent level. That is to say, there is virtually no forgetting.

THE REMINISCENCE EFFECT

There is one major modification that should be added to the general curve of forgetting. For a short period after the initial learning the memory may improve a little rather than decrease. This effect, which is the opposite to forgetting, is known as the reminiscence effect. It has been found that children who were given a poem to learn but not allowed to learn it to perfection remembered it better a day after learning than they did initially, often being able to recall lines they had not been able to remember at the time of learning.[2]

The reminiscence effect has been looked at by a number of different psychologists and in a number of different situations. Although it is a fairly common occurrence, it is not present in all learning situations. It seems to depend upon the nature of the material being learned, the method of testing, and the activities a person is engaged in between the initial learning and the retesting.

The time between learning and reminiscence also varies considerably. In a paired-associate test, in which subjects are presented with a list of paired words and tested for recall a little time later by being given the first word of the pair and asked to name the second, it is found that the reminiscence effect is strongest after about half a minute.[3] In learning lists of nonsense syllables, reminiscence has been found to be highest after about one minute.[4] Memory for photographs of faces was found to be best one and a half minutes after the initial viewing.[5] And in mechanical tasks reminiscence has been found to occur ten minutes after the initial learning.[6] It has also been found that the more meaningful the material and the greater a person's interest in it, the stronger is the effect. It is, for example, stronger with poems than with lists of abstract words, and stronger still if the poem is an interesting one.[7]

The exact reasons for the reminiscence effect are still not clear. Numerous theories have been put forward over the last fifty years, but none have satisfactorily explained all aspects of the phenomenon.[8] Inhibition theories suggest that during the initial learning recall performance is impeded by the task of learning, but that this effect dissipates afterward. According to this hypothesis it is not an improvement in retention that is being observed but a temporary improvement in recall. Consolidation theory, on the other hand, suggests that during the rest period the memory trace itself is being strengthened. The memory is being integrated and reinforced with other memories, and this unconscious processing adds to the permanence and strength of the record.

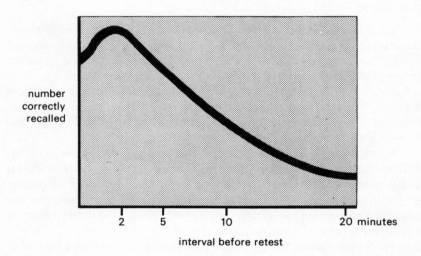

Figure 25 Forgetting curve for nonsense syllables showing reminiscence after 2 minutes. The improvement in recall is usually between 5 and 10 percent.

AN EXPERIMENT

Before going on to investigate how memory works, it will be useful for you to perform a simple experiment. The results will illustrate several important factors in memory. First, find yourself a pencil or something else to write with. Then read through the following list of words just once. Do not study them, just read each to yourself:

water, life, dog, line, home, mouse,
field, balls, rabbit, apple, sheep, head,
bone, year, goat, Maharishi, hill,
oar, donkey, shape, crop, wind, pig,
tool, cow, door, stone, flower, cat.

On the next page you will find a blank space. Write there as many of the words as you can remember, in whatever order they come to you. (If you feel bad about writing in books, a sheet of paper will do.)

PRIMACY AND RECENCY

You are unlikely to have recalled the whole of the list (for those who have, we shall be dealing with photographic memory shortly). Among the words that you have written down you will probably find that there are more from the beginning and end of the list. You are more likely to have recalled *water, life, flower,* and *cat* than *year* and *wind.* The increased probability of recalling the first two or three items is called the *primacy effect;* and that of recalling the last few items is called the *recency effect.* The two effects are shown together in Figure 26, in what is called a serial position curve.

The exact shape of the curve depends on a number of variables, such as the length of the list, the nature of the list—whether it is words, pictures, prose, or the learning of skills—and how much the person organizes the material to be learned and thereby improves memory throughout. In some cases primacy is the strongest effect, in others recency.[9] In any event, the general finding that the beginning and end of a learning session are remembered better occurs again and again in many different learning situations.

In the case of lectures the curve has been found to be more like that of Figure 27. Memory is good for material at the beginning of the

Write below as many words as you can remember from the list on the previous page.

lecture, being best a few minutes after the start. It gradually tails off during the lecture, but improves markedly again at the end.[10]

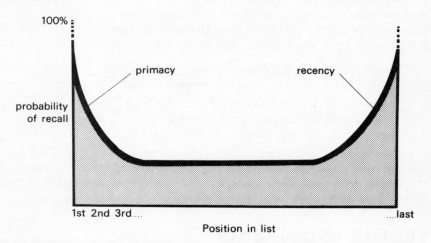

Figure 26 Serial position curve showing primacy and recency effects.

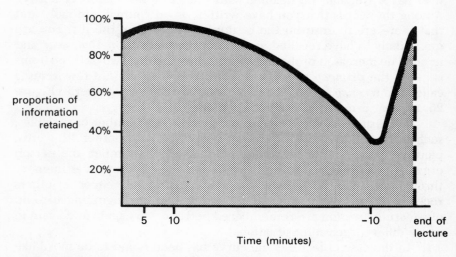

Figure 27 Recall during lecture. Memory for the beginning and end of lecture is almost perfect, but it tails off increasingly rapidly in the middle. (From E. J. Thomas, *Studies in Adult Education*, April, 1972. Reprinted with permission.)

DISTRIBUTION OF LEARNING

Ebbinghaus found that when he introduced short rest intervals between successive periods of practice, his learning efficiency improved. This was puzzling at first: It was expected that the rest periods would lead to forgetting and hence to reduced learning. The reason for the increase, it was later realized, lay partly in the reminiscence effect.

Immediately after learning, the memory was actually improving, so that when he returned to the task, more rather than less of the material was available as a basis for further learning. Supporting evidence for this comes from the finding that the greater the reminiscence effect, the greater the value of taking short breaks.[11]

The primacy and recency effects are two other factors that enhance the value of taking breaks. A single period of learning benefits from primacy and recency only at the start and finish. If the session is broken into a number of smaller blocks, with short breaks in between, there are more times at which primacy and recency effects can occur.

THE WARM-UP EFFECT

In physical activity a person always performs better when he has had a chance to warm up a little. The same is true of most mental activities. A warm-up effect is especially noticeable in learning where it has been found that retention is enhanced if a person has performed a similar task immediately beforehand. If, for example, people are given three lists of paired adjectives to learn (e.g. *blue–round; soft–high; . . .*) they will learn the second list faster than the first, and the third faster than the second, despite the fact that the lists are unrelated.[12]

A brief warm-up just before relearning has also been found to be very beneficial. In one experiment two groups of subjects were given lists of paired adjectives to learn. After twenty-four hours one group was given a short warm-up task before relearning, the other was not. The surprising thing was not that the warm-up group showed better retention, but that they showed *no forgetting, even improving slightly!*[13] In this case it would appear that, in addition to having a warm-up effect, the short practice before relearning had reestablished the appropriate mental "set" (see pages 203–6)—that is, their minds were "set" for the particular task to come. The implication is that much apparent forgetting may be simply due to changing one "set" for another.

THE VON RESTORFF EFFECT

In the memory experiment you did earlier most of you will have recalled *Maharishi*—it stood out from the rest of the list. This tendency to remember outstanding elements in a list is called the von Restorff effect.

Von Restorff found that three digit numbers were better learned if presented within a list of nonsense syllables than if surrounded by other numbers.[14] Thus in the first of the following lists the three-digit number is remembered better than the nonsense syllables, while in the second list the nonsense syllable is remembered better than the numbers:

TAJ	532
ZIN	147
DEC	938
RAX	HUQ
378	706
DAK	594
JAF	821

The effect has since been found to be true in any situation in which items stand out in some way from those around them, or are in any way surprising. Thus a brightly colored picture is better remembered than the black and white ones surrounding it, and the tall girl with husky voice will stick in your memory better than many other people.

One possible explanation is that the outstanding elements increase a person's attention, which in turn leads to better memory. An investigation of this possibility measured the galvanic skin response, a physiological measure of arousal, which was indeed found to increase significantly when the outstanding item was presented, though this does not prove conclusively that the increased arousal was also responsible for the improved recall.[15]

You may possibly find that you also remembered the words *goat* and *hill*—words positioned on either side of *Maharishi*. The higher arousal created by the outstanding word also effects the retention of those words close to it in the learning sequence. Thus the serial position curve of Figure 26 can be modified to include high retention for outstanding items and their neighbors:

THE MAGIC NUMBER SEVEN

In a memorable paper called "The Magic Number Seven, Plus or Minus Two," George Miller from Harvard showed that the immediate memory span appears to be limited in the number of items that it can hold.[16] He briefly presented people with short lists and immediately asked them to recall as many as they could. He found that whatever the items—whether they were numbers, words, colors, musical tunes, or any other items—most people could not correctly recall lists that had more than about seven items in them. To see this for yourself try remembering each of the following sequences of numbers. Just read each line through at a normal reading pace. Don't study them or try to remember them, just read each line through quickly and then look away or close your eyes and see how much of it you can remember. Or even better, if you have somebody else around, get them to read each list quickly aloud to you and see how many you remember each time.

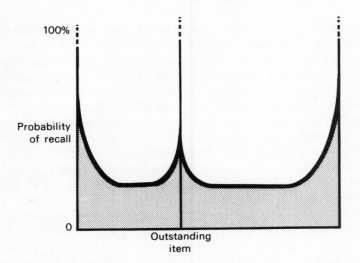

Figure 28 High recall of outstanding items, and increased recall of their neighbors.

```
3  8  7  4
5  1  3  4  9
6  2  8  7  4  1
9  5  0  2  1  3  6
2  9  4  0  1  7  5  8
3  0  1  4  9  6  8  2  5
1  4  9  2  5  3  1  7  8  4
```

It doesn't matter what the items are, whether they are numbers, words, or anything else. The immediate memory span seems to be somewhere around seven items. Thus if the list of words given on page 87 had been only seven words long or less, you would probably have recalled it all correctly and in the correct order. As it was, you probably only recalled a few of them, and even then probably not in the order presented.

Miller suggested that the immediate memory span was not limited by the amount of information contained in each item, but by the number of "chunks" that had to be remembered. In this respect, *4, dog,* and ☐ are all single chunks. Immediate memory seems to have the capacity for about seven separate chunks, and anything much more than this is lost.

Since it is the number of chunks that limits the immediate memory rather than the actual information content, it follows that effective memory span can be increased by reorganizing the material into larger (but not more) chunks. In his article Miller quotes an experiment by Sidney Smith in which he taught twenty subjects to recode items into larger chunks. He started with strings of binary digits—that is, strings of zeroes and ones—and found an average memory span of nine digits. Subjects were then taught to recode the digits in pairs renaming 00 as 0, 01 as 1, 10 as 2, and 11 as 3. Thus 10110100 would be recoded as 2, 3, 1, 0, and reduced from eight to four chunks. Once subjects had mastered the recoding, their binary digit span nearly doubled. Grouping in triplets, and recoding as the numbers 0 through to 7, they could increase their spans still further. Since the immediate memory span is seven, one would expect a capacity of around twenty-one binary digits after recoding in triplets. The increase was not, however, quite this large. This was possibly due to the extra load imposed by the encoding process itself.

To go further required considerable study, so Smith decided to follow the Ebbinghaus tradition and use himself as a subject. He learned recoding systems for binary digits in groups of four and groups of five, in the manner shown in Figure 29. His immediate memory span was larger than most people's, and he was able to remember about fourteen binary digits. When the digits were encoded in pairs, he could remember eighteen binary digits (nine chunks); in triplets, he could remember thirty-two binary digits (ten chunks); in quadruplets, forty (ten chunks). No extra value was gained from recoding in groups of five; his maximum span stayed at forty, (see Figure 30).

Now this is not just trickery. The mind remembers the number of chunks rather than the total amount of information. So organizing material into chunks is in fact helping the memory. Chunking is so natural that most people do it anyway without realizing it. Given the number 572317482, a person would probably regroup it as 572,317,482 and remember it as five hundred and seventy-two million, three hundred and seventeen thousand, four hundred and eighty-two. In doing this not only has a nine-figure number become three groups of three, but the individual digits have been given different tags—572 has become five hundred and seventy-two million rather than just five-seven-two million—which again helps memory. This is why we usually split telephone numbers up into several chunks; in the United States as 418-325-7162, and in many European countries as 41 83 25-71-62. Chunking in this way makes it easier to remember the list of ten digits, and when it comes to recalling a number, one recalls it chunk by chunk—area code, followed by exchange, followed by number.

Shown a long word such as *antidisestablishmentarianism,* people do not generally remember it as a sequence of twenty-eight letters— that would far exceed most people's immediate memory span. Instead, the letters are grouped together and stored as a number of larger units, probably something like *anti-dis-establish-ment-arian-ism.* Each part, being a familiar pattern, is treated as a single chunk. As children, most people did not learn the alphabet as a monotonous sequence from *A* to *Z,* but as organized units and subunits. The exact organization varies from one person to another; for some it may be *abcd, efg, hijk, lmnop, qrs, tuv, wx-yz;* for others, *abc, de-fg, hi-jk, lm, no-pq, rs-tu, vw-xyz.* This chunking reduced it to a smaller number of parts, and the patterns and rhythms set up also helped make it much easier to learn.

When listening to a story, people do not usually remember every word that is spoken: They build up themes and subthemes, extracting the essential features of the story. It is these larger units

Binary digits:	1 0 1 1 0 1 0 0 1 1 1 0			
Grouped in twos:	10 – 11 – 01 – 00 – 11 – 10			
Recoded as:	2 3 1 0 3 2			
Grouped in threes:	101 – 101 – 001 – 110			
Recoded as:	5 5 1 6			
Grouped in fours:	1011 – 0100 – 1110			
Recoded as:	11 4 14			

Figure 29 Recoding of binary digits (sequences of 0s and 1s in twos, threes, and fours). Each pair of binary digits can be equated with a number between 0 and 3 (inclusive); each triplet with a number between 0 and 7; and each quadruplet with a number between 0 and 15. Recoding in this way decreases the number of "chunks" to be remembered. "11, 4, 14" is more easily retained than "101101001110."

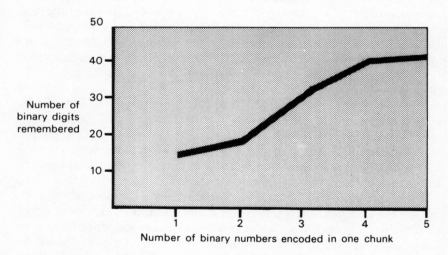

Figure 30 Effect of recoding into larger chunks on immediate memory span for binary numbers.

that are remembered. When later the story is recalled, these ideas are expanded, with varying degrees of success, into a word-by-word account.

APPLICATIONS AND ADVICE

Breaks. Any period of study or learning is best broken down into smaller chunks, with short breaks between each session. The actual size of each chunk will depend upon the type of material being studied. In practice, it is found that somewhere between fifteen and forty-five minutes is the best. If the chunk becomes too small, there is not sufficient meaning and internal coherence to gain a proper understanding of the material, and if it is too large, the full benefit of taking breaks is lost.

As to the question of how long the break should be, something of the order of five to ten minutes is best. It has been found that learning improves when the time between blocks is increased from thirty seconds to ten minutes, but no further improvement is gained by increasing the break period further.[17]

This finding can be understood in terms of the reminiscence effect. After a few minutes break, recall of the material actually will

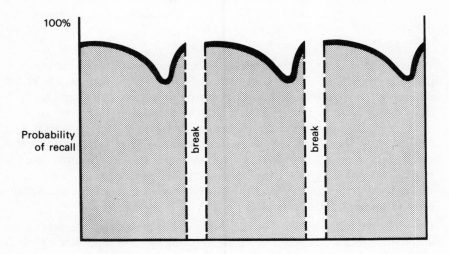

Figure 31 Retention curve when regular short breaks are taken.

have risen. Thus when one returns to study, he will remember *more* of the previous session than if he had simply gone straight ahead without a break, and comprehension and memory of the next section will be correspondingly improved. When regular short breaks are taken, the retention curve of Figure 24 changes to look like that of Figure 31.

The first thing to do when you sit down for a period of study is to plan the time, deciding how often you are going to break and when. And having done so, keep approximately to the schedule.

At certain times when you should be taking a break the study may be going excellently and it might seem tempting to continue on. In fact it is still better to take a break. It has been found that interrupting a task in which a person has become involved can lead to higher recall of the material—an effect known as the Zeigarnik effect after its discoverer.[18] Also, despite the fact that the understanding may be very good, the later recall of the material will be worse if the mind is not given a short break. *Understanding is not the same as remembering.*

During the breaks themselves you should take a complete rest from the type of work under study. If you merely switch to something similar, not only is the mind not given a real break, but numerous interfering associations will be made that will impede later recall. The best thing to do is to relax both mentally and physically and take some fresh air. The rest also helps the mind consolidate and organize the information gained, and it is important to let it get on with this in its own way.

Warm-Up. As far as study is concerned, a few minutes spent reviewing previous knowledge of the field and establishing what you want to know will have the dual effect both of warming you up to study and of "setting" your mind to the particular field concerned.

This also applies to the short breaks taken during a session. On returning to the study always spend a minute or two going over the previous session(s)—even though you only stopped five minutes previously. This quick review warms you up again and reestablishes mental set, bringing the memory of the previous section, now at maximum reminiscence, to the fore.

Lecturing, Giving Talks. Including regular breaks in a teaching or lecturing situation is going to make the subject more enjoyable as well as better remembered.

Since people will tend to recall the beginnings and ends of the session, it is best to try to arrange the material so that the most important points come when the memory is particularly high (see Figure 24). The high recall at the end can be used both to summarize the main points and to present a preview of important points to come after the break or in the next lecture.

In the middle of the lecture, particularly during the second half, when memory is at its lowest, it is good to give greater emphasis to important points, making them more outstanding—perhaps with visual aids or examples—to compensate for the lower recall.

The von Restorff Effect. This can be used to improve memory in a number of ways. Whenever you want to remember something, deliberately make the idea *stand out:*

- Exaggerate it. The more bizarre an idea is, the more arousing it is, and the more clear will be the memory.
- In writing or note taking, use outlining, bold print, color, and anything else that will make important points stand out.
- When reading, underline important points.
- Everything is unique. Emphasize its uniqueness in your mind, how it is different from everything else.

Figure 32

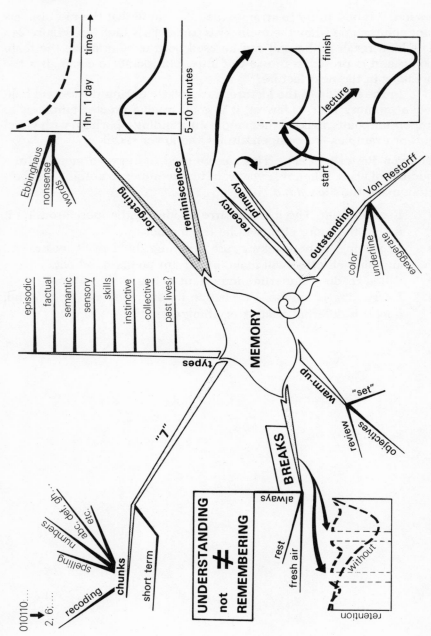

7.
Association and Organization in Memory

Why are associations important in memory?
Why is organization important?
How does principle seeking help memory?
Is principle seeking better than rote learning?
Why are meaning and significance important?
Does sleep learning work?

The power of association was realized by Sir Francis Galton in 1879. That year effectively marked the birth of experimental psychology: In Germany, Wilhelm Wundt, from Leipzig, established the first laboratory exclusively devoted to psychological studies, while Ebbinghaus was beginning his six-year experiment on the rate of forgetting. In the same year Sir Francis Galton took a walk down Pall Mall in London, a length of some 450 yards, and while he walked, he let his mind generate associations to everything he saw. During the walk he counted some three hundred objects on which his attention rested for a while, and recorded a considerably greater number of associative images. He wrote afterward:[1] "Samples of my whole life had passed before me. . . . Many bygone incidents, which I have never suspected to have formed part of my stock of thoughts, had been glanced at as objects too familiar to awaken the attention. I saw at once that the brain was vastly more active than I had previously believed it to be, and I was perfectly amazed at the unexpected width of the field of its everyday operations."

Many of us have probably received similar insights into the role of association in memory. When we cannot remember a friend's name, we may go through the alphabet trying first *A*, then *B*, then *C* and so on until the name is suddenly remembered. There may be places we have visited long ago about which we now appear to remember very little, yet if we were to revisit the place and see a few of the buildings and hear and smell the place again, we would probably find a whole flood of detailed memories streaming back. Or, in trying to recall a passage in a book, we may well find it easier first to recall when and where we read the book, where on the page the passage was, and other associations.

If it were not for the cues provided by association, one would have difficulty recalling anything. Memory would be like a vast library without a catalogue. Associations give some information about which part of the memory we should be looking in, and the more associations there are, the more specific the search can be. Associations may come from any direction and from any sense. Any one item in memory will probably have hundreds, perhaps thousands, of different associations.

The more associations we make when learning material, the easier it is to remember that material. Indeed, so powerful is the role of association that almost nothing will destroy it. The only things that will interfere with it are other stronger associations—apart, that is, from barbiturate overdoses, brain surgery, electric shock therapy, etc.

CONTEXT DEPENDENCY

The environment in which the learning takes place provides very important associations. As Victor Hugo once remarked, "Nothing awakes a reminiscence like an odor." Most people have probably used such environmental associations at one time or another to "jog" their memories. A typical example would be of the person who, while cleaning his teeth, thinks of a friend he should call. A minute later, when he gets to the phone, he finds he has completely forgotten who it was. He racks his brain but cannot recall it. So he goes back into the bathroom, but still he has no clue. He stands by the basin again: still nothing. So, checking that no one is looking, he starts cleaning his teeth again, and suddenly the memory comes back.

The seventeenth-century British philosopher John Locke quoted a particularly curious example of environmental association in the case of a certain young man learning to dance.[2]

> Having learned to dance, and that to great perfection, there happened to stand an old trunk in the room where he learned. The idea of this remarkable piece of household stuff had so mixed itself with the turns and steps of all his dances, that though in that chamber he could dance excellently well, yet it was only while that trunk was there; nor could he perform well in any other place, unless that or some other such trunk had its due position in the room.

There are many legendary anecdotes of a person having had a hard night's drinking and waking up with no memory whatsoever of the previous night's fun and games. But later, perhaps the next evening, when he gets drunk again, his memories come flooding back. This phenomenon was tested by giving people a number of tasks to learn—some while they were under the influence of alcohol, and some while they were sober. It was found that what was learned after drinking alcohol was remembered best when again under its influence.[3] Other experiments have shown the same to be true with people given heavy amphetamine or barbiturate doses.[4]

In an investigation of the effects of environment on memory, people were given lists of nonsense syllables to learn. Some of the subjects were then tested on the lists in the same room, others in a different room. It was found that memory was best with subjects tested in the same room as that in which they had originally learned the material.[5]

In another experiment sixteen divers were given lists of forty words to learn either while they were ashore or while they were ten feet down in the sea. When they were later tested on the lists, it was found that lists learned while underwater were recalled better underwater, and lists learned on land were recalled better on land.[6]

SUBJECTIVE ORGANIZATION

It has long been known that if a person is given a list of words to remember, he will later tend to recall them in clusters—words of similar meaning, or of the same sound, often being recalled together.[7] If you turn back to the words you recalled in the memory experiment on page

87, you will probably find that the names of animals may have been recalled in clusters. Yet if you look at the original list, you will see they were all separated from each other.

When subjects were given lists containing words from a few specific categories—for example, names of animals, vegetables, or professions—not only did they tend to recall items in clusters, but the more clustering that occurred, the better was the person's recall.[8] This suggests that a considerable degree of internal organization of the material is taking place, either consciously or unconsciously. This internal ordering is called *subjective organization*.

Endel Tulving from the University of Toronto devised an ingenious experiment by which to measure the degree of subjective organization taking place. He took sixteen words and constructed sixteen different listings of these words such that each word appeared only once in each of the sixteen different positions, and was followed by and preceded by each other word just once. Each list was read out aloud just once, and immediately after hearing it, the subjects were asked to recall as many words as possible from that list. This procedure was repeated with each of the sixteen lists. Tulving then analyzed the order in which the words had been recalled on each test, and he found the following results:[9]

1. Many of the words were followed or preceded by the same words on a number of different occasions, showing that a degree of subjective organization had taken place.

2. Subjective organization of the material increased as the experiment progressed, although the words were in a different order each time.

3. There was a positive correlation between the degree of subjective organization and the ability to recall the list—the greater the organization, the better the recall.

When we try to remember some new information, often we may repeat it again and again to ourselves. The phenomenon of subjective organization suggests that it is not the repetition itself that is helpful for memorizing, but that through repetition the mind is constructing patterns and imposing its own organization on the material. In addition, the repetition gives the mind a chance to make associative links where associations are not already obvious. Subjective organization is also enhanced by relaxation. This is yet another important reason for taking regular breaks during study.

The importance and the power of organization is shown by the fact that just the instruction to organize material is sufficient for it to be remembered. In one study subjects were given one hundred cards, on each of which was printed a word. Some of the subjects were told only to sort the cards into categories, while others were instructed to memorize the cards. When they later tried to recall the cards, the subjects who had merely been instructed to categorize the cards did just as well as those who had been told to try to remember them.[10]

PRINCIPLE SEEKING

Following are three lists of ten numbers (each therefore longer than the average immediate memory span of seven items). Study each list and memorize it in such a way that you could be sure of still remembering it correctly were you to be asked for it tomorrow morning.

(a)	0	1	2	3	4	5	6	7	8	9
(b)	8	6	4	2	0	9	7	5	3	1
(c)	1	8	4	5	7	2	0	9	3	6

The first list is easy; the sequence is already well known. To remember it you remember not the numbers themselves but the pattern —the digits 0–9 in their normal order.

The second is still moderately easy, once you see the principle underlying the sequence. It is the even numbers backward followed by the odd numbers backward, and again you remember the pattern rather than the numbers themselves.

The third is more difficult because the pattern is not so obvious. If you were to commit it to memory, you might do so by breaking it up into chunks. Or you may repeat the numbers over and over again allowing your mind, either consciously or unconsciously, to impose some organization upon them. Alternatively you may study the sequence further to discover the pattern and remember the rule. In the long run this will still be the most effective method.*

*The rule is: Add 3 to the first to get the third, add 3 to that to get the fifth, and so on for every other number. Subtract 3 from the second to get the fourth, subtract 3 from that to get the sixth, and so on. Ignore any "tens" digits. The odd items start with 1 (easy to remember) and continue from there by adding 3. The even items start with 8 and continue from there by subtracting 3. Got it?

George Karona, who wrote a whole book on the role of organization in memory, describes an experiment in which students were divided into two groups; one half was told to learn a sequence of numbers by rote, the other half was told to look for the principle. Both were given three minutes in which to do so. At the end of the three minutes there was little difference between the groups; 33 percent of the rote memorizers and 38 percent of the principle seekers recalled it perfectly. Three weeks later, however, the situation was very different. None of the memorizers could recall the list successfully, whereas 23 percent of the principle seekers still knew it perfectly.[11]

We continually use underlying principles and rules in remembering everyday facts. Most people do not remember by rote which years are leap years. Instead we usually remember the principle that leap years are those that are exactly divisible by four. And we may remember the additional principle that the centuries themselves are not the leap years, unless the century year is itself divisible by four hundred.

For the same reason long-distance information in the American telephone network was chosen to be 555-1212 rather than 641-8752. The pattern underlying the first number will be seen at a glance and remembered easily.

Another example of principle seeking is the remarkable memory of chess masters for board positions. If a chess position is shown to a novice for five seconds, he will probably only be able to put six or eight pieces back in their correct positions. A chess master, on the other hand, will probably be able to put 90 percent or more of the pieces back correctly. Whereas the novice tries to remember twenty or thirty individual chess pieces, the master sees the positions in terms of a few major configurations—that is, he has sought the underlying principles of the positions, and it is the configurations he remembers, not the positions. This is shown by the finding that when the pieces are just placed randomly on the board so that they no longer represent an actual game, the master does no better than the novice on this test.[12] Remembering the configurations rather than the positions themselves also has the advantage of reducing the information to a smaller number of chunks.

If you try playing chess blindfolded, or without a board and pieces, so that you have to rely solely on memory, you will notice that the configurations—lines of "power," areas of weakness—are remembered as much as, if not more than, the positions themselves. A blindfolded game is within the capacity of most average chess players and is an excellent mental exercise. For a while it was thought that to play three blindfolded games simultaneously was one of the greatest exertions of which the human memory was capable. But in 1933 Alexander Alekhine played thirty-two, in 1943 Najdorf played forty, and in 1960 the Belgian Master Koltanovski took on *fifty-six* simultaneous games blindfolded, winning fifty and drawing the other six[13]—a revealing glimpse into the fantastic capabilities of the human mind and memory.

MEANING AND ATTENTION

Another important way in which memory is organized is in terms of meaning. Meaning is an essential part of all thought processes, and it is meaning that gives order to experience. Indeed, the process of perception is ultimately one of extracting meaning from the environment. If there is only shallow processing of the material, little significance is extracted and the memory is poor. If the processing is deeper, more meaning is extracted, more meaningful connections are made with other ideas, and the memory is much stronger.[14]

Deeper processing requires conscious involvement with the material. If the mind is not attending, information will "go in one ear and out the other." The trace it leaves may well be too faint to be recalled in normal circumstances. The more that you consciously attend to something, the greater will be the depth of processing. The greater the depth of processing, the more meaningful the material becomes. The more meaningful it becomes, the better the memory. And the better the memory, the more opportunity there will be to make meaningful connections with new material in the future.

ASSOCIATIVE NETWORKS

Memory is not recorded like a movie film or tape recording, with each idea linked to the next in a well-defined temporal sequence. The information is recorded in vast interconnecting networks. Each idea or image has hundreds, perhaps thousands, of associations and is connected to numerous other points in the mental network.

There is now considerable interest in theories that regard human memory as a vast, intricately interconnected network. According to such models it is not letters, syllables, or words that are recorded, but concepts and propositions. The propositions are then related in various ways to other propositions, forming an associative or semantic network. According to such a model the act of encoding an event—in other words, the act of memorizing—is simply that of forming new links in the network, that is, making new associations.[15]

Such models not only tie in with most of the experimental findings on memory, they also explain the incredible versatility and flexibility of memory.

Memory is not like a container that gradually fills up, it is more like a tree growing hooks onto which the memories are hung. Everything you remember is another set of hooks on which more new memories can be attached. So the capacity of memory keeps on growing. The more you know, the more you can know.

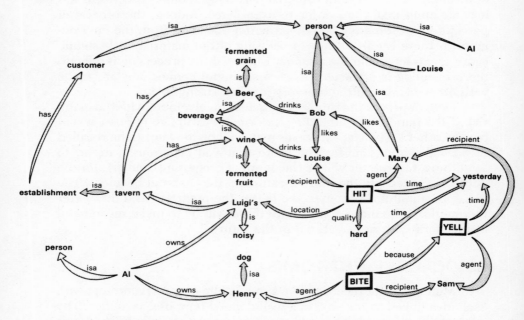

Figure 33 Semantic network representing a small set of interactions among Bob, Louise, Mary, Al, Henry, and Sam at Luigi's. The people and objects in the interactions are linked by lines showing their relationships, and the main activities are in circles. You can "read" it by starting with "Al," who owns Luigi's, a tavern . . . and Al's dog, Henry, bit Sam because. . . . (From R. H. Lindsay and D. A. Norman, *Human Information Processing*, New York and London: Academic Press, 1972. Used with permission.)

SLEEP LEARNING AND SUGGESTOPEDEA

In the fifties and early sixties there was a lot of interest in what was called sleep learning. The idea was that by playing a tape of material to be learned to a sleeping person, a large amount of the information could be digested and remembered. Experiments at the University of Florida showed that the average recall for five nights of material presented during deep sleep was 13 percent.[16] These and other experiments have concluded that learning occurs during sleep only to the extent that the subject is partially conscious. It therefore tends to disrupt sleep, and for this reason it has largely fallen from favor.

A related learning technique that is at present increasing in popularity is one known as suggestopedia. It was originally developed by Georgi Lozanof in Sophia, Bulgaria, in the 1960s. The technique used draws heavily upon yoga and hypnosis and incorporates such factors as deep relaxation, music, and psychodrama. The subject sits quietly in a chair and is taken to a very relaxed state. Then carefully chosen baroque music is played while the instructor (or tape) presents the material to be learned in the background. The student does not try to listen to the study material, the attention remains on the music. It is claimed that in this relaxed state the mind is able to absorb information much more readily and that material that would normally take two years at college can be learned in two or three months using suggestopedia. It has been claimed that this rapid assimilation of knowledge can be attributed to the enhancement of the activity in the brain's right hemisphere.[17]

APPLICATIONS AND ADVICE

Since the context of the original learning is an important associative cue to memory, it follows that the more distinctive and memorable you make the learning situation, the better will be your memory of the material studied. By becoming more conscious of the surroundings rather than just letting them slip by passively, and by deliberately associating the material studied with the situation itself, you will be forging stronger associative links and making it difficult for the material to be forgotten.

Also, by deliberately forming clear associations between ideas, you will be able to remember them much more easily. Advice on how to do this will be given in chapter 9.

For the purposes of recall, organization can be just as effective as deliberate learning. It is also much less tiring and considerably more enjoyable. If you can find any general pattern or rule in the things you need to recall, the recall will come much more easily and last a lot longer. Without looking back, see if you can remember the three lists of numbers given earlier in this chapter. (Hint for the third list: It began with 1.) If there is no obvious organization or order, try making up a rule that fits; creative ideas are usually remembered well.

There is no danger of your memory filling up. Indeed, the more you remember, the easier you will find it is to remember new things.

Figure 34

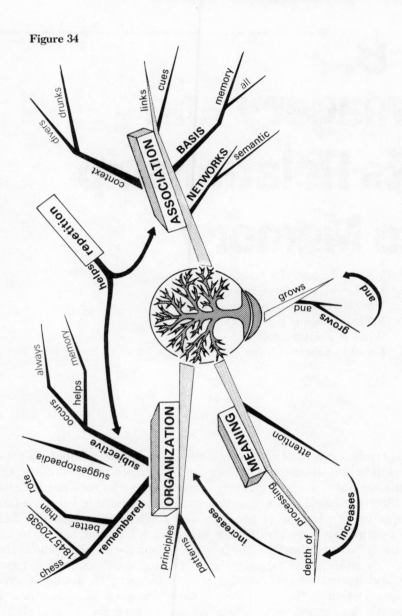

8.
Imagery and Its Relationship to Memory

What is imagery?
Does everyone have imagery?
How do images help memory?
Is visual memory perfect?
What is eidetic imagery?
Do only children have eidetic imagery?

Imagery is a sensory-type experience in the mind without an actual corresponding situation providing the immediate sense stimulus. One of the earliest surveys of imagery was conducted by Sir Francis Galton in 1883. He circulated a questionnaire to one hundred men, a large proportion of whom were distinguished in science or some other field. They were asked to recall their breakfast table as it had been that morning, and to describe the vividness and detail with which they could conjure up the experiences of hearing, smelling, tasting, touching, and feelings of cold, hunger, drowsiness, etc. He found an enormous variation in the degree of reported imagery. In some cases the subject's description was as lucid as the original scene, as clear and rich in detail as if the breakfast table were still in front of him. Other people had much vaguer images, and some reported no imagery whatsoever and did not believe it was even possible.[1]

Recent studies are now suggesting that everybody does in fact possess a considerable degree of imagery, whether, paradoxically, they are aware of it or not. In a study of five hundred people everyone reported having images of some kind. Ninety-seven percent reported visual images and 92 percent auditory images.[2] And even these figures are probably too low. If those few people who do not report visual imagery are asked to describe something, such as the Taj Mahal, they tend to break off in middescription to comment, "Yes, I *do* have visual imagery."[3]

To create a mental image is to "imagine," and the power of imagination is almost limitless. Although the situation has never been seen before, it is not difficult to imagine a green cat driving a car, making the sound of a brass band, and smelling of roses. This ability to put common images together in the mind to create new images is invaluable, if not essential to the process of memory.

IMAGERY AND MEMORY

Most people use imagery in memory quite naturally, often starting very early on in life. Some have various images associated with numbers. Often this involves a spatial arrangement of the numbers. They

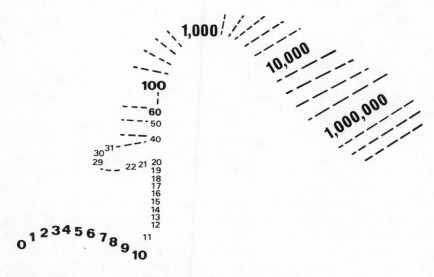

Figure 35 Example of number-form laid out in mental space.

may be strung out in a line, the line weaving its way through space, perhaps receding from the observer the higher the number. The individual numbers may vary in size, important points such as 10, 100, 500 and 1,000 appearing bigger than the others. Or they may vary in color, each number or group of numbers being a particular color. It has been found that about 80 percent of the population have some such "number form." Many people have similar forms for the alphabet, for the days of the week, the months of the year, etc.

This imagery may not appear very useful to the adult, but it was undoubtedly of immense benefit in early childhood. It probably helped one to learn the numbers, the alphabet, days of the week, etc. Although young children are not usually taught to use imagery, the mind finds it much easier to attach sensory associations of one form or another to abstract concepts and remember the image patterns created. It is in effect creating an additional degree of organization.

INTERACTIVE IMAGES

To investigate the power of imagery in memory, students were given twelve pairs of unrelated nouns, such as *dog* and *bicycle,* and told to associate the two by imagining a visual scene in which these two objects interacted in some way or another. Thus a person might imagine a dog riding a bicycle, being hit by a bicycle, or urinating on a bicycle. They were also given twelve pairs of words that they simply repeated aloud three times. In both conditions the time allowed for each pair was the same—eight seconds. Immediate recall tests showed that 80 percent of the imaged pairs were remembered correctly, whereas only 33 percent of the repeated pairs were remembered.[4] Thus by creating strong associative images the subjects had increased their recall two and a half times.

Another study investigated the importance of vividness in such imagery. When the images were vague and indistinct, recall was around 70 percent (still very much higher than that gained by rote repetition), but when they were "seen" vividly and distinctly, as if they were real, recall was around 95 percent.[5]

Other experiments on verbal memory have shown that words that evoke a strong mental image are far more easily remembered.[6] The more vivid the imagery, it seems, the more stable is the memory.

Imagery is valuable in memory because it strengthens associations and links. If the imagery does not actually link the ideas, it is of little value. This was shown by giving lists of word pairs, such as *dog–bicycle,* to two groups of people. The first group were told to create a strong visual image in which the two objects interacted in some way. The second group were also told to create a strong visual image but with the objects separated; for example, the objects could be pictured as being on opposite walls of a room. Recall tests showed that those who had produced strong *interactive* images recalled 71 percent of the words, whereas those who had formed separated images recalled only 46 percent of the words, which is only a little better than the 33 percent scored by rote repetition.

Imagery is most effective, therefore, when it is as vivid as possible and as interactive as possible.

Even when people claim to be poor visualizers, imagery can still be very valuable in helping memory. In fact, poor visualizers and good visualizers show the same improvement in memory when instructed to use imagery. The only difference is that the good visualizers tend to be much more confident of their memory than poor visualizers.[8]

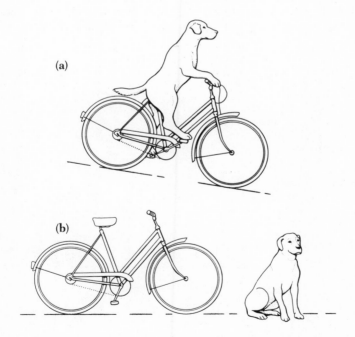

Figure 36 Dog-bicycle (a) connected, (b) disconnected.

VISUAL MEMORY

Visual images are generally much better remembered than words. So much so that visual recognition is practically perfect. In fact there is only one study that shows picture memory to be poor, and in that study the pictures were deliberately constructed to be as misleading as possible.[9]

In order to assess the potential of visual memory, subjects were shown a series of 2,560 photographic slides at the rate of one every ten seconds. These seven hours of viewing were split over several consecutive days. One hour after the last slide had been shown, the subjects were tested for recognition by showing them 280 pairs of slides in which one member of each pair was a picture from the original series, while the other was from a similar set but had never been shown to the subject. They recognized 85 to 95 percent of the original slides correctly. These high scores were maintained even when the presentation rate was speeded up to one every second, and even when the pictures were shown as a mirror image so that the right-hand side became the left-hand side. The experimenter commented that "these experiments with pictorial stimuli suggest that recognition of pictures is essentially

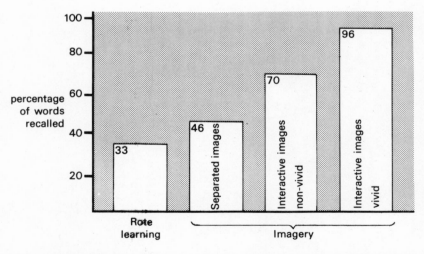

Figure 37 Effectiveness of imagery over rote learning of word pairs, and value of interactive and vivid images.

perfect. The results would probably have been the same if we had used 25,000 pictures instead of 2,500."[10]

In the foregoing experiment the pictures were recognized after an average interval of one and a half days. In another experiment subjects were tested immediately after presentation of some six hundred pictures, and recognition was then found to be 98 percent correct! Subsequent work in Canada expanded on this, presenting subjects with ten thousand pictures and measuring the extent to which the vividness of the picture affected recall. With vivid pictures the subjects were recalling 99.6 percent correctly.[11] When these results were extrapolated, it was estimated that if the subjects had been shown a million pictures rather than ten thousand, they would have recognized 986,300 of them!

These subjects were also tested on the effect of having to recognize the picture from a selection of thirty-two alternatives instead of having to recognize the correct picture from just a pair. This obviously made the task more difficult, but even with thirty-two alternatives, subjects were still 92 percent correct. Again it was concluded that "the capacity of recognition memory for pictures is almost limitless, when measured under appropriate conditions."[12]

PHOTOGRAPHIC MEMORY

Some people are able to look at a page of print for just a few seconds, then close the book and read it all back as if they were looking at a photograph of the page in their mind. The technical term for this ability is eidetic imagery, coming from the Greek *eidos* meaning "form" or "that which is seen." Eidetic imagery was widely studied up until about 1930, but virtually no more work at all was done on the subject until the recent interest in the role of imagery in memory.

The first work in this field was carried out by Galton in 1880. He studied boys from Charterhouse School and found that 18 out of 172 had the ability to see vivid eidetic images.[13] The work was taken further in the early part of this century by E. R. Jaensch in Germany and G. W. Allport in Cambridge, England.

Allport worked with children, generally in the ten-to-thirteen year age range. In a typical study he would place a picture on a dark gray background and leave it there for thirty-five seconds while the child looked at it carefully. The picture was then removed and the child was asked to look at the gray background alone and report what he saw.

Allport found that a large number of children behaved as if they were still actually seeing the picture, as if they had somehow remembered it photographically.[14] Most people have a very strong memory for pictures, but the imaging these children displayed differed from normal visual imagery in a number of respects.

1. The eidetic images were external, "out there." They were actually seen to be resting on the gray background on which the picture had originally been placed. And if the gray surface was folded or bent, then the eidetic image was likewise folded or bent.

2. The eidetic image was much clearer and stronger than a normal image. It tended to obscure the background it was projected against, rather as if a thin film containing a picture had been laid upon the background.

3. The eidetic image was much more persistent than a normal image. The children could maintain it for many minutes and in several cases come back to it weeks, or even months later. In this respect it differed from a visual afterimage—the sort of image you get from staring at a bright light bulb for a few seconds. Afterimages tend to fade rapidly, after half a minute or so. If particularly strong, they may persist for several minutes but never for weeks or months. In most afterimages the color is reversed—that is to say, one perceives complementary colors: red appears as turquoise, blue as yellow, and green as magenta, and vice versa. There is no such color reversal with the eidetic images. Furthermore, in the original viewing of the picture the children were encouraged to let their eyes rove all over it, whereas to create a good afterimage, it is necessary to keep the attention focused on a particular point of the picture.

4. The children reported a vast amount of detail in the image, often "seeing" items that had not been consciously noticed on the original viewing. Looking at their image, they could count the number of stripes on a zebra, for example, and do so correctly—something that is not possible with normal visual imagery. In one of the studies there was a street scene and in the background was an inn with the word *Gartenwirthschaft* written above the door. This German word was meaningless to the children and was not re-

ported when they first looked at their eidetic image, but when they were asked to look more closely, each of the children with strong eidetic images was able to see the small letters above the door. Some of them could spell the word out correctly, others nearly so. Moreover, they could read the letters off from right to left as easily as from left to right.

Although eidetic imagery has often been called photographic imagery, later experiments showed significant differences between the two. The eidetic image was found to be much more flexible than a photographic image. When, for example, a child was "looking" at an eidetic image of a picture containing a donkey and a manger, it was suggested to the child that the donkey was hungry. Immediately the child "saw" the donkey begin to walk over to the manger, bend his neck, and start eating.[15] In other cases subjects could make certain items in the picture bigger or smaller at will or rotate them to see what they looked like from the other side.

Another difference between eidetic imagery and "photographic" memory is that there may be additions, omissions, and distortions in the eidetic image. Despite the wealth of detail the image is generally not as exact as a photograph would be.

Eidetic images need not be limited to vision. It is possible to have an auditory eidetic imagery. One may, for example, be able to hear a symphony mentally, picking out all the individual instruments; or one may have a tactile eidetic image, being able to feel the image of a piece of fur with full clarity and richness.[16]

Later Work on Eidetic Imagery. Between 1930 and 1968 there were only two studies published on eidetic imagery. Since then there has been a renewed interest in the subject, one of the most remarkable experiments being to use pairs of computer-generated patterns of quasi-random dots. Although they appear to be random, these patterns are so designed that if one pattern is presented to the left eye while the other pattern is presented to the right eye, the two images fuse stereoscopically and a clear shape stands out in the middle of the combined pattern.

Instead of presenting the two patterns simultaneously to the right and left eye one pattern was presented to one eye on one day and the following day the second pattern was presented to the other eye. In one subject the eidetic imagery was so strong that she had retained the first

Figure 38 Two random dot patterns which when fused stereoscopically cause a shape to stand out from the background (from B. Julesz, *The Foundations of Cyclopean Perception*, Chicago: University of Chicago Press, 1971. Used with permission.)

picture in sufficient detail that it fused with the second picture and the hidden shape appeared, even though the eidetic image was being viewed twenty-four hours later.[17]

In a similar experiment children were shown the pictures (a) and (b) of Figure 39. They first looked at (a); then this was removed and they looked at (b). Those with strong eidetic images were able to superimpose the two and see the face depicted in (c). It is very difficult for a child to work out what the combined picture would look like and, indeed, they were often surprised when they suddenly saw the face.[18]

Eidetic imagery seems to be much more common in children than it is in adults. Estimates of its frequency of occurrence vary enormously. Some studies have suggested that 50 percent of children under the age of eleven possess the faculty, while others put the figure as low as 3 or 4 percent, or even zero percent. Such wide variability probably reflects the different types of tests used, the different criteria for eidetic imagery, and the varying cultural backgrounds of the children.

It is also difficult at first to get children to admit to having eidetic imagery. After a few years of schooling they soon become inhibited about saying that they see things which are "not really there"—not really there in the sense that other people cannot go up and touch and objectively verify their experience. People researching into eidetic imagery often have to spend some time with the child, gaining his confi-

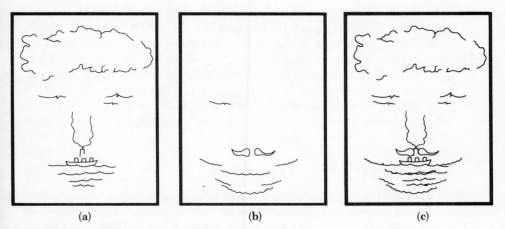

(a) (b) (c)

Figure 39 Eidetic children first were shown picture (a); it was then removed and picture (b) was exposed to view; (c) is the picture formed by combining the other two pictures. Eidetic imagers can remember one pattern and project it on to the second pattern at a later date, seeing the hidden shape. None of the children saw a face initially in the first picture, but many of them did when shown the second one, suggesting eidetic memory of the first.

dence, so that he will not feel silly, and not feel he is going to be laughed at or criticized, when he reports what he sees.

Several investigators have looked at the way eidetic images vary with age. Eidetic imagery seems to decrease fairly rapidly after about the age of ten, and by the time children are fourteen, they show about the same frequency of occurrence as do the rest of the adult population —that is, about 2 percent with moderate eidetic imagery and one in a million with very strong eidetic imagery.

This trend probably owes a lot to our educational systems. The emphasis on reading, writing, and arithmetic—that is, on the logical left-hemisphere functions—does not encourage strong visual imagery, which is a right hemisphere function. And, like any faculty not regularly used, eidetic imagery begins to atrophy.

The view that eidetic imagery is educated out of most individuals was first put forward in 1930 by E. R. Jaensch, one of the early researchers on the subject. He found that in special schools in which there was more emphasis on sensory activities, 80 to 90 percent of the children showed eidetic imagery.[19] This view is further supported by recent studies from other cultures in which children are not subjected to a predominantly verbal educational process. In several African cultures it has been found that eidetic imagery is retained through adulthood, with about 50 percent of the population showing the phenomena.[20]

Further evidence that adults may not have completely lost the faculty of eidetic imagery comes from some experiments in hypnosis. Adults under hypnosis were taken back to the age of seven. They were then presented with random-dot stereograms one at a time (see Figure 38), and several were then found to have eidetic imagery—though none of them did in the normal waking state.[21]

APPLICATIONS AND ADVICE

Possibly everyone has the ability of eidetic imagery latent within them, but in nearly all cases it has atrophied through lack of use—or rather, it has been educated *out* of our lives. Regular exercise of imagery by, for example, taking a moment to form clear interactive images of things you wish to recall, or imagining in as much detail as possible a place you were in earlier in the day, can revive some of these lost abilities.

Imagery can be developed by such exercises as the following: Sit comfortably and close your eyes. Relax easily. Now imagine yourself outside a building you know well—a friend's house, or if you are not at home, your own house. See how much of the image you can recall from memory. What is it built from? How many windows are there? What do the windows look like? Imagine the door. What color is it? What design is it? What is it made from? What is the door handle like? And what surrounds the door? Open the door and walk inside. Look at the walls—what color are they? What is on the floor? How does it feel to touch it? What furniture is there? Notice as much as you can. Spend some time just allowing your mind to roam around, letting images come up from memory.

Now imagine yourself picking up some object that is in the room. How does it feel—hard or soft? Is it hot or cold? What does it smell like? What color is it? Really get to know that object as if you were really there, looking at it from different sides and from above and below, using as many of your senses as you can.

When you feel quite comfortable with this exercise, you might try some more creative imagery and imagine yourself inside some solid object. For example, you might imagine yourself inside a brick of the wall, or inside the wood of a piece of furniture. Again imagine how it feels, what it looks like; are there any tastes or smells? Perceive as if you were really inside it.

Another useful exercise is to imagine an object changing in unusual ways. Imagine a glass of water, for example. Imagine it floating in the air in front of you, and then imagine it moving around in whatever manner you desire. Move it up to the ceiling, move it down and around. Imagine it turning upside down and the water staying in. Then try imagining the water changing color, becoming blue, then green, then golden. Let it change size. Imagine the glass becomes as tall as you, or imagine it becoming so small that it can sit on your fingernail.

Such exercises, if practiced regularly, will greatly enhance your power of imagery. As you begin to use imagery more in daily life, your overall memory will improve. And, as we shall see later (pages 215–216), the ability to form clear images can also be very useful in setting and achieving personal objectives.

In the animal kingdom, and in primitive man, memory evolved to record the routes and location of food, shelter, mates, and foes. Such a memory naturally uses associative imagery, with the result that associative imagery becomes the backbone of memory. It is only in relatively recent times that man has turned his memory to the recording of phone numbers, addresses, concepts, mathematical formulae, etc., all of which, being poor in imagery, are often poorly remembered. Their retention can, however, be greatly enhanced by the deliberate use of the natural capacities of memory and association, as will be shown in the next chapter.

Figure 40

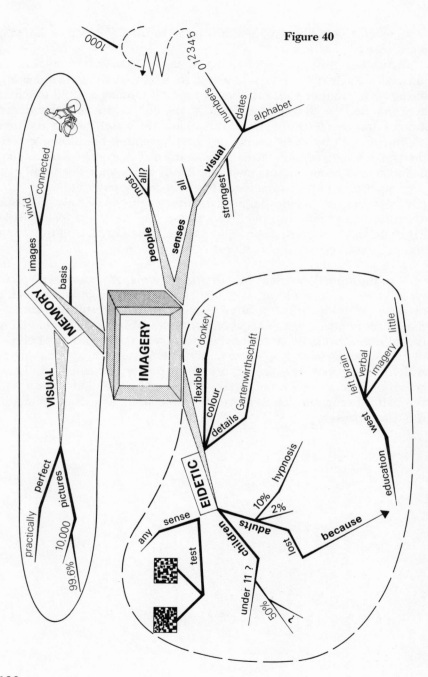

9.
Mnemonics

What are mnemonics?
How do they work?
Who first used them?
How to use simple mnemonic systems
Can they be used for anything?
Are mnemonics cheating?
Do some people have perfect memories?

The word *mnemonic* comes from the Greek *mneme,* "to remember"; a mnemonic is essentially any technique that helps people remember things better. It can be tying a knot in a handkerchief, a rhyme, a visual image, or any other aid.

The basis of virtually all memory techniques is the formation of a strong association. The association can be a link to some well-established memory, a link to a standard set of mental memory pegs, or a link between any previously unrelated ideas that need to be recalled together.

If, for example, you wanted to form a mnemonic between *apple* and *penguin,* you might form an image of a penguin with its head stuck inside a huge apple. You might like to try forming your own image connecting these two objects. Whatever the association, try to make maximum use of the factors that naturally enhance human memory:

Uniqueness. The association should be unique so that there will be no possibility of interference with other associations. It would not be very helpful to imagine a penguin eating an apple. Penguins do eat things (though not apples normally), and the image would not be so outstanding. But an apple eating a penguin, yes!

Exaggeration. The more exaggerated the image, the better. Make the apple huge. The more bizarre and outstanding an image, the more arousing it is and the clearer is the memory that results.

Sensory. For most people the image will be predominantly visual, since visual memory is usually the strongest, but smells, sounds, movements, etc., should be included wherever possible. See the penguin waddle, hear the crunch of snow, smell and taste the apple. The association can also be improved by making the image three-dimensional, in color and as vivid as possible.

Interactive. The connection between the objects should be the prime feature of the image. As we saw previously, disconnected images do not work so well: They must be closely connected. A penguin standing beside an apple is not a good association. It is much better to put it inside the apple.

Simplicity. The simpler the connection, the better. Apples and penguins both survive the cold well, but this would be too sophisticated a link for a mnemonic. Keep it childlike, unencumbered, and unique.

Creativity. Being creative involves you much more in the association and increases the depth of processing. The more original the image, the better will it be remembered. Indeed, the act of creation is essentially the same as that of memorizing— the forging of a link between two previously unassociated ideas.[1]

Sexual and Vulgar. Don't be afraid to make sexual or vulgar connections if they occur to you—and they probably will. Most people find such associations are remembered much better. No one else need ever know of your associations, so there need be no fear of embarrassment. Turn back to the memory experiment you did on page 87 and check whether you recalled the word *balls*, and if so, can you remember any helpful associations you had?

Involvement. Memory is intimately linked with conscious experience. The more strongly you experience something, the better you will remember it. So savor your mental image fully.

EARLY MNEMONIC TECHNIQUES

Mnemonic techniques were extensively used by the ancient Romans and Greeks. The Romans developed what is known as the systems of *loci. Locus (loci,* plural) is the Latin word for place and from it we have our word *location.* In the Roman system each item to be remembered was associated with a particular place in the surroundings. A person would first form a standard list of locations that he knew well. Maybe he would take his courtyard and make the pillar on the left the first *locus,* the ledge next to it the second *locus,* the tree the third *locus,* the statue the fourth *locus,* etc. Then, if the first item to be remembered were a horse, he might imagine a horse standing on top of the pillar, or standing up as a pillar. If the second item were a sword, then he could imagine a sword, perhaps standing on its tip on the ledge, at the second *locus.* And so on through the standard set of *loci.* To recall a given list, the person only had to go back and think of the pillar to get the first item, the ledge to remember the second item, and so on.

The Romans are said to have used this system extensively in memorizing speeches. Each of the topics to be remembered was associated with one of the standard places in the person's system so that he was able to give his speech in the correct order by merely running through the sequence in his mind as he spoke. The remnants of this system have descended into our own speech as "In the first place . . ." and "In the second place . . ."

The Greeks used a similar system of linking ideas with places. Our word *topic* comes from the Greek *topos,* which likewise meant "place." The topics to be discussed were the locations in the Greek memory system.

Many others since the early Greeks and Romans have used mnemonics. Thomas Aquinas used mnemonic systems in teaching his monks. They were used by some of the kings of England and France, and by Shakespeare, Francis Bacon, and Leibnitz. Children at school use them without any prompting, and they are the "secret" behind nearly all great "memory men."

PEG WORD SYSTEMS

Modern peg word mnemonics are based on similar principles to the early Roman and Greek systems, but the *loci* are now replaced by a standard set of objects that are each associated with a specific number. Thus the first item is linked to an image associated with 1, the second to an image associated with 2, etc.

In order to make it easy to remember which objects are associated with which numbers, mnemonic principles are applied to the choice of object. There are three principal ways in which this is usually done:

Number-Rhyme. The objects are chosen to rhyme with the numbers they represent. Thus one might have: 1–gun; 2–shoe; 3–tree; . . . ; 10–hen.

Number-Shape. Here the shape of the number is the cue: 1–pole; 2–swan; 3–breasts; . . . 10–Laurel and Hardy.

The Major System. Each digit is associated with a consonant, or similar sounding group of consonants. Most systems are based on a standard framework laid down in the seventeenth century:

1–t, d, th	(t and 1 have one downstroke)
2–n	(two downstrokes)
3–m	(three downstrokes)
4–r	(last letter of four)
5–l	(Roman for 50)
6–j, sh, ch	(j is mirror image of 6)
7–k, g (hard), ng, qu	(k is two 7s back to back)
8–f, v	(f in script looks like 8)
9–p, b	(9 reversed, or rotated)
0–z, s	(zero)

Images are then chosen which begin with the associated consonant— for example, 1–tie; 2–noah; . . .

This system is very powerful in that it can be easily extended to numbers beyond 10. The number 695, for example, would require the consonants, *j, sh* or *ch; p* or *b;* and *l.* Adding vowels, one might produce the word *ch*ap*el* as the key object for 695.

Providing each object is well linked to the item to be remembered, the capacity of such a system is almost limitless. In one study a girl with no special ability in memory was taught a similar system for the numbers one to a hundred. Using this, she was able to recall many lists of this length, usually with no errors whatsoever. In one test she was asked to recall alternate items in the series, which she did correctly. The experimenter then jumbled the list around and made her remember it in a different order, which she again did with almost complete success. Then without warning he asked her to remember the original order. She did so with only two errors.[2]

Another experiment extended the list to a thousand items. The images were presented in five hundred pairs and the subjects asked to form strong interactive images along similar lines to those just mentioned. They were presented with each pair only once. Yet afterward they were able to recall 99 percent of the words perfectly.[3] Subjects who are not instructed to form associative links seldom do better than 5 percent correct. Just one simple system had made recall twenty times better!

OTHER MNEMONICS

Many people use mnemonics spontaneously, probably without even realizing it. A person's name, Joy, for example, may have become stuck in the memory because the person was (or was not) a joyful character. At school one may have found it easier to remember that chalk is calcium carbonate by remembering that all three words begin with *c*. Such associations may seem silly and even trivial at the time, and people will not always admit to them, but it is these incidental and seemingly silly associations that are the very fabric of memory.

A powerful factor in memory is rhythm and rhyme, and these are often used in teaching children. The most obvious are rhymes like:

i before *e*, except after *c*,
or when sounding like *a*
as in *neighbor* and *weigh*

and

Thirty days hath September,
April, June, and November

Other common mnemonics used at school are ones like the English

Richard of York gained battles in vain

where the first letter of each word stands for the first letter of the colors of the rainbow (red, orange, yellow, green, blue, indigo, violet). And the popular one for distinguishing stalagmites from stalagtites:

When the tights come down, the mites run up.

What makes this particularly good and memorable is not only the rhythm and rhyme, but the little "naughtiness" involved.

Many students use mnemonics to help them remember their basic facts. A zoologist may remember how to distinguish a Bactrian camel from a dromedary camel by simply turning the initial letters on to their sides: ‬ has two humps, ‬ has only one. The imaginativeness and unique visual qualities of this mnemonic ensures that once seen, it is rarely, if ever, forgotten.

Mathematicians may remember the reciprocal of pi (0.318310) by simply remembering the phrase "Can I remember the reciprocal?" In this case the number of letters in each word determines the required numbers: *can* has three letters; *I,* one; *remember,* eight; *the,* three; *reciprocal,* ten.

Physiologists trying to remember the order of nerves that pass through the superior orbital tissues in the skull (lacrimal, frontal, trochlear, lateral, nasociliary, internal, abducens) probably find it easier to remember that "lazy French tarts lie naked in anticipation," the first letters of each word being the first letters of each nerve.

One can also use mnemonics for learning foreign languages. Most of the rules of grammar can be given mnemonic interpretations, and the vocabulary itself is always very much simpler to learn with associative images than by rote repetition. In learning French, for example, you might remember that the word for duck is *canard* by picturing yourself throwing a "can hard" at a duck, and that a rabbit is *lapin* by imagining one lapping a pan. Such associations do not usually give the correct pronunciation and spelling, but they are close enough to remind us of the words, and as such are highly efficient cues.[4]

ARE MNEMONICS CHEATING?

It is sometimes said that memory is of no use unless it comes through a thorough understanding of the material. Certainly understanding is valuable in that it helps to build up meaningful associations between the concept involved and one's whole body of knowledge. But rather than hindering understanding, mnemonics often help enhance it. New information cannot be related to other information if it is not available, and difficult material may be understood later on, if, that is, it has been remembered in the first place.

It has been said that there is no such thing as pure rote learning. Ultimately all memory is by some association or other. Mnemonic techniques are essentially making a fuller use of the brain's own natural memory functions, thus helping it in its task. It is not that mnemonics are cheating, but rather by not consciously using them, one is effectively hindering the learning process. The brain is, in the end, going to form associative connections whether you help it or not.

It is possible that some of the differences in learning proficiency among school children are attributable to the use of different memory strategies. It has been reported that the marked differences in learning between a group of normal children and a group of mentally retarded children can be largely eliminated when both groups are trained in learning methods, particularly in the use of associative mental imagery.[5] This has the somewhat revolutionary implication that "smart" people may simply be those who have discovered for themselves efficient learning strategies, and realized, either consciously or unconsciously, the value of associative imagery in learning.

MNEMONICS AND THE RIGHT HEMISPHERE

Some preliminary work has suggested that the use of mnemonic techniques brings the right hemisphere more into play. Straight verbal learning would tend to be associated with the left hemisphere. Visual imagery, on the other hand, is a function more associated with the right hemisphere. It was found that when one image from a mnemonically linked pair was presented in the left visual field, so that the information went to the right side of the brain, the time taken to remember the association was quicker than when the image was presented to the left side of the brain.[6] This supports the contention that mnemonic processes use the right hemisphere more than the left.

Mnemonic techniques have also been used to help people with brain disease. When the left side of the brain has been damaged and verbal functions impaired, memory often suffers. By learning visual mnemonic techniques, such patients have been able to improve their memory, making greater use of their healthy right hemisphere.[7] The use of mnemonic techniques is not only aiding the brain's own natural memory processes, it is also helping to integrate the functioning of the left and right hemispheres.

Piracetam, a drug originally developed as a possible cure for travel sickness, also appears to lead to improved memory. In the early 1970s experiments showed that it enhanced memory in animals, and it was given the name Nootropyl (meaning "toward mind"). Other studies showed that rats given piracetam appeared to have an increased facilitation of transfer of visual information between the left and right hemispheres.[8] Experiments on students showed that after being given the drug for a fortnight, learning abilities increased by 15 to 20 percent. When asked to distinguish between two series of words, one being presented to the left ear while the other was presented to the right ear, it was found that the students taking piracetam performed better than those taking a placebo, again indicating an increased integration of the left and right hemispheres.[9]

The important difference between this drug and mnemonic techniques, however, is that the drug leads only to a 15- to 20-percent increase, whereas mnemonic techniques improve memory several hundred percent.

"S." The power of associative imagery is brought out clearly in the case of a Russian newspaper reporter, Solomon-Veniaminovich Shereshevskii, who was studied by the Russian psychologist A. R. Luria over the thirty years from 1920 to 1950.[10] "S," as he is usually called for short, was sent to Luria by the editor of the newspaper for which he worked. Each day the editor would give the reporters lists of assignments including details of names, addresses, telephone numbers, etc. The other reporters would all take down copious notes, while "S" remembered everything perfectly without any notes at all. Initially he was surprised at the interest taken in him. He thought there was nothing unusual in the fact that he could easily recall what had been said to him, even right back to when he was a baby. "Did not everybody remember every-thing?" he asked.

Luria tested him in a number of ways, giving him lists of numbers, nonsense syllables, words, passages of foreign languages, and complex mathematical formulae to remember. He found no difference in the ability of "S" to remember, whatever the material. Luria worked up from short lists of twenty to fifty items to lists containing hundreds of items, and found that "S" still continued to remember everything per-fectly.

Not only was there no apparent limit to the capacity of his mem-ory, there was no apparent limit to its durability. Luria would some-times ask "S" to recall lists that he had tested him with fifteen to twenty years earlier. In one experiment "S" was read a list of several hundred repetitive nonsense syllables like these:[11]

ma	va	na	sa	na	va
na	sa	na	ma	va	
sa	na	ma	va	na	
va	sa	na	va	na	ma
na	va	na	va	sa	ma
na	ma	sa	ma	va	na
sa	ma	sa	va	na	
na	sa	ma	va	ma	na
etc.					

This was probably one of the most difficult tests he underwent. There is no obvious pattern and the similarity of the lines makes the task highly confusing. Nevertheless "S" not only recalled the full se-ries perfectly but when, eight years later, without any warning, Luria tested him again, "S" still remembered the list in its entirety, with no error.

In such cases "S" would pause for a moment, then commence "Yes, yes . . . this was a series you gave me once when we were in your apartment . . . you were sitting at the table and I at the rocking chair . . . you were wearing a gray suit and you looked at me like this . . . now, then, I can see you saying . . ." and then proceed to reel the series off perfectly.[12] This illustrates clearly the important associative clues pro-vided by the environment.

The means by which "S" accomplished these remarkable feats of memory was to use imagery. When he was given a random list of items to remember, he would spontaneously form a strong image of the item and associate it with some object along a road or street that he knew. As he mentally walked down the street, he would associate different items with different objects he encountered. Or if the item strongly suggested another location, he would see himself flying from one place to the other. Alternatively he would build up a story around the items. Thus when Luria asked him to remember a complex mathematical formula

$$\text{N.} \quad \sqrt{d.^2 \times \frac{85}{vx}} \quad \cdot \quad \sqrt[3]{\frac{276^2 . 86x}{n^2 v . \pi 264}} \quad n^2 b = sv \, \frac{1624}{32^2} \, .r^2 s$$

"S" used the following imagery:[13]

> Neiman (N) came out and jabbed at the ground with his cane (.). He looked up at a tall tree, which resembled the square root sign ($\sqrt{\ }$), and thought to himself: "No wonder the tree has withered and begun to expose its roots. After all, it is here that I built these two houses" (d^2). Once again he poked with his cane (.). Then he said: "The houses are old, I'll have to get rid of them ($\times$). The sale will bring far more money." He had originally invested 85,000 in them (85). Then I see the roof of the house detached (_____), while down below on the street I see a man playing the Termenvox (vx). He's standing near a mailbox, and on the corner there is a large stone (.), which had been put there to keep carts from crushing up against the houses. Here, then, is the square, over there the large tree ($\sqrt{\ }$) with three jackdaws on it (Ψ). I simply put the figures 276 here, and a square box containing cigarettes in the "square" (^{2}). . . . . etc.[14]

When he was asked to recall some such sequence, he simply started at the beginning of the journey or story and, going over it in his mind, "read off" the items as he came upon each successive image. In this particular case he was able to recall the mathematical formula in precise detail fifteen years later. When "S" describes his process in words, it may appear very cumbersome and lengthy, but remember that he was not using words in his mind, only images, and the sequence of images could be put together in his mind very compactly and quickly so that he could read off the mathematical formula from the images as fast as he could speak.

Occasionally "S" would appear to forget one of the items, but this turned out to be not a defect in memory so much as a defect in perception. He explained that the reason for the omission was that the image had become hidden in some way. This would occur if he had mentally associated the image with an area of the street that was not well lit and thus when he came to recall it, he could not "see" it clearly. In one case he omitted the word *pencil* from a series. And when this was pointed out to him he replied: "I put the image of the *pencil* near a fence . . . the one down the street. But what happened was that the image fused with that of the fence and I walked right on past without noticing it."[15]

"S" 's power of imagery was related to his remarkable synesthesia. In synesthesia the senses lose their boundaries and begin to merge with each other. Thus visual stimuli may evoke smells, tastes, and tactile sensations as well; and sounds may produce visual images. When presented with a tone at 50 Hz and an amplitude of 100 decibels, "S" saw

> a brown strip against a dark background that had red tongue-like edges. The sense of taste is like that of sweet and sour borscht.

For 100 Hz at 86 decibels, he saw

> a wide strip that appeared to have a reddish-orange hue in the center: from the center outwards the brightness faded with light gradations so that the edges of the strip appeared pink.

And with a 200-Hz note at an amplitude of 64 decibels, he saw

> a velvet cord with fibers jutting out on all sides. The cord was tinged with delicate, pleasant pink-orange hue.[16]

Synesthesia came spontaneously throughout his life. When asked if he would remember his way home from an institute where he had been conducting some experiments, "S" replied: "How could I possibly forget. After all, here is this fence, it has such a salty taste and feels so rough; furthermore it has such a sharp piercing sound."[17]

Synesthesia could also hinder his memory at times. If he were recalling images from a visual scene and Luria was saying yes to each correct recall, he would find that the word *yes* produced a smudge on the visual scene and he would have to move the image in order to see the next item clearly.

Curiously his biggest problem was how to forget. If "S" was recalling lists written on a blackboard, he had to be very careful not to recall lists written on the same blackboard in similar situations at other times. He tried various ways to overcome this difficulty, such as writing the items down on a piece of paper, believing that if he wrote them down, his mind would no longer feel it necessary to remember them. This is in sharp contradiction to most people's habit of writing things down in order to remember them, forming stronger associative bonds and increasing the depth of processing mentioned earlier. The solution that "S" finally adopted was surprisingly simple. He suddenly realized that if he did not want the list to be there, it would not appear. All it needed was for him to realize this, then once he set his mind on forgetting, he forgot.

Another curious feature about his mental processes was that "S" did not abstract information, or look for underlying principles, in the way that most people do. If given the following series to recall:

```
1  2  3  4
2  3  4  5
3  4  5  6
4  5  6  7
5  6  7  8
. . . .
```

he would proceed to form images of these numbers and associate them with other images in his normal manner. And after much effort and concentration he would proceed to recall the entire series perfectly. He did not make use of the obvious patterns in the numbers.[18]

Normally he found it very difficult to remember people's faces. He saw a face as a continually changing pattern of light and shade, which was never the same from one moment to the next. At different times people had very different expressions on their faces, making it exceedingly difficult for him to fix upon one definite concrete image. He was not remembering the abstraction derived from sensory experience, as most of us do, but was remembering the sensory experiences themselves.

"S" 's capacity may sound fantastic, but he was using abilities common to all of us. Indeed, the fact that he did not make much use of organization and principle seeking shows that even he was not using all his abilities—he was still working at only a fraction of his capacity.

APPLICATIONS AND ADVICE

Try making yourself a very simple peg system along the lines suggested on page 126, either choosing images that rhyme with the numbers, or images that have the same shapes as the numbers. Choose whichever you prefer, though it is best to stick to one system. The images you choose should all be of objects of one form or another, objects that are easily visualized. When you have found some image that links well with each number, you should find that you can remember all of them without any difficulty. If there is some difficulty with any particular one, go back and make sure that the association, that is, the rhyme or shape, is clear and simply connected to the number.

Now think up ten other objects—any objects you like. As you think of each object, link it with a number by forming some visual link and association between the object and the image you have associated with the number. Thus if your first object is an orange and you are using a rhyming system, then you want to link orange with gun (the image associated with number one) and you might imagine a gun shooting oranges or, even more unusual, a gun poking out of an orange. Remember to make the connection as absurd as possible, while keeping it simple along the lines indicated on page 126. Then take the next object you think of and link it with the image you have put to the number 2. Carry on doing this until you have linked ten objects to your peg system.

Now take a blank sheet of paper and write down the numbers 1 to 10 in any order you like and see if you can put an object to each number. First take the number, recall the image that rhymes with it or is of the same shape, and then see if you can recall what object was associated with that image. You will probably find that with very little trouble you will get nine or even ten correct—quite an amazing feat for the average memory (or is it?). If you fail to get any of the objects, or recall any incorrectly, check back and see if the imagery was really that absurd, visual, connective, simple, etc. You will often find your failures very instructive.

Then tomorrow see how many of the list you can still recall; you'll probably be very surprised.

Simple mnemonic systems such as the number-peg system can be very useful in daily life when paper and pencil are not easily available for jotting down lists, etc. Some people remember things they have to do the next day just before they go to sleep at night. They are faced with the choice of either getting out of bed, switching on the light, finding pen and paper, and writing them down, or else simply hoping they will still remember them in the morning. By using a simple associative system, you have only to form good clear associations between ideas and their respective pegs in the system and they will be fixed in the memory. The next morning you simply run through the list to recall the ideas that came the night before. The same applies to ideas that come while you are in the bath, driving the car, or at a dinner party.

It might be thought that only one set of items could be linked to the system at any one time, but the same system can in fact be used for two or three lists simultaneously without one set of items interfering with another. As well as the associations that are made deliberately, there are other very valuable incidental associations being made, such as the situation in which the links were made and the general topic of the list. These incidental connections keep the different lists firmly apart in the mind. One can have lists of shopping, lecture points, things to do, people to phone, etc., all linked to the same set of number rhymes and without any confusion. When lecture points are recalled, the images that come to mind will be those associated with the lecture point —those of the shopping list or people to phone are not being called for and will not come up.

Remembering Faces. One area of memory in which nearly everybody claims to have difficulty is remembering faces. One can be introduced to ten people, and within five minutes one has probably forgotten most of the names. Here again associative imagery is impressively powerful.

Instead of just passively hearing the person's name as you shake hands, you should consciously make a clear and simple association between the name and their face, or any other aspect that stands out or is relevant. Again use as many as possible of the factors that naturally enhance memory in order to make the association as vivid and lasting as possible. Thus if you were remembering first names, you might imagine Robin to have a bright red breast and Cheryl to have huge bunch of cherries hanging from her ears or, even better, from her nipples. With surnames one might imagine Mr. Campbell as sitting in a can of soup, Mrs. Evans floating in the heavens, Dr. Harrison in his surgery holding his hairy son, and Ms. Nixon with nothing but her knicks on.

What is important is to make the association strong and clear; really visualize the image as if it were really happening. And if you can link the image with some distinctive aspect of the person, such as the hair style or face shape, so much the better. This can normally be done in the second or two that it takes to be introduced. If an image does not readily come to mind, ask the person to repeat his name. In fact this is always a good policy, not only does it give you longer to make a good clear association, it forces you to be more conscious of the name.[19] When you use a simple system such as this, you will soon have little difficulty remembering twenty or more names straight off. When you do fail to recall a name, you will almost invariably find it is either because the image was not strong or ridiculous enough, or because you were not paying sufficient attention to the associative process at the time.

Absent-Mindedness. Another common complaint about memory is absent-mindedness. This again can be greatly reduced if you use strong associative imagery. If you find that you are always forgetting where you have put things, then the next time you put something away in a cupboard or drawer, make a strong bizarre image connecting the object and the place you are putting it and you will find it almost impossible to forget.

Absent-mindedness occurs when the mind is absent. You are probably only performing the functions semiconsciously. So become as conscious as possible of the event. If you have a tendency to leave your keys behind, imagine yourself using a huge colored key to open the door to go out. If the image is strong enough, then you will certainly remember your key as you start to go out.

As a general rule, whenever you want to remember something, create a simple image connecting the item with the reason for remembering it, making the link as unique, exaggerated, sensory, and original as possible, and you soon will be amazed at how easy it is to recall things you would otherwise have forgotten.

Figure 41

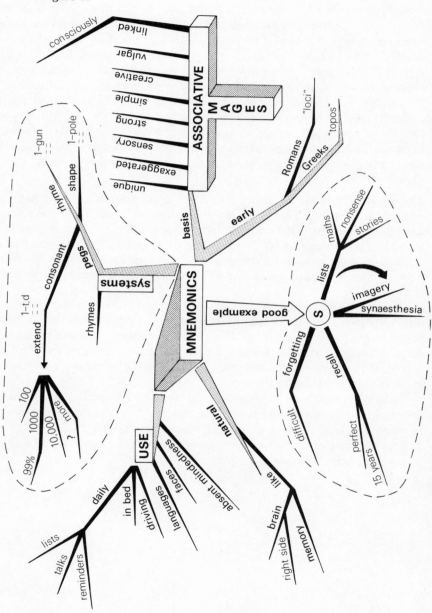

10.
The Brain's Record
of Experience

How are memories stored in the brain?
Can memories be transferred from one individual to another?
Can each memory be associated with a specific chemical?
Is learning the same as memory?
How does consolidation of the memory trace occur?
Why do we forget?
Why is regular review of studies valuable?

One of the first people to consider the subject of memory was Plato, in the fourth century B.C. He proposed what is known as the wax tablet hypothesis. According to Plato's theory, impressions are recorded in the mind in the same way that lines are etched in wax when a pointed object is drawn across its surface. With time the impression wears away, leaving a smooth surface once more. This Plato saw as the process of forgetting.

Since Plato, a wide variety of hypotheses on memory have been offered. For the first part of the present century memory theories were dominated by the idea of the cortical reflex arc. In this theory each memory trace consisted of a particular pathway among the neurons, new memories being laid down as new connections were made between the neurons. Since then, however, it has been realized that the brain does not function like a complex telephone exchange, as the cortical reflex arc theory supposes, nor do neurons appear to make numerous new connections each time a new memory is formed. Current theories suggest that the acquisition of memory is related to the inhibition and facilitation of the synapses throughout the brain. Specific memories are now thought to reside not in a particular synapse or pathway but in the pattern of electrical and chemical changes over the brain as a whole. The two most fruitful lines of research in this direction have been studies of the molecular basis of memory and the application of the principle of holography to memory. This chapter will look at the molecular basis; the next chapter at the holographic theory.

THE MOLECULAR BASIS OF MEMORY

Some of the first experiments to suggest a chemical basis of memory were performed by James McConnell, professor of psychology at Michigan University, in the 1960s. He worked with tiny flatworms (planarians) that he trained to react to light. He conditioned the worms to turn away from light by giving them an electric shock each time they failed to respond. When the worms were trained so that they reacted to the light at least 90 percent of the time, he cut the worms in half. As is common with such creatures the head end of the worm grew a new tail, and the tail end grew a new head. McConnell found not only that the head end still reacted to light, as expected, but also, rather surprisingly, that the tail end, having grown a new head, also reacted to light. He concluded that the learning to avoid light had been stored chemically in individual cells; not only in the brain, but throughout the body.[1]

Now it happens that planarian worms will, when they become very hungry, turn cannibalistic and eat their fellows—providing their victims are cut up into small enough pieces first. This provided McConnell with the chance to test his hypothesis further. If there was a chemical basis to learning that was distributed throughout the body, by training one worm to react to light and then cutting it up and feeding it to another untrained worm, the effect of training might be transferred. To his delight he found that the worms that had eaten the educated victims did significantly better (right from the very first trial) than the worms that had eaten untrained victims.[2]

Whether or not these findings prove a chemical transfer of memory is still a matter of debate. Some workers have failed to replicate

McConnell's results.[3] Others have suggested that there may be some other factor in the experimental procedure that made cannibal worms light sensitive.[4]

Meanwhile McConnell moved on to higher animals. In 1966 he started looking at memory transfer in rats. Rats, however, are not generally cannibalistic, and even if they were, the digestive process would almost certainly destroy any chemicals involved. Instead of feeding the trained rats to other rats McConnell took extracts from the brains of trained rats and injected the extracts directly into the brains of untrained rats. Again he found a very specific transfer of memory to be occurring, the injected rats learning the tasks much faster.[5] Other researchers had similar findings, not only in rats but also in such higher mammals as monkeys. The transfer is generally very specific. Thus if one group of rats is trained to react to the sound of a bell and another group trained to react to a puff of air, then a third group of rats injected with extracts from the bell-trained rats would avoid the sound of a bell but show no reaction to the puff of air, and vice versa.[6]

RNA AND MEMORY

The next step after McConnell's work was to look for the chemical, if any, being transferred. Attention initially turned to RNA (ribonucleic acid). This is a complex organic molecule, containing millions of atoms, which is found in all living cells. It is involved in, among other things, the production of proteins within the living cell. Strands of RNA copy the parts of the genetic code from DNA (deoxyribonucleic acid), and the information contained in the code determines specific sequences of amino acids. When strung together, the amino acids form proteins—the building blocks of life.

Early work showed that the RNA content of neurons increases following learning. Other experiments have since shown that when certain chemicals that inhibit the production of RNA are injected into the brains of animals, the learning is severely impaired or altogether eliminated.[7] Experiments with chemicals that enhance RNA productions have produced an improvement of learning.[8]

Initially it was thought that changes in RNA itself were responsible for memory and learning. It was proposed that a given pattern of electrical impulses impinging on a neuron might produce a slight but permanent change in the structure of the RNA molecules. This would affect the proteins being synthesized, and as a result there would be a change in the cell's functioning. This change would then be the basis of learning.[9] However, it now seems more likely that it is not the RNA itself that is important so much as the increased protein synthesis that results from the increased RNA. Thus many of the early failures to replicate McConnell's transfer experiments may have been due to researchers looking for the transfer of RNA itself, rather than the proteins synthesized by the RNA.

MEMORY MOLECULES

In the 1970s Georges Ungar, at the Baylor College of Medicine in Houston, not only found strong evidence that it is the synthesized proteins that are responsible for the transfer effect; he even managed to identify some of the molecules involved in specific types of learning.

Ungar trained rats to avoid darkness. Normal rats prefer dark areas to light, but in these experiments they received electric shocks every time they went toward a dark area of a box, so they learned to stay in the light area. He then injected extracts from the brains of the trained rats into untrained rats and found, as in similar experiments, that the untrained animals would also start to avoid the dark.

He then set about analyzing the brain extract to find the specific chemical responsible. Combining the extracts from four thousand rats, he found traces of a new protein—a string of some fifteen amino acids. He called this substance scotophobin, from the Greek *skotos,* "darkness," and *phobos,* "fear." To prove that this was indeed the chemical involved in the learning, he had chemists synthesize it from its basic elements. It was found that when the synthetic scotophobin was injected into normal rats, it produced the same avoidance of the dark as did the natural extract.[10] Even more remarkable is the finding by another research group that synthetic scotophobin produces dark avoidance in goldfish as well,[11] implying that it may be a universal coding.

Since then Ungar and his team have discovered an eight-segment chain of amino acids, which they call anelatim and which seems to be the specific chemical responsible for the habituation of rats to the sound of an electric bell. The specificity of the protein is shown by the fact that it was not found when the rats were habituated to the sound of a brass gong rather than an electric bell.[12]

In another series of experiments they analyzed the extracts from the brains of some ten thousand goldfish that had been trained to distinguish between the colors blue and green. They isolated another protein, called chromodiopsin, which appeared to be responsible for this particular color discrimination.[13]

These findings, if they continue to be corroborated, would imply that there may be a specific chemical substance associated with every single skill that it is possible to learn. As far as the number of different proteins are concerned, this is quite possible. Each protein is a string of amino acids, and there are 20 principal amino acids that can occur at any point on the chain. Thus the potential number of combinations is practically infinite. There are, for example, 20×20, or 400, different proteins possible containing two amino acids (20 possibilities in the first place and 20 possibilities in the second place). Similarly, there are 8,000 different proteins possible consisting of just three amino acids, and some 33.66 quintillion proteins like scotophobin consisting of fifteen amino acids. And these are still very elementary amino acid chains. Insulin, for example, still a comparatively simple organic substance, contains fifty amino acids, while more complex chains are known to exist containing some several thousand amino acids in sequence. The possible number of different proteins of this length, if written out in the normal way, would have a string of zeroes long enough to fill the next two pages of this book!

IS MEMORY THE SAME AS LEARNING?

Even if it were true that every behavior modification were associated with a protein chain, this would not prove that every *memory* had a similar basis. Learning and memory are not the same thing. Learning, as far as the foregoing experiments were concerned, consisted of training animals to react automatically to a certain given stimulus—a conditioning procedure. Memory, on the other hand, especially in humans, can be taken to include a much broader retention of information. Thus, to say we remember a person's face need only mean that in the right circumstances we might recognize that we have seen the face before. This is very different from the kind of learning that the foregoing experiments have been studying. In human terms, the rat and goldfish experiments are equivalent to training a person to jump in the air every time he saw a specific face until the reaction was so automatic that he would do it whatever the circumstances.

Not only is it extremely unlikely that everyday memory is encoded in the same way that conditioned learning appears to be: It is mathematically impossible. Even given the colossal number of different possible proteins, the variety of different facts we can remember is far greater still (although we cannot record everything simultaneously). This can be seen by observing that if memory worked by one protein encoding the memory for one fact, and the same protein were always used for the same fact, the ability to remember the amino acid sequence of any protein chosen at random would completely exhaust the capacity of such a memory, for the memory of each sequence would require at least one protein to encode it. Thus memory, in its broadest sense, cannot be based on a one-to-one correspondence with specific proteins. It is far more likely that it corresponds to patterns of chemical changes over the brain as a whole—something we shall be looking at further in the next chapter.

CONSOLIDATION

It seems probable that memory is encoded through the direct modification of synapses by proteins synthesized within the cell body. Although neurons produce several times as much protein as any other cell, none of these proteins is secreted: They are all used within the neuron itself. As we saw in chapter 3, many of the proteins travel rapidly down the axons, often at the rate of a few centimeters per day, to arrive at the synapse. The fact that they travel so fast means that very often a protein synthesized in the cell body can be at the synapse within only a few minutes. Thus, if proteins are involved in memory, it would seem that the distinction between short-term and long-term memory may represent the time taken for proteins to arrive at the synapse and consolidate the memory.

Whereas drugs that affect protein synthesis affect long-term memory, drugs that affect only electrical activity, leaving protein synthesis alone, affect only short-term memory.[14] Moreover, drugs that specifically affect the transfer of protein molecules down the axons have also been shown to affect long-term memory. The drug colchicine, for example, appears to block long-term retention by interfering with the microtubules (thin tubes inside the axons that carry the proteins from cell body to synapse), thus preventing the necessary changes at the synapses itself.[15]

Substantial evidence that the synapses are involved in learning has come from two different directions. First, learning can dramatically change the effectiveness of a synapse, decreasing its transmitting ability to zero or enhancing it considerably.[16] And second, the amount of transmitter substance at some synapses varies after learning, decreasing after the first day and then rising over the next week and declining again after two to four weeks.[17]

One possible way in which the proteins may affect the synapse is by occupying vacant sites in the grid system we previously looked at. The proteins would fit into vacant spaces in the grid and so influence the rate at which transmitter substances could be released into the synaptic gap. This would in turn affect the probability of the first neuron conveying an impulse across to the second one. Supporting evidence for this comes from experiments showing that after excitation the number of vacant holes in the grid does change significantly.[18]

A second stage of memory consolidation appears to occur during sleep, in particular during dreaming. Deprivation of dream activity has been found to lead to a decrease in memory for recently acquired material. Conversely, when a lot of learning has taken place, dream time tends to increase in the next night's sleep.[19] Thus, dreaming may

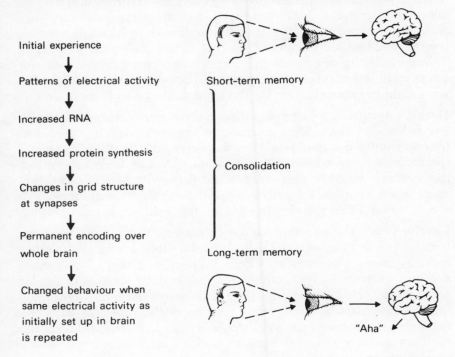

Figure 42 Some of the processes probably involved in the encoding of memory.

145

play an important part in helping to maintain a memory trace.

Proteins themselves last for only a few days and must continually be resynthesized. Therefore, the retention of a permanent memory is likely to involve a more permanent change than just protein synthesis. The protein changes at the synapse probably produce in the longer term permanent structural changes at the synapses, and these modifications may be taking place up to a week or two after the initial experience.

WHY DO WE FORGET?

Evidence from many different sources suggests that, for all practical purposes, our memory is virtually unlimited. Why then do we appear to forget?

Repression. One of the earliest theories of forgetting was Freud's hypothesis that forgetting is a result of repression. A period that has painful or anxiety-promoting associations is unconsciously repressed. If we cannot remember it, then we do not have to face up to its associations. Very occasionally this can result in a condition known as fugue, in which a person may lose all memory of his past. In mentally healthy people, however, although repression may sometimes occur, it only accounts for a very small amount of our forgetting. You probably cannot recall the last word of the previous chapter, but this is hardly the result of repression.

Decay. According to the decay theory, the memory trace itself gradually fades with time. Thus, if memory were encoded in changes in protein throughout the brain, then decay would take place as some of the proteins returned to their original state. As the decay progressed, the memory would become fainter and harder to retrieve. Although there is some evidence for decay, especially in short-term memory, it is now thought that interference plays a far greater role in forgetting.

Interference. The interference theory suggests that forgetting occurs because the memory can no longer be distinguished from all the other memory traces. The trace itself does not necessarily fade, but as more and more memories are accumulated, particularly those with similar associations, or of similar meaning, it becomes harder to recall the original material—in other words, the memories interfere with one another. Interference results not so much from an overcrowding of the memory as from a lack of suitable retrieval cues to distinguish one memory from another.

146

Search. Related to the interference theory of forgetting is the search theory. According to this, the retrieval of a memory is more of a problem-solving operation. Donald Norman shows that if a person were asked what he was doing on the Monday afternoon in the third week of September two years ago, his response might be as follows:

> Come on. How should I know?
> Okay. Let's see: two years ago. . . .
> I'd be in high school in Pittsburgh. . . .
> That would be my senior year.
> The third week in September—that's just after summer—that would be the fall term. . . .
> Let me see. I think I had chemistry lab on Mondays. . . .
> I don't know. I was probably in the chemistry lab. . . .
> Wait a minute—that would be the second week of school. I remember he started off with the atomic table—a big fancy chart. I thought he was crazy, to make us memorize that thing.
> You know, I think I can remember sitting . . .[20]

As the retrieval process continues and more and more clues are put together, it becomes easier to find the memory, although originally one may have been completely at a loss. According to the search theory, as with the interference theory, forgetting occurs as more and more memories are accumulated without sufficient cues to differentiate between them. Thus, it becomes harder and harder to find any one particular item in memory.

Set. Much apparent forgetting may occur as a result of changed mental preparedness, or "set." As was shown on page 89, a short warm-up task that resets the mind to a particular field can greatly enhance memory. Similarly, putting people back into a situation they were in some time before can invoke many forgotten memories.

APPLICATIONS AND ADVICE

There are several phases of memory consolidation:

1. During the first few minutes, as electrophysiological activity gives rise to protein synthesis

2. Over the next night's dreaming

3. Over the next week or two, as the synaptic changes are made more permanent

Repetition of the initial learning will always enhance memory, and it will be particularly valuable at these crucial stages of memory consolidation. It is therefore always a good plan to establish an organized system of review whenever you undertake any form of study or the remembering of any new material.

A good system is to have your first review of the material about five to ten minutes after the end of study.[21] This not only reinforces the consolidation of protein synthesis, it also makes the best use of the reminiscence effect, since memory is at its highest around this time. Research has shown that a five-minute review at this time considerably improves later recall.[22]

The second period of review should be about twenty-four hours later and should take only two to three minutes. This makes maximum use of the consolidation occurring during sleep, and will compensate for any initial decline in the memory trace.

The third review should be about one week later for two to three minutes. This will make use of the long-term reminiscence effect and stabilize the memory for a much longer period. There should be another review after about one month, again for two to three minutes, and a final review after six months. After this final review most material will be permanently recorded in memory. The consolidation can be further enhanced by appropriate study techniques and note-taking systems so that virtually all the required material can be recalled (see chapter 13).

The effect of such a review program is to reduce greatly the rate

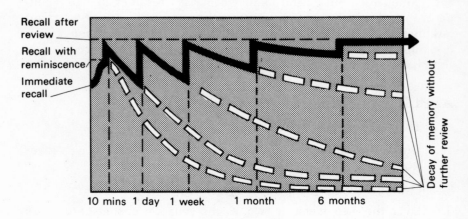

Figure 43 How organized review can keep results at a high level.

of forgetting. Instead of the memory dropping off rapidly by about 80 percent over the first twenty-four hours, it can be reinforced by reviews at the critical consolidation periods and at subsequent intervals, and it can be raised back toward, or even up to, the 100-percent line.

It may be thought that with continual study the reviews would accumulate and take over most of the study time. Actually, this is not the case. Supposing a person studied every day for one hour a day and set up a review program for this study. On any one day he would need to review the work from one day, one week, one month, and six months before.

Review of work done:	Time taken:
1 day before	3–5 minutes
1 week before	2–3 minutes
1 month before	2–3 minutes
6 months before	2–3 minutes
Maximum review time on any one day:	14 minutes

Thus a person spending one hour a day on study would need spend only a *maximum* total of fourteen minutes a day to complete all the necessary reviewing, and improve his memory many times over. This is the maximum because the information may often be recalled as a part of daily life or ongoing program of study, thus producing an automatic review of the material. A person studying as much as six hours a day, every day, still only needs spend a *maximum* of just over an hour each day reviewing the last six months' work in order to fix it permanently in his memory and so gain the greatest value from the study. If the extra 20 percent of time spent reviewing leads to an improvement in long-term memory from 10 percent to 90 percent, the overall gain in efficiency is about 750 percent. *Thus a few minutes devoted to review makes the hours spent studying effective and worthwhile.*

Figure 44

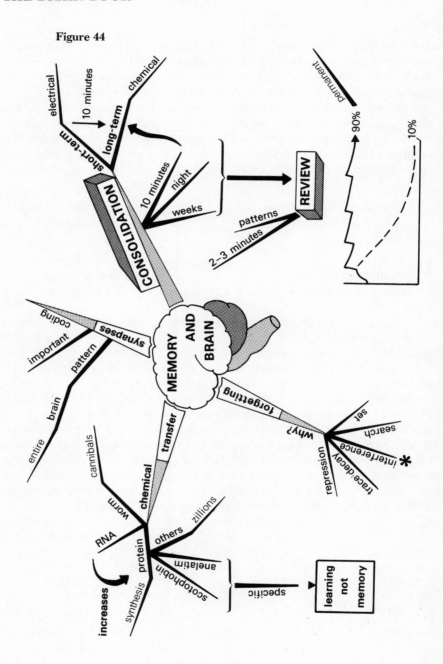

11.
The Holographic
Theory of Mind

What is a hologram?
How is it different from a photograph?
Is memory encoded holographically?
Is the mind a hologram?
Is the universe a hologram?

The term *hologram* was first coined by Denis Gabor in 1947 to describe a new photographic process he discovered and for which he was awarded the Nobel Prize in 1971. In a normal photograph the visual information is stored as a direct representation of the image, each point of the photograph corresponding to a particular part of the image. In a hologram the entire photographic plate stores a record of all the wave patterns produced by the object. The whole of the image is encoded at every point, hence the name *holography,* from the Greek *holos,* meaning "whole."

Gabor originally developed holography as a means of improving the resolution of photographs taken with electron microscopes, and the process did not find a wider use until the discovery of lasers some time later. Lasers produce coherent light, that is to say light in which all the

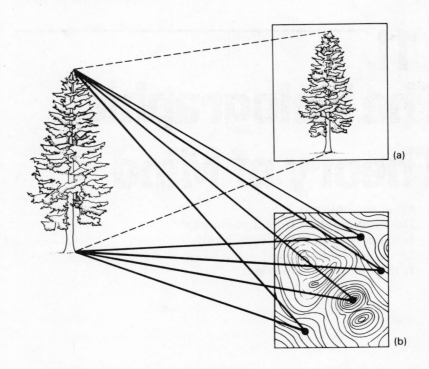

Figure 45 Difference between (a) ordinary photograph and (b) hologram. In an ordinary photograph each point of the object is represented by a specific point of the image. In a hologram the whole of the object is encoded at every point of the image.

waves are in step with each other. With coherent light it is very much easier to construct holograms and apply them to a number of different purposes.

To produce a hologram a laser beam is split in two. One half is directed straight to the photographic plate; the other is shone onto the object and reflected from it to the photographic plate. The plate then records the interference pattern produced by the meeting of the two waves. The image that is so recorded on the photographic plate bears little obvious resemblance to the object itself. If examined minutely, it looks more like fine waving bands of light and dark, something like a zebra's coat.

To reconstruct the image the hologram is simply reilluminated using the original laser beam, and a three-dimensional image of the original object appears floating in space where the original object was.

Itzhak Bentov provides a good analogy of seeing how a hologram stores information in his fascinating book *Stalking the Wild Pendulum.* [1] Imagine a pan full of water, into which you drop three pebbles. The pebbles produce three sets of circular ripples, each centered on the point where one of the pebbles hit the surface, and these ripples interfere to produce a complex pattern of waves on the surface. Now imagine you were to quick-freeze the surface and lift out the rippled sheet of ice. The whole sheet would contain precise information about where the pebbles struck. If the pattern were carefully analyzed, the different constituent waves could each be traced back to their source. Even if the sheet were shattered, each fragment would still contain all the necessary information. Taking a small section of the surface, you would be able to analyze what ripples had made up the pattern and work out where the three centers were. In a photographic hologram this reconstruction is done automatically by reilluminating with suitable laser light.

The hologram is the second most sophisticated information storage system known to mankind (the most sophisticated is the living brain). Thousands of different images can be recorded on the same plate, and each of them can be reconstructed from any part of the plate. The reconstructed images are three-dimensional, and looking at the hologram from different angles gives different views of the image.

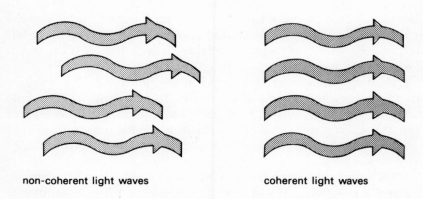

non-coherent light waves   coherent light waves

Figure 46 Noncoherent light (waves out of step) vs. coherent light (waves peak and trough together).

IS MEMORY RECORDED HOLOGRAPHICALLY?

Karl Pribram, from Stanford Medical School, and several other researchers have investigated the possibility that memory may be stored in the brain along holographic principles. In this case individual memories are not stored in specific networks of neurons or at specific synapses but are distributed throughout the whole brain. The fact that different areas of the brain are linked by thousands of parallel pathways provides a basis for the neurological equivalent of coherent activity, and any rhythmic firing would tend to enhance the phenomenon. As the patterns of electrical activity are consolidated by chemical changes, the experience becomes permanently encoded. Any one memory would be encoded as a pattern of chemical changes over trillions of synapses— and possibly glia cells as well—and each synapse would be involved in billions of different memories. Pribram's case is supported by the many striking similarities between human memory and holograms, suggesting that similar principles may indeed underlie both.

Distribution of Memories. Karl Lashley first demonstrated that memory appeared to be distributed throughout the brain rather than localized at specific sites. He trained rats to run mazes and then removed various parts of their brains. But whichever part he removed, he could not remove the memory; by removing successively larger and larger chunks he could only impair the memory to a greater degree. From this he developed two theories: the theory of "mass action," which stated that the intensity of recall depended upon the mass of the brain left intact; and the theory of "equipotentiality," which held that the memory was distributed evenly throughout the brain.

The same phenomena are found in the hologram. The image is stored over the whole plate and every chip from it contains the whole information. The only loss that occurs is a loss in detail and clarity. An image which is reconstructed from a small chip of the hologram will not be as sharp, nor contain as much detail as the original, but the image itself will still be there.

This brings out another important distinction between the human brain and a computer. If just one tiny connection in a computer is altered, the whole informational content may be significantly changed, even upset and destroyed. Both holograms and memory, though, are very resistant to damage.

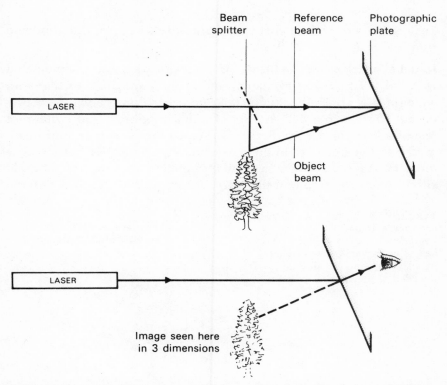

Figure 47 Creation of hologram (top). Light reflected from object meets unreflected light (reference beam) and interference produced is recorded on photographic plate. Reconstruction of image (bottom). When plate is developed and reilluminated with original light, a three-dimensional image is seen standing in position originally occupied by object.

Multiple Images. Many different images can be stored in one holographic plate. Having recorded one image, the plate only has to be rotated by one or two degrees in order to record a second image which will not interfere with the record of the first one. As well as rotating the plate through any number of angles the frequency of the light used can also be changed to record different images. So by varying the angle and the frequency it is possible to record many thousands of complete three-dimensional images on one plate—and of course many thousands are also recorded on each chip. It may sound fantastic, but it is just this kind of fantastic phenomena that we find in the brain—millions of images each stored throughout the brain and each clearly differentiated from the rest.

Initial Conditions and Context. If a holographic plate is illuminated with light of the same frequency and at the same angle as that with which it was originally illuminated, the original image will be reproduced. Change to a different set of initial conditions and a different image is brought out. Earlier it was shown the same is true of memory, that the initial conditions are important cues for retrieving a memory. It is much easier to recall information if a person is put back, either mentally or physically, into the original situation. Thus the

Figure 48 Three pebbles dropped in a bowl of water set up interference patterns which contain all information about where pebbles fell, much as an image is recorded in a hologram.

Interference pattern produced by waves from 3 stones

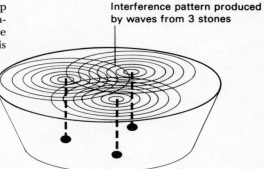

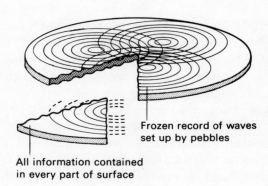

Frozen record of waves set up by pebbles

All information contained in every part of surface

drunk remembers what he did when he gets drunk again, and Locke's young man remembers how to dance only when the trunk is in the room.

Association. Closely connected with the phenomenon of initial context is that of association. It has been seen how all memories are linked by numerous associative connections, and that by thinking of one half of an association the other half will spontaneously spring to mind. Exactly the same phenomenon occurs in holograms. If, in forming the hologram, the first beam is also reflected off an object instead of going straight to the plate, the interference pattern recorded is that produced by the interaction of the waves from the two objects. On reilluminating the plate with light reflected from one of the objects, the image of the second object is reconstructed. Thus association, one of the most important factors in human memory, is also an intrinsic characteristic of holograms.

Recognition. When a hologram is illuminated with coherent light reflected from the original object, or something very similar, a bright spot is observed in the hologram rather than an image; the intensity of the spot corresponds to how well the new image resembles the original one. Here we have a close parallel to recognition. When the original object, or something very similar, is perceived, we have a subjective "flash," a sudden bright point in our consciousness, and the stronger the "flash," the clearer the recognition.

Capacity. One of the most remarkable features of both the hologram and of human memory is their remarkable capacity. Just one cubic centimeter of a photographic hologram can store ten billion bits of information. The human brain is fifteen hundred times as large, and the proteins involved are much smaller than the silver grains in photographic film. Human memory capacity is probably several thousand times greater still. It can probably store something on the order of a quadrillion (1,000,000,000,000,000) bits of information. If all this were given over to memory, the brain would have the ability to record a thousand new bits of information per second for every second from birth onward and still have only used a fraction of its memory potential after seventy-five years. [75 (years) × 365 (days) × 24 (hours) × 60 (minutes) × 60 (seconds) × 1,000 (bits per second) = 2,365,200,000,- 000.] Some of this capacity is taken up by the brain's programs. But even if they took up 90 percent of the capacity, you would still have enough left to record a hundred bits a second—which is probably sufficient capacity to remember most of the experiences that happen during a lifetime.

IS THE MIND HOLOGRAPHIC?

Not only does memory appear to function on holographic principles, but so does perception. The mathematics of holography involves the use of what are called Fourier transformations. These are mathematical equations that transform the object shape into the coded pattern. Similar transformations occur naturally within human perceptual processes.[2]

A nerve fiber connecting the retina of the eye to the brain is attached to several cells in the retina. These cells constitute its receptive field. The nerve responds differently to different cells in its field, so that if the nerve's activity is recorded while a point of light is moved

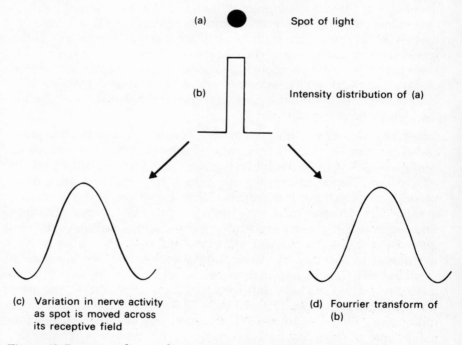

(a)   ●   Spot of light

(b)   Intensity distribution of (a)

(c) Variation in nerve activity as spot is moved across its receptive field

(d) Fourrier transform of (b)

Figure 49 Response of nerve from retina to spot of light at different points in its receptive field compared with Fourrier Transform of intensity distribution.

across the field, the activity varies as shown in Figure 49. It has been shown that the pattern of activity is in fact the Fourier Transform of the intensity (b).[3] In other words, the brain is making a coded image, and the coding is similar to that which takes place in a hologram.

Other experiments have investigated the electrical response that occurs when the pinpoint of light is replaced by a regularly undulating pattern of light and dark bands. Again it is found that the activity that results relates closely to the Fourier Transform of the input.[4] Research has also shown that hearing, taste, smell, and touch are also analyzed by the same mathematical process.

It has been surmised that the brain probably uses some technique of deconvolution, similar to the processes used to bring out the detail in the blurred photographs of planets radioed back to earth. If the brain did not use some such technique, it would be difficult to understand how we could see as clearly as we do.[5] Such processes are also based on Fourier Transforms. Scientists studying the radar phenomena in bats have found that the only known mechanism that matches the bat's performance is one based on holographic processing. Subsequent research supports the existence of holographic processes in insects, birds, and fish.[6]

IS THE UNIVERSE A HOLOGRAM?

Several scientists have suggested that reality as we know it may be constructed on holographic principles.[7] Physicist David Bohm hypothesizes that the underlying reality is one of pure vibration, a primal frequency realm, which is beyond time and space—analogous to the frequency patterns in a hologram. Any observation or awareness of the world is a concretization of this underlying "reality." A perception by the brain is, in effect, one particular image reconstructed from the infinite number stored in the hologram. It appears to us as real because we can only encompass one particular manifestation at any particular time, and since the hologram is all-pervading, we are usually obliged to see the same "reality" as everyone else.

Such an idea is not new to physics. In the submicroscopic world of quantum physics, objects only have well-defined positions and velocities when they are observed. When not being observed, an object can be in any one of an infinite number of possible states—in fact it is generally said to be in all the states at once. The act of observation, however, forces the mathematical equations to condense out in one particular solution—what mathematicians call the *eigen*-value—and one of the tasks of quantum physicists is to assess the various probabilities of an object appearing in any particular state. If this is so of the submicroscopic world, it is probably also true of the world in which we live our daily lives. It is our being conscious of the world that forces it to adopt a particular reality.

Karl Pribram has argued that a holographic model of "reality" is able to explain telepathy, precognition, clairvoyance, psychokinesis, healing, and most other phenomena that appear to contravene the laws of space and time. These laws are themselves only constructs imposed by our particular concretization of the underlying frequency realm.

This model also makes sense of Jung's phenomenon of synchronicity, in which unrelated events often show striking coincidences. According to a holographic model, there exist underlying patterns and symmetries, but we do not see them because we do not see the realm beyond space and time. The symmetries nevertheless appear in our particular concretization of reality as unexplained coincidences.

Transcendental experiences can also be explained by this model. The person who, deep in meditation, passes beyond the many activities of the mind and experiences a timeless, spaceless realm in which all things are one would appear to be coming into direct contact with the underlying frequency realm. This could explain why people in such states appear to have access to knowledge not available in the ordinary waking state. It would also support the claim sometimes made by people in touch with this level of reality that anything is possible. If we do construct our own reality, it is only a small step to constructing it in any way we imagine. We have only to allow the individual mind and its imagination to resonate with the underlying reality—with the field of all possibilities—for anything to be possible.

Such theories, fascinating as they are, are still highly speculative. The holographic theory of memory itself is not universally accepted. It is still incomplete, and in the future we might see new, even more powerful, theories arising to explain the nature of human consciousness, as the human brain tries to catch up with its own subtleties.

Figure 50

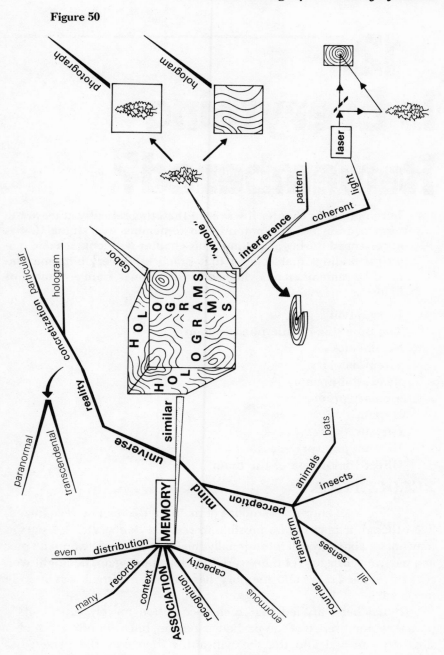

12.
Is Everything
Remembered?

In the previous chapter it was seen that, theoretically at least, the human brain has the potential to remember everything that is experienced during a lifetime. This chapter will look at some empirical findings that suggest that practically everything may indeed be remembered. Evidence for this comes from a number of fields:

Recognition
The tip-of-the-tongue phenomenon
Mnemonics
Visual memory
Incidental memory
Memory prodigies
Hypnosis
Dreams
Death-type experiences
Direct stimulation of the brain

RECOGNITION

There is an enormous amount of material that can be recognized, even though it may not be possible to recall it deliberately. A person may not be able to recall intentionally the faces of people whom he met at a party a year ago. Yet if he were to meet them again, he might well recognize the faces. The memory has not been lost; it was merely inaccessible.

It has been argued that such recognition merely represents a partial remembrance of the particular person, but very often in such a situation one will find that he will also notice how the person has changed; or, if it is another person who looks very similar, he may notice that there is something different about the face. He may not be able to pinpoint the difference, but the fact that he notices there is a difference shows that many of the minor details have also been remembered, although they may not be consciously recalled.

Several psychologists have tried to measure the difference between intentional recall and recognition. In one experiment subjects were presented with a list of one hundred words five times. When asked to recall the list, they scored about 30 percent. When, on the other hand, the subjects were asked to recognize the one hundred words mixed with one hundred unrelated words they scored 96 percent correct.[1] This still leaves open the possibility that under more suitable experimental conditions they would have recognized even more, perhaps even 100 percent.

In another experiment people were given lists of words to remember and asked to recall the list three times. It was found that they tended to recall about the same percentage of words on each successive test, but the actual words they recalled varied considerably. Only half of the words recalled appeared in all three tests.[2] This again shows that people remember considerably more than they can recall at any one time.

THE TIP-OF-THE-TONGUE PHENOMENON

One may sometimes be absolutely certain that he knows something yet still not be able to recall it. Often the first letter or even first syllable of a word may be known and it will be "on the tip of the tongue," yet still not recalled.

In a study of this phenomenon experimenters read out definitions of obscure English words and asked people to supply the word. Whenever a person was "seized" by a tip-of-the-tongue state, they asked him to say all the words that came to mind. Although the subjects would have failed on a straight recall test, they were able to produce considerable information about the word—for example, first letters, number of syllables, syllabic stress, suffixes and prefixes—and when they were actually presented with the word, they recognized it immediately.[3]

MNEMONICS

Mnemonic techniques such as those discussed in chapter 9 show that when maximum use is made of imagery and association, memory can be almost perfect. For example, see if you can write down next to the numbers 1 to 10 below the ten items you associated with each of the numbers in the mnemonic exercise given on page 135.

1.
2.
3.
4.
5.
6.
7.
8.
9.
10.

Given a list of one hundred words, few people will be able to recall more than about a quarter of them. Using a simple number-peg system, a person can usually remember all one hundred words perfectly, and in order, and such systems can be easily extended to one thousand words[4] and probably up to ten thousand or more.

VISUAL MEMORY

It was also seen that visual memory is considerably superior to verbal memory. On tests of ten thousand pictures, subjects recognized 99.6 percent of them correctly. As one researcher commented: "The recognition of pictures is *essentially perfect*" (see pages 114–115).

INCIDENTAL MEMORY

In a common type of memory experiment a subject is given a list of words to learn, which he does with varying degrees of success. If, however, some years later, the subject is asked to recall the experiment, he may not remember one of the words. He may well, however, remember the laboratory, what kind of day it was, the clothes he had worn, where he was sitting, who the experimenter was, whether he was friendly or unfriendly, who the other subjects were, and maybe the type of experiment involved. Ironically the person has remembered everything except that which he was asked to remember. One might ask which is the better test of memory capacity: the partial recall of a meaningless, dissociated, nonorganized, boring list of words or the wealth and breadth remembered about the meaningful, multiply associated, interesting events taking place in the environment.

Most psychological tests of memory are misleading if they are taken as an indication of memory capacity. They are generally only elucidating the mechanisms of memory, and in order to elucidate any one particular mechanism, one has to eliminate all other mechanisms that might confound the experiment. Ebbinghaus, for example, in his pioneering experiments mentioned earlier, systematically eliminated all the natural clues and aids to memory in order to measure forgetting. If he had included association, organization, and all the other natural cues, he would probably have found very little, if any, forgetting. Moreover, the majority of memory tests used by psychologists use lists of words or nonsense syllables, yet verbal memory is not nearly so good as visual memory. And few memory experiments would condone the use of mnemonic techniques that helped the person remember. Memory has been studied at its worst, not at its best.

MEMORY PRODIGIES

The remarkable memory of the Russian mnemonist "S" has already been looked at in chapter 9. "S" was not a unique case, although he was one of the most studied cases. Another Russian could memorize 150 poems and recall word for word a story read to him just once several weeks previously. His memory for nonsense syllables appeared perfect, though he did not have any of the synesthesia that "S" did.[5]

The late A. C. Aitken, professor of mathematics at the University of Edinburgh, "easily" remembered the first thousand decimal places of the value of π—forward and backward. Like "S," he could recall lists of words used in memory tests twenty-seven years earlier and had nearly perfect verbatim recall for stories over the same period.[6]

An American named Daniel McCartney, living in the nineteenth century, showed similar prodigious powers. At the age of fifty-four he could still tell instantly what he had been doing on every day since childhood, and could also give the exact date, the weather conditions during the day, and say what he had eaten for breakfast, lunch, and supper on that day. He was also a mathematical prodigy able to give the cube roots of numbers up to millions almost instantly. Yet due to poor vision he could neither read nor write.[7]

Many other similar cases exist, some of them well-known people.

Themistocles remembered the 20,000 names of the citizens of Athens. Xerxes was supposed to be able to recall the 100,000 names of the men in his army. Cardinal Mezzofanti, living in the nineteenth century, was said to be able to speak between seventy and eighty languages, including Latin, Greek, Arabic, Spanish, French, German, Swedish, Portuguese, English, Dutch, Danish, Russian, Polish, Bohemian, Serbian, Hungarian, Turkish, Irish, Welsh, Wallachian, Albanian, Illysian, Sanskrit, Persian, Georgian, Armenian, Hebrew, Chinese, Coptic, Ethiopean, Alyssian, and Amharic. Most of them he could speak fluently.[8]

There were also many Polish Jews called Shass Pollaks who remembered the exact position on the page and the exact page of every word in the twelve large volumes of the Talmud.[9] Indeed, the Talmud was originally handed down solely by memory, as were the even longer Vedic scriptures of ancient India.

HYPNOSIS

Another indication of the phenomenal capacity of human memory comes from experiments on hypnosis. Most people appear to have forgotten much of their early childhood, only a few isolated instances remaining. But in all likelihood the memories have not been erased; it is just that people cannot normally get in contact with them again. When an adult is hypnotized and "taken back" to his early childhood, he will often be able to remember the names of other children in his kindergarten class and be able to give detailed descriptions of them.

David Cheek, from San Francisco, has taken the regression back further and retrieved memories from childbirth itself. He found that his subjects made movements exactly like those of a fetus in childbirth, movements not commonly seen in adults. Cheek himself had been an obstetrician and he conducted an experiment with three adults whom he had delivered twenty years earlier; under hypnosis he took them back to birth. They were then asked for reports of birth experiences, including the positions they took up, which arm extended first, etc. He checked his own notes on the deliveries and found that their descriptions coincided exactly with his own detailed notes of the births.[10]

Cheek also found considerable evidence that people can remember what was said at the time of their birth.[11] As well as throwing more light on the capacity of human memory, this also poses an interesting question: Has language developed sufficiently in the womb for a newborn baby to understand what is being said even if he does not react, or are the words simply stored in memory and understood later?

One of the most amazing examples of memory being retrieved under hypnosis has been reported from Yale University. A bricklayer who ten years previously had worked on a special neo-Gothic building using distinctive bricks was hypnotized and asked to describe a certain brick in a certain wall. He was able to describe the color of the brick, noting that it had been burned a shade too much in the kiln, that it had a purple pebble embedded in the clay in the lower left-hand corner, and that the brick had a slight swelling at the upper right-hand corner that matched the hollow of the brick just above it. The experimenter checked with the actual brick and found that these details, and many others the bricklayer also supplied while under hypnosis, matched perfectly with the brick in question. Moreover, he had laid some two thousand bricks that day, and it is very likely that he would have been able to recall any other of the bricks with equal clarity.[12]

Several police forces are now beginning to use hypnosis in the investigation of crime. In Israel witnesses of terrorist attacks have, under hypnosis, been able to give detailed descriptions of the people involved. Los Angeles police have used hypnosis to solve a number of crimes. In one rape case the victim was able to recall under hypnosis the licence number of her assailant's car.[13]

Under hypnosis people can often recall events that took place while they were apparently unconscious, for example, under an anesthetic during an operation. In one memorable anecdote a woman clearly remembered the surgeon saying, "Well, that takes care of this old bag." She took this to refer to her, though the surgeon was in fact referring to the ovary he had just removed.[14]

In another case reported from Johannesburg a patient accurately recalled that while under deep anesthesia the doctor had exclaimed that it might not be a cyst after all: It may be a cancer![15]

David Cheek likewise found that patients remember a considerable amount of what happens during operations and now uses this to a positive end. He deliberately talks to his patients during anesthesia, giving them positive, optimistic reports on the surgery and suggestions that recovery would be rapid with little pain. He found that the suggestions worked and such patients stayed in the hospital for an average of only eight and a half days, compared with eleven days for patients who were not spoken to under anesthesia.[16]

DREAMS

Further evidence that we may remember far more than we can consciously recall comes from dreams. When people take the trouble to record systematically their own dreams, they may find very detailed memories of the past coming back. Often they may be about episodes they thought had been entirely forgotten. The probable reason why a lot of people do not remember many of their dreams is that there is little association between the world of dreams and the world of daily life. When dreams are suddenly recalled, it is often because of a chance association, and it may well bring back a detailed memory of a dream from several nights or several weeks before. Possibly all our dreams are also recorded in memory, but we do not have the right cues at hand with which to recall them.

DEATH-TYPE EXPERIENCES

Another quite remarkable insight into the capacity of memory comes with the "life review" that some people experience when on the point of death. People who, for example, were rescued from drowning at the very last moment have reported that as they approached death, the whole of their life appeared to flash before them in a moment.

Ten years ago a person suffering a serious heart attack would probably have died. Recent advances in medical treatment have now made it possible to resuscitate a person, even though his heart may have stopped beating for several minutes, and so bring him back from the edge of death. Studies of a number of such cases in which people have temporarily died or been on the brink of death have found many clear instances of this "review" phenomenon. Typical experiences are:

> . . . it was like looking through a volume of my entire life and being able to do it within seconds. It just flashed before me like a motion picture that goes tremendously fast, but I was fully able to see it, and able to comprehend it.

> . . . it shot right by me from the earliest things I can remember right up to the present and it all happened within a short time.

> It was just all there at once, I mean, not one thing at a time, blinking off and on, but it was everything, everything at one time.[17]

An analysis of over a hundred cases of near death from accidents such as mountain-climbing falls, car accidents, and explosions, found that *in half the cases* there was a vivid replay of memory. One woman, who swerved to miss an oncoming car, lost control, and found herself heading toward a bridge pillar, suddenly experienced a dreamlike calm and "saw an endless stream of past experiences—there must have been hundreds—flow through my mind. They were all pleasant. During all of this, time stood still."[18]

Such experiences not only indicate that very little, if anything, is ever forgotten, they also show that the brain can work at speeds many times faster than those to which we are accustomed. Maybe it is because closer to death, the person is freed from the need to keep in touch with the world around him, and the mind starts working at its own natural rate.

DIRECT STIMULATION OF THE BRAIN

Other evidence for the virtually unlimited capacity of human memory comes from the studies of Wilder Penfield and his colleagues at the Montreal Neurological Institute. Because there are no pain receptors inside the brain itself, operations on the brain are often performed with only a local anesthetic to numb the skull, with the patient remaining fully conscious throughout the surgery. During one thousand brain operations between 1936 and 1960, Penfield and his colleagues used this fact to try and ascertain the specific functions of different areas of the cortex. Using fine electrodes they would stimulate a point of the brain with a small electric current and ask the subject to report what he experienced. They found that when they stimulated areas on the side of the brain—what is called the temporal cortex—the patient often reported specific experiences of the past.

The fantastic wealth of detail that Penfield was able to bring forth again suggests that our brains may well be recording everything that happens. The memories elicited were rich in detail, very vivid, and could come from any part of the person's life. Patients would often feel that they were "there," reliving the scene as it happened, often with sight, sound, smell, and touch all present and integrated. One patient, for example, reported:

I was in an office somewhere. I could see the desk. I was there and someone was calling to me—a man leaning on a desk with a pencil in his hand.[19]

Moving the electrode just one millimeter away would usually bring forth a completely different memory.[20]

It is unlikely that the points stimulated were the points at which those specific memories were recorded. The points stimulated were in the "association areas" of the cortex, areas involved in the processing and integration of information, and it is most likely that the stimulation was creating a specific pattern of electrical activity that corresponded to a retrieval cue for a specific memory. The memory itself, though, as we saw in the previous chapter, is very probably distributed throughout the brain.

Each of the lines of evidence discussed in this chapter show that we remember far more than we may ordinarily be aware of. Taken together, they suggest that our memories are vastly greater than we usually imagine. They do not prove we remember everything, but given that the brain has sufficient capacity to do so, it is a possibility.

Figure 51

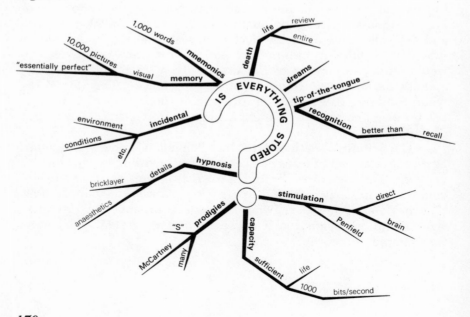

13.
Note Taking

How are ideas linked?
What are key words?
Can note taking be improved?
Are mind maps the answer?
How are mind maps made?
When are mind maps used?

As noted in chapter 1, the human brain is very different from a computer. Whereas a computer works in a linear, step-by-step fashion—albeit very fast—the brain works associatively as well as linearly, carrying on thousands of different processes at the same time, comparing, integrating, and synthesizing as it goes. Thus a person often finds that in conversation his mind is not behaving linearly but racing on in different directions, exploring new ideas and the ramifications of what is being said, and at the same time taking in subtle changes in intonation, body position, facial expression, the eyes, etc., as well as the linear sequence of words.

Association plays a dominant role in nearly every mental function, and words themselves are no exception. Every single word has numerous links attaching it to other ideas and concepts. You have only to take a simple word and start writing down any associations that come to your mind to see that this is true. Given only a minute or two, most people will quickly generate ten or twenty different associations to the word. And these ten or twenty associations are by no means exhaustive. The same word given to ten different people will usually produce sets of associations with very few words in common. Even nonsense syllables have associations. *Boc* is meaningless according to the dictionary, but sit down with a paper and pencil and it is easy to generate several different associations.

Considerable use of this associative power of words is made in creative writing. Part of the art of creative writing is to produce associative images that go beyond the text itself. These offshoots are not linear; they have no well-defined temporal sequence but occur while one is reading, in parallel. Both the writing or reading of such a text tends to make fuller use of the right half of the mind. Scientific writing, on the other hand, tends to be primarily linear, making more use of the left hemisphere. The aim of a scientific paper is not to produce numerous images and send the mind soaring off on other ideas, but to be as specific and linear as possible so that only the one desired idea comes across.

KEY WORDS

We saw earlier that words that had greater significance, had greater meaning, were more outstanding, and generated stronger images were very much easier to remember. When we read, we automatically pick out these more memorable words from the text, and the rest of the material is generally forgotten within a second or two. Thus, take the following sentence: "Astronomers are now suggesting that black holes may not, after all, be entirely black, but may in fact be capable of radiating energy." The key ideas in this sentence, the words that are most memorable and contain the essence of the sentence, are *astronomers, black holes, not black, radiating energy*. The rest of the words are merely grammatical constructions and emphasis; they are not necessary for recall.

Key words tend to be the nouns and verbs in a sentence—though sometimes adjectives and adverbs may be significant enough to become key words. Key words are generally concrete rather than abstract. It has been found that concrete words generate images faster than abstract words—one and a half seconds faster on the average—and that the images they generate are richer and have more associations.[1] For this reason they are better remembered.

In a study by Michael Howe at Exeter University students' notes were examined and the ratio of key words to non–key words measured. It was found that the higher the percentage of key words present in the notes, the better was the recall.[2] Because of their greater meaningful content key words "lock up" more information in memory and are "keys" to recalling the ideas. In the foregoing case you have only to recall the two keys *black holes* and *radiating energy* to unlock the memory of the main idea contained in the sentence.

So that you can get a feel of key words, go back and count how many words in the above three paragraphs of this chapter are actually key words.*

When a young child begins to speak, he starts with key words, stringing them together directly—for example "John ball," or "Susan tired." It is not until later that sentences are expanded and non–key words included to give expressions such as "I want to play with the ball" or "Susan is feeling tired."

We see the same pattern in the historical development of written language. The earlier written languages tended to contain a much higher percentage of key words. This was probably because there was a shortage of material on which to write, scribes being limited to carving on stone or writing on bark or dried leaves; hence it was essential to use words as efficiently as possible. Thus in a Latin sentence there are a higher proportion of nouns and verbs; prepositions, conjunctions, and pronouns are often integrated into the word endings—hence the more complex grammatical structure of Latin. If we go back further to the ancient Indian language of Sanskrit, we find that sentences consist almost entirely of key words. Yet in Sanskrit there is no loss of meaning or significance; if anything, it is more flexible than modern languages.

KEY WORDS AND NOTE TAKING

Although people such as "S" could remember everything that was said without writing anything down, most people find that taking notes helps their recall. Michael Howe in his investigation of students' notes found that items that were noted were six times as likely to be remembered as items that were not written down.[3]

*About thirty.

Taking notes serves several functions besides the simple storage of information. Indeed, simply getting every word down without attention to meaning and significance can often interfere with subsequent memory of the material. In addition to being a means of storing information, taking notes (as opposed to mere copying) performs the valuable functions of

> encoding the information;
> imposing organization upon the material;
> allowing associations, inferences, and interpretations to be jotted down;
> bringing attention to what is important; and
> bringing attention to what is written.

These are all very valuable for later recall. It has also been shown that the longer the lecture or study session, the more valuable are notes.[4]

The subject of note taking is, however, rarely studied, let alone taught. Thus, although much of a student's life is concerned with the taking of notes, he is seldom, if ever, given much guidance on how best to do so. Most people start out by writing grammatically correct phrases and sentences. Over time they gradually refine these, developing their own shorthand notation and abbreviations in order to make the notes more efficient, making important items outstanding by underlining. Even so, conventional notes still tend to be very cumbersome and inefficient compared with what is possible with key-word notes. When students are asked to take notes in whatever way they have found to be the most efficient and effective, it is usually found that only 5 to 10 percent of the words written are actually key words.

Since it is the key words that are remembered, notes such as those in Figure 52 have a number of serious disadvantages:

1. Time and energy are wasted in taking the notes.

2. Other information may be missed while the student is busy noting.

3. Time is wasted reading the notes.

4. Further time is wasted sorting out key words from irrelevant words.

As well as serving as an (information storage) system, (notes) also allow one to (encode) the information, (organise) it, make (associations) and (inferences) and think about what is (significant.)

Figure 52 Conventional linear notes. Only the key concepts (circled) are really necessary.

5.   Key words are dissociated (a) visually, (b) in time—this decreases comprehension and memory.

6.   The attention wanders more easily.

7.   Review is lengthy and laborious.

In short, conventional notes are more like a system to aid forgetting rather than a system to help remembering.

Since we do not remember complete sentences, it is a waste of time to write them down. It is the key words that are recalled, and it is the key words that should be abstracted and recorded. In selecting the key words, a person is brought into active contact with the information. He is not simply copying down material in a semiconscious manner but is becoming immediately aware of the meaning and significance of the ideas, analyzing them, and forming images and associations between them. The memory process is thereby given tremendous help.

MIND MAPS

Most people who have ever had difficulty remembering something from their notes have probably noticed that they may well be able to remember where it had been written on the page, with what other ideas it was associated, and any outstanding visual associations, such as accompanying diagrams. The memory is in fact working excellently, recalling all possible associations, meaningful connections, and outstanding factors. The reason that the recall is difficult is because the notes were not initially made with an awareness of what would be good for recall.

Notes in neat lines may be highly commendable as far as the writing of essays is concerned, but they offer little foothold for memory. In the system of mind maps, developed by Buzan,[5] all the various factors that enhance recall have been brought together in order to produce a much more effective system of note taking. To make a mind map one starts in the center of the paper, with the major idea, and works outward in all directions, producing a growing and organized structure composed of key words and key images. (See, for example, the summary mind maps at the end of each chapter.)

Organization, association, clustering, visual memory, outstandingness, and other phenomena that naturally facilitate human memory can be used to make mind maps more effective in the following ways:

Organization. The brain spontaneously imposes its own subjective organization on all the material it remembers. Even when the material is completely random, subjective organization aids recall. The more we deliberately organize the material, the more we are helping the memory process. In making mind maps the organization is made concrete in the structure of the pattern.

Moreover, the very activity of organizing the material is itself helpful to memory. Having to work out where a given piece of information fits into the pattern as a whole, and how it interconnects with other areas, brings you into more immediate contact with the note-taking process than do straightforward linear notes. This increases the depth of processing and so makes for better memory.

The fact that mind maps often take on an organiclike structure reflects their organized nature. An organism is an organized array of living cells. A billion cells put together in a jar do not create an organism; it is the interrelation and organization of the elements that is important. In the same way, it is the organization and interrelation of

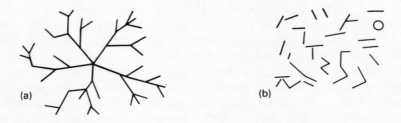

Figure 53 (a) Structured pattern; (b) less structured pattern.

the elements in the notes that give mind maps their organic structure and their value.

Key Words. Key-word notes are far more effective than phrases or sentences. The brain automatically drops the inessentials, and we should do the same in note taking. So only record the key ideas. This has several additional advantages:

1. The bulk is significantly reduced.

2. The recorded words are rich in imagery.

3. The very act of extracting the key words involves you more in understanding the material and further increases the depth of processing.

Association. Since words and ideas that are closely associated are recalled together, it helps memory if they are put together visually in the notes. This reinforces the association and results in a natural clustering of ideas into themes.

Since all the ideas in any one set of notes will be related to the theme of the notes, it is best to start with a key word for the overall theme in the center of the page. The center should be a strong visual image so that everything in the pattern is associated with it.

Clustering. As well as having a well-defined center, a mind map will naturally tend to have a number of subcenters radiating from it, and from these a number of sub-subcenters, and so on. In most practical situations there are seldom more than seven or eight subcenters, so the material can be organized into a number of easily remembered chunks. Similarly, the number of chunks radiating from each subcenter again will usually be within the immediate memory capacity.

Visual Memory. Since visual images are much better recalled than words, the more visual the mind map is made, the better. This can be done in a number of ways:

1. Each word should be printed rather than written in script. This gives the word a clearer visual image, makes it more easily remembered and less likely to be confused with other words. Lower-case letters are better than capitals, since they are more easily read and give better shape recognition.[6] However, where

the word is to be made more outstanding, capitals can be used with good effect.

2. Each of the key words should be printed on a line and each of the lines joined to other lines to give structure to the pattern. The initial inclination might be to join the words up by lines, but this is less flexible. It creates a weaker visual structure than does writing words along the lines themselves, and tends to produce networks that close in on themselves, making additions difficult.

3. Colored images are much better remembered than black and white ones. Therefore, use as many colors as possible in a mind map. Different colors can be used for different themes. They can also be used to make specific parts of the map outstanding. The more daring you are with color, the better.

4. The mind maps can be given depth. The centers and subcenters can be given three-dimensional shapes, providing the map with a more solid visual structure.

5. Use other images besides words. Whenever a simple visual image comes to mind, use it. If diagrams and pictures are part of the material, include them as part of the pattern.

6. Use arrows to link and associate different areas in the pattern.

7. Groups of words can be outlined or their background shaded to hold them together as a unit.

Outstandingness. Whenever an item is outstanding in some way or another, it is better remembered. When you make mind maps, every center should be unique; you should use different key words, different colors, and different shapes. Wherever parts of the pattern stand out, they will be better remembered.

Conscious Involvement. The more you participate actively and consciously in the note-taking process, the better. Mind maps intrinsically are more fun and spontaneously hold the attention more. Wherever possible, think of original ways in which to note the material. The greater the originality and creativity, the greater the interest, and the better the memory. Wherever you have been particularly creative in a pattern, you will always remember that part well. Try to be creative throughout.

With conventional linear notes spontaneous associations have to be held over until you reach the place where they are relevant, and by then the idea may well have been forgotten. Because mind maps are growing the whole time in all directions, associations can be included as soon as they arise. With mind maps the faster you go, the better.

Everybody's memory is a personal affair. We each have our own associations and our own mnemonics. So allow your pattern to be personal, including your own codes and symbols as much as possible. Remember only to use key words and key images. When you look for key words, always remember that they are primarily nouns, and they contain the essential substance of an idea. It might be a good exercise to go back and pick out the key points on mind mapping from the last 4 pages. As you do so, compare them with the mind map in Figure 54, which contains the basic information contained in these pages. As well as showing you how a mind map is created, it will also serve as a very useful review of this section.

WHY USE MIND MAPS?

You will notice that mind maps are reminiscent of the semantic memory structures we looked at on pages 105–106. The similarity is no accident. Since they include as many of the natural memory processes as possible, the mind maps are beginning to take on the same structure as that of the memory itself. A mind map works in the same manner as the brain itself. It is therefore an excellent interface between the brain and the written or spoken word.

Paradoxically one of the greatest advantages of mind maps is that they are seldom needed again. The very act of constructing a map is itself so effective in fixing ideas in memory that very often a whole map can be recalled without going back to it at all. A mind map is so strongly visual and uses so many of the natural functions of memory that frequently it can be simply read off in the "mind's eye."

APPLICATIONS OF MIND MAPS

Whenever information is being taken in, mind maps help organize it into a form that is easily assimilated by the brain and easily remembered. Thus they can be used for noting books, lectures, meetings, interviews, telephone conversations, etc. (fig. 55).

Whenever information is being retrieved from memory, mind maps allow ideas to be quickly noted as they occur, in an organized manner, obviating the relatively laborious process of forming neat sentences and writing them out in full. They therefore serve as a quick and efficient means of review, and so keep recall at a high level.

In a study of note taking in which recall was tested after review, it was found that good notes were "definitely useful for review, but poor notes were not."[7] Howe compared the review value of mind maps using shape, color, boxes, and different letterings with ordinary prose notes and found that recall rose by 50 percent with mind maps.[8]

In another instance a college lecturer in English was concerned that "of the 300 or so books I have read in the last 10 years on Theology, Philosophy, Psychology, Health, Nutrition and Literature, only the haziest of notions of their contents remained in my memory. And yet I had understood almost everything in these books when I read them. . . . [I now realize] understanding is *not* remembering." Using mind maps and a systematic procedure of review and rereview, he reports that "in two days I had three or four patterns of all I needed from the book. . . . It was interesting to find a note at the end of the book saying that it had taken me two weeks to read it in 1969. From two weeks to two days, *with* [mind maps], was quite an improvement."[9]

Because of the large amount of association involved in mind maps, they can be very creative; they tend to generate new ideas and associations that have not been thought of before. Every item in a map is in effect the center of another map, and one could go on generating maps *ad infinitum.*

Mind maps are very valuable in any planning or organization, whether it is of books, reports, lectures, meetings, study, daily tasks, or future activities. In this case do not try to put the material into a linear form until all the relevant information has been retrieved and incorporated into the pattern. Then go over the pattern labeling the branches (1), (2), (3), etc., according to whatever order seems appropriate. By leaving the linearization to last, you avoid the messy problems that arise

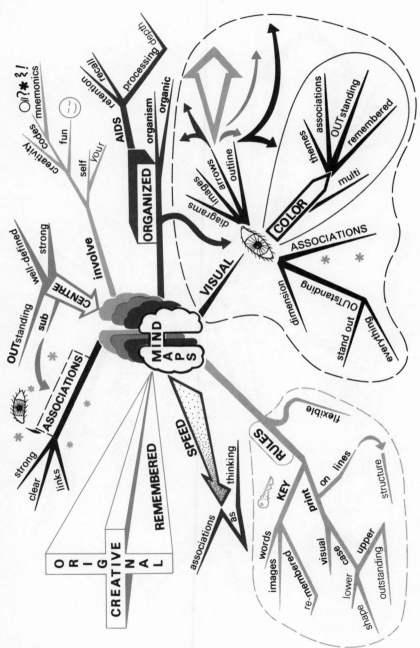

Figure 54 Mind maps on mind-mapping.

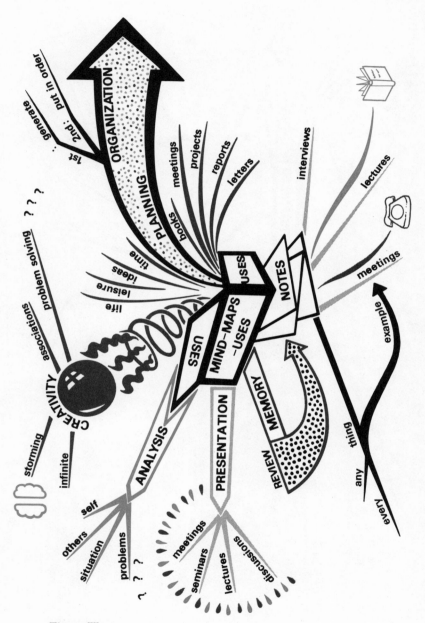

Figure 55

in lists when you start shuffling things around as you recall later points.

The creative potential of a mind map is very useful in brainstorming, either individually or in groups. If you are looking for a solution to a problem, you need only start with the basic problem as the center and generate associations and ideas from it in order to arrive at a large number of different possible approaches, many of which you would never have thought of if you had approached the problem linearly. In this situation do not discard "useless" solutions immediately. Put them into the pattern, as they may themselves later generate useful associations.

Mind maps can also be valuable in giving presentations and lectures. If the key points to be covered are put up in front of the group, it makes it easier for the others to follow. It also helps the lecturer keep to his themes and know where he is going (fig. 56).

Mind maps can be used with great effectiveness in almost any instance where one would normally write or jot down words. Even a book, which is a long linear list of ideas when it appears in print, can be approached as a series of mind maps in the writing stage. This book, for example, was not written from beginning to end as a series of sentences; it was drawn as a set of 7 major mind maps, springing from which came some 150 minor maps. All of the basic work was done in mind-map form. It was only when the book was finally being prepared for printing that it was transposed into a linear form.

In short, mind maps can be used in virtually any situation where there is a flow of information between the mind and the outside world, no matter which direction the flow (fig. 57).

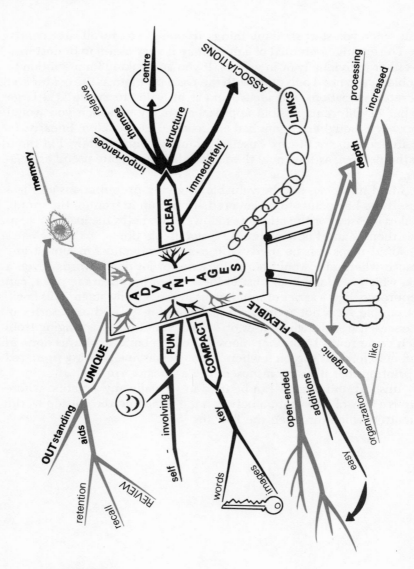

Figure 56

184

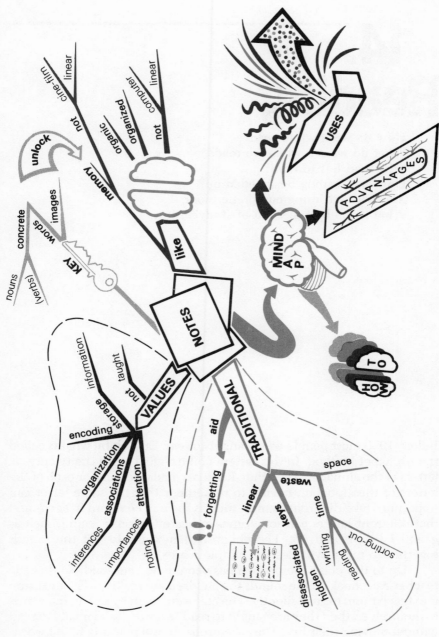

Figure 57

14. Reading

How do we learn to read?
What do we see when we read?
Why read left to right?
How can reading be speeded up?
And without losing comprehension?
What is the best method of study?

Before 1950 most people were taught to read English by what is called the Alphabet Method. In this system children first learn the twenty-six letters of the alphabet. They then learn particular sounds for each of the letters of the alphabet, having to remember that the same letter can sometimes take different sounds, such as the *c* in *civil* and in *cavil,* and that different letters can sometimes indicate the same sound, such as *g* and *j* in *gib* and *jib.* The children then learn to put the sounds together to make syllables and simple words.

Up to this point the process has been done "out loud" so that the teacher can check on the sounds the children are making. The next step is to teach them to read silently. The children begin by saying the words to themselves, then they are taught to read "silently," and finally to read without moving their lips. They are probably still pointing to the words they read, and so the last stage in this method is to persuade the children to stop pointing at the words and to read with their eyes alone.

Further progress is made by giving the child progressively more complex books, expanding his vocabulary and knowledge of grammar, so that by the time he leaves junior high school he can hopefully read most of the material he encounters.

Unfortunately this method has several disadvantages. A major handicap is the complex relationship of the letters and the sounds they represent, which slow down a child's rate of learning. As one reading teacher put it, "*Hay*' is for 'apple,' *bee* is for 'book,' *Sea* is for 'confusion.' "

Since the 1950s a wide variety of techniques have evolved that have attempted to overcome the failing of the Alphabet Method. One of the most common of these is the "Look-Say Method." The child is given pictures of a familiar object, such as a cup, and underneath it in large letters is written its name, *cup*. Initially the child is not taught the alphabet but simple words and their associated sounds and meanings. Other techniques have concentrated on adding extra symbols to the normal alphabet so that there is a more direct relationship between the letters and their sounds. In the "Initial Teaching Alphabet," or i.t.a., the twenty-six letters of the English alphabet are augmented by eighteen additional signs so as to cover most of the phonetic range of speech. And in the Diacritical Marking System the normal alphabet is used with additional signs to indicate how letters should be pronounced. In another system, the Color System, the normal twenty-six-letter alphabet is used and each letter is printed in one of forty-eight different colors, each color indicating a specific sound. The current trend is toward combining the best elements of each system, making full use of imagery, color, association, and other factors that help learning.

All these systems undoubtedly have their own advantages, but they are concerned only with teaching basic recognition of letters and words. They do not of themselves help children to increase their "silent reading" speed, to read more effectively, nor to remember what they read.

Children are normally considered to have learned to read once they are reading silently without moving their lips and without tracing the words with their fingers. But in terms of the fantastic amount of visual information that the brain can take in and retain, they are all very poor readers.

Most of us, even as adults, "hear" the words we are reading. We may not go so far as to subvocalize the words—that is, "say" them to ourselves—but the sound of the word is still there. Most people cannot "hear" more than around two hundred to three hundred words per minute, and this rate becomes a limit to our normal reading speed. We have simply not been taught how to read visually. This would speed up our reading to several thousand words per minute. Nor have we been taught how to maximize both our comprehension and our retention of what is read. Learning to read is seen as learning to recognize the letters and put them into words. Yet these are really only the first stages in the reading process.

The word *reading* comes from the Anglo-Saxon *raedan,* "to advise oneself." It does not mean just the ability to interpret the symbols on a page and know the words they form; it is also the ability to advise oneself of the meaning and significance of what is being seen. Buzan, who advocates a similar broader interpretation of reading, defines it as a seven-stage process:

1. Assimilation of the visual data by the eye

2. Recognition of the letters and words

3. Understanding; relating the words being read to the meaning of the passage as a whole

4. Comprehension; relating the information to one's whole body of knowledge

5. Storing the information in memory efficiently and effectively

6. Recalling the information where and when it is needed

7. Making effective use of the information and communicating it successfully to others; and also communicating it to oneself, that is, thinking clearly[1]

By this definition we can see that most standard approaches to reading deal mainly with the first two stages. Comprehension tests may measure the third and fourth to some extent, but children are given little help on *how* to comprehend and integrate the material properly, nor on how to ensure it is remembered.

THE EYE AND ITS MOVEMENTS

In order to understand how we read and how reading may be improved, we must first look a little at how the eye works.

Light entering the eye is focused by the lens onto the retina, which lines the inside of the eye. The retina itself consists of hundreds of millions of tiny cells responsive to light—equivalent to the population of the U.S.A. squeezed onto a postage stamp. Some cells, the cones, respond to specific colors; others, the rods, to the overall light intensity. These cells are connected to a web of nerves extending over the retina, and these nerves relay information directly back to the brain. In fact, the retina is not really separate from the brain, it should be properly thought of as an extension of the cortex.

The center of the retina, called the fovea, is a small area in which the cells are much more tightly packed. These two thousand cones are packed into an area less than one tenth of a millimeter square. The perception of images falling on the fovea is much sharper and finer than elsewhere on the retina. When we are looking directly at something,

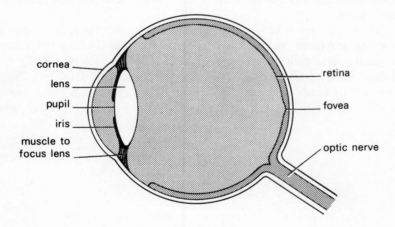

Figure 58 Simplified diagram of the human eye. The retina contains several hundred million light-sensitive cells. They are most closely packed at the fovea, the center of the visual field where vision is most acute (a quarter of a million cells per square millimeter).

the light from that object is falling on the fovea. The fovea sees less than one forty-thousandth of the total visual field. If you are looking at a line of print from a distance of two feet, only about three letters are in this central field of vision, and only those few letters are seen perfectly at any one time. The further images are from the fovea, the less clear the vision becomes, until at the periphery of the visual field you receive only very faint visual impressions.

The fact that we see most clearly that which we are looking at directly has two important implications for reading:

1. The eye must move along the text so that different parts of the line are brought into focus at the fovea.

2. To see anything clearly, the eye actually has to stop moving for a fraction of a second in order that a still image can rest on the fovea and be transmitted back to the brain.

Thus the eye takes short gulps of information. In between it is not actually seeing anything; it is moving from one point to another. We do not notice these jumps because the information is held over in the brain and integrated from one fixation to the next so that we can perceive a smooth flow.

The first person to discover that the eye did not move smoothly was Professor Javal, at the University of Paris, in 1879—that historic year again. Javal called these movements *saccades,* French for "jerks," and since then psychologists have talked of these movements as "saccadic eye movements." The eye is rarely still for more than half a second.

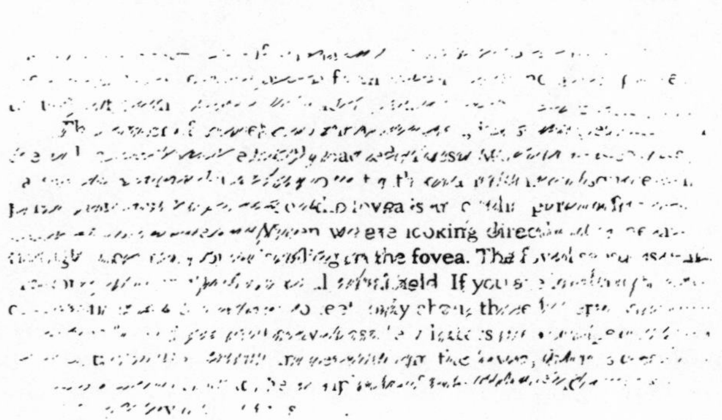

Figure 59 Print as seen by the eye.

Even when you feel the eye is completely still (as when you look steadily at the period at the end of this sentence), it will in fact be making a number of small movements around the dot. In fact, if the eye were not continually shifting in this way, the image would rapidly fade and disappear.

EYE MOVEMENTS IN READING

The first attempts to carry out a detailed study on the speed of the eye movements, the duration of the stopovers, and the number of fixations per line were by Edmund Huey, who published his pioneering work, *The Psychology and Pedagogy of Reading,* in 1908.[2] To this day it remains one of the most comprehensive and accessible studies on reading.

Huey found that the eye takes about a quarter of a second to move from one point of fixation to the next. Thus it is limited to about four fixations per second. Each fixation of an average reader will take in two or three words, so that to read a line of this book probably takes between three and six fixations. The duration of the stops and the length of the jumps will vary considerably, according to both the material being read and the individual's skill. The more skilled the reader, the more will be taken in by a single fixation.

You can see for yourself the way the eye moves during reading by asking a friend to read from a book, holding it up in the manner shown in Figure 60 so that you can watch the eyes as they move along the line.

The visual information is picked up by the eye in a few hundredths of a second, and is quickly sent on its way to the brain. The brain itself takes between a quarter and a half of a second to process and recognize the visual data. While this is taking place, the eye is already moving on to the next point of fixation, and often on to further fixation points. Thus the eye will usually be a phrase or two ahead of what one is conscious of reading.

Although the sharpest perception occurs at the fovea, images that are off-center are still seen but less clearly. This off-center vision is called peripheral vision. We often talk of it as "seeing out of the corner of the eye."

Peripheral vision performs a most valuable function during reading. Words that lie ahead of the current point of fixation will be partially received by the eye and transmitted to the brain. On the basis of this slightly blurred view of what is coming, the brain will tell the eye where

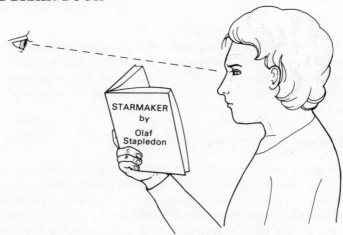

Figure 60 Watch someone reading and observe his eye movements.

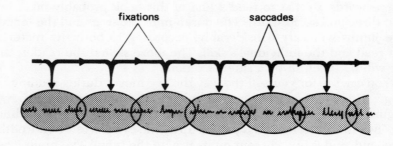

Figure 61 The eye moves along a line of print in steps, taking in the section of the line which is at the center of vision at each fixation.

to move to next. Thus the eye does not move along the line in a regular series of jumps but skips redundant words and concentrates on the most useful and distinguishing parts of the text.

Most readers do not continue to read along the line in a steady sequence. Much of the time their eyes are jumping back to check on words already "read," and even on words in the preceding line. This back-skipping is called regression. Generally the more skilled the reader, the less regression there is. In a study of five thousand readers it was found that 25 percent of the eye movements made by children were regressive, as were 15 percent of those made by adults.[3] Many of these regressive movements are unnecessary. They are not based on lack of comprehension so much as apprehension and fear that one may have missed something.

Huey found that the fixation points tend to be concentrated toward the middle of a line of print. When the eye goes to a new line, it does not usually start at the beginning; instead it starts a word or two in from the edge. The brain has a good idea of what is to come from the sense of the previous lines and only needs to check with peripheral vision that the first few words are as anticipated. Similarly the eye usually makes its last fixation a word or two short of the end of a line, again making use of peripheral vision to check that the last few words are as expected.

WHY READ LEFT TO RIGHT?

What we see to our left (the left visual field) falls on the right retina of each eye and is transmitted to the right side of the brain. Conversely, the right visual field of each eye is transmitted to the left side of the

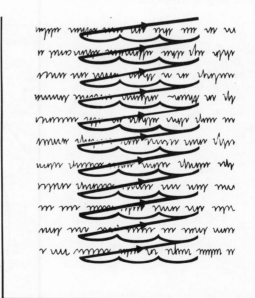

Figure 62 Typical eye movements down a page of print, concentrated more toward center of page.

brain. Since the left hemisphere is better at verbal tasks, whatever lies in the right visual field will have its verbal content processed more quickly than that which lies in the left. Experiments have shown that when words are briefly flashed to either the left or right visual fields, the words flashed to the right are recognized more quickly than those flashed to the left.[6]

If a person is reading from left to right, the material that has not yet been read, but which is nevertheless being processed peripherally, is being received by the left side of the brain, more specialized at verbal processing. Reading right to left, on the other hand, results in the material yet to be read being processed by the right hemisphere, which is not as good at verbal tasks, with the result that the brain would have a poorer idea of what is to come.

This implies that it is intrinsically easier to read languages written from left to right. Studies of different systems have shown that not only is left-right reading more efficient, it is also better for the brain itself. The two halves of the brain of the left-to-right readers become more adept at working together and better able to integrate verbal and spatial tasks. The two halves of the right-to-left readers' brains did not work together so well.[5]

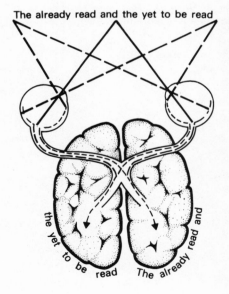

Figure 63 Schematic diagram of the visual processing of a line of text. When reading left to right, the material yet to be read is taken in with peripheral vision and analyzed for content by the linguistic left hemisphere. This helps the brain decide the best next point of fixation and increases the efficiency of reading.

RECOGNITION

Once the visual information has been received by the brain, it has to be recognized and given meaning. As soon as the data arrive at the visual cortex at the back of the brain, they undergo feature analysis. The data are broken up into their basic constituents of lines, curves, and angles, the whole process taking only a few hundreths of a second.

To some extent, letters are recognized on this basis. Experiments have shown that when letters are briefly flashed onto a screen and a person is asked to call out what the letter was, any wrong letters called out tend to be letters with similar features; a *P,* for example, may be confused with a *B,* or an *F.* [6] Further evidence for feature recognition comes from the finding that when a person is required to search for a particular letter among a series of letters, he takes much longer when the other letters contain similar features to the letter searched for. [7]

Feature analysis cannot, however, explain how 𝒜 ⤲ ℸ *a* ⧉ ⧸ are all easily recognized as the letter *A.* Here the features involved vary considerably from one typeface to the next. It appears that letters are also recognized holistically, that is, as informational wholes in their own right.

Not only are individual letters recognized holistically, but common words are often recognized and treated as single units. As far back as 1886 it was discovered that people were better at recognizing a series of letters flashed briefly before them if the letters formed meaningful words. [8] It has also been found that a person who is a little too far away from a word to be able to recognize the individual letters can still recognize the word as a whole. [9] Words can also be recognized when they are in peripheral vision and the individual letters are too blurred to be recognized. [10] As with letters, words that have their own characteristic shape are more easily recognized than words with shapes similar to others.

Earlier it was shown that immediate memory span depends on the number of "chunks" rather than the information content. The same is true of reading. When we read, we can take in about five chunks at a time. A chunk may be a single letter, a syllable, a word, or even a small phrase. The more meaningful the material, the easier it is to understand, and the larger will be the chunks. Strings of random letters such as *krplztgf* are read very slowly, letter by letter. Nonsense words such as *bidnolleck* that approximate English words in structure will probably be read syllable by syllable. A phrase such as *the differentiated effects of temporal neocortical resections on overtrained and nonovertrained visual habits in monkeys (sic)* that is difficult to understand will be read word by word. But an easy passage will be "chunked" into groups of words and phrases.

REDUNDANCY

There is a large amount of redundancy in printed English, and much of the material can often be omitted without any loss in meaning. Much of each letter's structure is redundant and phrases can still be read ~v~n th~u~h parts of ~a~h letter may be missing The brain knows that only certain arrangements of lines and curves are going to occur and fits in the letters according to the general gist of the whole thing. It is this redundancy that allows a pharmacist to read a doctor's prescription. The reason many people find doctor's prescriptions illegible is that they are searching for the correct word out of millions of possibilities. The pharmacist making up the prescription has only to pick the right word from a few hundred possibilities. This means that the writing need contain less information and that more of it is redundant.

Not only can parts of the letters be omitted, but whole letters can be dropped. Sntncs wtht vwls cn b rd, and so can th.se wi.h eve.y fif.h let.er mi.sing. Similarly every fifth word . . . be omitted from a . . . without losing the meaning. The general meaning and grammatical structure of a sentence, help the reader anticipate what is to follow. A sentence that begins "We write more words than necessary for . . ." is unlikely to be followed by words such as *cat, visitors, plastic,* or *philodendron.* It is much more likely to be followed by such words as *comprehension, recognition,* or *understanding.* The reader has to determine merely whether the word is one out of ten rather than one out of millions. Only a little information is needed, and this information can usually be gained from peripheral vision, without having to fixate upon the word itself.

By helping us anticipate what is to come, redundancy speeds up the reading process. We read what we expert to read, and the faster, more expect reader will probably have corrected the errors in this sentence without realizing it.

A very simple and convenient way of examining the normal reading process is to read material upside down. This slows down the process sufficiently for you to begin to become aware of the operations involved.

At first it seems very strange. You may start by reading syllable by syllable, much as a child does at first, then after a few lines you begin to take in complete words more easily, and later simple phrases become readable. As you continue, you will find your reading speeding up and will probably notice that you do not read the whole of a word—probably the first letter or two and the last letter or two are sufficient and you guess at the rest, only coming back to it if in the light of the rest of the sentence you realize your guess was wrong. And where you come across phrases that are very common, you will find yourself reading them quite rapidly. You may also begin to notice how the eye fixates on the most distinguishing features of a word or phrase. By slowing down the reading process in this matter you become directly aware of the importance of context. If you continue to practice like this for ten minutes or more, you will find reading steadily speeding up as you get more proficient at reading larger chunks at a time.

SKILLED READING

Reading speed can be increased considerably by

eliminating regression;
expanding the focus of fixation;
making greater use of peripheral vision;
making greater use of redundancy;
increasing motivation;
previewing the material; and
using the right side of the brain as much as the left.

Early speed-reading techniques were based on tachistoscope training. A tachistoscope is an instrument for presenting very brief flashes of a picture. In speed-reading techniques the tachistoscope gives a brief glimpse of a few words from a line and then moves on to show the next few words. Regression becomes impossible, and since more words are included in each flash, the subject is forced to take in progressively larger units with each fixation. Using such techniques it is possible to increase a person's reading speed from 250 or so words per minute to 500 or 600 words per minute.

Doubling your reading speed may sound a considerable achievement, but it is not, in fact, that large an increase. With modern techniques of skilled reading it is possible to increase your rate to 2,000 or more words per minute. Two limiting factors in the tachistoscopic approach are that it does not develop peripheral vision, nor does it make use of many of the findings about how we assimilate and recognize written material.[11]

VISUAL GUIDES

A visual guide is a pointer, such as the blunt end of a pencil or a fingertip, moved along underneath a line of print. To many people it might seem a backward step to start using a visual guide again. Were we not taught very early on at school that pointing to the words as we read only slows us down? How then is it being claimed to speed up reading?

Try moving your finger backward and forward as fast as possible. You will probably find you can do so at least five times a second, which is ten times faster than the eyes normally move along a line of print. So following the finger cannot in itself slow down reading. The reason children are discouraged from pointing to the words as they read them is that stopping to point *at each individual word* can indeed slow up the process. But if instead of pointing at each word the finger is moved along smoothly underneath the line of text, it can actually speed up reading.

A visual guide improves reading in three ways:

1. If the eye is trained to follow the visual guide, then most unnecessary back-skipping is eliminated.

2. Deliberately speeding up the visual guide will help the eye to move along faster.

3. The number of fixations is limited to about four or five per second. As the eye moves faster, it is encouraged to take in more words with each fixation. This increases the meaningful content of the material so that comprehension actually improves.

A visual guide used in this way in practical situations has been found to increase reading speeds by an average of 50 percent.[12] In one study it was shown that a visual guide halved regression (from 1.37 back-skips per ten words to 0.77) and increased the span of fixation by 60 percent (from 2.15 words to 3.50 words). Together these two improvements led to an increase in speed from 274 words per minute to 465 words per minute.[13] This is already approaching the level normally attained by several weeks of tachistoscopic training!

EXPANDED FOCUS

Since written English is highly redundant, a large proportion of the information in a text can be absorbed through peripheral vision. Words that are highly likely to occur in a given context do not have to be checked by looking directly at them—peripheral vision can check that they are what is expected even while the eye is fixating elsewhere. Thus, many skilled readers do not read along each line but read from side to side of the center of the page, taking in most of a line in one glance.

The central area of clear vision extends not only in a horizontal direction but also vertically. Although we may not realize it, when we look at a word in a line, we are also getting a fairly clear impression of the words a line or two above and below. Very fast readers make use of this and can take in two or more lines with one fixation.

Visual guides are again very useful for developing peripheral vision. Instead of moving the guide along individual lines, move it down the middle of the page, following it with the eye. The high redundancy in written language often allows you to use the incomplete peripheral information and still gain as much understanding as you would by fixating on each word or phrase.

Making a fuller use of peripheral vision, the skilled reader is able to get a better idea of the general sense of what is to follow, and this also helps to speed up reading. Furthermore, with this broader overview it is easier to understand and integrate the material. This is why many people find that as soon as they start speed reading, their comprehension actually increases. They have a broader perspective of what they are reading, and since they are reading faster, the short-term memory for what has just been read goes back several sentences further and those words being read are understood within a larger immediate context.

The importance of context in aiding both understanding and speed becomes apparent if you try reading the following passage as it stands:

With hocked gems financing him, our hero bravely defied all scornful laughter that tried to prevent his scheme. "Your eyes deceive," he said. "It is like an egg, not a table." Now three sturdy sisters sought proof. Forging along, sometimes through calm vastness, yet more often over turbulent peaks and valleys, days became weeks as many doubters spread fearful rumors about the edge. At last, from nowhere welcomed winged creatures appeared, signifying momentous success.

Each sentence is simple enough; the grammar is straightforward, and the words are common. The reason you probably found yourself reading it slowly was because you simply had very little idea of what it was about. And if you did manage to make sense of it, it was probably only after much time spent reading it several times through (or of looking down here first). But once you know that it is about Christopher Columbus discovering America, you can read it much more easily, much faster, and remember it better.

In addition to the redundancy in letters and words mentioned earlier, whole phrases, and even sentences, are sometimes redundant. Often sentences are only elaborating on other sentences or putting them in different words; they can be omitted without loss of meaning. The efficient reader will recognize this from various clues in the text and skip ahead, checking with just a glance or two that no new information is being added. Since the main theme of a paragraph is often stated at the start, many skilled readers read only the first sentence of a paragraph, doing so with one or two fixations, merely checking the rest of the text with peripheral vision.

Obviously the degree to which skimming is possible depends largely on the type of text being read. In very condensed concise passages it may well be necessary to read every sentence. Conversely, with highly redundant material it may not even be necessary to check each paragraph. The important thing is to be flexible. Go slowly when you need to and fast whenever you want to and the material allows you to.

HIGH-SPEED TRAINING

In high-speed training the reader is forced to scan pages of print at speeds many times faster than normal reading. The reader starts by moving the visual guide as fast as physically possible along each line, not worrying if very little is absorbed. Then he begins moving the guide down the page, increasing the pace every few minutes until he is spending only one second on each page. At this speed very little, if anything will be absorbed. After about five minutes of high-speed training, the person goes back to reading at what he takes to be a normal speed. He will probably find, however, that he is reading at double his usual speed and yet with the same or even greater comprehension.

This training breaks the habit of reading at a set pace. It is rather like driving down a highway at eighty miles an hour for a long period, and then being asked to slow down to thirty miles an hour. If you try to do this without looking at the speedometer, you will probably think you are at thirty when in fact you are still doing fifty.

High-speed training has two other advantages: It encourages you to see the key words in the text; and it brings the right side of the brain into the reading process.

When you first start high-speed training, spending only a second on each page of the book, everything seems to be a blur and nothing is absorbed. But after a few minutes an interesting phenomenon may occur. You may find that a few of the words are in fact being seen. This by itself is not remarkable. What is significant is that the words that are being picked out are generally the nouns and verbs in the text. Moreover they are often the key nouns and verbs. The fact that these words are being picked out implies that, although the page of print is not being consciously read in detail, most of the page is nevertheless being processed by the brain. And being processed in only a second! The high-speed training develops this ability to extract the relevant words from a page.

A person learning to read finds it easy to stop saying the words aloud and not difficult to stop subvocalizing (moving the throat); but many people find it difficult to stop hearing the words they are reading, and this limits their speed to 250 or so words per minute. High-speed training breaks the habit. At a page a second you cannot hear many of the words, but you can still take in the page visually, for visual processing is many times faster. This shift in processing corresponds to a shift from the left hemisphere to the right. When you slow down again to "normal" speeds, the right hemisphere stays enlivened, words continue to be taken in visually, and reading is correspondingly faster. It is only when the shift is made from auditory to visual reading that high speeds become possible. Indeed, it could be said that until you have made this shift, you have not fully learned to read.

Florence Schale, at Northwest University, has integrated many of these different approaches to skilled reading and taught them to large numbers of people. She found that most people were capable of reading at what would normally be considered very high speeds: two thousand or more words per minute. In a study of fifteen hundred people she also found fifteen people who, after suitable training, were capable of reading at even higher rates of twenty thousand words per minute—and still with a comprehension rate of 70 percent or more! (Seventy percent is good: People reading at "normal" speeds or two hundred or three hundred words per minute seldom score better than this.) The most advanced subjects were able to take in two columns of print simultaneously by scanning down the center of the page. The readers themselves did not claim to have "photographic" memory, but they reported that the key words in the passages stood out and that they read enough key words to complete the thoughts of the passage meaningfully. One subject, a fifteen-year-old girl, could even scan material at the rate of eighty thousand words per minute, with 100 percent comprehension![14]

APPLICATION TO STUDY

It is of little value to be able to read at two thousand or even twenty thousand words per minute if half an hour later 90 percent of the information has been forgotten. Reading, as was expressed in the expanded definition on page 188, includes not only the assimilation and recognition of the written material but also understanding, comprehension, retention, recall, and communication.

The principal reason many people find themselves forgetting what they have read is that as children they were rarely given guidance on memory and study. The most common approach to study of a new text is a linear one, typified as the "start and slog" approach. The reader opens the book at page 1 and reads the book through to the end—if, that is, he does not give up out of boredom or fatigue halfway through. This might seem the obvious approach, since most books do appear to start inside the front cover and end just before the back cover. But a linear approach is, in fact, an inefficient use of both the reader's time and knowledge and has a number of serious disadvantages:

- Time is wasted going over material that is already familiar.
- Time is wasted covering material that is irrelevant to the study in question.
- Time may be wasted wading through large chunks of text only to find that the author has conveniently summed up the essence of a chapter in a short summary at the end.

- The reader has no overall perspective until he *finishes* the text, and possibly not even then.
- Association and organization are poor, and this leads to poor recall of the information.
- Any information that is retained is usually disorganized; it is seldom well integrated with the rest of the book nor with the reader's whole body of knowledge.
- Motivation is low and the reader tends to become bored, dull, and tired. The more tired he becomes, the less efficiently he reads, the less he remembers, and the less motivated he will be to read again.

Numerous books have been written on the subject of study, and nearly all agree that a book should be approached as a whole. The reader should start with some sort of plan and overview in order to get a general feel of the ground, setting definite goals and aims, selecting relevant portions, and rejecting irrelevant ones. A linear approach to study is like going shopping by systematically walking along each street, going into every store, and walking through every floor of each store picking up here and there any items required. Holistic study, on the other hand, parallels the normal activity of shopping. One prepares a list of what is required, goes only down the relevant streets, window-shopping as one goes to get a preview of what is available, selecting the few stores that contain all that one needs.

In approaching any sort of study, the following practices will all be valuable:

1. **Plan the session.** Do not just rush into the text, but set aside a definite time and definite areas to be covered.

2. **Review your current knowledge of the subject.** This increases expectancy of what is to come, bringing to the fore the relevant mental hooks, which improves the retention of what is being read. The best way to do this is to make a quick mind map of your current knowledge.

3. **Establish objectives.** This sets the right mental hooks in advance. In addition it helps you select the relevant and reject the irrelevant.

4.   **Overview the material.**   This clarifies the aims and goals and gives you an overall perspective of the subject covered. It also makes use of the "warm-up" effect (see page 89). During overview you should not be reading any of the text itself. Look at:

> **Title and subtitle.**   They are not trivial. Their implications may affect your approach to the book.
>
> **Author.**   If he is known to you already, you have a good idea of the level at which the book will be pitched. You may not need a popularization, for example.
>
> **Date of publication.**   This will indicate whether the material is up to date, where that is pertinent.
>
> **Table of contents.**   Study them carefully. You will begin to have a general feel for the layout of the book and which parts are going to be of greatest interest and relevance.
>
> **Index.**   Indexes are not only valuable for finding passages. Quickly running through the index at this stage will give you a fuller idea of the topics covered and how much attention is paid to each.
>
> **Diagram, pictures, graphs, and other visuals.**   Visual information is better absorbed and remembered than verbal information (see pages 114–115) and often summarizes large portions of text.
>
> **Dust-jacket flaps/back cover.**   These provide a good overview.
>
> **Preface.**   Nearly always written last, it will, if short, often provide an excellent summary, and usually a statement of purpose for the book and/or a note on the author's perspective on the subject.

All the foregoing will probably take a minute of two yet will save you many times this. You will begin to know how much of the book is going to be valuable and will not be wasting time on irrelevancies, repetitions, and that which you already know. If, for example, you practice hang-gliding as a regular hobby and pick up a book entitled *A Guide to Hang-Gliding,* you may well find after a minute's overview that there is nothing in the book new to you.

You will have effectively read the book in a minute and need spend no more time with it.

5. **Preview.** Get a close feel for the book as a whole by flipping through, looking at:

> Beginnings and ends of chapters.
> Subsection headings.
> Summaries the author may have provided.
> Anything else which catches the eye—bold print, italicized sections, etc.

6. **Practice high-speed training.** It is good to precede in-depth study with five minutes of high-speed reading. This not only increases "normal" reading speed but encourages the use of the right side of the brain. During the high-speed training you will be unconsciously absorbing a considerable amount of the text. An extra five minutes here can save an hour or more later.

7. **Study in depth.** This is the stage for filling in details not provided by the overview and preview. Again treat the book as a whole. It will often be more effective to go through the book quickly ten times, gradually building up knowledge, than to slog through from the beginning. Psychologists call this the lag effect. It has been found that when the same information is repeated during the same learning session, the material is better remembered the more separated are the repeated presentations.[15] In addition, difficult passages may often become clear in the light of later sections. In other instances the mind may be working subconsciously on the argument and spontaneously come up with an understanding of it later on. Flexibility is of utmost importance here; different types of books will require different approaches.

8. **Mark and underline.** Despite most people's inhibitions, marking books can be very valuable. Mark the text in preparation for notetaking. If the book is not yours, use a *soft* lead pencil and remove the marks later with a soft eraser; it would take a forensic expert to discover you. If it is your own book, do not be afraid to use different colored pens; it helps memory and distinguishes different themes and topics.

Underlining key words, or otherwise making them more outstanding, has been found to greatly enhance students' performances, resulting in better short-term and long-term comprehension than does straight reading,[16] and also that students who regularly use underlining during reading score significantly higher on recall than those who do not.[17]

9. **Be prepared to reject.** Omit sections that are

> irrelevant;
> already familiar;
> padding;
> repetition;
> outdated; or
> excess examples.

Also reject false arguments. Robert Thouless, in *Straight and Crooked Thinking,* [18] lists thirty-eight dishonest tricks to watch out for. Some of the principal ones are:

> using emotive words to bias the reader
> quoting well-known names to "prove" a point
> denigration of opponents rather than their arguments
> generalization from the particular
> false premises
> undefined sources
> proving by analogy
> misuse of statistics

10. **Take regular breaks.** Taking a five-minute break every thirty or forty minutes increases retention of the material. Break regularly even when the study is going excellently. *Understanding well is not necessarily remembering well.* After each break take a minute to review the previous work. This consolidates the retention. Rest during the break. Especially rest the eyes by cupping them in your palms. The hand should not touch the eye but simply form a little dome over it. This practice soothes the eyes and gives them complete rest.[19]

11. **Make mind maps.** Mind maps increase comprehension and integration of knowledge; they are easier and quicker to make than

conventional notes, are better remembered, and are more fun. After you finish a book, take a five-minute break; then go through the book making detailed pattern notes, relating points to previous knowledge wherever possible. Remember to use color, imagination, outstanding features, shape, outlining, absurdities, etc., as much as possible.

12. **Review.** Regular review consolidates memory. Making detailed mind maps serves as the first immediate review and makes maximum use of the reminiscence effect. It helps integrate the material and gives an overall perspective. Review again, after one day, one week, one month, and six months, by running through your pattern in your head. This ensures that you will remember virtually everything.

The best way to review is again to use mind maps, as described in the previous chapter. At the end of a study session, if you're not already working with a mind map, it is good to prepare comprehensive notes in map form.

The preparation of the mind map can count as the first review, and once that is completed, many of the details will already be firmly implanted in your memory. At the subsequent reviews it is enough to go over the pattern mentally, checking that you can still recall all the details, referring back to the pattern whenever you are vague.

A good way to organize all the reviews is to keep a file of all your mind maps. Each map should be marked with the date of its next review, and they should all be ordered by date. Each day look at the top of the file to see if there are any for review. Once you have reviewed them, put a new date on them and reinsert in the corresponding place in the file. In this way the patterns will automatically arrive at the top as they are needed.

Or, if the patterns are filed by subject, go through all the files regularly to see whether any patterns are due for review.

THE BEST CONDITIONS FOR STUDY

Heat.   Most central heating systems keep the temperature between 68 and 70 degrees Fahrenheit. This may be comfortable as far as the body is concerned, allowing a person to work with only a shirt or cotton dress, but it is a little too warm for the brain. The brain works best when the surroundings are at a temperature of 65 degrees Fahrenheit (18 degrees Celsius). You may need to put some more clothes on if you have been used to working in warmer conditions, but it will be worth it in terms of increased mental clarity.

Light.   The human eye is capable of a remarkable range of adaptation, being able to accommodate variations in intensity of several million fold. Once the eye has adjusted, it can read under the brightest sunlight or by a dim candle flame. In order not to put too heavy a strain on the eyes, however, something in between is more advisable—shade on a bright day, or a well-lit room at night.

Natural daylight is better than artificial illumination. It contains the full range of the visible spectrum and is much more restful as a result. Artificial light tends to give an unbalanced spectrum, and some forms of fluorescent lighting may be limited to a very narrow band of wavelengths. This puts an undue strain on certain cells in the retina and leads to more rapid fatiguing of the eye.

Daylight also has the advantage of providing a diffuse illumination. If you are working out of the direct rays of the sun, the light is coming from many different directions and does not cast harsh shadows across the page. If possible, windows should be to your left (for right-handed people) so that a shadow of your writing hand will not fall across the page. It is best not to work directly in front of a window, for every time you glance up out of the window, the eyes are forced to make a rapid accommodation to the change in light intensity, and this can result in eye strain.

Similarly with artificial light, it is best to work in as diffuse a light as possible, one reflected from the ceiling and the wall rather than directed straight onto the paper. This gives a greater evenness of light and avoids tiresome reflections from any shiny objects there may be on the desk. If spotlights are used, they should be used in conjunction with a good general illumination. A single spotlight may help to concentrate the attention on the page, but it is not good for the eyes. It creates a very uneven brightness over the table itself, which means that every time you glance away, the eyes again have to accommodate to a rapid change in intensity, this time to darkness rather than brightness.

Posture. The fatigue felt after a period of study is partly mental fatigue, partly eye fatigue, and partly a result of muscular effort and tension. The least tiring study position is an upright one with the back very slightly bent forward. Sitting with an absolutely straight back can, if you are not used to it, add tension to the back muscles.

Chairs should be high enough that the thigh is horizontal and the lower leg at a right angle to it with the feet resting comfortably on the floor. If the seat is too high the chair edge exerts pressure on the leg obstructing blood circulation. If too low, the thighs are tilted up and the weight of body pressing down on the top of the thigh again causes tiring pressure.

This does not mean you have to have chairs made especially for you. A little adjustment with cushions or foot rests will usually be sufficient.

Table height should also be attended to. Too low and you will begin to slouch, with tension and fatigue in the back. Too high and your arms will be pushing up into your shoulders.

Thus reading in its broadest sense is far more than recognizing letters and putting them together to form sentences. Reading also needs to be efficient. We need to be able to go faster where we need to, comprehend better, remember what we have read, and apply it usefully in long term. Moreover, as much attention needs to be paid to how and where we study as to the art of reading itself if the best use is to be made of the time spent reading.

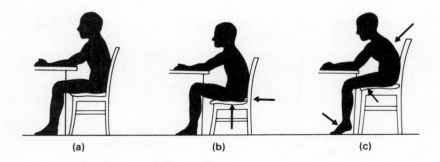

Figure 64 Sitting positions (a) good; (b), (c) bad (arrows show tension points).

Figure 65

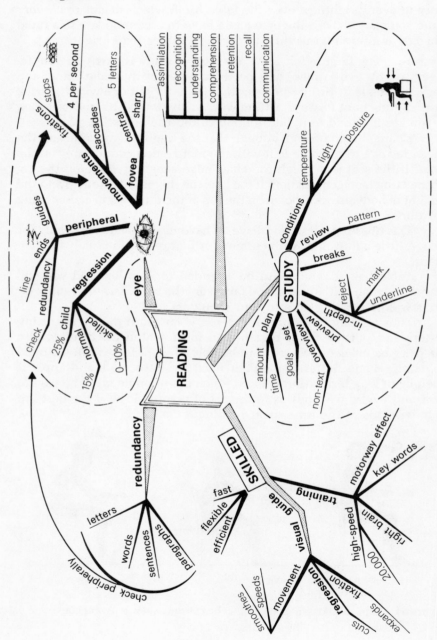

15.
Belief and Set

What is mental "set"?
How does belief affect our lives?
Can it actually change people and society?
Does positive thinking work?
How much is it used in sports?
Can it cure illnesses?
Can a person alter his body's functioning through "set"?
Can one also alter the world around one?

If you have just bought a new coat, you may start noticing a lot more people wearing the same or similar coats. The number of such coats may not have increased significantly, but your mind has become tuned to these particular coats and picks them out from the crowd. This is an example of what psychologists call set. The mind will tend to pick out whatever it is "set" for.

If we are expecting someone to call us on the telephone, we will immediately recognize their voice on the other end. If, on the other-hand, we are not expecting them and have not heard from them for some time, it may be a little while before we recognize the voice. Or again, the postman may be easily recognized when we see him standing outside the door early in the morning, but it may be much harder to recognize him when we meet him on a holiday in Spain. These are examples of negative set—missing that which is not expected.

Psychologists have measured the role of set in perception by asking people to recognize words flashed briefly before them and giving them different expectancies of what was to come. In one experiment, subjects were very briefly shown the name of an animal, such as *horse.* One group was told that they were going to see the name of an animal, another group that they were going to see the name of a flower, and a third group that they were just going to see a word. Those who were expecting to see the name of an animal recognized the word most quickly and made the least errors. Those who were expecting any word did second best. And those who were expecting to see the name of a flower did worst of all, reacting more slowly and making more mistakes.[1]

In a similar experiment using single letters it was found that if the flashes are made very brief indeed, the subject could still be correct nearly every time if the choice was between two letters, for example, *A* or *B,* but almost always incorrect when the choice was one out of twenty-six.[2]

Thus, set can be deceiving in that you may sometimes see what you expect to see even when it is not there. Magicians rely heavily upon this. They get you to expect them to do one thing, and you see them doing that—for example, burning your five-dollar bill—even though they are really doing something different. Because of your set you miss the little "tricks."

Set will often continue for some time after the initial expectation. When people are asked to recall as many names as possible beginning with a certain letter—*T,* say—they will still be set for names beginning with *T* several hours after the experiment has ended. The task remains at the "back of the mind" and as soon as a *T* name appears, even in a completely different setting, it will stand out.[3]

The same can happen in daily life. A person may have had a name on the tip of his tongue but not have been able to recall it. Later he may hear the name incidentally in conversation or read it somewhere and immediately recognize that this was the name he could not remember. Although it was not being consciously looked for, the mind had remained "set" for it.

Set affects virtually everything we see and do. Any belief system will make a person "set" to notice those events and facts that support their belief and miss those that do not. This is why two people can hold completely opposite views about religion, politics, education, the state of the economy, the mind, or the nature of reality and each find, *from his own experience,* that the world is the way he believes it to be. They have unconsciously selected the supporting evidence. This can be very comforting, but it also leads to bigotry and prejudice. Mark Brown, in his book *Set Thinking—Why Dogs Look Like Their Owners,* suggests that a good way to offset this is occasionally to try holding the opposite belief. By doing this you can make sure you are seeing both sides of the situation and not becoming "over-set" in any particular direction.[4]

As to why dogs tend to look like their owners, and vice versa, this also is a matter of set. Any outstanding qualities in the one "set" you to notice those qualities in the other. If you meet a pudgy man with a boxer dog, you will be more likely to notice if he has a squashed nose himself, or if the dog is also overweight. You will pick out any ways in which they are similar but probably not notice the hundreds of ways in which they are unlike each other.

Set can also affect the way you see other people. If you have just had an argument with someone, you may feel that he is the most selfish and uncompromising of people, and when you next meet him, you will be "set" to notice his bad points. Conversely, when you are "head over heels" in love, the other person is the best in the world; in your eyes he can do nothing wrong.

Not only does set affect the way we see other people, it can sometimes change the other person for better or for worse. A study of over one hundred children measured the extent to which the parent's expectancy of a child's ability affected the child. Of those children whose mothers had rated them below average and predicted that they would remain so, only 7.7 percent were free from emotional disturbances at the ages of ten to eleven. Whereas, of those children whose mothers rated them above average, 46.2 percent were free from symptoms. This relationship was independent of other factors, such as the educational level of the parents, their occupations, ages, the type of delivery or family size, suggesting that it was indeed a direct influence of "set."[5]

Similarly, at school a teacher's expectancy of a child's ability can often determine the child's actual performance at school. If a group of children is divided into two groups of equal aptitudes but their teachers are told that children in one group have high IQs and are expected to excel at school whereas the other children are academically poor, the first group will do much better than the second. This effect, known as the Pygmalion effect, has been borne out by numerous studies, not only in school, but in business, psychiatry, medicine, politics, social relationships, and other situations.[6]

Some of the effect may be due to the teacher's being set to notice the achievements of the bright children and the failures of the dim ones. In a now legendary experiment psychology students were given two groups of rats. One group was said to be intelligent and trained, the other group dumb—though, as with the children, both groups were identical. The results of the students' experiments showed that the intelligent rats performed much better in the mazes than did their "dumb" fellows.

With children some of the effect may also be due to the children becoming set as a result of the teacher's attitudes. A "dumb" child may pick up, either directly or indirectly, that he is not thought to be very bright and become "set" to this "fact." As a result he is quick to notice his failures and slower to notice his successes, and his negative set is reinforced. The child does actually come to perform less well than a child in the "bright" group.

Overall social trends can even be affected by set. If, for example, the majority of people believe that the country is on the verge of collapse, that extremists are about to take over, that ecological disaster is around the corner, and that doom is sure to come, then doom is far more likely to come—particularly when these attitudes are reinforced through the media. One recent study showed that even the quality of news bulletins can affect a person's attitude to others. People who heard positive bulletins, recalling the good news of the day, showed more positive feelings toward other people than did people whose news was full of gloom and despair.[7]

A major report by Willis Harman and colleagues at the Stanford Research Institute came to the conclusion that society tends to move toward the dominant image propagated through the media and the educational system. They concluded that if humanity is to survive the next few decades, it is essential to reaffirm the positive sides of human potential and "set" society for a positive future.[8]

MENTAL SET AND STUDY

In the previous chapter it was advised that, as part of the preparation for study, you should quickly review your knowledge of the field and set goals for the session. These both have the value of establishing a strong set for the subject, making it easier to recognize relevant points and easier to understand and recall them.

This review is best done with a quick-sketch mind map. Put the subject under study at the center of the map and spend just half a minute or so very quickly sketching the key words associated with the subject, in order to give a rough but comprehensive outline of the field. Even if it is a completely new field to you, you will nevertheless have some associations connected to the subject and sketching these down in a quick pattern will bring out the right hooks and prepare the mind for further study of the subject.

The more clearly your aims and goals are defined, the stronger will your mental set be. Again, the best way to do this is to jot down a very quick pattern, fitting in any associations that come to mind. Very often we have been conditioned out of the habit of asking questions, usually through a fear of appearing stupid or of being told to keep quiet. But questions should not be thought of as exposing one's ignorance so much as opening oneself to knowledge. Questioning is in fact a very natural method of gaining knowledge. The young child seems never to stop asking questions: Who? What? Why? When? Where? How? . . .

Another advantage of establishing a strong mental set before reading or studying is that you are also effectively setting yourself against that which you do not need to know or which is irrelevant. As was mentioned earlier, you are less likely to notice something if you are positively not expecting it than if you are expecting almost anything.

SET IN SPORT

Considerable interest is now being shown in the role of mental set in sports. Alan Richardson in Australia, investigated the effects of mental imagery on basketball players. He took three groups of students. The first group practiced basketball throws for twenty minutes every day. The second group did no physical practice but instead spent twenty minutes a day imagining that they were throwing the ball into the basket. As with physical practice, this group tried to correct their shots when they "mentally" missed the net. The third group had no practice whatsoever. After three weeks it was found that the group who had practiced mentally had improved by the same amount as the group who had practiced physically—about 24 percent—while those who had no practice whatsoever had not improved at all.[9]

Looking closer at the mental practice group, Richardson found that each individual's improvement was related to his ability to control his mental image. One of the players, for example, found that, although he could visualize the basketball court quite vividly, he could not bounce the ball in his mind; it tended to stick on the floor. This player was not helped very much by mental practice. Those subjects who were able to "feel" the touch of the ball as well as "see" it were much more successful. And those who were able to "hear" the bounce of the ball as well were even more successful.

In another series of experiments Richardson asked a group of gymnasts to perform mental training for a "single leg upstart on a high bar." As with the basketball players, those who practiced mental training improved considerably over those who did not. Again, the vividness of the images and the control they were able to exert in their images were reflected in the improvement in physical practice.[10]

Such mental training not only increases a player's confidence and prepares him for a given situation, it also directly affects his muscles. It has been shown that when a person imagines an activity to be taking place, small electrical changes can be detected in the associated muscles, despite the fact that there may be no physical signs of movement.[11]

Mental imagery has also been used in the training of skiers. The subjects, all competition skiers, were put into a relaxed state and then told to visualize the practice of racing techniques, slalom turns, course concentration, etc. Whenever they made mental faults, they were told to go back and correct them mentally. The practice was so effective that when it came to selecting a team for the race events, the coach chose only those who had used mental imagery.[12] Similar techniques of mental setting were used by the gold-medalist skier Jean-Claude Killy, who always practiced mentally if he was not able to practice physically.

Tennis is another sport in which mental set can be very effective. Billie Jean King used mental imagery before her matches, imagining every conceivable situation that could occur on the courts and mentally making sure she could cope with them, practicing in her mind all the awkward shots. Similarly Virginia Wade "saw" herself on the center court at Wimbledon, and "knew" she could get there. In his book *The Inner Game of Tennis* Timothy Gallway, himself a professional tennis player, suggests that when one is practicing difficult shots, he should first of all practice them mentally. The player is to first look at where he has to hit the ball, then close his eyes and imagine the ball leaving his racket and hitting the target. Having done this several times and having corrected any misses, the player opens his eyes and *without trying* to hit the target, without any control, trusts his body to carry out the action perfectly—letting "the serve serve itself."[13]

Mohammed Ali's continual prefight banter ensured him a strong mental set for success. He seldom allowed the possibility of failure to enter his mind, not only setting himself to win but simultaneously setting his opponent to lose. When he predicted correctly, every fight that Ali won provided yet more material with which to "remind" his opponents that they were bound to lose.

Similar results have been found with golf, motorcycle racing, and other sports.

Conversely, negative set can produce limitations in sport. For a long time weight lifters could not break the 500-pound barrier. The top people were around the 499-pound mark. They thought, "Nobody else had done 500 pounds, so how can I?" When Valery Alexis finally lifted 500 pounds, he was fooled into it. The scales were rigged to show 499.9 pounds when the weight was in fact 501.5 pounds. He lifted it. And once the barrier was broken and everyone knew "it could be done," many others followed. Their set had shifted from negative to positive.[14]

Arnold Schwarzenegger, five times Mr. Universe, believes that body building is very much in the mind: "As long as you can envision the fact that you can do something, you can do it—as long as you really believe it 100 percent."[15]

SET AND HEALTH

One of the first people to recognize the power of the mind in curing disease was the sixteenth-century Swiss physician Paracelsus. He believed that imagination could cure illness as well as produce it, and although he interpreted many of the theories in terms of good and evil spirits, his methods of healing were in essence a mental setting for health.

Most medical systems have realized that set can play an important role in sickness and health. The person who thinks of himself as prone to sickness is more likely to get sick than the person with a healthy, optimistic attitude. Most forms of treatment are in fact helped by an optimistic attitude on the part of the patient.

This was the basis of Emile Coué's therapy, which was very popular in both Europe and America in the 1920s. His treatment involved the frequent repetition of the phrase "Every day, and in every way, I am becoming better and better." Though very simple, it appeared to be extremely effective.

Often belief alone is enough to effect a cure. Patients given placebos, inert chemicals such as sugar or white flour disguised as a drug, will sometimes recover as well as patients given drugs, providing, that is, the patient is made to believe that the placebo is some "wonder drug." In one study a doctor gave injections of distilled water to patients with bleeding peptic ulcers, telling the patients that he was giving them a new drug that would cure them. Seventy percent of the patients showed excellent results lasting over a year.[16] In another experiment a patient was given the drug ipecac, which normally produces nausea and vomiting. In this case, though, the patient was told that the drug would *prevent* the nausea and vomiting that he already had. And it did.[17]

Jerome Frank in his book *Persuasion and Healing* points out that until the middle of this century most treatments prescribed by physicians were chemically inert and were not themselves killing bacteria and viruses: "The history of medical treatment until relatively recently is the history of the placebo effect."[18]

Cancer in particular is one illness where set can have important consequences. There is a general set throughout Western society that cancer is a killer, and once it is diagnosed in an individual, the negative set becomes a personal one—particularly if it is reinforced by a prediction that the patient concerned has only six months, or whatever, to live.

A prediction of death can in itself sometimes be enough to bring death about. In the Murngin tribe of northern Australia the headman can tell a tribesman that he will die in two days, and almost invariably the person is dead before the forty-eight hours are up. Scientists investigating such cases have found no evidence of physical illness in the corpse. When, however, a dying tribesman is told that the sentence has been lifted, he generally recovers with no ill effects.[19]

Similar principles have been applied in one of the more promising approaches to the treatment of cancer. Carl and Stephanie Simonton give their patients a positive setting for survival, showing them many cases of spontaneous remission, educating them on the body's own self-healing potential, and getting them actively to visualize the body becoming well again. As a result 30 percent of their patients have shown a complete recovery and another 45 percent have become well on the way to recovery.[20] Although their work is still only in the preliminary stages, these are very much higher success rates than those attained with conventional cancer treatment.

Another field of medicine in which "set" has been used to great advantage is childbirth. Dr. Grantly Dick-Read, a strong advocate of natural childbirth, believes that an important factor in easing birth is to give the mother a much more positive image of birth, thereby preventing the "fear–tension–pain syndrome."[21] In Western society young women are continually exposed to negative mental setting about the pain and suffering of childbirth. The resulting fear of giving birth leads to resistant actions in the womb, muscular tension, disturbed blood flow to the uterus, buildup of waste products in the tissues, and eventually to pain. Here the fear of pain actually produces pain. In many primitive societies, on the other hand, where there is no cultural tradition that childbirth is painful, women seem to give birth with little sign of distress; for many it can even be a blissful transcendental experience.

PHYSIOLOGICAL CONTROL OF THE BODY

There are many stories of Indian yogis and fakirs who have been able to produce remarkable changes in their bodies merely by mentally setting themselves for those changes. One yogi was able directly to change the temperature of two patches of skin on the same hand, making one hotter and the other colder simultaneously. Although the two areas were only a couple of inches apart, they showed a temperature difference of 10 degrees Fahrenheit. The hot area looked bright red, while the cold area of the palm looked ashen gray.[22] In such cases the yogi usually achieved the result by strong visualization, imagining one side of the palm to be burned by a hot coal, the other to be frozen by ice.

The Russian mnemonist "S," discussed earlier, also used his remarkable powers of imagery to accomplish similar feats. Not only was he able to control the temperature of his hands, he was able to raise or lower his heart rate by imagining himself running for a train or lying flat in a bed.[23] He was able to alter the size of his pupils by visualizing varying degrees of light, and he could change the alpha-wave patterns in his brain by visualizing a light flashing in his eyes.[24]

He could also use imagery to control pain. He described how at the dentist, for example, he would sit there and "when the pain starts, I feel it . . . it's a tiny, orange-red thread . . . I'm upset because I know that if this keeps up, the thread will widen until it turns into a dense mat . . . so I cut the thread, making it smaller and smaller until it's just a tiny point, and the pain disappears."[25]

In the West there has been a growing interest in the technique of biofeedback, by which a person can change such physiological parameters as blood pressure, skin temperature, brain activity, and other factors previously thought to be beyond individual control. The person does not try to change the physiological parameters, rather he tries to find a mental state that produces the required change, and he is able to observe whether or not he is successful by information "fed back" from monitoring instruments. Imagery has been found to play an important part in biofeedback. Skin temperature can be changed by imagining oneself to be hot or cold; and blood pressure and muscle tension can be lowered by imagining relaxed conditions.

A few people have gone further to suggest that mental imagery and belief can actually change the world around. Here we get into the field of miracles and superhuman powers, such as walking on water and levitation. Such things may not be altogether impossible,[26] but more objective studies of their occurrence is needed before we can begin to understand how they might occur.

APPLICATIONS AND ADVICE

One's own self-image is a form of mental set. The person who has a low opinion of himself, say, as someone who never really succeeds, is set to notice his failures more than his successes. He notices those aspects that reinforce his self-image and, believing himself to be a failure, puts less energy into trying to succeed. Conversely, someone who is optimistic about his potential will be quick to notice his successes, slow to notice failure, and less put off by failure. This is the basic principle behind the many techniques of positive thinking.

Numerous books have been written on the subject of positive thinking and remarkable claims have been made for its effectiveness in everyday life.[27] But it has been largely ignored by traditional psychology, presumably because most of the cases have been anecdotal in character and because the books on the subject were aimed at the mass paperback market rather than academics.

The essential process behind positive thinking is first to set yourself goals and then to imagine them having been achieved. It is not just a question of setting goals, but of "seeing" in your mind's eye the goals being fulfilled. The importance of this can be understood in terms of mental set. If the goal is merely a thing to be desired in the future, then the set for it is still negative—it has *not yet* been achieved—and experiences will be unconsciously selected that support that set. Imagining as strongly as possible the fulfillment of your dreams as already having occurred sets you positively for events and opportunities that will support your goals.

Most systems recommend that this imagination be done while in a relaxed state, either sitting quietly and letting yourself sink into a dreamy, peaceful state, or while in that no-man's-land between waking and sleeping last thing at night and first thing in the morning—the hypnagogic and hypnopompic states. The probable reason for this is that it affects the deeper semiconscious levels of the mental activity that we are more in contact with during these states. Although the actual mechanics are not clear, it presumably works in much the same way as a posthypnotic suggestion.

This unconscious mental set then acts as a form of preprogramming throughout daily activity, with the result that a person again starts noticing those factors that support his set, and also the opportunities for actually realizing it. Thus, if a person had used some technique of positive thinking for self-confidence, he would not only begin to feel more self-confident, he would actually begin to act more self-confidently. He would have a greater aura of self-confidence, which would be noticed by others and fed back to support his new set.

A general rule in most positive thinking systems is never to say "I can't," but to think of ways in which you can. Even when you cannot see how a certain goal could be achieved, deliberate setting is still very valuable. The unconscious thinking levels will be preprogrammed for the goal and often work out ways and means by which it can be achieved and throw up solutions "out of the blue," which your more rational mind would never have thought of.

Problem Solving. The same principles can be used with a problem that has been defying solution, or with a difficult decision. First try to solve it. Get all the relevant information on hand. Then, if no solution is forthcoming, turn it over to your subconscious mind.

An easy way to do this is to have the problem in your mind before you drift off to sleep. But don't worry about it or try to solve it. Just be aware of the nature of the problem and the relevant factors and imagine it being solved. Feel how it would be if the problem were solved, and let your attention dwell upon this as you drift off to sleep. You may find you wake up in the morning and the answer suddenly flashes into your mind. Or maybe later in the day it will suddenly come up.

The reason why this happens less often when a person goes to sleep worrying about a problem or trying to solve it is that they are worrying if there is a solution and go to sleep knowing that they have not found a solution, which keeps the mind negatively set.

Waking Up. Another simple way set can be used before going to sleep is setting a mental alarm to wake yourself up on time in the morning. Various techniques have been suggested for this, ranging from drawing the required time on your forehead to banging your head on the pillow the relevant number of times, for example, seven times for seven o'-clock. A less drastic and more effective way is to wait until you are about to drift off to sleep, then imagine a large clock in front of you with the hands at midnight and see and feel yourself dragging the hands round to the required time, and imagine yourself waking up at that time fresh and alert. This technique can be remarkably accurate. People often find themselves waking within a minute or two of the "set" time.

The specific mental mechanics of this are still not clear. It is, however, known that the body has an accurate biological clock and probably the subconscious mind connects into it in some way.

This technique is also useful as a starting point in "setting" yourself generally. Most people find it a fairly easy technique to master, and the fact that it works "sets" you generally for your potentials in this area. When you come to try setting yourself for something else, you already know something about the effectiveness of such techniques and so have a more positive set toward them. The more you go on, the more you realize that very much more is possible.

Stopping Smoking. An important factor in breaking many habits is the belief that you can do so. A person is less likely to be able to give up smoking if, in the back of his mind, there is the feeling that it cannot be done. They have tried before and failed, so why should this time be any better? How often do people say, "I would like to, but I am too addicted"?

Most of the different methods for stopping smoking give you a framework whereby you can begin to cut down or stop, plus a system to believe in. "It worked for me, try it." Or, "Proved by thousands." And the more strongly a person comes to believe in a system, the more effective it is likely to be.

In gaining a positive set toward giving up smoking, sympathetic friends are invaluable—particularly friends who have done it them-selves and can reaffirm that it is possible, and also friends who can encourage you through difficult phases when the old mental set raises its head again. Also positive suggestion that you are giving up smoking will help considerably.

Unsetting Depressed People. Many depressed people get themselves into a spiral of negative thinking. Because of their depressed set they interpret the words and actions of others in a pessimistic light. Throughout the day little incidents seem to confirm that everyone is against them, that they cannot cope, or whatever; the negative set is reinforced.

Some of the standard treatments used for depression attempt to break this viscious circle by giving drugs that elevate the patient's mood, with the hope that with a different mental perspective the person can begin to see things in a better light.

Another promising approach, and one without the side effects often found with antidepressant drugs, is to talk to the patients and get them to see themselves as winners rather than losers. The therapists go through events in the patients' lives showing them that their negative interpretation of themselves may not be based on fact and that a positive interpretation is often more plausible. This breaks the negative feedback spiral and often overcomes the setting for failure and hopelessness.[28]

Getting Set Up. Since virtually everything we perceive or do is affected to varying degrees by our set, it follows that we can apply the principles of positive setting almost anywhere: to getting out of bed on the right side and generally enjoying life; to seeing the good sides of other people —which not only helps them become more positive but also reaffirms your own positive set for humanity; to getting a promotion, a raise, or another job; even to meeting interesting new friends.

William James, one of the fathers of twentieth-century psychology, said that the greatest discovery of the nineteenth century was not in the realm of physical science but in the power of subconscious mind tinged by faith. The faculties of imagination and belief remain the least known and least used of all mental faculties. Yet they are also the most powerful. They are probably the key to our future evolution, both as individuals and as a species. If the human brain is the spearhead of evolution, these faculties are its tip.

Figure 66

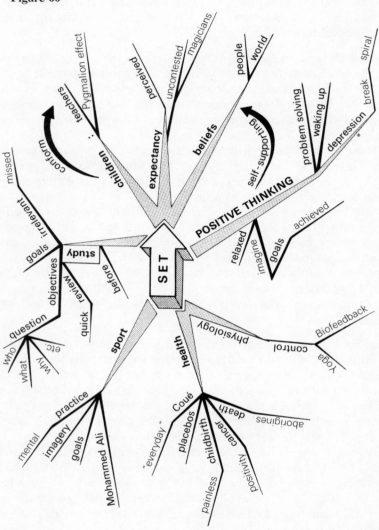

16.
Review

Since review is of utmost value in helping the brain remember new material, this final chapter is devoted to a review of the whole book. It is a good idea to get some colored pens and a large sheet of paper and make your own mind maps as you go.

The human brain is the most complex and most powerful information processor known to man.

Unlike an electronic computer, the brain can carry on a thousand different functions simultaneously, continually cross-referencing and integrating new information. Though many times more powerful and flexible than a computer, the brain weighs only three and a half pounds. Its complexity far surpasses that of modern technology. A transistorized brain would completely fill Carnegie Hall and one using microelectronics would still fill a large room.

The human brain is the most evolved system on this planet. It is the spearhead of evolution. The extent to which we use its potentials determines the extent to which we, both as individuals and as a race, progress.

Over the last two decades tremendous advances have been made in our knowledge of the brain and its functioning. Brain studies are now at the frontier of science and involve specialists from many different disciplines. Yet despite all that is being discovered, we are still a very long way from a full understanding of the brain.

As human beings we have hardly begun to use our brain's full potential. At school we were not taught how the brain works, and we never learned to use it properly in study, reading, memory, and other daily tasks.

BRAIN DEVELOPMENT

The brain is unlike any other organ in the body in that:

- Its internal structure is always changing and developing as a result of experience. This gives it an unlimited capacity for learning.
- The brain's cells do not generally reproduce themselves. Thus the same neurons are with you for life.

There are two major periods of brain growth:

1. Eight to thirteen weeks after conception. During this period the full complement of cells are being formed.

2. Six months after conception till the age of two, when the neurons are making most of their major connections. During this phase much of our basic learning takes place.

Considerable learning takes place while the child is still in the womb. The basic sounds and rhythm of language, for example, are acquired at this stage.

At birth the child is an intelligent, sensitive, perceptive, feeling being—far from a dumb animal.

The young brain is making millions of new connections each day as the young child absorbs its environment, and a rich environment is invaluable in helping it develop quickly and fully. Studies of gifted children reveal that many of them benefitted from a rich early environment, with a diversity of stimulation. In cases where parents have deliberately given their babies rich and varied environments, the children have often grown up with remarkable mental abilities. Although "supernormal" by conventional standards, this should be the "normal" pattern of development.

NEURONS

Each human brain contains some 10 billion neurons, which is more than there are people on this planet. Spreading from each neuron are hundreds, sometimes thousands, of fibers connecting the neurons to one another.

The junction of two of these fibers is called the *synapse*. There are estimated to be over 10 trillion synapses in one human brain. It is through the synapse that one neuron interacts and communicates with another, and these junctions, although only a few thousandths of an inch across, are the most important points in the nervous system.

As well as transmitting electrical pulses, some of the fibers (the axons) also carry proteins and other molecules down to the synapse, where they modify its ability to transmit pulses. This modification probably plays an essential role in memory.

In addition to its 10 billion neurons the brain also contains 100 billion glia cells, which surround every neuron, insulating it and nourishing it.

There are also millions of tiny blood vessels bringing the brain's much needed oxygen. Although only 2 to 3 percent of the body by weight, the brain consumes 20 percent of the oxygen intake. Much of this energy goes into the production of proteins and other molecules used at the synapse.

STRUCTURE

The brain can be divided into many different regions. The main parts, starting with the "oldest," are spinal chord, brain stem, cerebellum, midbrain, and cortex.

The cortex, which covers most of the brain's surface, is responsible for such higher mental functions as thinking, perception, decision making, and will.

THE TWO HALVES OF THE BRAIN

The cortex is divided into two distinct halves:

- The left side generally prefers to function in a linear, analytic mode and is more concerned with verbal abilities and logical thinking.
- The right side generally prefers to function in a simultaneous, synthetic mode and is more concerned with spatial abilities and creative thinking.

Most people in Western societies tend to use the functions associated with the left side more than those associated with the right. But this is not an intrinsic dominance; it is probably the result of cultural and educational systems that emphasize the faculties associated with the left.

Ideally we should be using both sides equally, as many great thinkers (Einstein, for example) seemed to do. The integration of the two sides is enhanced by meditation and by deliberately using the faculties associated with the right in reading, writing, etc.

Although the left brain controls the right side of the body and vice versa, it does not seem that left-handed people use the right side of their brains more, nor that their brains are reversed.

The qualities associated with the left and right sides of the brain are reflected in most cultures throughout the world with a symbolism of right and left—for example, good/bad, matter/spirit.

AGING

It is a common misconception that intellectual abilities necessarily begin to decline after the age of twenty. Neurologically speaking, there is no reason for abilities to decline: They should keep on improving throughout most of life. The apparent decline is probably due mainly to

a lack of use; and
an expectancy of decline.

Polymaths and others who have made full use of their brains throughout life show no deterioration with age.

Although many older people claim that memory for recent events deteriorates as they get older, there is little experimental evidence to support this. Possibly they appear to remember more of their childhood and youth because these periods were more novel and outstanding. Recent memories can be enhanced and the apparent decline reversed if one maintains an active interest in the present.

RECOVERY OF FUNCTION

It has long been accepted that the young brain can adapt and change its structure in response to injury or other physical changes. It has only recently been realized that the adult brain also shows considerable adaptability.

Studies of people who have suffered severe head injuries show that, given time, the brain will compensate for the damage, eventually recovering many of the destroyed functions. This recovery is enhanced by

specific retraining programs; and
retraining as soon after the injury as possible.

If damage occurs very gradually, as with some brain diseases, the brain can adapt as the damage progresses so that very little loss of function may be noticed.

CARING FOR YOUR BRAIN

In order to make the most of your brain you must keep it healthy. Regular exercise and rest are both essential, as is a well-balanced, wholesome diet.

MEMORY

Of all our mental faculties, memory is the most important and is involved in everything we do.

Although recall of an event generally fades with time, it may actually increase a little for a few minutes after learning. This is known as reminiscence (fig. 67a).

In any learning situation the beginning and end of the session are remembered better (primacy and recency).

So are outstanding items (fig. 67b).

Taking regular breaks during any study or learning increases the overall recall. Breaks take maximum advantage of primacy, recency, and reminiscence.

You should break once every forty minutes at least, and for about five to ten minutes (fig. 67c).

During breaks, rest, relax, take some fresh air, etc.

After a break do a quick review of the previous session(s). This warms you up mentally and also gets you mentally "set" for the subject.

Even when study seems to be going well, it is still good to break. *Understanding is not necessarily remembering.*

Chunking. Immediate memory is limited to about seven "chunks" of information. Most people can remember about seven numbers in a row, seven colors, seven shapes, or seven of any other items. So if you need to remember more than seven items, it is better to organize them into a smaller number of chunks.

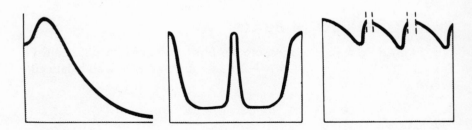

Figure 67 (a) (b) (c)

Association. This is one of the most important factors in human memory. Memories are linked by association and any one thought will have many ideas and images associated with it. Thus, memory is not recorded linearly as in a film but is a vast, intricately interconnected network.

Associations are like hooks on which more memories can be attached. So rather than filling up, memory capacity actually *expands* as more and more things are remembered.

Organization. Organization is also very important in memory. Unconsciously the mind organizes any new material into groups and patterns. The greater the subjective organization, the better the memory.

Consciously looking for underlying patterns and principles is more effective than rote learning. It is the ordering of the material that the mind remembers. Chess masters, for example, remember the configurations on a board, not the individual positions.

The more consciously you are involved with anything, and its meaning and significance, the greater the depth of processing; the greater the organization; and the better the memory.

Sleep Learning. Although moderately effective sleep learning tends to wake a person up, modern approaches such as suggestopedia put a person into a *wakeful,* relaxed state and are much more effective.

IMAGERY

Most people possess imagery to varying extents, and with most of the senses, though visual imagery is generally the strongest.

Memory of visual images is essentially perfect. Shown ten thousand pictures, people can recognize 99.6 percent correctly.

One reason that the potential of human memory has been underestimated in the past is that psychologists have used verbal memory, which is poorer than visual memory, and deliberately eliminated the natural tools of memory, such as association, meaning, and organization.

Everyone's memory can be improved by making a greater use of imagery. When two images are associated, they should be made to connect and interact as directly and vividly as possible.

Many children possess the ability of eidetic imagery. They are able to maintain a strong, full-color visual image of a scene and "see" the details in it for some time afterward, sometimes even days. Most children, however, lose this capacity as they grow up, probably because our educational system is orientated more toward the verbal faculties associated with the left hemisphere than the visual ones of the right. Hypnotic regression back to childhood has shown that some adults still have eidetic imagery as a latent faculty.

MNEMONICS

A mnemonic is any technique for increasing memory. They were first used extensively by the ancient Greeks and Romans.

The basic principle underlying all mnemonics is to make a strong association with the thing to be remembered. As much as possible, the associations should be unique, exaggerated, sensory, simple, creative, and outstanding. A little vulgarity often helps.

A simple system for remembering lists is the number-rhyme system, in which the numbers one to ten are given rhyming images, such as one–gun, two–shoe, etc. (itself an easy mnemonic), and each element of the list associated with one of the images. Such a technique is invaluable for remembering odd things when there is no pencil or paper handy.

Rhymes and rhythm are very useful in remembering things; they provide a patterned framework for the words involved. Many simple mnemonics used at school are based on rhymes. Most people also use apparently "silly" mnemonics for remembering many everyday things.

Mnemonic principles can be used for learning both the vocabulary and grammar of foreign languages, for remembering faces, and for remedying absent-mindedness in general.

Mnemonics are not cheating. They are making a fuller use of the imagery capacities of the right side of the brain and the natural associative properties of human memory. Far from being "silly," they are eminently sensible.

The Russian mnemonist "S" displayed a near perfect memory. Studies showed that he spontaneously used the principles of mnemonics throughout everyday life, forming strong vivid associations with everything he encountered. This was enhanced by his natural capacity for synesthesia, by which visual images would automatically conjure up smells, sounds, tastes, and tactile sensations. "S" still remembered long, monotonous lists of nonsense syllables fifteen years after the experiment.

MEMORY STORAGE

Experiments on the transfer of memory from one animal to another suggest that there is a chemical basis to learning. In some cases specific proteins have been identified that correspond to specific learning. Scotophobin, for example, is synthesized in rats trained to fear the dark, and when injected into other rats, it causes them to fear the dark also.

Despite the fact that there are zillions of different proteins that could be synthesized, this is still very much less than the zillions upon zillions of possible things we could remember. It is not therefore possible that each incidental memory could be related to a unique protein. *Memory is different from learning.*

The synapses between neurons play a fundamental role in memory. Learning almost certainly results in some of the brain's trillions of synapses' changing their ability to transmit impulses, and the pattern of these changes over the whole brain determines the specific memory.

HOLOGRAPHY AND MEMORY

A hologram is unlike a photograph in that every part of the image affects every part of the plate. They are records of the patterns produced by the interference of a pure coherent beam of light, as from a laser, with the same beam reflected from an object.

Holograms possess the following special features:

- The whole image may be reconstructed from any part of the hologram.
- Images are "recalled" by reestablishing the same initial conditions (frequency and angle of incidence of coherent light).
- If the reference beam is also reflected from an object when creating the hologram, the two objects will be permanently associated, and one will "recall" the other.
- Illumination with the beam reflected from the object will produce a bright spot (or flash) of recognition.

The hologram closely resembles human memory in its functioning, and it may well be that memory works along similar principles. The same mathematical transformations have been discovered in the brain, and a holographic model also explains the virtually unlimited potential of human memory. In fact not only memory, but perception and the mind generally, may be based on holographic principles.

CONSOLIDATION AND REVIEW

The initial short-term memory of an event probably sets up coherent patterns of electrical activity in millions of pathways over the brain as a whole. This corresponds to the interference pattern in the hologram. These electrical changes probably result in changes in protein synthesis in the neurons and, as these proteins are conveyed down to the synapse, in changes in the transmission characteristics of the synapse. Over time, particularly if reinforced, these changes become permanent. This is known as *consolidation* of the memory trace.

The initial consolidation probably occurs within ten minutes of the event. Further consolidation takes place over the day, during sleep, and over the next few weeks. It also takes place every time the initial experience is repeated.

Review is therefore imperative for efficient memory. It is a good idea to take a few minutes to review about ten minutes after the initial study, and again after one day, one week, one month, and six months. This makes maximum use of consolidation and ensures that memory of the subject is essentially perfect.

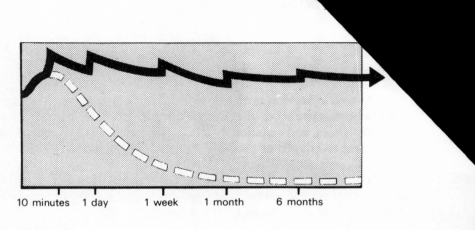

10 minutes   1 day   1 week   1 month   6 months

Figure 68

IS EVERYTHING REMEMBERED?

Evidence from a number of sources—

virtually unlimited storage capacity;
excellent recognition;
near perfect visual memory;
tip-of-the-tongue recall;
power of mnemonics;
amazing wealth of incidental memories;
memory prodigies, such as "S";
hypnotic regression to childhood;
near-death experiences;
dreams;
direct stimulation of the brain—

suggests that the brain may well record every experience.

There are several theories as to why we appear to forget many of our experiences: repression, decay, interference, confusing cues, and loss of mental set. They are probably all responsible to some extent. They can be compensated for by making maximum use of imagery, organization, association, and other natural attributes of memory, in everything we do.

n information storage system, efficient notes
e information, organize it, make associations
usly think about what is significant, thereby
cessing.

The key words in any sentence are the words that hold most of the information content. They are the words that are remembered, and when recalled they "unlock" the meaning again.

Key words are usually nouns and verbs. They are concrete and specific, and generate strong images.

The more key words there are in notes, the more useful they are and the better they are remembered. Ideally, notes should be based on key words and key images.

Traditional notes, in neat linear sentences, waste space, waste time in recording and reviewing, disguise and dissociate the key words. They aid forgetfulness rather than memory.

The brain does not generally work in a linear step-by-step manner but processes many streams of information at once, making numerous associations and connections as it goes. Mind maps reflect this nature of the brain and are therefore an excellent interface between the brain and the outside world.

In making mind maps:

use key words and images;
print the words rather than use script;
put the words *on* lines;
use one word per line;
make the pattern outstanding;
be creative and original;
use color, dimensions, imagery, and imagination;
have strong well-defined centers and subcenters;

use arrows and other means to show connections;
use personal codes, mnemonics, and associations;
be involved with the pattern and have fun.

Mind maps can be used in any situation where you want to put pen to paper—and in many more.

They have advantages over ordinary notes in being:

visual and easily remembered;
flexible and open-ended;
clear in themes, structure, and relative importances;
unique and outstanding;
compact;
fast;
organic like the brain;
fun and enjoyable;
creative.

READING

There are many different systems of learning to read, but they all suffer from the disadvantages that reading stops at "silent reading." This does not bring in the right, "visual" half of the brain, so reading speeds stay around two hundred words per minute—a small fraction of what they could be. Moreover, comprehension, understanding, recall, retention, and communication of the material are hardly taught.

The following is an expanded definition of reading:

1. Assimilation—the eye taking in the information

2. Recognition—of letters, words, simple phrases

3. Understanding—in the immediate context

4. Comprehension—in the overall context

5. Retention—in memory

6. Recall—at a later date

7. Communication—to others or self (thinking)

The Eye and Reading. The *fovea* is the small central area of the retina where perception is clear and sharp. It sees only one degree of the visual angle, i.e., about half a dozen letters at normal reading distance.

The eye can only see when it is still, relative to the object seen, thus during reading it makes a series of jumps (saccadic movements), stopping (fixating) to allow new parts of the line to cast an image on the fovea. The eye can make a maximum of about five jumps per second.

Normal readers take in about two or three words with each fixation. Skilled readers may take in two or three lines.

Although vision is clearest at the fovea, the rest of the visual field is still seen in varying degrees of clarity. This is known as peripheral vision. It is used

to read the beginnings and ends of lines without actually fixating there (making use of the redundancy in written English);
to guide the eye on to the next most useful point of fixation;
to give skilled readers a good idea of what is in the next few lines.

Most people skip back to reread words they have already seen. This is called regression. In young children as much as 25 percent of eye movements are regressive. Most regression comes from fear and apprehension, not from actual misreading. The more skilled the reader, the less the back-skipping.

Contrary to popular opinion, a visual guide will not slow down reading if it is moved along smoothly under a line of print. A visual guide alone can speed up reading to around five hundred words per minute by

eliminating the tendency to skip back;
speeding up the eye so that more is taken in with each fixation.

In high-speed training the reader is forced to "read" at speeds far beyond those at which he can consciously absorb any of the meaning. This brings into use the right "visual" hemisphere and encourages the perception of key words. On returning to "normal," reading is two to three times faster—and with equal if not greater comprehension.

Study. Plan the session and check heat, light, and posture. "Set" the mind by quickly reviewing what is already known.

> Set objectives
> Overview
> Preview
> Practice a few minutes high-speed training
> Treat the text as a whole
> Underline and make outstanding important points
> Reject what is already known or irrelevant
> Reject false arguments
> Break regularly
> Make mind maps
> Review

MENTAL SET

A person tends to see what he expects to see and to miss what he is not expecting. This is known as "set."

Because of "set" many beliefs about the world or other people are self-validating. A person notices that which supports his belief.

A person tends automatically to fulfil the image and goals he sets for himself. If disaster always seems to be occurring, it may well be because of a pessimistic self-image. Conversely, deliberately "setting" for positive goals can bring success. To get the most from positive thinking, be clear on your goals and visualize them actually happening.

Many sportspeople use mental practice to improve their performance. Again the more vividly the practice sessions are imaged, the more benefit is gained.

Positive thinking has been very valuable in the treatment of depression. Helping the patient to see events in an optimistic light breaks the negative spiral of depression.

Belief is also important in physical health. Most medical treatments work better if the patient (and doctor) believe in them. Often inert chemicals (placebos) will work just as effectively as drugs and antibiotics—providing that is, the patient is convinced of their efficacy.

Many people have been able to exercise control over their physiology, raising the temperature of patches of skin, for example, merely by holding the image of that change firmly in their minds.

Belief and imagination, although little understood, are perhaps the most important of all human faculties. With them rests the potential for our continued evolution and progress. They are the tip of the spearhead of evolution.

Chapter Notes

THE SPEARHEAD OF EVOLUTION

1. Peter Russell, "Analysis of Accessions in Cambridge University Library," unpublished report, 1976.
2. See, for example, Lyall Watson, *Supernature* (London: Hodder & Stoughton, 1973).
3. See, for example, Russell Targ and Harold Puthoff, *Mind Reach* (New York: Delacorte, 1977).
4. *Brain-Mind Bulletin* 2 (16):2.
5. Beatrice T. Gardner and Allan R. Gardner, "Teaching Sign Language to a Chimpanzee: 1. Methodology and Preliminary Results," *Psychonomic Bulletin* 1 (2):36.
6. Ann J. Premack and David Premack, "Teaching Language to an Ape," *Scientific American,* October 1972, pp. 92–99.
7. Carl Sagan, Harvard University, personal communication, October 1977.
8. Karl Witte, *The Education of Karl Witte, Or the Training of the Child,* trans. L. Wiener (London: Harrap, 1915).
9. P. Solomon, ed., *Sensory Deprivation: A Symposium* (Cambridge, Mass.: Harvard University Press, 1961).
10. Marcelle Gebber "Psychomotor Development of African Children in the First Year, and the Influence of Maternal Behaviour," *Journal of Social Psychology* 147:185–195.
11. Winifred Stoner, *Natural Education* (London: John Lane and Bodley Head, 1923).
12. "The Edith Project," *Sunday Times* (London), April 17, 1977.

13. Quoted in Marilyn Ferguson, *The Brain Revolution* (New York: Bantam, 1973), p. 266.
14. Daniel J. Davis, "Birth Order and Intellectual Development," *Science* 196:1470–72.
15. " 'Head Start Pays Off," *New Scientist,* March 3, 1977, pp. 508–509.
16. "Should Children Be Pushed into Early Learning?" *Psychology Today* (UK edition), September 1977, pp. 32–37.
17. Reported in *Times* (London), June 16, 1976.

THE BRAIN'S DEVELOPMENT

1. John Lilly, *The Mind of the Dolphin* (New York: Avon, 1969).
2. John Barratt, personal communication, 1972.
3. Robert L. Fantz, "The Origins of Form Perception," *Scientific American,* May 1961.
4. Tom Bower, "The Object World of the Infant," *Scientific American,* October 1971.
5. Tom Bower, "Competent Newborns," *New Scientist,* March 14, 1974, pp. 672–75.
6. Quoted in Marilyn Ferguson, *The Brain Revolution* (New York: Bantam, 1973), p. 274.
7. Roger Lewin, "Developing brains," *New Scientist,* June 13, 1974, pp. 686–89.
8. Mark Rosenzweig, "Environmental Complexity, Cerebral Change and Behaviour," *American Psychologist* 21 (4):321–32.
9. William S. Condon and Louis W. Sander, "Neonate Movement Is Synchronised with Adult Speech," *Science* 183:99–101.
10. Ronald Laing, *The Facts of Life* (London: Allen Lane and New York: Pantheon, 1976).
11. "A Gentle Entry into Life Has Its Advantages," *New Scientist,* November 25, 1976, p. 449.
12. *Brain-Mind Bulletin* 2(23).
13. See *New Scientist,* October 24, 1974, p. 268.
14. Brian Cragg, "The Development of Cortical Synapses During Starvation in the Rat," *Brain* 95:143–50.
15. Roger Lewin, "The Poverty of Undernourished Brains," *New Scientist,* October 24, 1974, pp. 268–271.
16. "Stimulating Homes Cancel Brain Damage in Malnourished Children," *New Scientist,* January 1, 1976, p. 108.
17. John Spudich and Dan Koshland, "Non-Genetic Individuality: Chance in the Single Cell," *Nature* 262:467–71.
18. John J. Sherwood and Mark Nataupsky, "Predicting the Conclusion of Negro-White Intelligence Research from Biographical Characteristics

of the Investigator," *Journal of Personality and Social Psychology* 8:53–58.

TEN BILLION NEURONS

1. Irene Gore, "The Meaning of Ageing," *New Scientist,* March 21, 1974, pp. 756–57.
2. Marian Diamond, "The Ageing Brain: Some Enlightening and Optimistic Results," *American Scientist* 66:66–71.
3. K. Akert and K. Pfenninger, "Synaptic Fine Structure of Neural Dynamics," in *Cellular Dynamics of the Neuron,* ed. S. H. Barondes (New York: Academic Press, 1969), pp. 245–60.
4. Robert O'Becker, *Genetic Psychological Monographs,* no. 2 (1971), pp. 177–235.
5. Paul Weiss, "Neuronal Dynamics," in *Neurosciences Research Symposium Summaries,* ed. F. O. Schmidt et al., vol. 3 (Cambridge, Mass.: MIT Press, 1969), pp. 255–84.
6. S. H. Barondes, "Synaptic Plasticity of Axoplasmic Transport," in *Neurosciences Research Symposium Summaries,* ed. Smith et al., pp. 249–54.

THE TWO SIDES OF THE BRAIN

1. K. U. Smith and A. J. Akelaitis, "Studies on the Corpus Callosum," *Archives of Neurological Psychiatry* 47:519–43.
2. Michael S. Gazzaniga, J. E. Bogen, and Roger W. Sperry, "Observations on Visual Perception After Disconnection of the Cerebral Hemispheres in Man," *Brain* 8:221–36.
3. Michael S. Gazzaniga, "The Split Brain in Man," *Scientific American,* August 1967, pp. 24–29.
4. Ibid.
5. Ibid.
6. David Galen and Robert Ornstein, "Lateral Specialisation of Cognitive Mode: An EEG Study," *Psychophysiology* 9 (4):412–18.
7. Doreen Kimura, "The Assymetry of the Human Brain," *Scientific American,* March 1973, pp. 70–78.
8. Thomas G. Bever and Robert J. Chiarello, "Cerebral Dominance in Musicians and Non-musicians," *Science* 185:537–39.
9. Hadyn D. Ellis and John W. Shepherd, "Recognition of Upright and Inverted Faces Presented in the Left and Right Visual Fields," *Cortex* 11:3–7.
10. Gillian Cohen, "Hemispheric Differences in Serial versus Parallel Processing," *Journal of Experimental Psychology* 97:349–56.

11. Stuart Dimond, *The Double Brain* (London: Churchill Livingstone, 1972), chapters 6 and 10.
12. M. L. Taylor, "A Measurement of Functional Communication in Aphasia," *Archives of Physiological Medicine and Rehabilitation* 46 (1-A):101–107; and P. Marcie et al., "Les réalisations du langage chez les malades attients de lésions de l'hémisphère droit," *Neuropsychologia* 3:217–45.
13. J. Wade and T. Rasmussen, "Intracarotid Injection of Sodium Amytal for the Lateralisation of Cerebral Speech Dominance," *Journal of Neurosurgery* 17:266–82.
14. *Brain-Mind Bulletin* 2 (24).
15. "Why Children Should Draw," *Saturday Review,* September 3, 1977, pp. 11–16.
16. Ibid., p. 14.
17. Dimond, *Double Brain,* pp. 139–49.
18. C. Branch, B. Milner, and T. Rasmussen, "Intracarotid Injection of Sodium Amytal for the Lateralisation of Cerebral Speech Dominance: Observation in 123 Patients," *Journal of Neurosurgery* 21:399–405.
19. Sandra F. Witelson, "Sex and Single Hemisphere; Specialisation of Right Hemisphere for Spatial Processing," *Science* 193:425–26.
20. "Man's Sexist Brain," *Sunday Times* (London), June 25, 1976.
21. Quoted in Daniel Goleman, "Specialist Abilities of the Sexes: Do They Begin in the Brain?" *Psychology Today*, November 1978, p. 59, from Diane McGuinness and Karl Pribram, in *Cognitive Growth and Development—Essays in Honor of Herbert G. Birch*, ed. Morton Bortner (New York: Brunner/Mazel, 1979).
22. Juhn Wada and Alan Davis, "Fundamental Nature of Human Infant's Brain Assymetry," *Canadian Journal of Neurological Sciences* 4 (3): 203–207.
23. Arthur Deikman, "Bimodal Consciousness," *Archives of General Psychiatry* 25:481–89.
24. Robert Ornstein, *The Psychology of Consciousness* (San Francisco: Freeman, 1972).
25. A. Werner, "Note on the Terms Used for 'Right Hand' and 'Left Hand' in the Bantu Languages," *Journal of the African Society* 4:112–16.
26. Bernard C. Glueck and Charles F. Stroebel, "Biofeedback and Meditation in the Treatment of Psychiatric Illnesses," *Comprehensive Psychiatry* 16:303–21.
27. David Orme-Johnson and John Farrow, eds., *Scientific Research on the Transcendental Meditation Program* (New York: MIU Press, 1977), pp. 187–207.

THE EVER-ADAPTABLE BRAIN

1. Quoted in Maya Pines, *The Brain Changers* (New York: Signet, 1975), p. 197.
2. C. Doyle Haynes et al., "The Improvement of Cognition and Personality after Carotid Endarterectomy, *Surgery* 80:699–704.
3. M. R. Rosenzweig, E. L. Bennett, and M. C. Diamond, "Brain Changes in Response to Experience," *Scientific American,* February 1972.
4. Quoted in Marilyn Ferguson, *The Brain Revolution* (New York: Bantam, 1973), p. 198.
5. William R. Russell, *Explaining the Brain* (Oxford, England: Oxford University Press, 1975), p. 115.
6. E. K. Warrington and H. I. Sanders, "The Fate of Old Memories," *Quarterly Journal of Experimental Psychology* 23:432–42.
7. Helen C. Franklin and Dennis M. Holding, "Personal Memories at Different Ages," *Quarterly Journal of Experimental Psychology* 29:527–32.
8. Stuart Dimond, *The Double Brain* (London: Churchill Livingstone, 1972), pp. 95–110.
9. R. E. Saul and R. W. Sperry, "Absence of Commissurotomy Symptoms with Agenesis of the Corpus Callosum," *Neurology* 18:307.
10. H. L. Teuber, "Recovery of Function After Lesion of the Central Nervous System: History and Prospects," *Neurosciences Research Program Bulletin* 12 (2):200.
11. Ibid., p. 205.
12. A. R. Luria, *The Man with a Shattered World* (London: Jonathan Cape, 1973).
13. J. H. Wepman, *Recovery from Aphasia* (New York: Ronald Press, 1951).
14. Teuber, "Recovery of Function After Lesions of Central Nervous System," p. 204.
15. Ibid.
16. Glen Doman, *What to Do About Your Brain Injured Child* (London: Jonathan Cape, 1974).
17. Glen Doman, *How to Teach Your Baby How to Read* (New York: Doubleday, 1975).
18. Moshe Feldenkreis, demonstration at the May Lectures, London, 1974.
19. Paul Pietsch, "Shuffle Brain," *Harpers* 244:44.
20. Quoted in Ferguson, *Brain Revolution,* p. 294.
21. G. E. Schneider, "Development and Regeneration in the Mammalian Visual System" in *The Genesis of Neuronal Patterns,* ed. M. V. Barkley, D. S. Famborough, and D. M. Farnborough, *Neurosciences Research Program Bulletin* 10:287–90.
22. Geoffrey Raisman, "The Reaction of Synaptogenesis in the Central and

Peripheral Nervous System of the Adult Rat" in *Neuronal Mechanisms of Learning and Memory,* ed. M. R. Rosenzweig and E. L. Bennet (Cambridge, Mass.: MIT Press, 1976), pp. 348–351.

23. Clarence D. Cone and Charlotte M. Cone, "Induction of Mitosis in Mature Neurons in Central Nervous System by Sustained Depolarisation," *Science* 192:155–58.

24. Brian S. Scott, "Effect of Elevated Potassium on the Time Course of Neuron Survival in Cultures of Disassociated Dorsal Root Ganglia," *Journal of Cellular Psysiology* 91:305–16.

25. Quoted in Ferguson, *Brain Revolution,* p. 264.

26. M.R. Rosensweig, P.A. Ferchmin, and E.L. Bennett, "Direct Contact with Enriched Enviroment Is Required to Alter Cerebral Weight in Rats," *Journal of Comparative and Physiological Psychology* 88:360–67

27. *New Age Journal,* November 1977, p. 24.

28. A. H. Ismail and L. E. Tratchman, "Jogging Your Personality into Shape," *Psychology Today* (UK edition), August 1976, pp. 24–28.

29. Robert Shaw and David Kolb, "Reaction Time Following the Transcendental Meditation Technique," in *Scientific Research on the Transcendental Meditation Program,* ed. David Orme-Johnson and John Farrow (New York: MIU Press, 1977), pp. 309–15.

30. Andrew Rimol, "The Transcendental Meditation Technique and Its Effects on Sensory-motor Performance," in *Scientific Research on Transcendental Meditation Program,* ed. Orme-Johnson and Farrow, pp. 326–30.

31. Ibid.

THE PSYCHOLOGY OF MEMORY

1. Hermann Ebbinghaus, *Memory,* trans. D. H. Ruyer and C. E. Bussenius (New York: Teachers College Press, 1913).

2. B. P. Ballard, "Oblivescence and Reminiscence," *Quarterly Journal of Experimental Psychology* 16:265–92.

3. Lloyd R. Peterson, "Short-Term Memory," *Scientific American,* July 1966, p. 95.

4. L. B. Ward, "Reminiscence and Rote-Learning," *Psychological Monographs* 49 (220).

5. B. Milner, "Visual Recognition and Recall After Right Temporal-Lobe Excision in Man," *Neuropsychologia* 6:191–209.

6. G. A. Kimble and B. R. Horenstein, "Reminiscence in Motor Learning As a Function of Length of Interpolated Rest," *Journal of Experimental Psychology* 38:239–44.

7. Ballard, "Oblivescence and Reminiscence."

8. J. Mohan, "Reminiscence: A Review," *Psychologia (Kyoto)* 9:157–64.

9. Richard C. Atkinson and Richard M. Shiffrin, "The Control of Short-term Memory," *Scientific American,* August 1971, pp. 82–90.
10. E. J. Thomas, "The Variation of Memory with Time for Information Appearing During a Lecture," *Studies in Adult Education,* April 1972, pp. 57–62.
11. C. I. Hovland, "Experimental Studies in Rote-Learning Theory: Comparisons of Distribution of Practice in Serial and Paired-Associate Learning," *Journal of Experimental Psychology* 25:622–33.
12. L. F. Thune, "Warm-up Effect As a Function of Level of Practice in Verbal Learning," *Journal of Experimental Psychology* 42:250–56.
13. A. L. Irior, "Retention As a Function of Amount of Pre-recall Warming Up," *American Psychologist* 4:219–20.
14. H. von Restorff, "Über die Wikung von Bereichsbildungen im Spurenfeld," *Psychologisch Forschung* 18:299–342.
15. See Alan D. Baddeley, *The Psychology of Memory* (New York: Harper & Row, 1976), p. 269.
16. George A. Miller, "The Magical Number Seven, Plus or Minus Two: Some Limits in Our Capacity for Processing Information," *Psychological Review* 63:81–97.
17. H. Pieron, "Recherches expérimentales sur les phénomènes de mémoire," *L'Année Psychologique* 19:91–193.
18. B. Zeigarnik, "Das Behalten erledigter und unerledigter Handungen," *Psychologisch Forschung* 9:1–85.

ASSOCIATION AND ORGANIZATION IN MEMORY

1. Francis Galton, "Psychometric Experiments," *Brain* 2:148–62.
2. John Locke, *An Essay Concerning Human Understanding* (1690, reprint ed., London: Everyman's Library, Dent, 1961).
3. D. W. Goodwin et al., "Alcohol and Recall: State Dependent Effects in Man," *Science* 163:1358.
4. Quoted in Marilyn Ferguson, *The Brain Revolution* (New York: Bantam, 1973), p. 64.
5. J. Greenspan and R. Raynard, "Stimulus Conditions and Retroactive Inhibition," *Journal of Experimental Psychology* 53:55–59.
6. D. R. Godden and A. D. Baddeley, "Context-Dependent Memory in Two Natural Environments: On Land and Underwater," *British Journal of Psychology* 66:325–32.
7. W. A. Bousfield, "The Occurence of Clustering in the Recall of Randomly Arranged Associates," *Journal of General Psychology* 49:229–40.
8. W. A. Bousfield, B. H. Cohen, and G. A. Whitmarsh, "Associative Clustering in the Recall of Words of Different Taxonomic Frequencies of Occurence," *Psychological Reports* 4:39–44.

9. Endel Tulving, "Subjective Organisation in Free Recall of Unrelated Words," *Psychological Review* 69 (4):344–54.

10. George Mandler, "Organization and Memory," in *The Psychology of Learning and Motivation,* vol. 1., ed. K. W. Spence and J. S. Spence (New York: Academic Press, 1967), pp. 327–72.

11. George Katona, *Organizing and Memorizing* (New York: Columbia University Press, 1940), pp. 188–90.

12. A. D. DeGroot, "Perception and Memory Versus Thought; Some Old Ideas and Recent Findings," in *Problem Solving,* ed. B. Kleinmuntz (New York: Wiley, 1966).

13. Arthur Koestler, *Heel of Achilles* (New York: Random House, 1975), p. 230.

14. F.I.M. Craik and R. S. Lockhart, "Levels of Processing: A Framework for Memory Research," *Journal of Experimental Psychology (General)* 104:268–94.

15. D. A. Norman and D. E. Rumelhart, *Explorations in Cognition* (San Francisco: Freeman, 1975), p. 374.

16. Quoted in Ferguson, *Brain Revolution,* p. 73.

17. Maralyn Ferguson, ed. "Suggestology to be explored in U.S.," *Brain-Mind Bulletin* 1 (5): 1–2.

IMAGERY AND ITS RELATIONSHIP TO MEMORY

1. Francis Galton, *Inquiries in the Human Faculty and Its Development* (London: Macmillan, 1883).

2. P. McKellar, "The Investigation of Mental Images," in *Penguin Science Survey,* ed. S.A. Barnett and A. McLaren (London: Penguin, 1965).

3. Quoted in Alan Baddeley, *The Psychology of Memory,* (New York and London: Harper & Row, 1976), p. 225.

4. Quoted in Gordon Bower, "Mental Imagery and Associative Learning," in *Cognition in Learning and Memory,* ed. L. W. Gregg (London and New York: John Wiley, 1972), p. 67.

5. Ibid., p. 69.

6. A. Paivio, "Mental Imagery in Associative Learning and Memory," *Psychological Review* 76:241–63.

7. Bower, "Mental Imagery and Associative Learning," p. 69.

8. Baddeley, *Psychology of Memory,* pp. 222–23.

9. A. G. Goldstein and J. E. Chance, "Visual Recognition Memory for Complex Configurations," *Perception and Psychophysics* 9:237–41.

10. Ralph N. Haber, "How We Remember What We See," *Scientific American,* May 1970, p. 105.

11. R. S. Nickerson, "Short-Term Memory for Complex Meaningful Visual

Configurations: Demonstration of Capacity," *Canadian Journal of Psychology* 19:155–60.

12. Lionel Standing, "Learning 10,000 Pictures," *Quarterly Journal of Experimental Psychology* 25:207–22.
13. Quoted in A. Richardson, *Mental Imagery* (New York: Springer, 1952).
14. G. W. Allport, "Eidetic Imagery," *British Journal of Psychology* 15: 99–120.
15. H. Kluver, "Studies on the Eidetic Type and on Eidetic Imagery," *Psychological Bulletin* 25:69–104.
16. C. R. Gray and K. Gunnerman, "The Enigmatic Eidetic Image: An Initial Examination of Methods, Data and Theories," *Psychological Bulletin* 82:383–407.
17. C. F. Stromeyer and J. Psotka, "The Detailed Texture of Eidetic Images," *Nature* 225:346–49.
18. Baddeley, *Psychology of Memory,* pp. 222–23.
19. E. R. Jaensch, *Eidetic Imagery* (London:). Routledge and Kegan Paul, 1930.
20. Gray and Gunnerman, "The Enigmatic Eidetic Image."
21. *Science News* 108:168.

MNEMONICS

1. Tony Buzan, personal communication, 1976.
2. J. Ross and K. A. Lawrence, "Some Observations on a Memory Artifice," *Psychometric Science* 13:107–108.
3. *New Scientist,* May 16, 1974, pp. 386–88.
4. Harry Lorayne, *The Memory Book* (London: W. H. Allen, 1975), p. 57.
5. Buzan, *Use Both Sides of Your Brain* (New York: E.P. Dutton, 1977), pp. 59–80.
6. Gordon Bower, "Analysis of a Mnemonic Device," *American Scientist* 58:504.
7. I. W. Pleydell-Pearce, personal communication, 1973.
8. *Archives of Neurology* 26:25.
9. O. Burešová and J. Bureš, "Piracetum Induced Facilitation of Interhemispheric Transfer of Visual Information in Rats," *Psychopharmacologia* 46:93–102.
10. *Sunday Times* (London), March 21, 1976, p. 13.
11. A. R. Luria, *The Mind of a Mnemonist* (London: Jonathan Cape, 1969).
12. Ibid., p. 51.
13. Ibid., p. 12.
14. Ibid., pp. 49–50.
15. Ibid., p. 36.
16. Ibid., p. 23.

17. Ibid., p. 38.
18. Ibid., pp. 59–60.

THE BRAIN'S RECORD OF EXPERIENCE

1.   J. V. McConnell, R. Jacobson, and D. M. Maynard, "Apparent Retention of a Conditioned Response Following Total Regeneration in the Planarian," *American Psychological Abstracts* 14:410.
2.   J. V. McConnell, "Memory Transfer Through Cannibalism in Planaria," *Journal of Neuropsychiatry* 3(supplement 1):42–48.
3.   A. L. Harty, P. Keith-Lee, and W. D. Morton, "Planaria: Memory Transfer Through Cannibalism Reexamined," *Science* 146:274–75.
4.   Georges Chapouthier, "Behavioural Studies of the Molecular Basis of Memory," in *The Physiological Basis of Memory*, ed. J. A. Deutsch (New York and London: Academic Press, 1973), pp. 1–25.
5.   J. V. McConnell, T. Shigehisha, and H. Salive, "Attempts to Transfer Approach and Avoidance Responses by RNA Injection in Rats," *Journal of Biological Psychology* 10 (2):32–50.
6.   G. Ungar, "Chemical Transfer of Learning; Its Stimulus Specificity," *Federation Proceedings, Federation of American Societies for Experimental Biology* 25:109.
7.   J. L. McGough and L. Petrinovitch, "Effects of Drugs on Learning and Memory," *International Review of Neurobiology* 8:139–96.
8.   Ibid.
9.   H. Hydén and H. Egyhazi, "Nuclear RNA Changes in Nerve Cells During a Learning Experience in Rats," *Proceedings of National Academy of Science* 48:1366–75.
10. G. Ungar, L. Galvan, and R. H. Clark, "Chemical Transfer of Learned Fear," *Nature* 217:1259–61.
11. Reported in Marilyn Ferguson, *The Brain Revolution* (New York: Bantam, 1973), p. 291.
12. *Brain-Mind Bulletin* 1 (10):1.
13. Ibid.
14. J. F. Flood and M. F. Jarvik, "Drug Influences on Learning and Memory," in *Neural Mechanisms of Learning and Memory*, ed. M. R. Rosenzweig and E. L. Bennett (Cambridge, Mass.: MIT Press, 1976), pp. 483–507.
15. J. Cronly-Dillon, D. Carden, and C. Birks, "The Possible Involvement of Brain Microtubules in Memory Fixation," *Journal of Experimental Biology* 61:43–54.
16. Quoted in Maya Pines, *The Brain Changers* (New York: Signet, 1973), pp. 159–61.
17. J. A. Deutsch, "The Cholinergic Synapse and the Site of Memory," in *The*

Physiological Basis of Memory, ed. J. A. Deutsch, (New York and London: Academic Press, 1973), pp. 59–76.

18. K. Akert and K. Pfenninger, "Synaptic Fine Structure and Neural Dynamics," in *Cellular Dynamics of the Neuron,* ed. S. H. Barondes (New York: Academic Press, 1969), pp. 245–60.

19. V. Bloch, "Brain Activation and Memory Consolidation," in *Neural Mechanisms of Learning and Memory,* ed. Rosenzweig and Bennett, pp. 583–90.

20. P. H. Lindsay and D. A. Norman, *Human Information Processing* (New York: Academic Press, 1977), pp. 379–80.

21. Tony Buzan, *Make the Most of Your Mind,* (London: Encyclopaedia Britannica, 1977), pp. 46–48.

22. F. J. DiVesta and G. S. Gray, "Listening and Note-Taking," *Journal of Educational Psychology* 63:8–14.

THE HOLOGRAPHIC THEORY OF MIND

1. Itzhak Bentov, *Stalking the Wild Pendulum* (New York: Dutton, 1977, and London: Wildwood House, 1978), pp. 11 and 14.

2. Karl Pribram, *Languages of the Brain* (Englewood Cliffs, N.J.: Prentice-Hall, 1971).

3. Karl Pribram, "The Neurophysiology of Remembering," *Scientific American,* January 1969, pp. 73–86.

4. C. Blakemore and F. W. Campbell, "On the Existence of Neurons in the Human Visual System Selectively Sensitive to the Orientation and Size of Retinal Images," *Journal of Physiology* 203:237–60.

5. Paul Greguis, ed., *Holography in Medicine* (Guildford, England: IPC Science and Technology Press, 1976).

6. *Ibid.*

7. *Brain-Mind Bulletin* 2 (16):1–3; and Robert M. Anderson, "A Holographic Model of Transpersonal Consciousness," *Journal of Transpersonal Psychology* 9 (2):119–28.

IS EVERYTHING REMEMBERED?

1. J. C. McGaugh and L. Petrinovitch, "Effects of Drugs on Learning and Memory," *International Review of Neurobiology* 8:139–96.

2. E. Tulving, "The Effects of Presentation and Recall of Materials in Free-Recall Learning," *Journal of Verbal Learning and Verbal Behaviour* 6:175–84.

3. R. Brown and D. McNeil, "The 'Tip-of-the-Tongue' Phenomenon," *Journal of Verbal Learning and Verbal Behaviour* 5:325–37.

4. Tony Buzan, *Speed Memory* (Devon, England: Newton Abbott, 1977), pp. 86–123.

5. E. Hunt and T. Love, "How Good Can Memory Be?" in *Coding Processes in Human Memory*, ed. A. W. Melton and E. Martin (Washington, D.C.: Winston/Wiley, 1972), pp. 237–60.
6. Quoted in A. D. Baddeley, *The Psychology of Memory* (New York and London: Harper & Row, 1976), pp. 365–67.
7. J. H. Creighton, "A Prodigy of Memory," *Knowledge* 11:275.
8. *World of Wonders* (London: Cassel, 1892), p. 4.
9. George M. Stratton, "The Mnemonic Feat of the 'Shass Pollak,' " *Physiological Review* 24:244–47.
10. David Cheek, *American Journal of Clinical Hypnosis* 16:261–66.
11. Ibid.
12. Quoted in John Pfeiffer, *The Human Brain* (London: Gollanz, 1955), p. 84.
13. *Brain-Mind Bulletin* 2 (23):1 and 3.
14. Ralph N. Haber, "How We Remember What We See," *Scientific American,* May 1970, p. 105.
15. Quoted in Marilyn Ferguson, *The Brain Revolution* (New York: Bantam, 1973), p. 161.
16. Ibid.
17. Raymond Moody, *Life after Life* (New York: Bantam, 1976).
18. Russell Noyes and Roy Kletti, "Depersonalisation in the Face of Life-Threatening Danger: A Description," *Psychiatry* 39:19–27.
19. W. Penfield and L. Roberts, *Speech and Brain-Mechanisms* (Princeton, N.J.: Princeton University Press, 1959).
20. W. Penfield and P. Perot, "The Brain's Record of Auditory and Visual Experience: A Final Summary and Discussion," *Brain*, 86:595–702.

NOTE TAKING

1. Vernon Gregg, *Human Memory* (London: Methuen, 1975), p. 50.
2. M. J. A. Howe and J. Godfrey, *Student Note-Taking As an Aid to Learning* (Exeter, England: Exeter University Teaching Services, 1977).
3. M. J. A. Howe, "Using Students' Notes to Examine the Role of the Individual Learner in Acquiring Meaningful Subject Matter," *Journal of Educational Research* 64:61–63.
4. P. Weiner, "Note-Taking and Student Verbalisation as Instrumental Learning Activities," *Instructional Science* 3:51–74.
5. Tony Buzan, *Use Your Head* (London: BBC Publications, 1974), p.25. In America, the book is entitled *Use Both Sides of Your Brain* (New York: E.P. Dutton, 1977).
6. M. A. Tinker, *Bases for Effective Reading* (Minneapolis: University of Minnesota Press, 1965).
7. J. Hartley and S. Marshall, "On Notes and Note-Taking," *University Quarterly,* no. 28, pp. 225–35.
8. Howe and Godfrey, *Student Note-Taking As an Aid to Learning*.

9. Edward McCarthy, Ware College of Further Education, personal communication, 1978.

READING

1. Tony Buzan, *Use Your Head* (London: BBC Publications, 1974), p. 25. In America, the book is entitled *Use Both Sides of Your Brain* (New York: E. P. Dutton, 1977).
2. Edmund Huey, *The Science and Pedagogy of Reading* (1908; reprint ed., Cambridge, Mass.: MIT Press, 1968).
3. E. A. Taylor, "The Spans: Perception, Apprehension and Recognition," *American Journal of Opthalmology* 44:501–507.
4. G. Geffon, J. L. Bradshaw, and G. Wallace, "Interhemispheric Effects on Reaction Time to Verbal and Non-verbal Visual Stimuli," *Journal of Experimental Psychology* 87:415–22.
5. Martin Albert, "Cerebral Dominance and Reading Habits," *Nature* 256: 403.
6. G. A. Miller, "Decision Units in the Perception of Speech," *Institute of Radio Engineering Transactions on Information Theory* 8:81–83.
7. E. E. Smith and K. T. Spoehr, "The Perception of Printed English: A Theoretical Perspective," in *Human Information Processing*, ed. B. H. Kantowitz (Hillsdale, N.J.: Lawrence Eribaum Association, 1974), p. 235.
8. J. M. Cattell, "Time Taken Up by Cerebral Operations," *Mind* 11:220–42.
9. Huey, *Science and Pedagogy of Reading*, p. 74.
10. Ibid.
11. John J. Geyer, "An Eye Movement Measure of Reading Efficiency," in *Reading: Process and Pedagogy*, ed. G. B. Schick and M. M. May (Milwaukee, Wisc.: National Reading Conference, 1970), pp. 168–71.
12. Tony Buzan, Encyclopaedia Britannica Annual Conference, Vienna, 1977.
13. B. Schmidt, "Changing Patterns of Eye Movements Among Students in Reading Classes and Composition-Literature Classes," in *The Psychology of Reading Behavior*, ed. G. B. Schick and M. M. May (Milwaukee, Wisc.: National Reading Conference, 1969), pp. 38–41.
14. Florence C. Schale, "Two Gifted Readers—A Preliminary Study," in *Psychology of Reading Behavior*, ed. Schick and May, pp. 282–89.
15. L. R. Peterson, "Short-term Verbal Memory and Learning," *Psychological Review* 73:193–207.
16. D. J. Willmore "A Comparison of Four Methods of Studying a College Textbook" (Ph.D. dissertation, University of Minnesota, 1966).
17. E. K. Adams, "Underlining: The Graphical Aid to College Reading," in *Reading: Process and Pedagogy*, ed. Schick and May, pp. 12–22.

18. Robert Thouless, *Straight and Crooked Thinking* (London: Pan Books, 1974).
19. W. H. Bates, *Better Eyesight without Glasses* (New York: Holt, Rinehart and Winston, 1940).

BELIEF AND SET

1. W. R. Garner, *Uncertainty and Structure As Psychological Concepts* (New York: Wiley, 1972).
2. Quoted in Ian Hunter, *Memory* (Baltimore: Penguin, 1970), p. 33.
3. Ibid., p. 228.
4. Mark Brown, *Set Thinking—Why Dogs Look Like Their Owners*. In press, 1979.
5. *Brain-Mind Bulletin* 2 (23):2.
6. Robert Rosenthal and Leora Jacobson, "Teachers' Expectancies: Determinants of Pupils IQ Gains," *Psychological Reports* 19 (1):115–18.
7. *New Age Journal,* January 1978, p. 19.
8. Willis Harman et al., *Changing Images of Man* (Stanford, Calif.: Stanford Research Institute, 1973).
9. A. Richardson, *Mental Imagery* (New York: Springer, 1952; London: 1969, Routledge and Kegan Paul,) p. 56.
10. Ibid.
11. Edmund Jacobson, *How to Relax and Have Your Baby* (New York: McGraw-Hill, 1965), p. 110.
12. Richard Suinn, "Coaching the Olympic Imagination," *Psychology Today* (UK edition), August 1976, pp. 29–30.
13. W. T. Gallway, *The Inner Game of Tennis* (New York: Random House, 1974), p. 59.
14. Arnold Schwarzenegger, "Powers of Mind," *New Age Journal,* January 1977, p. 43.
15. Ibid.
16. J. Frank, *Persuasion and Healing* (Baltimore: Johns Hopkins University Press, 1961), p. 66.
17. Ibid.
18. Ibid.
19. Ibid.
20. O. C. Simonton and S. Simonton, "Belief Systems and Management of the Emotional Aspects of Malignancy," *Journal of Transpersonal Psychology* 7 (1):29–47.
21. G. Dick-Read, *Childbirth Without Fear* (New York: Harper & Row, 1968).
22. Quoted in Mike Samuels and Nancy Samuels, *Seeing with the Mind's Eye* (New York: Random House, 1976), p. 222.

23. A. R. Luria, *The Mind of a Mnemonist* (London: Jonathan Cape, 1969), p. 140.
24. Ibid., p. 143.
25. Ibid., p. 146.
26. Peter Russell, *The TM Technique,* 3rd ed. (London: Routledge and Kegan Paul, 1978).
27. See, for instance, Napoleon Hill, *Think and Grow Rich* (North Hollywood, Calif.: Wilshire Books, 1966).
28. Aaron Beck and Marion Kovacs, "A New Way to Cure Depression," *Psychology Today* (UK edition), June 1977, pp. 31–35.

Suggested Further Reading

The following books are general reading going more deeply into the topics discussed in this book. They are not, apart from a few exceptions, academic references.

THE SPEARHEAD OF EVOLUTION

Buzan, Tony. *The Evolving Brain.* Newton Abbot, England: David and Charles, and New York: Holt, Rienhart and Winston, 1978.

Doman, Glen. *How to Teach Your Baby How to Read.* New York: Doubleday, 1975.

Englelman, Therese. *Give Your Child a Superior Mind.* London: Leslie Frewin, 1966.

Rowlands, Peter. *Gifted Children.* London: J. M. Dent, 1974.

THE BRAIN'S DEVELOPMENT

Brierly, John. *The Growing Brain.* London: National Foundation for Educational Research, 1976.

TEN BILLION NEURONS

Pribram, Karl. *Languages of the Brain.* Englewood Cliffs, N.J.: Prentice-Hall, 1971.
Rose, Stephen. *The Conscious Brain.* New York: Knopf, and London: Penguin, 1973.

THE TWO SIDES OF THE BRAIN

Brown, Mark. *Left Hand, Right Hand.* Newton Abbott, England: David and Charles, 1978.
Dimond, Stuart. *The Double Brain.* London: Churchill Livingstone, 1972.

THE EVER-ADAPTABLE BRAIN

Luria, A. R. *The Man with a Shattered World.* London: Jonathan Cape, 1973.
Stein, D. G., et al. *Plasticity and Recovery of Function in the Central Nervous System.* London: Academic Press, 1974.

THE PSYCHOLOGY OF MEMORY

Baddeley, Alan. *The Psychology of Memory.* New York and London: Harper & Row, 1976.
Gregg, Vernon. *Human Memory.* London: Methuen, 1975.

ASSOCIATION AND ORGANIZATION IN MEMORY

Brown, Mark. *Memory Matters.* New York: Crane-Russett, and Newton Abbot, England; David and Charles, 1978.
Katona, George. *Organizing and Memorizing.* New York: Columbia University Press, 1940.

IMAGERY AND ITS RELATIONSHIP TO MEMORY

Jaensch, E. R. *Eidetic Imagery.* London: Routledge and Kegan Paul, 1930.
Richardson, A. *Mental Imagery.* New York: Springer, and London: Routledge and Kegan Paul, 1952.
Samuels, Mike, and Samuels, Nancy. *Seeing with the Mind's Eye.* New York: Random House, 1976.

MNEMONICS

Lorayne, Harry. *The Memory Book.* London: W. H. Allen, 1975.

Luria, A. R. *The Mind of a Mnemonist.* London: Jonathan Cape, 1969.

Yates, F. A. *The Art of Memory.* London: Routledge and Kegan Paul, 1966.

Buzan, Tony. *Speed Memory,* Newton Abbott, England: David and Charles, 1977.

THE HOLOGRAPHIC THEORY OF MIND

Bentov, Itzhak. *Stalking the Wild Pendulum.* New York: Dutton, 1977, and London: Wildwood House, 1978.

Pribram, Karl. *Languages of the Brain.* Englewood Cliffs, N.J.: Prentice-Hall, 1971.

IS EVERYTHING REMEMBERED?

Luria, A. R. *The Mind of a Mnemonist.* London: Jonathan Cape, 1969.

Moody, Raymond. *Life After Life.* New York: Bantam, 1976.

NOTE TAKING

Buzan, Tony. *Use Your Head,* London: BBC Publications, 1974; published in U.S.A. as *Use Both Sides of Your Brain.* New York: Dutton, 1977.

Howe, J. A., and Godfrey, J. *Student Note-Taking As an Aid to Learning.* Exeter, England: Exeter University Teaching Services, 1977.

READING

Buzan, Tony. *Speed Reading.* Newton Abbott, England: David and Charles, 1977.

Huey, Edmund. *The Psychology and Pedagogy of Reading.* London: MacMillan, 1908. Reprint. Cambridge, Mass.: MIT Press, 1968.

Smith, Frank. Understanding Reading. New York: Holt, Rinehart and Winston, 1971.

Two good review papers, together covering most of the research on eye movements in reading, are:

Rayner, K. "Eye Movements in Reading and Information Processing," *Psychological Bulletin* 85 (3): 618–60.

Tinker, M. A., "Recent Studies of Eye Movements in Reading," *Psychological Bulletin* 55: 215–31.

BELIEF AND SET

Brown, Mark. *Set Thinking—Why Dogs Look Like Their Owners.* In press.
Hill, Napoleon. *Think and Grow Rich.* North Hollywood, Calif.: Wilshire Books, 1966.

Index